Screenwriter's & Playwright's Market

includes a 1-year online subscr~
Screenwriter's & Playwright's Market on Wri~

D0795761

WritersMarket.com
WHERE & HOW TO SELL WHAT YOU WRITE

THE ULTIMATE MARKET RESEARCH TOOL FOR WRITERS

To register your
2010 Screenwriter's & Playwright's Market book and
START YOUR 1-YEAR ONLINE GENRE ONLY SUBSCRIPTION,
scratch off the block below to reveal your activation
code, then go to www.WritersMarket.com. Click on
"Sign Up Now" and enter your contact information
and activation code. It's that easy!

SW-M50JN15

UPDATED MARKET LISTINGS FOR YOUR INTEREST AREA

EASY-TO-USE SEARCHABLE DATABASE

DAILY UPDATES

RECORD KEEPING TOOLS

INDUSTRY NEWS

PROFESSIONAL TIPS AND ADVICE

Your purchase of *Screenwriter's & Playwright's Market* gives you access to updated
listings related to this genre of writing. For just $9.99, you can upgrade your
subscription and get access to listings from all of our best-selling Market books.
Visit www.WritersMarket.com for more information.

WritersMarket.com
WHERE & HOW TO SELL WHAT YOU WRITE

Activate your WritersMarket.com subscription to get instant access to:

- **Updated listings in your writing genre** — Find additional listings that didn't make it into the book, updated contact information and more. WritersMarket.com provides the most comprehensive database of verified markets available anywhere.

- **Easy-to-use searchable database** — Looking for a specific magazine or book publisher? Just type in its name. Or widen your prospects with the Advanced Search. You can also search for listings that have been recently updated!

- **Personalized tools** — Store your best-bet markets, and use our popular record-keeping tools to track your submissions. Plus, get new and updated market listings, query reminders, and more – every time you log in!

- **Professional tips & advice** — From pay rate charts to sample query letters, and from how-to articles to Q&A's with literary agents, we have the resources freelance writers need.

- **Industry Updates** — Debbie Ridpath Ohi's Market Watch column keeps you up-to-date on the latest publishing industry news, so you' always be in-the-know.

YOU'LL GET ALL OF THIS
WITH YOUR INCLUDED SUBSCRIPTION TO
WritersMarket.com

To put the full power of WritersMarket.com to work for you, upgrade your subscription and get access to listings from all of our best-selling Market books. Find out more at www.WritersMarket.com

2010 2ND ANNUAL EDITION

SCREENWRITER'S & PLAYWRIGHT'S MARKET.®

Chuck Sambuchino, Editor

WRITER'S DIGEST BOOKS
CINCINNATI, OH

Publisher & Editorial Director, Writing Communities: Jane Friedman
Managing Editor, Writer's Digest Market Books: Alice Pope

Writer's Market Web site: www.writersmarket.com
Writer's Digest Web site: www.writersdigest.com

2010 Screenwriter's & Playwright's Market. Copyright © 2009 by Writer's Digest Books. Published by F + W Media, Inc., 4700 East Galbraith Rd., Cincinnati, Ohio 45236. Printed and bound in the United States of America. All rights reserved. No part of this book may be reproduced in any form or by any electronic or mechanical means including information storage and retrieval systems without written permission from the publisher. Reviewers may quote brief passages to be printed in a magazine or newspaper.

Distributed in Canada by Fraser Direct
100 Armstrong Avenue
Georgetown, ON, Canada L7G 5S4
Tel: (905) 877-4411

Distributed in the U.K. and Europe by David & Charles
Brunel House, Newton Abbot, Devon, TQ12 4PU, England
Tel: (+44) 1626 323200, Fax: (+44) 1626 323319
E-mail: postmaster@davidandcharles.co.uk

Distributed in Australia by Capricorn Link
P.O. Box 704, Windsor, NSW 2756 Australia
Tel: (02) 4577-3555

ISSN: 1944-2823
ISBN-13: 978-1-58297-633-4
ISBN-10: 1-58297-633-3

Cover design by Claudean Wheeler
Production coordinated by Greg Nock

fw
media

Attention Booksellers: This is an annual directory of F + W Media, Inc. Return deadline for this edition is December 31, 2010.

Contents

SUBMITTING YOUR WORK

PERSPECTIVES

From the Editor

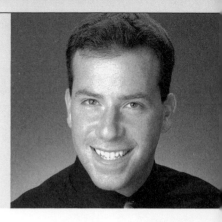

Fade in:

Welcome to the brand new, completely updated second edition of *Screenwriter's & Playwright's Market*—the comprehensive market resource for screenwriting and playwriting from Writer's Digest Books.

After the first edition of this book came out last year, readers wrote to me with their thoughts—and I was listening. You wanted more articles and instruction from the pros, and I've brought you more articles and instruction from the pros. Lots more, to be exact. We have culled together more than 160 pages of informative articles to go with our 600 listings for agents & managers, contests, theaters, and writers' conferences.

Inside this book, you'll find articles on the craft—and more so, the business—of writing. These articles, covering a whole host of topics, can help both new and experienced writers navigate the road to Hollywood with success. Looking to summarize your script? Check out script manager Mike Kuciak's advise on writing the logline (page 29). TV writers shouldn't miss advice on writing for existing shows, provided by writer and producer Ellen Sandler (page 70). If you've finished your stage play and want to know what's next, check out playwright Liza Lentini's article on "Once Upon a Playwriting Idea" (page 33). And these articles are just the beginning. Look at the Table of Contents to see everything we've pulled together.

Concerning the listings, they're detailed to let you know all the needed ins and outs of each market. We tell you how to submit to certain script managers, what different contests are looking for, who's speaking at which conferences, and how to send work to each theater so it gets a fair read. There's much more, but you'd be better served to leaf through the pages than have me keep talking.

Please continue to stay in contact with me at screenwriter@fwmedia.com, passing along success stories, improvement ideas, and news from the scriptwriting world. Perhaps I'll see you at a writers' conference down the road!

Chuck Sambuchino
Editor
Screenwriter's & Playwright's Market
screenwriter@fwmedia.com

How to Use This Book

Seeing your screenplay or stage play come to life can be an overwhelming task, whether you're a brand new writer or have credits in another category on your résumé. More than likely, you're eager to start pursuing agents and anxious to hear your words spoken aloud by actors. But before you go directly to the listings in this book, take time to familiarize yourself with the worlds of writing for screen and stage. By doing so, you will be more prepared in your search and ultimately save yourself effort and unnecessary grief.

Read the articles

The book begins with feature articles that explain all about the craft and business of screenwriting, TV writing and playwriting. The articles are organized into four sections appropriate for each stage of the search process: *Getting Started*, *Sitting Down to Write*, *Submitting Your Work* and *Perspectives*. You may want to start by reading through each article, and then refer back to relevant articles during each stage of your search.

Decide what you're looking for

Listings in this book are markets for screenwriters, TV writers and playwrights. Make sure you know what you're writing and who you want to contact. If you're looking for representation, for instance, the **Managers and Agents** section lists each rep's contact information and explains what type of work the agency represents as well as how to submit your work for consideration.

If you want to test your writing's meddle against others, look through the **Contests** section and try and claim a top prize. The section will show you competitions of all shapes and sizes (not to mention possible entry fees), so check them all out before firing away material.

Frequently Asked Questions

1 **Why do you include producers/agents who are not seeking new clients?**
This book is designed to be a comprehensive resource, and we include some listings simply so writers know they exist and know not to contact them at this time. When we do not, writers will contact us and ask why a particular market/agency was not included in the book.

2 **Why do you exclude fee-charging agents and producers?**
No WGA-endorsed managers or agents will charge an upfront fee to review work. They make money when you make money by taking a small percentage of what writers earn. Beware anything such as "marketing fees," "evaluation costs," "submission fees," or any other euphemism. If you pay a company money to review your work, you may very well get your stuff read, but they still have no legal binding to do anything besides say, "No thanks."

3 **Why are some contests and producers not listed in *Screenwriter's & Playwright's Market*?**
For starters, we don't have infinite space to list everything, so we can only list as much as the page count will allow. Some markets may not have responded to our requests for information. And still others have contacted us personally, requesting to not be listed.

4 **Can I submit my work simultaneously to different contests or different agents?**
Typically, yes. Check the listings and individual websites to see if any individual or company requires an "exclusive submission," meaning they want to be the only person to be reviewing it for a period of time.

5 **If I have a literary agent, do I need another representative for my film work?**
If you simply want to sell the movie rights to your book(s), then your literary agent will likely pair up with a co-agent in California to make that deal—meaning you don't have to do a thing. If you want to sell screenplays and stage plays but your agent has no expertise in those areas, you may indeed need another rep.

6 **Why didn't the contest or agent return my material?**
There are a number of reasons why this occurred. Your submission could have been addressed wrong or gotten lost in the mail—never even reaching its destination. More than likely, though, the recipient (contest, producer, etc.) has a policy of not returning submissions. They are usually recycled to avoid time spent mailing materials back.

7 **Why don't you list more foreign listings and agents?**
It's not that we don't want to—it's just that this is a new book and we've tried to compile as much useful information as we can. As the database grows, we will start to have more Canadian and other international listings. On this subject, keep in mind that when dealing with international listings, you must 1) include an international reply coupon instead of American stamps if you want something mailed back; and 2) be positive that the market in question accepts submissions from writers of all countries, and not just native scribes.

Utilize the extras

Aside from the articles and listings, the book offers a section of **Resources**. If you come across a term with which you aren't familiar, check out the Resources section for a quick explanation. Also, note the gray tabs along the edge of each page. The tabs block off each section so they are easier to flip to as you conduct your search.

Finally—and perhaps most importantly—are the **Indexes** in the back of the book. These can serve as an incredibly helpful way to start your search because they categorize the listings according to different criteria. For example, you can look for script agents by name or according to their specialties (romantic comedy, horror, etc.). Plus, there is a **General Index** that lists every agent, contest and conference in the book.

Listing Policy and Complaint Procedure

Listings in *Screenwriter's & Playwright's Market* are compiled from detailed questionnaires, phone interviews and information provided by the markets. The industry is volatile, and listings will change frequently—and sometimes, dramatically. Agents quit. Contests fold. Play competition deadlines get moved up one month. We rely on our readers for information on your dealings with the screenwriting and playwriting industries. If you find changes in information or evidence of any shady dealing, please contact the editor of this book at: Editor, Screenwriter's & Playwright's Market, 4700 E. Galbraith Road, Cincinnati, OH 45236, or e-mail us at screenwriter@fwmedia.com.

Listings are published free of charge and are not advertisements. Although the information is as accurate as possible, the listings are not endorsed or guaranteed by the editor or publisher of *SPM*. If you feel you have not been treated fairly by someone listed in this book, we advise you to take the following steps:

- First try to contact a listing representative. Sometimes one polite follow-up e-mail can clear up the matter. Politely relate your concern.
- Document all your correspondence with the listing. When you write to us with a complaint, provide the name of your manuscript, the date of your first contact with the listing, and the nature of your subsequent correspondence.

We will keep your letter on file and keep the concern in mind when attempting to contact them and verify their information. The number, frequency and severity of complaints will be considered when deciding whether or not to delete a market's listing from the next edition.

Screenwriter's & Playwright's Market reserves the right to exclude any listing for any reason.

Screenwriting Basics

The Scoop on Writing for a Visual Medium

by Chuck Sambuchino

Making a living as a screenwriter is a challenging endeavor to say the least. And if you're reading this, you've no doubt at least toyed with the idea of trying to tackle Hollywood and seek success in the realms of screenwriting and TV writing. This is an ambitious goal, so it's vital that you're well prepared for what lies ahead. And like in all things, it's important that you work smart—to make sure your time and effort is well spent.

So before you type the words "Fade In" on your computer (or at least go any further on the script), read on to learn the basics about writing for the screen.

IS IT A SCREENPLAY?

Here are some questions to ask yourself before you begin.

Can you create a compelling visual story?

Writing for movies and TV means writing with visuals in mind. It means telling your story through images just as much—if not more than—through words. Whether your tale is set on an exotic island or in a run-down apartment complex, you must help the reader imagine your scenes as you write them on the page.

Is the length right?

Feature-length screenplays run from 90-130 pages. If you feel yourself

---

CHUCK SAMBUCHINO is the editor of *Screenwriter's & Playwright's Market*. He also edits *Guide to Literary Agents* (www.guidetoliteraryagents.com/blog) and oversaw the third edition of *Formatting & Submitting Your Manuscript*.

Getting Started

Scripts to Read

Recently, the Writers Guild of America compiled their list of the top 101 screenplays of all time. Though we don't have enough space to list them all, here are the Top 20.

1   *Casablanca*

2   *The Godfather*

3   *Chinatown*

4   *Citizen Kane*

5   *All About Eve*

6   *Annie Hall*

7   *Sunset Boulevard*

8   *Network*

9   *Some Like It Hot*

10   *The Godfather: Part II*

11   *Butch Cassidy and the Sundance Kid*

12   *Dr. Strangelove*

13   *The Graduate*

14   *Lawrence of Arabia*

15   *The Apartment*

16   *Pulp Fiction*

17   *Tootsie*

18   *On the Waterfront*

19   *To Kill a Mockingbird*

20   *It's a Wonderful Life*

Also, know that each year, the Academy of Motion Picture Arts and Sciences nominates 10 screenplays for awards—five for the Best Original Screenplay Oscar, and five for the Best Screenplay Adapted from a Previously Published Work Oscar. Any nominated script is that year's créme de la créme in terms of screenwriting, and worth checking out.

really struggling with length, you may have a good story that's just not a screenplay.

Are you making your story a screenplay just to make money?

Yes, there is money to be made in Hollywood—plenty of it, if you're good enough. But that's not a good enough reason to become a scriptwriter. As you develop your ideas, plot and character, pay attention to the medium where you most feel yourself drawn. Sometimes, a story is suited best as told through a novel, or as told through a series of TV episodes. Forcing a concept into the form of a screenplay for money's sake may produce an awkward finished product.

Is your idea strong enough?

As you'll read in these pages, the idea for your movie must be strong or else you're already in a tough spot. If you consider yourself a writer who prides himself on things such as the quality of your prose, the complexity of your language and the mystique of your narrative, then you may want to stay away from screenwriting (at least for now). Scripts are processed quickly by readers and producers in Hollywood, so make sure that you're dealing with a concept that doesn't need a lot of preface before a reader can grasp what it's about. Are there exceptions to this? Of course. But you can never count on being that rarest-of-rare exception.

Are you OK with letting others change your ideas?

Perhaps in no other medium of writing is work changed so much—and so drastically—as in screenwriting. Scripts can be purchased for the concept alone; following the purchase, your work may be completely rewritten (a "page one rewrite") in accordance with a producer's vision of how to develop your idea in a different direction. Of course, this doesn't always happen—and the more success you have, the less it will—but you must prepare yourself.

Do you have a thick skin?

Here's an expression you'll hear more than once in this lifetime: "That's Hollywood!" The expression is used when someone gets ripped off, has their ideas stolen, has a deal fall through, or has a project stuck in Development Hell, etc. The stereotype that Hollywood is filled with sharks did not materialize for no reason. It's a slick business out west, and you'll meet plenty of people interested more in money than your creative artistry or livelihood. Enter the waters at your own risk.

How I Broke In: 5 Tips for Writers

by Trai Cartwright

I was one of those writers who developed into a jack-of-all-trades: I was a studio development exec and a feature film producer; I consulted for production companies, movie stars and independent writers; I judged contests; and of course, I wrote (a few of my scripts were even optioned). There are many paths to getting paid in Hollywood, and mine took me in directions both surprising and strange (like the time I helped the stunt coordinator on a major feature rewrite a big chase sequence!). It wasn't easy, and it didn't happen overnight.

Here are five things I did along the way that can help you get on the road to success in Tinseltown:

1. **I picked up the phone.** If you can talk intelligently about your script and not waste anyone's time with stammering, high-maintenance demands or amateur theatrics, you can get your script read. Simply find out who is in the market for your kind of script, aim for the assistant to a junior executive, practice your 30-second pitch, pick up the phone and pretend to be a player, too. And by the way, the assistants will actually *read* your script because they are looking for the one that will catapult them into the office with a window.

2. **I treated assistants like my best friends.** Treat them well, and you may just slice and dice your way through the tangle of Hollywood without ever having to talk directly (or be avoided studiously) by an executive. And that's not a bad thing.

3. **I worked for free. A lot.** Once I'd had some on-the-job training with a studio production company, I was in a position to help others. I put as much energy into other people's projects as I did my own because that's how Hollywood works. You do favors, and then when it's your turn, people do favors for you. Plus it's a great education.

4. **I lived in LA.** You don't have to live in Hollywood to be a screenwriter, but it helps. You can absolutely sell your first screenplay living in Topeka, but if you want to be a contender for writing jobs or plan on pitching specs, think about moving. You can't take meetings at the drop of a hat if you're a plane ride away.

5. **I realized the importance of finding a niche.** Probably the most important advice I wish I'd gotten as a young writer: Pick a specialty and then hone it until I did it better than anyone. My early years as a writer involved a lot of experimenting; I had the voice, but I didn't have the theme. Over the years, I'd written a script in every major genre. This helped make me a great consultant, able to work with any kind of writer, but it didn't make me the most successful screenwriter. Don't get me wrong—I was happy with my successes—but if I had to do it over today, I would have focused on the one genre I most dearly wanted to write for the rest of my life and then I would have rode for broke.

Trai Cartwright (www.craftwrite.com) is a script consultant and contest judge who has had multiple scripts optioned. She now lives in Colorado.

And lastly: Do you love movies?

They say the best writers are great readers, and the same is true in this medium. To be a screenwriter, you must watch plenty of movies—and enjoy watching them. But if you're talking about making a living as a screenwriter, you're beyond simply "watching" films and TV shows. Now you must become a student of them. Break stories down; dissect them; reverse engineer a successful plot to figure out why things worked the way they did. Ask yourself: Do you have the patience to watch a good movie a second (and third and fourth . . .) time to deconstruct why it entertained you the first time through?

ADAPTING YOUR WORK AND OTHERS'

Adaptations are a tricky thing, and not to be rushed into. If you want to adapt an already-existing work, then you need to secure the rights to that story—a complicated process involving time and money. If you want to write about a true story and real people, that means securing life rights—another not-so-simple task.

Some writers compose scripts based on already-existing franchises or ideas, such as the next Batman movie or a script for *Ghostbusters III*. This is dangerous because the characters and concepts are not yours, and there is almost nothing you can do with the screenplay, even if it's good. There is only an infinitesimal chance it will sell, and managers may be unwilling to even look at it as a writing sample because they fear some legal repercussion when distributing the work around town.

Writing scripts for existing TV shows, on the other hand, is common and encouraged. It's a common way for TV writers to get their talent noticed and land a job.

Adapting your *own* work is a practical route for novelists and other writers. If your novel sells but Hollywood fails to snatch up the film rights and hire a screenwriter, you can always try writing the screenplay adaptation yourself. The odds are against success here, though, as novelists tend to get too close to their work and fail in adapting it to a vastly different medium. Peter Benchley's adaptation of his own novel, *Jaws*, for example, was a huge disappointment, and the script wasn't used. But then again, John Irving won an Academy Award for adapting his own book, *The Cider House Rules*.

Since you weren't commissioned to adapt your own work, you'll be writing it on spec, meaning that no money is promised or guaranteed. If done well, adapting your own published work into screenplay form can be a double boon for writers, as it may start the ball rolling on getting a film produced, and the adapted screenplay can serve as a writing sample to get you more assignments in Hollywood, if you ever considered making the jump.

LIVING IN HOLLYWOOD

One of the great things about being a freelance writer or novelist is that you can live anywhere. It's no coincidence that so many freelancers live in some nice area near Portland, or in Santa Fe, or on 25 acres in New Hampshire. But can you make a career out of screenwriting and live outside LA? It's possible, but not likely. Hollywood is a place of meetings and lunches, schmoozing and networking, discussions and assignments. You need to be close by, or at least be able to jump on a plane to California at a moment's notice.

It is definitely possible to begin your career in Hollywood and *then* move elsewhere, as you've already had face-to-face meetings with plenty of important contacts and they know your name.

PERSEVERANCE IS MANDATORY

A screenplay is no short story. It's a 110-page monster that will consume your life for quite a while—and that's just while writing it. After that, you'll be dealing with rewriting, queries, synopses, research, managers, pitching and everything else. Add it all up and you're looking at a lot of time dedicated to a single project. Make sure that you're ready to commit yourself to your writing or you could end up just another writer who has two-thirds of a finished screenplay sitting in a desk drawer somewhere, promising himself every Jan. 1 that *this* is the year it gets finished and makes the rounds.

While dedication and heart is mandatory with any medium of writing, you must also be brave and strong to wheel and deal in Hollywood, as you fight not only tough odds, but also a lot of people who will knock you down just to get ahead.

So—if you've read all this and still think that the medium of screenwriting is the best fit for your story—as well as a good fit for your career goals—then carry on, my wayward son. Let's get to work on advancing your writing career, and maybe you can be *commissioned* to write the next Batman movie.

Screenwriter FAQ

*The Pros Chime In on Some Common
(and Not So Common) Questions*

by Robin Mizell

What's the best way to break in to the screenwriting business?

You should never underestimate the importance of writing short films to get noticed. It goes against what you may have read in all the books, but you should really write scripts on spec and try to sell them. And Hollywood is the place to be in terms of getting meetings and meeting people who can give you a job. You don't necessarily have to move here with no prospects, but you can set up some meetings with some studios and maybe arrange a vacation around a visit. There's a lot of groundwork to cover, so have plenty of ideas ready to go when you get here and pound the pavement until you get your foot in the door.

—*Kevin Brodbin's first script was* The Glimmer Man. *Later, writing with Frank Capello, he turned the Hellblazer comics into* Constantine.

Are there jobs for freelance TV scriptwriters?

I gave out two assignments to assistants the first year. Frequently, the assistants on shows are writers who haven't gotten breaks yet. So if there's a script available to be written outside of a staff, the assistants are typically the first ones to get it. That's why people who are interested in writing for television take assistant jobs: 1) You learn how the process works, and 2) It puts you in a place where you can put a script on someone's desk and they can see your work. Then they may toss you a script when an opportunity comes up.

—*Allison M. Gibson has worked as writer on NBC's* Parenthood; *the creator, executive producer, and writer for WB's* Reba; *and a consultant on UPN's* Rock Me Baby.

ROBIN MIZELL (robinmizell.com) is a literary agent and the founder of Robin Mizell Ltd., Literary Representation. She was formerly an editor for *Screenwriter's & Playwright's Market*.

Advice from the Picket Lines

A year after receiving a bachelor's degree in film studies from the University of Colorado Denver, Liz Lorang decided to make the trip to Los Angeles to march on the picket lines with members of the Writers Guild of America, West, who were demanding a more favorable residuals agreement for their contributions to dramatic works distributed online. Lorang hoped to meet some of the writers who worked on her favorite television shows. If she talked to them while they were picketing, she thought, maybe they could offer her a little advice about launching her career as a scriptwriter.

Here is Lorang's account of what she learned by visiting the frontlines and marching in solidarity with other writers.

"The most important tip I received while speaking with writers is that while you're looking for work it's important to make sure you have amazing samples—both spec scripts and a script for an original TV series.

It's also all about who you know. If you don't have any connections, be adamant about making some. Most of the writers I spoke to were fortunate to know someone in the industry who helped them get started. Whether it was a showrunner, or simply a writer's assistant on a show, writers took full advantage of connections and worked their way up from the lowliest of assistants to full-fledged staff writers.

The great thing about L.A. is that it is obviously full of people in the film and television industry. When it comes to television writers, there is a definite community that supports and helps new and existing writers find work and keep working. Film screenwriters are more on their own in terms of having a screenplay produced. It could be said that a screenwriter is more of a lone wolf battling the Hollywood institution, while television writers have more of a network of people to rely on, partially due to the teamwork that goes into writing a show with a group of people. While on the picket line, I saw that the writers were interested in what others were working on and gave tips and advice to one another.

I love living in Denver and am not too excited about the thought of living in L.A and away from my immediate family. One writer informed me that it is simply necessary to live in L.A. during staffing season and pilot season, about four or five months out of the year—roughly between the months of March and July. After that, it's possible to write for a show by telecommuting.

Regardless of their backgrounds, the writers I met were all steadfast and dedicated to making it as writers in Hollywood. Even those who were out of work, not just because of the strike, were working on projects, keeping in touch with those they knew in the industry, and figuring out how to get work. Persistence is key, above anything else. Whether working or not, it's vital to keep writing, not only to polish your skills, but simply for the enjoyment of it."

Liz Lorang lives and works in Denver, and is writing a spec script she hopes will attract the attention of a Hollywood producer.

As someone who writes for plays, TV, and film, how do you feel that writing for each medium is different and unique?

The differences come down to what the audience can see. In plays, the audience gets the big picture. They can't see things close up. Words that the actors say are the most valuable commodity there. In TV, you've got a small screen, one step up from a play. Spoken words are important, but not as much as on the stage. The camera becomes transitional. It gives the writer more freedom to explore the relationship between a character and his/her various settings. In film, someone's quick glance can be the size of a building wall. You may not need as many words there because the minute features of the actors can tell the story and emotions without having to spend so much time explaining things to the audience.

—*Clay Stafford is a playwright, producer and screenwriter living in Nashville.*

Do networks or studios ever develop shows by newcomers?

It's rare, almost never, that a studio or network will even meet with a person with no TV experience, and even less likely they'd actually give money to a new writer to develop or produce their own series. Sometimes writers can cross over from feature film writing, but less so from theater. It happens, but you really have to earn your chops.

Staff writing is like an apprenticeship. If you're smart and attentive and lucky enough to work for people who allow you to be part of the process, you can learn everything you need to know. Once you have a sense of how a show operates, you can use that experience when you pitch to a studio or network, and they can trust you with the hundreds of thousands of dollars it costs to shoot a pilot. ·

—*Molly Newman is an Emmy Award-winning television writer and producer whose credits include* Frasier, Murphy Brown, *and* The Larry Sanders Show.

Is it challenging to write on a project where there are so many hands trying to stir the pot?

It's a whole different challenge, but yes, it is a challenge. Something like *Spider-Man*, there's a lot more people involved and, therefore, a lot more opinions and more possibilities for conflict. *Spider-Man* was a job I was up for and very, very much wanted. The studio was clear with everybody that nobody just gets this job handed to them, you have to come in and impress us. It was an audition. So I did as much prep work as I could, and I found all the relevant sections of the various comics that I was interested in, and put it all up on big poster boards, and went in there and pitched my little ass off. Happily, I got the job. Never underestimate the power of office products.

—*David Koepp has worked on many franchise hits, series, sequels, and blockbusters, including* Jurassic Park, Mission Impossible, Spider-Man, *and* Indiana Jones and the Kingdom of the Crystal Skull.

What's a frequent obstacle for scriptwriters, and how should they deal with it?

In terms of the writing process, it's all about conquering procrastination. If you're serious about writing, you need to give yourself a block of time to write—before work, on vacation, or leave your job for a month. It's like going to the gym. Everybody says they want to go to the gym, but they never do unless there's a specific time or a reason or a friend picking them up. Don't get overwhelmed with screenwriting how-to books, because there's no real, one way to do it. Just write the script. Write it long and write it big, then trim it back and fix it. Just get something down on paper.

—*Dan Fogelman created and co-produced the sitcom* Like Family, *wrote and produced* Lipshitz Saves the World *and* The 12th Man *for television, and created the film scripts for* Cars *and* Fred Claus.

Playwriting Basics

Know the Dos and Don'ts Before Diving In

by Chuck Sambuchino

Stage plays are a medium all their own, no matter if you're writing a 10-minute script, a one-act, or a sprawling three-hour masterpiece. Plays are minimalist in nature, and rely heavily on excellent storytelling and compelling characters. The world of playwriting is typically one of little money and long hours—but a big payoff. In this medium, words reign—so a writer's snappy dialogue or in-depth character drama can come front and center, without worrying about how many producers want to change the script or add in a gratuitous sex scene to attract a new audience demographic.

Read on to discover the basics of plays and playwriting, and know whether that story you're concocting is best fit for the stage.

IS IT A PLAY?

Here are some questions to ask yourself before starting to create your story as a stage play.

Can the story move forward using a combination of dialogue and emotion?

Perhaps the greatest tool for any playwright is dialogue. That's most of what a play is: spoken words. A novel can have pages upon pages of description and characters' interior thoughts/monologue; meanwhile, films are a visual medium, where images are paramount. On stage, however, special effects are hard to come by, and you won't have a John Williams score in the background to help convey mood or tension—hence, the emphasis on dialogue and character.

CHUCK SAMBUCHINO is the editor of *Screenwriter's & Playwright's Market*. He also edits *Guide to Literary Agents* (www.guidetoliteraryagents.com/blog) and oversaw the third edition of *Formatting & Submitting Your Manuscript*.

Can you show exposition, backstory and setting through dialogue without making it sound like a paragraph in a book?

All you've got is a stage. Flashbacks are feasible, but complicated. Montages are not realistic. If one of your characters is supposed to enter a lush garden with plants and vines, you probably won't have a detailed set that reflects that.

Plays to Study

The best way to learn how to compose a great play is to read other great plays and analyze them. Your first step should be visiting the official Tony Awards Web site (www.tonyawards.com), which will reveal works nominated and awarded the honor of "Best Play" each year. Obviously, any of these works are of great caliber and worth a look. Outside of those with Tony nominations and anything by William Shakespeare, the following works should be sought out at the bookstore or online:

- *Angels in America*, by Tony Kushner
- *Arcadia*, by Tom Stoppard
- *Cat on a Hot Tin Roof*, by Tennessee Williams
- *Crimes of the Heart*, by Beth Henley
- *Dark of the Moon*, by Howard Richardson
- *A Doll's House*, by Henrik Ibsen
- *Fences*, by August Wilson
- *Glengarry Glen Ross*, by David Mamet
- *'night, Mother*, by Marsha Norman
- *Oedipus Rex (Oedipus the King)*, by Sophocles
- *Our Town*, by Thornton Wilder
- *Pygmalion*, by George Bernard Shaw
- *Six Degrees of Separation*, by John Guare
- *A Streetcar Named Desire*, by Tennessee Williams
- *The Cherry Orchard*, by Anton Chekhov
- *The Death of a Salesman*, by Arthur Miller
- *True West*, Sam Shepard *Waiting for Godot*, by Samuel Beckett.

Keep in mind that older plays are likely in the public domain, as their copyright has long since expired. For example, Shakespeare's works are free to read online, and it's easy to find works by Oscar Wilde, as well, among others. Here are a few starter Web sites to check out when searching for plays posted online:

- The Literature Page: www.literaturepage.com/category/plays.html
- Classic Reader: www.classicreader.com/
- The Virtual Library for Theatre and Drama: vl-theatre.com/list4.shtml
- Pro-play: www.singlelane.com/proplay/
- Chiff's Databases: www.chiff.com/art/theater/scripts.htm
- Simply Scripts: www.simplyscripts.com/

A playwright must describe the characters' surroundings through dialogue, but not overdo it. If you spend two minutes describing the view of the ocean, it can get boring for the audience.

Are you prepared to be a marketer and advocate for your play, helping out wherever needed?

If you sell a screenplay, the work is now completely out of your hands. Try walking into a meeting of big-wig executives and suggesting a design for the movie poster—then you can enjoy being escorted from the building. Plays, on the other hand, often need all the help they can get. Plays that are produced by small- or medium-sized theaters need volunteers (read: you, the playwright) who will assist in publicity and marketing, from designing fliers to writing the press release.

Can you engage an audience?

One of the most common mistakes of storytelling in any medium is releasing too much information too fast—commonly called an "information dump." Writers do not need to explain everything about the characters and the world they inhabit right at the beginning of the work. Audience members want to be more than spectators—they want to be *part* of the play and its happenings, as it helps them forget they're simply sitting down and watching actors.

Do not underestimate the value of having the audience ask questions. By not explaining things fully—meaning, you limit exposition and never hit the nail on the head—you connect with audience members and allow them to mentally engage the story, figuring things out for themselves. "When something is spelled out, or told directly to us, it simply becomes less fun because our participation is denied," says playwright Michael Wright, in his book, *Playwriting in Process*. "Imagine being told just before a game starts that 'your team will lose by one point on a missed shot with one second left in the game.'"

"THE PRACTICALITIES OF THE THEATER"

Cast size

Cast size should always be on your mind. Musicals, children's theater, and big-budget productions aside, theaters will usually look for plays with small cast sizes. A small cast requires less money for actors (especially when you're dealing with unions) and less hassle in getting people together for rehearsals. An old playwriting joke tells of a meeting between a writer and a producer. The producer asks, "How many actors will be needed for this play?" The writer responds, "That's the good news. Just one!" The producer pauses and says, "See if you cut that number down, then call me back."

Keep in mind that what's important here is a small *cast* size, not a small number of roles. David Lindsay-Abaire's play, *Wonder of the World*, for example, requires seven actors, but has many more characters than that. Six of the characters are major, and all the minor characters (such as a waitress, a helicopter pilot, a cop, etc.) are played by a seventh actor, who changes appearances.

Embracing simplicity

Plays are not superhero movies, and one of the biggest and most common amateur errors is to try to force a movie onto the stage. "When you have a scene, you have to write with the practicalities of the theater in mind," says Ted Swindley, creator of the musical *Always . . . Patsy Cline*. "Plays are not movies. You can't say, 'Scene 1: The Peer at Lake Michigan; Scene 2: A Skyscraper Penthouse; Scene 3: Central Park.' That is a nonrealistic play. Frankly, there are a lot of logistical things that producers will look at in a script. They may say, 'This is an interesting play, but it's got too many characters, it's too many costumes, it's got too many props.'"

When you're writing a play, keep basic things in mind. Is this set change possible? Do I really need to include these props in this scene? If a character is in a wedding dress in one scene, then the next scene requires them to be on their honeymoon, dressed casually, how will that transition work? Don't underestimate simplicity. "There are two reasons that certain plays are repeatedly produced," Swindley says. "One is that they make money and that they become popular—that's just economics . . . But there's also a practical reason why plays are done: They're really good plays that are really simple to produce. (Playwright) David Mamet's a prime example. Brilliant writer—simple to produce. It's all about his language."

Limiting stage directions and description

Looking back at Shakespeare's plays, it's astounding to see the lack of stage directions. Characters enter; they leave; many die—and that's about it. While playwrights today definitely have more leverage, stage plays are not a medium where you can describe action in depth. For example, if two characters fight, simply say, "They fight." Writing down a paragraph or two full of blow-by-blow action is the exact thing *not* to do.

Ideally, your play will be produced many times on many different stages—and the directors that tackle your work will not want to put on the exact same interpretation of another director; same goes for the actors. Directors will often black out some or all of a play's stage directions, so they can

8 Things That Can Ruin Your Play

Don't sabotage your work! Avoid these eight poisonous pitfalls that can get your work rejected:

1. Neglecting character arc and development. Not all characters can have a whole, dramatic arc throughout the story, but the most important characters must change.

2. Using poor transitions. When a scene change means we're in another country two years later, it must be done well, or you'll leave the audience perplexed. The play *Closer*, by Patrick Marber (made into a movie in 2004), follows four characters over the course of a few years, yet you never feel confused as to how much time has elapsed because the writing is good.

3. Beating the moral or message over the head of the audience. They're smarter than you think they are.

4. Using a cliché storyline. If you have a plot that's simple, such as a love story or a family member dying of cancer, it must have extraordinary characters and dialogue. Ask yourself: What makes your take on this story unique, different and special?

5. Not properly formatting your play, whether than means not including a cast of characters, not numbering pages, or simply not centering text that should be centered.

6. Being sloppy. Your text should have no typos, unless you're spelling out words phonetically for a reason. Make sure your submission is neat and professionally bound. If a contest turns down your submission and happens to send you the copy back, examine the play. If pages are bent and it's obvious that the play was indeed read, then don't send that same copy out again.

7. Creating too many long monologues. There are times and places for these, but four-page speeches don't often happen in real life.

8. Writing a conflict or scene a certain way "because it happened that way" in real life. A play must be entertaining to an audience, be it a drama or comedy. Writing about your own experiences is fine, as long as it's not simply a cathartic effort for you, but rather an entertaining play for the audience.

create their own vision of how to block the action. By the same token, if you feel you must preface every line of dialogue with an emotion, such as "nervous" or "holding back tears," you're limiting how actors can interpret your words.

Getting Started

WHY WRITE PLAYS?

Playwriting is not an easy business by any means. First of all, money is scarce. There is a reason that community theaters close: Attendance is down. The ease of things such as DVR, Netflix and the Internet has provided even more reasons to stay in on the weekends rather than catch a show. After all, you can turn off a bad movie, but you can't turn off a bad play, which is perhaps why fewer people go to the theater. This is why plays must be good. They must be entertaining. They must pull you in through conflict, drama and emotion.

So if it's difficult and there's very little money if any, why do it? Because there's nothing like being behind the last row of audience seats (usually while pacing and biting fingernails)—and hearing a house laugh ripple through the venue. There's nothing like hearing a large crowd be dead silent at the exact moment where you hoped they would be.

Plays celebrate the written word, and quality is not just appreciated, but expected. With plays, the writer and his words truly reign.

Long Live the Idea

Finding a Great Concept

by Pamela Wallace

Creating a good movie is all about the idea. No matter how many hot stars you use or how much you spend on special effects or how over-the-top you make the marketing campaign, the secret to box-office success is an original, compelling story.

Before leaving Disney to co-found DreamWorks studios, Jeffrey Katzenberg drafted a memo that raised the bar for what movie executives call "high concept." The term referred to a fresh idea that could be summarized in a sentence or two: easy to understand, easy to sell to an audience. Katzenberg kicked high concept up a notch, insisting that only scripts with ingenious, powerful core ideas that could succeed without brilliant execution deserve the label.

Katzenberg wrote that stars, directors, writers, hardware and special effects can influence the success of a film. But these elements work only if they serve a good idea. In essence, he said, "The idea is king."

AIM FOR WIDE APPEAL

A great idea needs to translate into a compelling story. This happens when a central character goes through a transforming experience the audience can relate to. In *Raiders of the Lost Ark*, cocky Indiana Jones is humbled by the realization that there are forces even he shouldn't challenge. *Tootsie* is about a man who becomes a better man by pretending to be a woman. A successful story will stir emotions in its viewers, making them laugh or cry (both, in really good movies) or shriek in horror.

Deceptively simple, but universal ideas connect best with audiences:

The Logline: Boiling It Down

A **logline** is a one-sentence description of what a story is about. Though "logline" is typically a Hollywood term, being able to concisely explain what your story is about is a universal concept—and that's why you need to know how to do it. Loglines are short, catchy, and mandatory.

Loglines are designed to be simple—that means one sentence, ideally. Two-sentence loglines are generally acceptable, but a reason should be clear why the story can't be summarized in one.

> Two best friends who crash weddings as a way to pick up women find themselves breaking their own rules when they both fall head-over-heels for ladies at a high-profile reception.
> —*Wedding Crashers*

> To track down a serial killer, an ambitious female FBI agent-in-training seeks help from an imprisoned psychiatrist, who is both a manipulative genius and a serial killer himself.
> —*Silence of the Lambs*

> After he kills several assailants in an act of self-defense, a small-town restaurant owner suddenly finds himself being terrorized by the mob, who believe he is actually a former mafia killer who disappeared decades ago.
> —*A History of Violence*

> A no-name boxer is plucked from obscurity (and the streets of Philadelphia, more literally) when he is given the opportunity to fight the World Heavyweight Champion.
> —*Rocky*

> Thirty years after he failed to save President Kennedy, a veteran Secret Service agent must stop a psychopathic assassin from killing the current president.
> —*In the Line of Fire*

> After being kicked out of their sport for fighting, two rival male figure skaters must join forces to compete in a pairs skating competition.
> —*Blades of Glory*

OK, so you can craft witty dialogue and your characters are interesting in an existential sort of way. You're proud of your writing—but can you boil the tale down into one or two intriguing sentences? If you can't, you're in trouble. Every reader, manager and executive who sees your query or picks up your script will first peruse the logline, seeing if the story is interesting enough to warrant more attention.

Is it fair to judge a whole body of work on one sentence? Perhaps not, but it's somewhat understandable. Studios are in this business to make money, and they do so by people going to see their movies. But if they produce a film that's not easily summarized for viewers, then they can't get butts in the seats. No money. And *that's* why you need a solid logline.

underdog triumphs (*The Karate Kid*), revenge (*Dirty Harry*), triumph of the human spirit (*The Color Purple*), coming-of-age (*Stand by Me*). "Connect with the viewer" is the mandate of every successful film.

Once executives and producers buy into a screenplay's central idea, their focus shifts to the next big issue: Is the story castable? In other words, are the leading roles appropriate for "bankable" stars? Or is the idea strong enough that you don't need stars (as in *Independence Day*)? Has this idea proved commercial in the past? Or, even better, is it a fresh take on a proven commodity?

The next deal-making issue is the audience. Who will want to see this movie? Will this idea appeal to a broad demographic? Production costs for a major summer release usually exceed $100 million, meaning a major film must be able to pull in at least two demographic segments of moviegoers to recoup expenses.

Typically, studios target a primary audience, then go after a secondary and possibly tertiary group. *George of the Jungle* demonstrates this strategy. Ostensibly, George was a kid flick—after all, it was based on a cartoon character. But sexy Brendan Fraser—wearing nothing but a loincloth—combined with a witty script peppered with adult humor, turned a broad comedy into an entertaining movie for teens and enjoyable entertainment for adults (especially women).

The necessity of a great idea is borne out every year by the films that achieve the best profit vs. cost ratio. Small, relatively low-budget films often top the profit-making list above higher-profile movies. In 1997, a little British movie called *The Full Monty* cost a mere $3.5 million to produce but was the revenue ratio champ. In fact, that year's top five profitable films were each made for less than $6 million. What they lacked in bankable stars and special effects, they made up for with universally appealing concepts.

FINDING THE GREAT ONES

Where do winning concepts come from? I pull ideas from many sources—newspaper and magazine articles, my friends' lives, the lives of people in the news, my own life or unrealized fantasies. My concept for *Witness* came from reading news stories about an Amish baby, killed accidentally when non-Amish teenage boys threw rocks at the infant's carriage. As a mother myself, I ached for the parents. The idea for my CBS movie *Borrowed Hearts* reflected my childhood desire for the father I didn't have. On other occasions, I indulged my most romantic imaginings while writing three romance novels that were subsequently adapted into movies for the Showtime channel.

The common thread for all these projects was a subject or thought that touched my heart, that made me want to explore more deeply the feelings it evoked. I've tried to write stories that were market-driven, but they've never worked. I believe that's true for most writers. For an audience to love a movie, the writer has to love what he's written.

HIGH-VOLTAGE INSPIRATION

I know I'm on to a viable idea by the jolt of excitement I feel when it hits. It's heartfelt, it's deep, it's powerful. I'm compelled to grab the nearest pen and jot down as much as I can before it escapes.

Recognizing an idea with real film potential is part inspiration and part physical sensation, and it points to the essence of our creative energy. The best ideas are often the most intimate and personal. We resist examining these sensations because of the pain or fear they dredge up. This force is the core strength of the story that we want to communicate to the audience.

When *Borrowed Hearts* sold, the production company executive asked how I came up with the idea. I was reluctant to disclose that the story I wrote—a man "rents" a family for business purposes then falls in love with the single mother and her daughter—came from my therapist's suggestion that I get in touch with my inner child. When I couldn't "talk" to my imaginary younger self, I, instead, considered what that little girl would have wanted more than anything: a father. The plot evolved smoothly from there.

Borrowed Hearts was the No. 1-rated TV program of the week it aired, and the fourth-highest-rated TV movie of the season. All of that from a simple but profound childhood longing. When you're fighting through the difficulties of writing a screenplay, return to the initial idea. Why did it touch you? What do you want to express in the story? Never lose sight of that.

Your personal approach to an idea makes it uniquely yours. No other writer would explore that particular story exactly as you would. Your internal associations with an idea make it emotionally powerful. Ultimately, it's that power that makes your idea king.

100 Writing Prompts

Looking for Ideas? We've Got You Covered

by E.L. Collins

1. A teenager finds out that his father was a priest and his mother a nun.
2. "I'm here to answer the ad in the paper."
3. "Seriously, I was eating at the same restaurant as him, and let me tell you, he didn't look like such a 'badass' to me."
4. A woman awakens to find herself levitating above the bed.
5. During the State Fair Opening Ceremonies, a prize-winning animal is kidnapped.
6. A group of salesmen on their way to a company retreat decide to stop and investigate a strange-looking suitcase on the side of the road.
7. "If we have this conversation, It's going to end badly for you. Consider that a fair warning."
8. "I'm sorry, sir, but she checked out last night."
9. A stay-at-home dad joins the neighborhood "mommies club."
10. "C'mon, let's try it. They test this stuff all the time to make sure it's safe."
11. "Do you ever feel like you just haven't got the common sense that everyone else was born with?"
12. While traveling abroad, a nurse finds herself on a tour bus with an expectant mother who begins to go into labor.
13. "I'm sure that's an urban legend."
14. A PR firm's newest client becomes a public relations nightmare.
15. "I've seen enough monkeys for one day, thank you very much."
16. A young woman must run errands while wearing an embarrassing and inappropriate outfit.
17. You arrive at your office to find that your personal belongings have been boxed up.
18. "Thanks for seeing me. I need to discuss something important, and I didn't want to do it over the phone."

E.L. COLLINS is a Virginia-based writer and freelancer. These prompts excerpted with permission from *The Writer's Book of Matches: 1,001 Prompts to Ignite Your Fiction* (Writer's Digest Books).

19. "Mom, Principal Sanderson is on the phone. He wants to talk to you."
20. A journalist doing a story on what it's like to live on death row begins to fall for one of the inmates she's been interviewing.
21. What appears to be the fuselage of a strange aircraft is uncovered during the site excavation for a future strip mall.
22. A nurse in a mental hospital discovers that a well-known missing person is being held there against her will.
23. "I think you're out of options."
24. "Are you following me?"
25. You win a seat on the first commercial space shuttle flight.
26. After a near-death experience, a young man is haunted by visions of a beautiful yet terrifying afterlife.
27. While serving a long tour of duty overseas, a soldier becomes distraught that he can't remember his wife's face.
28. A family member disappears while vacationing on a cruise ship.
29. "It would be best if you put that back where you found it, sir."
30. An alcoholic attends his first social event since leaving rehab.
31. Though paralyzed by his fear of heights, a man considers bungee jumping to impress someone.
32. A renowned psychic finds that her powers of precognition have vanished.
33. It is discovered that the pie in a small-town diner has curative properties.
34. After watching Eminem's movie *8 Mile*, a mild-mannered businessman is inspired to participate in a rap battle.
35. "If you can guess what I have in my pocket, you can have it."
36. A philanthropist's plane crashes in the jungle, where the native tribe he has fought so hard to protect begins hunting him.
37. "I just want to kiss him. I know it's the wrong time, the wrong place, but I don't care."
38. The morning after a heavy snowfall, a single man sees a set of footprints leading away from his house.
39. After falling asleep on his shift, a prison guard awakens to find that all of the cells are empty.
40. After completing a solo camping trip, a woman gets her film developed and discovers that several of the photos are of her … sleeping.
41. A man's doorbell rings. He looks through the peephole to see a figure wearing a yellow jumpsuit and a motorcycle helmet with wings painted on each side.
42. "At least I'm walking out of this alive."
43. A psychiatrist is offered a large sum of money to treat a patient, but he must first sign a contract stating that he will never reveal the patient's identity to anyone. If he does, the consequences will be severe.
44. "Helpful hint: Wait until you're sober before trying that again."
45. "So they can't get the landing gear down and we were up there just circling for, like, three hours."

46. "I can't believe you've taken up jogging. What about our pact?"
47. A young woman loses her ability to speak, save for one word.
48. "Oh I'll propose a toast to the happy couple, all right..."
49. In the middle of the night, a man rolls over just in time to see his wife pull on a pajama top. In the moonlight, he notices bruises/marks on her arms that weren't there when they went to bed.
50. "It's always the quiet ones, you know."
51. "You have ten seconds..."
52. Two high school sweethearts arrange to meet for a drink fifteen years after graduation.
53. "Mom, you've got to stop dragging me into the middle of things."
54. A man in a business suit, briefcase handcuffed to his wrist, stands on a quiet beach watching the sunrise.
55. "Yeah, she's got two kids, but so what?"
56. An unstable, institutionalized woman believes herself to be a time traveler. She vows to escape to return to her own era.
57. An infertile woman wants a child so badly that she starts to contemplate some unthinkable options.
58. "I'm going to disappoint you. But you knew that already."
59. "None of that 'eye for an eye' bullshit. I just want him dead."
60. While surfing porn on the Internet, a man comes across a picture of his wife.
61. "You'll notice my wife doesn't drink."
62. A woman discovers that her boyfriend's apartment is bugged with surveillance equipment.
63. "Who are these women who keep calling the house? And why do they call you 'Mr. President'?"
64. On his way to propose to his girlfriend, a man is approached on the subway by four youths.
65. A married woman attends a teamwork training retreat with several co-workers. Upon arriving, an attractive man from her office suggests that they start an affair.
66. A radio talk jock plans a farewell show as his station prepares to change to a soft rock format.
67. A drug addict's only supplier is killed in a police raid.
68. A woman learns that one of her young daughters has used a home pregnancy test.
69. "Whatever you do, don't go outside."
70. A telemarketer begins to receive telephone threats from the customer she just called moments before.
71. "You need special permission to view this material."
72. Two friends decide to ditch school for the day and explore the nearby sewer tunnels.

73. After practicing his act for years, a man finally gets the chance to audition for a television variety show.
74. A riot breaks out at a candlelight vigil for a dead rock star.
75. "Remember how you said my marriage wouldn't last a year? Well..."
76. "How much do you know about guns?"
77. A young man of North-African descent, but who has lived in the United States almost his whole life, is deported back to the country he never knew.
78. A therapist at a battered women's shelter is beaten up by her boyfriend.
79. "She lost the baby."
80. Big tobacco announces that smoking increases penis size.
81. A Florida game warden volunteers to work undercover to apprehend members of an alligator-poaching ring.
82. "Can you *please* turn the camera off?"
83. A young man works his way into an apprenticeship with a slick salesman.
84. An architect is informed that his current project bears an uncanny resemblance to a "haunted" hotel destroyed decades earlier.
85. "Well, he said we were pretty drunk at the time."
86. Faced with poverty, a retired exotic dancer concocts a plan to take Broadway by storm.
87. An ant decides to take his revenge upon the man who stepped on his family.
88. "Is it true what they say about you?"
89. A frustrated artist finds himself temporarily inspired after committing an act of violence.
90. You're secretly in love with your best friend's wife, and you suspect she feels the same way about you.
91. A woman walks into a grocery store, but when she walks out, many things have changed.
92. A teenage girl's dead grandmother starts appearing in her dreams and revealing family secrets.
93. "How am I supposed to go to the bathroom with this on?"
94. A man gets out of bed one morning and discovers that he's a foot shorter that the day before.
95. Believing the floating lights in his backward to be fireflies, a young boy accidentally traps a fairy in a Mason jar.
96. An accountant believes that his "sick" co-worker has been killed by her husband.
97. "You won't believe what I just got in the mail."
98. "They said I'd never walk again. Ha—what did they know?"
99. While on a camping trip, a little boy strays from his family and happens upon a carnival in the middle of nowhere.
100. "I don't care if this is a recorded threat. If you come near my wife again, I will kill you."

Writing the Logline

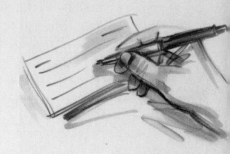

Boil It Down to One Sentence

by Mike Kuciak

The logline is an incredibly important creative and marketing tool in the film industry. Loglines are especially useful to screenwriters and the people who represent them. Loglines help to shape and sell scripts, acquire representation, attract elements and market the finished product to the movie going audience.

However, as vital as loglines are, all too frequently I encounter writers who don't even know what a logline is, much less how to write one. Let's change that.

WHAT'S A LOGLINE, AND HOW DO YOU WRITE ONE?

A logline is a one-line summary of the story. Every once in a while I see a two-sentence logline, but it's rarely good. When it comes to loglines, the tighter and more cohesive, the better. For example, here's a logline that could work for *Raiders of The Lost Ark*:

> An archaeologist adventurer battles Nazis for the lost ark, a holy artifact with the power to tip the scales of World War II.

It's not genius, but it does the trick. You know from reading it:

a) Genre
b) Concept
c) Time Period
d) The Hero
e) The Villains
f) The Risk (What's at stake?)

MICHAEL KUCIAK is vice president of acquisitions at management/production company AEI (*Joe Somebody, Life or Something Like It, The Truth About The Canal Street Brothel*). He spends every day chasing the perfect logline.

Pretty good for one little line. If I wanted, I could expand the logline a bit to include the feel and/or inspiration:

> In an homage to Depression-era serial adventures, an archaeologist battles Nazis for the lost ark, a holy artifact with the power to tip the scales of World War II.

You can tweak the same logline for different uses. For instance, say I'm sending the script to an actress's agent for consideration. I might massage the logline to:

> An archaeologist teams up with his tough and beautiful old flame to battle Nazis for the lost ark, a holy artifact with the power to tip the scales of World War II.

Notice that from one incarnation to the next, I'm not just adding. Trying to jam too much stuff into one line just muddles it. A muddled logline makes the movie seem muddled. Sometimes writers say they can't write a logline for their script because the story is oh-so-complex/character-driven/ whatever. "Sell my art in one line?" they snort. "Impossible!" This excuse is complete bullshit.

When writers complain they can't apply a logline to their script, it tells me they haven't thought out the unifying idea of their story. *The Matrix* is a pretty twisty movie with a super-high concept, but:

> When a hacker discovers that all of reality is a computer simulation, he fights to bring down the machines enslaving humanity.

Again, not brilliant but it works. How about a movie almost completely driven by its characters and dialogue with lots of plot twists, like *The Big Lebowski*?

> An ex-hippie loser and his bowling alley friends deal with colorful Hollywood characters while pursuing a briefcase full of $1 million in stolen ransom money.

In this example, I spent more time talking about the characters. I glossed over the twisting plot—it's impossible to even touch on without drowning the logline in details. One school of thought suggests always mentioning the genre at the top of the line. *The Big Lebowski* would be something like:

> Character-driven comedy about an ex-hippie loser and his bowling alley friends who deal with colorful Hollywood characters while pursuing a million-dollar ransom.

A CONCISE EXPLANATION

If you're pitching to someone who is specifically looking for a certain kind of project, he knows upfront the script is something that might interest him. A side note: There is no benefit to writing a logline that tricks people into reading the script. If you retooled *The Ring*'s logline so it sounded like a character-driven comedy, all you're going to earn is a script thrown in the trash. I've read a lot of vague, wishy-washy loglines. Things like:

> Two people face trials in a difficult time.

This explains absolutely nothing. What is it? *The Blues Brothers? Heavenly Creatures?* Typically, these examples appear when the writer a) doesn't know how to write a logline; b) doesn't know what story he's trying to tell; or, c) thinks, by being vague, people will request it to find out what the script is about.

The c) school of thought couldn't be more wrong. No one in the industry can drop an hour just to solve the mystery of a random logline. Notice that in every example, the hero's doing something: striving, battling, searching, etc. It implies an active, dramatic project.

Strong loglines are an indication of a strong writer—solid nouns. Active verbs. Sleek sentence structure. An exciting idea. If your logline includes all of these elements, the possibility of industry professionals asking to see more of your work is much better. Also, make sure the logline pertains to the majority of the story and not just the coolest part or the climax. At times I'll get queries with loglines that sound interesting:

> After his best friend dies on the battlefield, a soldier strives to deliver his friend's last letters and falls in love with the widowed wife.

The script arrives ... and almost the whole thing is about a guy trying to launch his poetry career in a coffee shop filled with kooky characters. The logline pitched me something that doesn't happen until the very end.

LOGLINES VS. TAGLINES

Occasionally, writers confuse the logline with the tagline. A tagline is what you find on the movie poster or the DVD box. It's supposed to tease and lure, not explain. Taglines are generally written by the marketing department for use in advertising movies. My personal favorite is the one for *The Killer*: "One Vicious Hitman. One Fierce Cop. Ten Thousand Bullets."

Another example, the tagline for *Ghostbusters*: "Who Ya Gonna Call?" The logline, on the other hand, would be something like:

Getting Started

A sci-fi comedy about three scientists who open a ghost extermination service and end up saving New York from a powerful demon.

Vastly different animals. If you pitched the logline to talent reps and studio execs, they would get the project and be able to judge accordingly. If you just kept saying, "Who ya gonna call?", their answer will be: "Not you."

THE DATE TEST

There are a couple of tricks to writing loglines. My favorite is pretending I'm on a date, standing in front of the marquee, deciding what movie to see. There's an action-comedy I really want to catch, but she's going to ultimately decide.

I ask, "What about this action-comedy?"

She replies: "Maybe, what's it about?"

If I say, "It's much too complex and character-driven to explain," I'm probably not going to see it.

If I say, "It's about two people who face difficult situations," I'm probably not going to see it.

If I say, "It's, uh, a romantic drama with strong female characters," I might get to see my action-comedy; but, after the movie she'll think I'm either stupid or a liar. Either way, no more dates for me.

However, if I was able to explain it—concisely describing the major aspects of the movie—and also sell it, make it sound like a really cool, funny, exciting movie, there's a good chance I'll see the action-comedy. My date might say she's not interested in a film like that or just doesn't like action-comedies across the board. Fair enough, because there is also a horror movie I'd like to see ...

I'd also like to point out that those little white "coming attraction" pamphlets you can pick up in the theater lobby are filled with great loglines. You don't think you can wrap up your whole story in a line? If you can't, the people who write those loglines certainly can. Practice with well-known movies—titles you love and know. After a while you'll get the hang of it and will not only be able to write a workable logline, but also one that sings and sells your script.

Once Upon a Playwriting Idea

Making Your Concept Stage-worthy

by Liza Lentini

This article is not about how to get over your fear of writing—but it could be. After all, *fear* is the number one reason folks don't finish what they start, or even begin the story they want to tell. When I was a young idealist, starting to teach my own workshop in New York City, I never, ever suspected that at the beginning of every new class I would have to prep myself for at least one person pulling me aside and telling me: "I shouldn't be here. Can I get my money back? I can't write a play to save my life. I don't want to bother trying." My response? *Go ahead and leave, then.* The earth will continue to turn on its axis, the sun will still rise tomorrow, and everyone will get on with their lives without noticing you decided to cop out. My point is: There are no excuses.

In order to approach writing a play, you must have a burning idea—something inside you that demands to be portrayed on stage. From that great idea comes an even greater story, and with that story, you can build your play. You may only perceive a glimpse of a scene or a mysterious character, you may not know what your play is called or how it ends, and all that is perfectly fine. Better, in fact. Because by the time you finish reading this article, you'll have the answers to those questions, and have learned to conquer fear by bringing in its arch nemesis: *fun.*

GET YOUR CHARACTER IN CHECK

The debate over which comes first—a play's character or its plot—is

LIZA LENTINI'S (www.lizalentini.com) plays have been performed at The Cherry Lane Theatre, PS122, The Women's Project, and The McGinn/Cazale Theatre, among others, garnering a multitude of honors and awards. She is the founder and creative director of Elephant Ensemble Theater, a charitable organization that brings performances to children in hospitals. Liza is currently writing a book called *How to Write a Play in 8 Weeks or Less*, which details her unique no nonsense method, the same she teaches in her NYC workshop.

endless. We don't have to resolve that here and now, but what you *do* have to do, is pick your central character. That is, who your play is about. This may not be as obvious as you think, as your central character may not be the most colorful, the most loveable, or even the most interesting (to you). Your central character will, however, be the one main character who learns something by your play's ending. The reason an audience member purchases a ticket to spend (roughly) two hours with your play is because they want to discover something. The eyes through which you allow them to make this discovery belong to your central character.

Peter Filichia is a critic for the *Star-Ledger* in New Jersey. He writes a column three times a week (www.theatermania.com/peterfilichia), and he's a man who believes that the more playwrights know about their characters, the better. "Make sure your characters are real; I always suggest filling out a job application for them," he says. "Get a pad of job applications from your local stationery store, one ideally for a low-level job. Those tend to be the ones that ask questions such a height and weight, and that starts a playwright thinking: Is my character overweight? How has that affected him? Is he embarrassed by it? Happy eating no matter what the consequences? Is he short? Is he adversely affected by it, aware that the best jobs go to the tall people? Or is he/she combative as a result of it. Pretty soon you'll find that who your characters are will put them in situations in which they'll either thrive or have to extricate themselves. And, as an exercise, how about putting your characters in situations that they'll never encounter in the play—just to see how they'll react in such circumstances. You'll learn even more about them!"

Eventually, you will need to know all you can about your central character, but for now, choose a name that suits their personality, decide on their age and general disposition, and let's get started—playing.

CHILD'S PLAY

Let's try something—a game that requires you act on impulse, and resolve to be fearless and have a good time. This game is based on a classic children's story, no story in particular. If you've never read a children's story before (as one student told me), then either go out and read one or wing it. If you've ever done Mad Libs as a child, you be even better prepped for the silliness that awaits you.

I created a template which allows you to go wherever the story takes you. Even though the story here is a classic "hero conquers evil" whimsical tale, don't let that limit your story to a G rating. Don't be fooled by the simplistic language, and do not feel as though your story has to make too much sense.

Right now, I am writing a play about a guy who makes an awkward homecoming after being sent away from his family for the first 30 years of his life. Here's an example of my story:

Once Upon a time, there lived a little girl/boy named <u>Frank</u>. Only very special people knew that this little person had a gift. S/he could <u>drink more alcohol than anyone thought was humanly possible</u>, like no one else in the world. More than anything s/he <u>loved to play with other's people's psyches</u> and hated to <u>dwell on his horrific childhood</u>, which would end up being very important later in life.

Now you give it a try. Let your character out for the first time to roam and play. You do not have to read the template beforehand. Give yourself 20 minutes. Ready? Go.

MY STORY

By _____

Once Upon a Time, there lived a little girl/boy named _____. Only very special people knew that this little person had a gift. S/he could _____, like no one else in the world. More than anything s/he loved to _____ and hated to _____, which would end up being very important later in life.

Growing up, _____ had a great/exceptionally difficult time. (Tell us why: _____)

The one thing S/he wanted more than anything was _____. S/he tried many ways of getting his/her dream. To name a few ways: _____ _____.

One day, his/her life completely changed because of _____. This launched him/her on a great adventure. The first major thing that happened was _____ and that amazing thing led to another amazing thing, _____.

For a minute, it looked as though _____ was well on his/her way toward achieving his/her ultimate goal of

_____, but then a big monster came along in the form of a _____. This monster was a pretty major problem. Our hero tried so many different ways to get rid of the monster, to name a few: _____.

For now, it looked as though the monster was behind him/her. "Gee, I think I'm going to achieve my dream after all," s/he thought to his/herself. "But now I'm finding I have a few philosophical questions I need to answer about life." Though this was unexpected, our hero went about trying to solve some major philosophical questions about life, like: _____. The way s/he went about solving them was by _____ and _____ _____. By making this effort, s/he got closer to his/her ultimate goal without even knowing it.

Our hero was having quite a journey. Along the way, s/he made some friends named _____. They were really important because they helped our hero to _____ _____. Our hero needed his friends, because otherwise he couldn't _____.

But before any real success could be achieved, an evil demon got in the way. This one took the form of a _____. Our hero could see the glorious glow of _____ on the horizon. He tried to get away from the demon by using all of these very skillful skills like _____ and _____. It did/didn't work, and that lead our hero to _____.

But s/he persevered! Sometimes at night s/he found him/herself longing for _____, but comforting his/herself with _____. Little did s/he know, another mini-adventure was just around the corner. The sight of his/her dream (also known as _____) could now clearly be seen, but not touched. First our hero had to prove him/herself a warrior by _____ and _____. This made him/her feel _____. He then took action to _____ which proved his loyalty to his ultimate goal more than anything else.

What followed was like an explosion. Our hero did/didn't see it coming. All of a sudden, all the good, all the strength that was helping our hero make this journey just fell away. It was as though missiles were being thrown at his/her and s/he was expected to dodge them all alone. Here's how s/he did it: _____ _____. Pretty impressive, huh?

When the storm calmed, our hero was very tired. S/he decided s/he needed to _____ in order to feel human again.

And then, unexpectedly, the dream was there, right before him/her. It was/wasn't what s/he had expected. It had evolved into _____. What made it evolve was the way s/he had _____. At the end of this marvelous and incredibly journey, our hero was changed. Before, s/he was _____. Now, s/he was _____ _____. S/he decided that the one thing that was most important in life was _____. (Or, s/he never really understood that the meaning of life was _____ and took the lesser route of _____.) Our hero was/wasn't victorious.

THE END

OUR FRIENDLY NEIGHBORHOOD PLOT POINTS

If I had told you at the very beginning that you were about to plot out your story, you may very well have run away screaming. But that's exactly what you've just done. Chances are good that the template's language and phrasing isn't appropriate for your play's ultimate narrative, and so it's now your job to create a comprehensive narrative—one that represents your goals for your script, as well as your central character's goals (what he or she ultimately wants) which will serve as the driving force for your story.

Plot's basic skeleton is constructed of 5 main parts:

1. Introduction: when we find out who the characters are in your play, what the general setting is, and why we're all watching.

2. Rising Action: When each and every character is fighting to achieve their immediate goals and, most likely, coming up with obstacles. (Conflict creates drama—always remember that.)

3. Climax: When we see all of that wonderful conflict come to a head; it's usually a moment of great discovery.

4. Falling Action: When you allow your audience and your characters, whomever is left standing, to take a breather, digest what has just happened, and what will follow, once the curtain comes down

5. Resolution: or the *denouement*, is your last chance as a playwright to let the audience take home a message. It's Linda Loman's "Attention must be paid," in Arthur Miller's classic *Death of a Salesman*. It's the moral; it's the message. It's the end.

THE "PERFECT PLAY" MYTH

All that said, playwriting is one of the only places you truly can create your own world. Often my students will ask me if their plays have to be conventional, and I always shoot them a quick "Heck no!" with extra emphasis on the "no." I wouldn't tell anyone to do something I wouldn't do myself, and my plays have been as far from conventional as possible. Just because we're using words like plot and structure, doesn't mean your play has to adhere to any of the rules of kitchen sink realism or those that are presented as "well-made plays." The best theater takes soundly structured ideas and makes them fresh and personal. When Samuel Beckett wrote *Waiting for Godot*, people famously flew *out* of the theater. At the time, they may not have been ready for his idea of plot, but his play certainly has one. And he found an original way to tell a story on stage that revolutionized theater forever.

"I think a great story is one in which you care about the characters and really want to keep reading/watching in order to see what will happen to them," says Liz Frankel, literary manager at The Public Theater. "There is a clear dramatic question hovering above the action, so you know roughly where the story is headed, but you can't predict the ending and find it both surprising and fitting when you get to it. The best story is one that you feel that you have never heard before, or heard told in this particular way. Great stories do not have to be told in linear or naturalistic fashions and, of course, many great plays break all the rules and are compelling anyway."

And when Frankel reads a play that falls short, when the playwright doesn't follow through and go all the way, it's a disappointment. "I feel frustrated because I wanted to know more than the author told me," she says. "And it's especially frustrating to see writers leave out the details necessary to bring their stories to life only in order to create a compact 90-minute drama. Sometimes, a play needs to be two hours long (or more!) in order to reach its own potential and provide a satisfying experience for its audience."

John Clinton Eisner, artistic director and co-founder of the Lark Play Development Center, agrees—believing playwrights have an obligation to take risks and follow the beat of their own drummer. "Playwrights are natural leaders in any evolving society, bringing people face to face in the theater to learn about alternative perspectives and to inspire shared visions of the future," he says. "For these reasons, it is critical for playwrights to be attentive to their own passions and driving interests, rather than to dwell on what they perceive to be the demands of the market. The genuine artifact in theater is authentic emotional truth rooted in recognizable experience. Audiences know it when they see it; you can't fool them. Playwrights who remain true to themselves and their most deeply held values, while, at the same time, embracing an active dialogue with creative collaborators and audiences, are lightening rods for humanity against the storm of progress. It is a strange melding of iconoclasm, idiosyncrasy and a profound need to connect with others that makes for success in the theater in life as well as art."

So, a great big congrats goes out to you. You've accomplished so much in so little time today. You're on your way towards writing a new play! Just remember to keep fun at close hand, in case that killjoy called fear rears its ugly head again.

Formatting Your Script

Make Your Work Look Professional

by Charles Galvin

The best part about writing a novel may be the simple formatting. It's all in block chunks, page after page. Easy peasy. Scripts, meanwhile, follow rigid guidelines when it comes to how things should appear on the page, and poorly formatted material is likely to be thrown in the trash.

You may be saying, "But a good story will see its way through." It may—but it's hard for your script to get read when it's in the recycle bin. Incorrect formatting of a screenplay or play is an obvious sign of an amateur. Producers and agents are used to reading scripts that follow the rules. It helps them read quicker—so make sure you follow them, too.

"If you want your script to stand out from the crowd in a good way, you want to make sure it doesn't stand out from the crowd just because of how it looks," says Gregory K. Pincus, a screenwriter (*Little Big League*) and TV writer. "If your script looks like you know what you're doing, you'll pass the first 'smell' test and, with luck, you can hook people with your story."

Don't skip a dream sequence just because you don't know how to write it. Don't avoid flashbacks because you're not sure if everything looks A-OK on the page. Tackle it all—by reading the guidelines below.

STARTING OFF

Title Page: Starting about a quarter from the top of the page is the title, centered and capitalized. A few lines below the title will be the credit line, centered, using both upper and lower-case. This line should simply say "By," or "A Screenplay by." A couple lines beneath the credit line should be your name, centered. In the bottom right hand corner of the page, be sure

---

CHARLES GALVIN is a former assistant editor for *Screenwriter's & Playwright's Market*.

Formatting Screenplays

Use a header. Include your name, the script title, and the page number.

SAMBUCHINO/OCTOBER SURPRISE   25

EXT. POLICE PRECINCT–DAY

These slugs introduce the location and time of day.

Civilians and police officers mill in and out. Down the street walks BILLY VAN RAYNE, 20s, tall, powerful–maybe even a bit dangerous. He looks at the police station, hesitating.

Capitalize characters as they are introduced.

BILLY

Now or never.

He pulls something out of his pocket. It's a HANDHELD TAPE RECORDER.

Capitalize key actions and objects.

VOICE (O.S.)

Need some help?

Billy looks to see a BEAT COP, 30s, eyeing him suspiciously.

Center character names for dialogue.

BILLY

Indent dialogue.

No thanks–I'm okay . . .

Billy walks up the steps toward the precinct front door.

When one scene continues directly into another, use this abbreviation.

INT. POLICE PRECINCT–DAY–CON'T

Billy enters. The first person he sees is an obese DESK SERGEANT, who is trying to answer questions from a Russian SKINHEAD.

DESK SERGEANT

I don't know what else to tell you. You'll have to go to the courthouse for further instructions. After that–

SKINHEAD
(in Russian)

I still cannot understand you!

DESK SERGEANT (CON'T)

–we may be able to work something out. That's all I can tell you. As you can see, I'm very busy.

To specify emotions or specific actions while speaking, center it and use parentheses.

(calls out)

Next!

INT. CAPTAIN RYBAN'S OFFICE–THAT MOMENT

RYBAN

You can use other slug variations besides "Night" and "Day," though don't get carried away. Common variations include "That Moment," "Early Morning," and "Dusk."

Don't leave "hangers."

Sitting Down to Write

Formatting Plays

Play formatting has its various little differences from screenplays. After the title page, you will want to include an informational page that contains the following:

1. **Characters**. Names of all characters with a one-sentence description, such as "Baby Joe's mother; a housekeeper who likes to keep things simple."

2. **Time**. How much time elapses during the course of the play? One night? Five years?

3. **Synopsis**. Keep this story summary as short as you can. Consider it a "logline."

4. **History**. Show the play's development. Was it read or workshopped yet? Has it had a production? If so, where?

This line designates the page, the act, and the scene (in that order).

The Snowflake Theory   Page I—I—I

ACT I
Scene 1

Tell what happens before the lights come up.

SETTING: MARGE's kitchen. Only a table and chairs are needed. On the table are two sets (different colors) of plastic unbreakable dishes and two sets of flatware. It's Wednesday, Feb. 26, 2003.

BEFORE RISE: Sounds of MARGE removing dishes and flinging them to the floor.

Explain what's going on when the lights come up.

AT RISE: Action continues. Nothing is breaking. MARGE becomes more and more frustrated. She throws the flatware at the dishes. Finally, Marge gives up and sits.

Center character names for dialogue.

                              MARGE
You are where you are. That's what Manny always said.

Keep all dialogue pushed left and have it wrap all the way across.

Indent action and stage directions. Have it in parentheses.

                              (MARGE opens a garbage bag and starts throwing everything in. REBECCA enters in a coat.)

                          REBECCA
It's not garbage night.

Capitalize character names.

to include your contact information (address, phone number, e-mail, etc.). Many times, the contact will actually be your representation, so include that instead, if applicable.

Margins: Before you start, be sure to set the proper page margins. One inch from the top, bottom, and right, one and a half inches from the left. These criteria apply to all pages except the title page.

Font: The standard is Courier font, size 12. Filmmakers expect the same font in every screenplay they read, both for visual comfort and for the purpose of judging length. A different font is a quick way to irritate somebody who reads dozens of scripts a day, not to mention a sign of a writer's inexperience. Every page of text is usually translated to mean one minute of film. Changing the font will throw off the movie's estimated length.

Tense: Other than dialogue, always write action and description in the present tense: "The bomb *explodes*. Jane *is* thrown from the passenger seat."

Page Numbers: Be sure to number all of your pages. This will help in determining screen time as well as serve as a reference for the reader. To be safe, also include a header, which will contain the film title and your last name.

GETTING INTO IT

"Fade In": The official beginning to each and every screenplay. This is probably one of the only—if not *the* only time—a screenwriter should include camera instruction in your writing. In fact, including camera directions, such as "zoom out," "dolly in" or "match cut," is a serious sign of a novice.

Scene Heading/Slug Line/Scene Slug: Each scene begins with basic information that is found in the heading. This part tells whether the scene is interior or exterior (INT. or EXT.), where the scene is taking place, and what time of day it is. All of this information should be left-justified and set in upper-case. The most traditional way to handle the time of day is simply stating "day" or "night." While other options are still acceptable, producers will often count the number of "day" scenes vs. "night" scenes to help estimate a budget, as shooting at night costs more money.

Scene Description: This information follows the scene heading. It is brief and written in sentence case. Don't get carried away here. Script readers like to see "white space" on a page—meaning that they don't want to read thick paragraphs of description and action. Keep it simple.

Dialogue: A character's dialogue is noted by centering the name in upper-case letters directly above their lines. In some cases, it is necessary to indicate how a line should be read using one or two descriptive adverbs.

If necessary, these are placed in parentheses directly underneath the character's name, above their lines.

THE NITTY-GRITTY

Some screenwriting devices are not essential to writing a screenplay. In many cases, a writer can fall in love with things like montages or flashbacks. Overuse or misuse of certain techniques can detract from the screenplay, so if you are going to try something, make sure to do it the right way.

Montages, Dreams, Flashbacks, or Fantasy Sequences: Obviously, these are different elements in a screenplay, but they are introduced using the same method. For example, to indicate one of these sequences, write "BEGIN MONTAGE" in the scene heading. Any shots or descriptions to be included should be clear and concise. When finished, be sure to indicate "END MONTAGE."

Simultaneous or Dueling Dialogue: In scenes where two or more characters speak at the same time, their dialogue can be listed on the page next to each other. It is also acceptable to indicate in the scene description that they are both talking, and to place one dialogue above the other.

Phone Call: Dialogue between characters on the phone can be showed in one of two ways. One way is to cut back and forth while each character speaks, showing both on the screen at different times (or even splitting the screen to show both characters at the same time). The other way is to show only one character on screen but still have the other character's voice heard through the phone. In this case, the character's name should be followed by a parenthetical indicating (ON PHONE) to specify that they can be heard but not seen.

Where to Read Scripts

The best way to see how the intricacies of a script are laid out and formatted is simply to look at other scripts. Here are some online locations where you can see professional scripts for free:

- Simply Scripts: www.simplyscripts.com

- Daily Script: www.dailyscript.com

- Drew's Script-o-Rama: www.script-o-rama.com

- The Internet Movie Database: www.imdb.com

V.O. and O.S.: In some cases, a character will not be onscreen yet will still be talking and a part of the scene, such as when a character is narrating. This is voiceover—and noted by writing (V.O.) next to the character's name above the dialogue. When a character offscreen is talking, use the notation (O.S.) next to their name.

Fading Out: You may have times at the end of a screenplay—or in the middle—where the screen fades to black. This is a common technique when large spans of time elapse. Avoid overusing fade-outs. Along with "fade to black," you can also "fade to white," such as at the end of *Total Recall* (so *was* it a dream?).

And the rest: Your title page should be on card stock—slightly thicker paper. Use card stock for the back page as well to give it a clear beginning and end. As with most submissions, only print on one side of the paper. Lastly, scripts are usually three-hole punched and bound by two brads.

Effective Dialogue

Using Speech for Stage and Screen

by Dr. Philip Zwerling

There are just three ways for us to know the inner workings of a character in a script: from what others say about them, from what they say about themselves, and from what they do. Clearly what a character does is immensely more important, and truthful, than what they say. A woman may tell her friend how much she loves her fiancé in scene one, but if the audience sees her lustfully kissing a strange man in scene two, we learn two things about her character: that she doesn't love her man, and that she lies to her friends.

But though scriptwriting is inherently a visual medium, there is still a vital role for the spoken word—especially with playwriting. Dialogue has three main functions:

1) to reveal character
2) to move the plot forward
3) to create conflict

All scripts need dialogue, just not as much as most writers throw in. As Aristotle said, "Drama is the imitation of an action"—and your script must place primacy on action. Learn to use dialogue effectively and sparingly. Seek the visual image first and the spoken words second. Do we want to see our character John speaking in detail and at length of all the ways he loves character Jill? Or do we want to see him take her in his arms and kiss her passionately? And then see whether she slaps him or returns his kiss with even greater ardor?

PHILIP ZWERLING is assistant professor of English and Creative Writing at the University of Texas Pan American and a published and produced playwright.

THE IMPORTANCE OF DIALOGUE

"Good dialogue," Jeffrey Hatcher writes in *The Art and Craft of Playwriting*, "is both expressive and economical … It must deliver exposition (what has happened). It must depict action (what is happening). It must promise future action (what may happen)." As an example of good dialogue, Hatcher uses one of Regina's short speeches from Lillian Hellman's *The Little Foxes*. Imagine Bette Davis delivering these lines in the movie version of that play: "I'm smiling Ben. I'm smiling because you are quite safe while Horace lives. But I don't think Horace will live. And if he doesn't, I shall want seventy-five percent in exchange for the bonds. And if I don't get what I want I am going to put all three of you in jail."

Hellman's brief dialogue tells us a lot: 1) it reveals Regina as a rapacious plotter unconcerned for the health of her husband, Horace; 2) it hints at a shady financial scheme in the past; and 3) it builds the conflict with Ben for the future.

Yes, it also contains exposition—and exposition is a slippery eel for any writer. You may want to use dialogue to pass on to your audience information they need. Regina, for example, tells us Horace is dying and that she knows about Ben's arrangement with Horace. However, Hellman couches the exposition in the form of threat, which is perfectly natural to the plot and the character speaking.

Gone Are the Old Ways

In the mid-19th century, there was a common theatrical convention. When the curtain rose at the theatre, the audience often saw two maids tidying up an ornate drawing room and the dialogue went something like this:

MAID #1

Let's tidy up quickly, Berenice. The whole Barnewell family is returning from the weekend in London at any moment.

MAID #2

Do you think Madam Barnewell knows about her husband's affair with that notorious West End actress, who has ensnared so many married men?

MAID #1

I hope not since the Madam has such a jealous and violent nature.

MAID #2

And what will they say when they learn George, their oldest son, proposed marriage to that Fitwell woman from the wrong side of the tracks?

MAID #1

Or that young Tabitha, their 19-year-old daughter still pines for that rich
Lord Bromley, who is as old as her own father.

At which point a doorbell is heard ringing off stage and the aforementioned
characters slowly enter the drawing room, the audience already well
informed of their backgrounds and about all the conflicts to come. Such
use of exposition has happily gone the way of the feather boa, waistcoats
and high starched collars. Likewise Shakespeare's soliloquies, in which a
character unburdens himself in directly to the audience, are things of the
past.

Avoiding Dialogue Crutches

While dialogue does inform an audience about what characters want and
think, exposition must be used sparingly and dribbled out in small amounts
rather than dumped on an audience in large chunks. Remember that one
character does not tell another character what that second character already
knows (as in the example of the maids above). The rule of thumb is: If a
character is speaking only so that the writer can deliver information to
the audience, they should not speak. Note again that Regina's speech may
contain exposition, but it also reveals character, increases the conflict, and
moves the plot forward in a natural way.

Beware as well of a direct address to the audience and the use of Voice
Over narration for screenplays. In class, I don't allow students to use either
technique. I also don't allow them to have characters who talk to themselves.
It's true that well received movies like *American Beauty* and *Adaptation* use
Voice Over and it's true that some people talk to themselves in real life, but
it's too easy for a writer to rely on these techniques to provide exposition,
inner thoughts, and transitions. I'd rather make students (and you) work
harder by working without these crutches. Once you've mastered the craft
without them, you can choose to use them when they make sense rather
than when you need them.

CRAFTING REALISTIC SPEECH

Dialogue comes realistically from character. An American will speak
differently than a Ukrainian, a neurosurgeon differently than a dishwasher,
and someone from the Victorian Age differently from someone from the
Age of Aquarius. Before you can write dialogue, you must define your
character.

I always make out a character sheet for each of my creations. I decide
physical characteristics: gender, age, ethnicity, height, eye and hair color,

etc. Their social characteristics: economic class, educational level, politics, hobbies, etc. and the psychological: ambitions, frustrations, moral standards, bad habits, most prized possession. And finally I write down three things that make this character different from every other character of the same age. Always ask yourself what makes your character different and unique, not what makes them like everyone else. Who the character is will determine what they say and how they say it.

To get a feel for how people really talk, I assign my students to go out and eavesdrop on two or more people and to take notes on the conversation unobtrusively. Students quickly learn that 1) real people do not usually speak in complete sentences or use perfect grammar; and 2) that real conversation has lots of pauses, digressions, and radical changes of direction. I have the students take that "discovered dialogue" and use it to write a scene. Their feel for realistic dialogue increases quickly.

If you listen and take notes, you'll uncover more bits of astounding dialogue than you can use because people really do say the most amazing things.

A UNIQUE VOICE AND SUBTEXT

Every character comes from you but they can't all sound like you. The serial killer, the femme fatale, the whiny nine-year-old come from your imagination and somehow are part of your persona but each one needs to have a unique voice of their own. That voice will come out of your character chart and your observations. When students come to me with dialogue for a nine-year-old character but the vocabulary and syntax sound like a college student, I send them out to talk to some real nine-year-olds and take notes.

Also, don't limit yourself to "pristine" or "perfect" dialogue. In real life, people trail off, interrupt one another, misspeak, and stammer. They may use "uh's" and "um's" in their speech.

And here's the ironic part: What a character doesn't say is often more important than what they do say. Scriptwriting is like drawing a blueprint or forming skeleton for a scene on stage or screen. Making movies and plays is a collaborative effort between the writer, the actors, the director, and the designers. The writer needs to give the actors room to develop a character. Use dashes, commas, semi-colons and ellipses, beats, and pauses to allow the actor and director to flesh out the character and deliver the subtext. Subtext is what a character is really saying and feeling beneath, between, or in contradiction to the words they are mouthing. Because that's the way we communicate, or fail to communicate, in real life.

For example: what happens when John shows up for work after a really bad weekend. His wife, Anne, just left him. His dog died. He's behind on his mortgage. John runs into his best friend, Fred, at the water cooler. Do you think he shares all these details with his friend? I don't think so. The conversation is likely to happen like this:

> FRED
>
> Hey, man, how was the weekend?

> JOHN
>
> Um … OK, I guess.

> FRED
>
> Whadja do?

> JOHN
> (distracted)
>
> Uh...not much, not much.

> FRED
>
> Carol and I made reservations for Bermuda next spring.
> (snaps fingers)
> Hey, maybe you and Anne could join us!

> JOHN
>
> Wait—what?

> FRED
>
> Bermuda. Next spring. You and Anne?

> JOHN
>
> Yeah, yeah, I can ask her. But, uh … probably not, come to think of it. I should, uh, I should get back to work. I'll see ya, Fred.

SHOW DON'T TELL

When you've scripted your scene, then considered voice, exposition, and subtext, do two more things quickly. Rewrite your scene as narrative. Take all the spoken words out. In the scenario above it might read like this:

> *The camera follows John through his home. He stops in front of a closet and we see that it is almost completely empty. Only a few women's clothes remain on hangers that are jumbled about as if someone tore the clothes off hastily. John moves to the bedside and*

we see a framed photo of him and Anne in happier times. John turns the photo face down. John walks down the hall. He finds his little dog's rubber bone toy, picks it up and sadly throws it in the trash can, which is already full of empty liquor bottles. Cut to John's office: John runs into Fred at the water cooler. Fred looks happy and we see him talking. John looks downcast. He is not listening. John slowly walks away. Fred walks over to some other coworkers and relays concerns about John's behavior.

Second rewrite: draw five pictures to tell the same story with no dialogue or narrative. It's all right if you can't draw—use stick figures! It could look like this:

Picture 1: John sits on the bed with his head in his hands
Picture 2: An empty clothes closet
Picture 3: A trash can full of empty liquor bottles
Picture 4: John and Fred at the water cooler
Picture 5: Fred talks to co-workers and motions in the direction of John.

Now rewrite your original scene with dialogue but allow the pictures to show us more than the words tell us.

Rewriting

*Three Deadly Pitfalls and
How to Avoid Them*

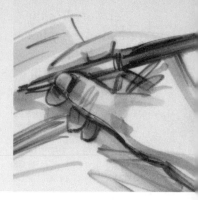

by John Robert Marlow

For most of us, the real magic comes not in the first draft, but in the second, or third. Or tenth. Even screenwriting luminary Terry Rossio states flatly: "I'm just an average writer. But I've learned the trick of applying what talent I possess many times over to a project, elevating it a little each time…. Essentially, I am an abundantly talented editor."

Ideally, rewrites are about improving and refining what's already on the page—catching things that, in the throes of creative passion, we didn't stop to notice. As Terry points out, this is often more like editing than anything else. Having written and professionally edited (or "doctored") both scripts and novels for the better part of a decade, I've come to learn that certain missteps occur more frequently than others. This article will cover a few of the most common mistakes: things every writer should look for when rewriting a script—or novel, for that matter.

PITFALL #1: REPETITION

This is a literary sin that creeps up on the best of writers. Professionals notice on their next pass—and correct the problem before anyone else sees the script. Amateurs don't notice, or correct.

As a general rule, avoid using the same word (or similar words) multiple times in quick succession. Oft-repeated words include he, she, him, her, his and hers ("He pulls *his gun*, sticks Harry's *gun* in *his* belt, and sneaks down the hall."). Character names can also be repeat offenders, this typically happens when a name is used in dialogue and then in narration, or vice versa. (BRENDA: *Linda*, wake up. / *Linda* hears the voice, as if in a dream.).

JOHN ROBERT MARLOW is an Academy-honored screenwriter, script consultant, novelist and editor. John's online Self Editing Blog (http://selfeditingblog.com/) provides useful tips for screenwriters and book authors. His *Lonely Keyboard* website (http://lonelykeyboard.com/) contains extreme-length interviews with working screenwriters.

Worst of all is the "double," where the same word repeats twice in a row—often at a sentence break. ("Bill hands the crocodile to Bob. Bob screams when it bites his arm off at the shoulder. Shouldering his backpack, Bill bends down and picks Bob's arm up off the street.")

Even widely-spaced repeaters can present a problem. In general, the more unusual the word or phrase, the less often you can use it. No one's going to notice that you used the word "man" or "woman" two pages ago—but throw in "hermaphrodite" on page 6, and you can be sure that readers who encounter "hermaphrodite" on page 110 will remember having seen it before.

Also keep an eye out for "William Shatner moments," in which one character—Captain Kirk, for instance—immediately parrots the dialogue of another character; this technique is so overused it's become a joke (intentionally so in *The Long Kiss Goodnight*).

Deliberate repetition is another matter—as where a particular character has a trademark phrase (used to great effect in *The Italian Job*), one character is mocking another (Otto in *A Fish Called Wanda*), a character habitually stutters (Ken in *A Fish Called Wanda*) or is stuttering under extreme stress (most often fear, grief, or anxiety; the Edward Kimberly reveal in *Tootsie*), or you're using a turnaround line ("What if there were no tomorrow?" and "That's not happiness to see me, is it?" in *A Perfect Murder*).

As a writer, you're expected to have a lot to say. You're also expected to have an unusually large vocabulary with which to say it. Repetition flies in the face of both expectations. It's like having two chins, when you should have only one: it makes you look bad. So give your writing a facelift and dump those doubles—along with your other repeats.

PITFALL #2: TRANSITIONS

Transitions are probably the single biggest source of confusion in unproduced scripts. And by "transitions," I don't mean formatted transitions like CUT TO: and DISSOLVE TO:, but story transitions. Few scripts relate events in a continuous flow, from start to finish. Sometimes the story moves back in time (as with flashbacks); more often it jumps forward, sparing the reader the dull details of ordinary life. Frequently, the transition will take the reader from one location and set of characters to another. Each of these transitions has its place—and each is fraught with peril.

Problems arise when the reader is not crystal clear on time, place or characters present. This kind of situation arises when everything is clear in the writer's head, but perhaps not quite so clear on the page. As with typos, we as authors tend to fill in the blanks: Because we know how it's supposed to read, that's the way we see it—even if some of the details were left off the page. The moment someone else picks it up—someone not intimately familiar with the story, and so unable to fill in the blanks—confusion reigns.

To avoid this, be sure to orient the reader *immediately* each time you jump to a new time or place. Part of this involves the proper use of slug lines (INT. or EXT. LOCATION / SUBLOCATION – TIME-OF-DAY). If you've got scenes in two different bedrooms, don't call each of them INT. BEDROOM; make one INT. JACK'S HOUSE / BEDROOM and the other INT. JILL'S APT. / BEDROOM. Using the same slug for multiple locations does more than confuse the reader—it also interferes with breakdowns, which affect budgeting, shot lists, and so on. The same goes for characters; absent some good reason to keep things secret (that killer hiding in the closet, for example), tell the reader which characters are in the new scene before going into dialogue.

When jumping to a later time at the same location, use something like "—LATER" or "—MOMENTS LATER" (no quotation marks necessary, naturally) as your time-of-day in the slug. If you're jumping to the next day, indicate this with a new time-of-day (—MORNING, when the last one was —NIGHT). When skipping more than a day, you may want to use a super on its own line: "SUPER: Three weeks later…" and then put your new slug on the following line.

When jumping backward in time, *always* use a super or scene header in preference to a slug, because the potential for confusion is massive. SUPER: 36 hours earlier… would be one way to do this (and the way it was handled onscreen in *Iron Man*). FLASHBACK: on its own line would be another (you might even want to underline or boldface the word to make sure it isn't missed). If you then jump back to the present, you *must* indicate this with another super (SUPER: The present) if that's what you used for the first jump, or another scene header (BACK TO SCENE:, which can also be underlined or bolded). *Iron Man* required neither because we never jumped forward from the past; instead, we stayed there until past became present.

If you're jumping a ways with both time and place, or opening with a scene from the past, a super like this may be in order: SUPER: Las Vegas, 36 hours earlier. When dealing with these situations, ask yourself: Is there any possible way that any of these details (time, place, characters present in the scene) could be misread or misinterpreted? If so, rewrite for clarity.

PITFALL #3: UNINTENDED MEANINGS

This is as true on the page as is it is in life: You say one thing, your listener hears another, and trouble soon follows. They heard every word you said, and accurately, too—but they took those words to mean something very different from what you intended. Consider the following passage:

"His eyes bounce between Teddy, Mandy, the girl, the geologist, then back to Franklin." Read literally, this tells us that "his eyes" are flying around the room, bouncing between characters like a pinball between posts. And while it's true that very few readers are going to take this literally, many will nonetheless read it the wrong way. When that happens, the reader is taken out of the moment, plucked from the world of the story like Dorothy from Kansas, or Neo from the Matrix. Readers will then stop, go back, and read it again to clarify—or they will laugh. Either way, the spell we've worked so hard to weave is now broken; the reader who a moment ago didn't know the real world existed, now marveling at our ineptitude.

When I first read the aforementioned "bouncing eyes" line (in a script I'd been hired to edit), it conjured up images of John Anderton in *Minority Report*, chasing his freshly-dropped eyeballs as they rolled down the corridor at Precrime. Not the image you want bouncing around inside your reader's head.

You might expect such unintended meanings to be rare, but this is not so. Most manuscripts have at least a few multiple-choice sentences. Many are unique to the stories in which they appear. Still, when you've read enough scripts, you begin to notice that certain grammatically dangerous situations lend themselves to particular variants of this problem.

One that pops up consistently goes something like this: Our heroes—call them Dick and Gwendolyn—are being hunted by armed thugs in an old warehouse. Dick ambushes Thug One and takes his gun. Telling Gwendolyn to stay put, Dick moves forward, gun at the ready. Suddenly, Thugs Two and Three appear. The next line is: Dick shoots Gwendolyn a glance. Tense scene, mounting suspense, edge-of-the-seat reading and then—Dick shoots Gwendolyn?

Of course not, but, thanks to unfortunate grammar, that's your reader's first impression. It doesn't matter how skillful you've been to this point, or how much suspense, drama, and reader involvement you've managed to create; it's all gone, right there. Shot to hell, you might say, along with poor Gwendolyn. The good news is, the heroine will recover. The bad news is, your script may not.

More often, unintended meanings are mundane, and lead readers astray on such simple matters as choreography (specific physical actions and the order in which they occur), or the identity of the character performing a specific action.

As writers, we're expected to have a remarkable facility with language. With few exceptions (political speechwriting and several ex-president come to mind), we are in the business of *making ourselves perfectly clear*. Unintended ambiguity—"multiple choice sentences" that can be read in more than one way—do a disservice to both reader and writer.

As you rewrite, keep this question in the back of your mind: Is there any possible way to misread this sentence? If the answer is yes, rephrase it. Hunt dual meanings down without pity, or remorse, or fear. Then terminate them—before they terminate you.

POLISH YOUR WORK

To paraphrase *Body Heat*'s Teddy Lewis: "Any time you go to write a decent script, you got fifty ways you can screw up. You think of twenty-five of them, and you're a genius." Like Terry Rossio, I claim no particular brilliance—but after reading thousands of scripts, I'd be an idiot if I didn't see patterns emerging: where and why things tend to go wrong, and what it takes to set them right.

Ultimately, writing is a bit like life: the more we keep at it, the better we get. We celebrate our victories, but often learn more from our mistakes. After a while, if we're paying attention, we begin to learn from other people's mistakes. This article—and the online Self Editing Blog (http://selfeditingblog.com/)—are my way of passing along what I've learned.

Chris Vogler

A Master Storyteller Talks Character, Craft, Pacing and Plot

by Jenna Glatzer

Chris Vogler is a writer and story consultant. His book, *The Writer's Journey: Mythic Structure for Writers* is based on an influential memo he wrote while analyzing scripts for the Walt Disney Company in the 1980s. He was invited to consult on Disney animation projects including *Aladdin*, *The Lion King*, *Hercules*, and *Fantasia 2000*. His website for his consulting company, Storytech, is www.thewritersjourney.com

Your book, *The Writer's Journey*, was inspired by Joseph Campbell's *The Hero with a Thousand Faces*. What drew you to his book?

As a young film student at USC, I was on a kind of vision quest, looking for guidance and a unifying system to organize the chaotic world of writing. I knew there had to be some order to it. I had already sensed some of the patterns in myth and movies when a film professor pointed me in the direction of Campbell's book. It was one of those life-changing experiences, hitting me like a bolt of lightning and completely re-organizing my brain. In that same semester, the first Star Wars movie was released, further clobbering me with the possibilities of Campbell's ideas.

Your book explores storytelling in terms of the "Hero's Journey." How do you answer critics who complain that writers should never follow formulas?

I agree with them. I hate formulaic movies, especially those that follow the Hero's Journey model formulaically. I don't see it or use it as a formula. It's not a cookbook recipe that you can follow to whip up a good screenplay. Instead, it's a map of the human territory that underlies storytelling, on

JENNA GLATZER (www.jennaglatzer.com) is a freelance writer of books, magazine articles and more. She is the founder of Absolute Write (www.absolutewrite.com).

which you can plan a unique journey that will follow a completely original path while still touching at the classic stations and crossing points that are present in any human experience.

I don't say it's the only way to tell a story or communicate with an audience. I do say that almost any story or work of art can be interpreted in the language of the Hero's Journey, because it's a universal description of just about anything that can happen to a human being.

How does your method differ from the traditional "three-act structure"?

My approach is based on the three-act model that Syd Field articulated and which is still the most practical way for filmmakers to communicate amongst themselves. The difference is that I see the long second act naturally breaking down into two distinct movements—one leading up to a central event or crisis (Syd Field's Midpoint, my Central Ordeal) and one trailing away from the central event. The first movement of Act II is the preparation for the Central Ordeal, and the second movement is the consequences of that central event. So you end up with a structure of four movements, Act I, Act IIa, Act IIb, and Act III.

Of course these are just conveniences—ways to talk generally about things that are never so neat and tidy in practice. The *story* tells you how many acts or movements it needs. Maybe you choose to think of it as one continuous, seamless flow of images; maybe you discover it needs 26 acts, movements, or chapters; maybe you don't spend one second thinking about how many acts it has. The best rule for structuring is "What happens next?" Your obligation is to be constantly, unrelentingly interesting—not perfectly structured.

How can a writer develop an anti-hero with whom audiences will empathize?

Just make them good characters, meaning they should have all the human equipment—hopes, dreams, fears, flaws, blessings, etc. Maybe they started out as optimists or innocents who got burned by life. They are wounded in some way. Maybe they had noble aspirations that got crushed or corrupted. They should have some flamboyant, colorful, flashy, charming, or skillful aspects. They can be appealing by their contempt for the hypocrisy of conventional heroes or society itself. They can be attractive because they get to express something the audience feels deeply and strongly. They fulfill some wish: to see the crushing authority of the world defied, to escape from social restrictions, to act on impulse without inhibition.

One of the key steps in the Hero's Journey is the "meeting with the mentor." Can you give us examples of characters who function as mentors?

Obvious mentors are benevolent guides and teachers like those in *Goodbye, Mr. Chips* and *Mr. Holland's Opus*, or the Jedi masters in the Star Wars series. The caddy in *The Legend of Bagger Vance* or Patrick Stewart's character in *X-Men* are mentors to their young heroes. Sometimes mentoring is less obvious and may be combined with other jobs like that of villain or antagonist, because we can learn a great deal from our opponents. That's the case in *Bedazzled*, where The Devil is trying to win the hero's soul but also serves as a teacher and guide for him, showing him in the long run what's really important in life. In romantic stories, you can look at the lovers as mentors for each other, each guiding the other to a deeper understanding.

How can a writer give enough backstory without stagnating the story?

Give the backstory in pieces as a series of reveals or surprises. Give it on the run, while people are *doing* something active, so the story doesn't stop. Let it come out of conflict, so that people blurt out backstory in the heat of an argument or have it pulled out of them with great difficulty. Use visuals, props, costumes, and sets to reveal backstory without words. A house full of trophies will tell us someone has a sports background without a word of dialogue.

Behavior can reveal backstory. It's especially effective if people refuse to answer questions, change the subject, or squirm when casual questions are asked about their backgrounds. Raise questions about background but leave some unanswered and let the audience do some of the work—they might fill in a more interesting backstory than can be provided with explanations and dialogue.

Must every script have external conflict, or can an entire script be based on the hero's internal conflict?

Even in the most internalized of stories, it's good to have some external sign of the inner turmoil, even if it's just a spilled coffee cup or a stuck window.

It's just realistic that inner conflict will find expression outside of the person in the form of disagreements, misunderstandings, and physical struggles. However, once in a while you might create an interesting contrast between a placid exterior environment and a raging inner conflict.

How can a hero prove his or her character arc is complete?

Character arc is another one of those convenient terms used to pummel writers in story meetings. Of course, you do have to demonstrate that a protagonist has learned a lesson, made a choice, or evolved to a new level, after passing through a series of logical, believable steps that evoke some conflict or emotion. One way to dramatize a character change is to show that the hero is able to do something at the end of the story that was impossible at the beginning (accept herself, forgive someone, be a team player, stand up for herself, find love, overcome an obstacle, defeat an opponent, reach a goal). You might ask: Has the hero gone through all the logical stages of learning about this problem? As a storyteller, have I explored all the possibilities inherent in this situation?

What are some of the most common mistakes you see new screenwriters make?

Over-explaining and over-writing. They give a lot of unnecessary detail because they are afraid their audience—the readers of the script—won't get it. We get it. Give your readers credit and let them participate. It's amazing what you can leave out and still achieve full communication.

On the other hand, some new writers take too much for granted, and don't spend enough time setting up and emphasizing their main character. Sometimes I don't know who the story is about for 40 or 50 pages because the characters are introduced with equal emphasis. Remember that writing is also directing—directing the audience's attention. "Look here. Now look here. Look at this—it's important."

In writing for Hollywood, is it ever advisable to write an open-ended story?

Hollywood favors "closed-loop" stories in which the loose ends are tied up and all plot threads are neatly resolved, like comforting fairy tales designed to reassure a child. However, Hollywood also adores novelty and variety, so a story that breaks the "rules" and isn't so neatly tied up may attract attention. You can be sure it will be severely tested in the much-hated development process, where all the conservative tendencies of the business will try to tack on a happy ending or a "satisfying" conclusion, but once in a while, the open ending works for Hollywood—especially in certain genres like horror, science fiction, or film noir where the whole concept may be to challenge conventional, comforting patterns of closure and resolution.

What are your responsibilities as a script consultant?

I have to read the script with an open mind, trying to evaluate it on its own terms. I try to think of what will bring out the writer's true intentions. Then I write notes or prepare for a meeting with the writer and producer, in which I look for a "big idea"—one unifying, overall insight that will bring the most positive development to the idea. Then, if the script is relatively close to production, I might go over it page by page to raise questions and make suggestions. I also evaluate the project—what's the best format for this story, novel, feature script, TV series, animation? What's the best path for getting it produced?

Anything further you'd like to add?

Adapt or die. Anybody wanting to keep working in this business should be very open-minded and adaptable. Screenwriting seems to be quickly dissolving and blending into other forms, such as writing for the Internet, creating computer game scenarios, and designing hybrids of movies and amusement park rides. A small number of people will be able to make their living entirely from writing Hollywood feature films; most writers will make a living by creating all sorts of things in all sorts of places. For example, designing Web sites is an infant art form, about where cinema was in 1900, and who knows what it will turn into? Some of my work lately has been in advising Web site and game designers on how to put the techniques of drama, myth, and film into the experiences they create.

The first generation of people who grew up in a world where computers were taken for granted may have new preferences in drama and entertainment. Screenwriters may have to adapt to their rhythms. Open-ended stories may become more popular. Young people may not be responding to movies as they used to simply because movies are finite, they go in one direction and they come to an end, whereas the possibilities of the computer are endless—literally something you can be immersed in all the time. Movies may evolve into much more complex, flexible, and open-ended forms, as is happening already with DVD versions that include alternate scenes and background material. We've always desired to see around the edges of the frame, to extend the movie experience and be able in some sense to live in that movie, and the future will allow us to indulge this even more.

Sitting Down to Write

Blake Snyder

*The Late Great Spec Screenwriter's
Advice is Therapy for Scribes*

by Robin Mizell

When he was starting out as a screenwriter more than 20 years ago, Blake Snyder relied on the advice in the pages of *Writer's Digest*. Later in his life, *he* was the professional giving instructions and providing moral support to aspiring writers and groups all over the world. Sadly, Snyder passed away in 2009 at the much-too-young age of 52. Though he passed one, his advice and enthusiasm for writing and the success of others will live on.

Snyder, a prolific scriptwriter, spent two decades writing for Hollywood—a time during which he sold plenty of spec scripts, including the screenplay he co-wrote for Disney's *Blank Check* and an as-yet unproduced script called *Nuclear Family*, for which he signed a million-dollar deal with Steven Spielberg. Along the way, Snyder picked up tips and tricks from talented writers, and started enjoying the process of pitching a script. Possessed of an analytical mind and an intuitive understanding of audiences' instinctive reactions, he began to dissect what worked versus what was not effective in scripts, loglines, pitches, and the final product—movies. Before long, he'd codified each aspect of good screenwriting. "It just evolved sort of naturally," he explained. "People would ask me for advice on things, and I found myself giving the same advice again and again. So, I just put it down in a book."

The end result was a how-to book on screenwriting called *Save the Cat! The Last Book on Screenwriting You'll Ever Need*. The book focused on demystifying the storytelling process, and emphasized that structure and the initial idea are crucial in creating a successful script. The book went viral, becoming an underground hit as scriptwriters discovered it and began

ROBIN MIZELL (robinmizell.com) is a literary agent and the founder of Robin Mizell Ltd., Literary Representation. She was formerly an editor for *Screenwriter's & Playwright's Market*.

SAVE THE CAT!
The Last Book On Screenwriting You'll Ever Need!

BLAKE SNYDER

recommending it to other industry professionals, including managers, agents, and producers. By mid-2008, *Save the Cat!* was in its 12th printing and had sold more than 30,000 copies. "To me, it was just a labor of love," Snyder said, "and something that's really changed my life."

The book's success within the writing world allowed Snyder to connect with writing groups everywhere—online and in person—as he happily shared his tips on storytelling. Through his Web site and blog (www.blakesnyder.com), as well as his spin-off lectures and workshops, Snyder gave advice to film writers of all ages and skill levels. And *The Cat*'s popularity even spawned more titles: "There's even a sequel to *The Last Book on Screenwriting You'll Ever Need*," said Snyder. His second book is *Save the Cat! Goes to the Movies*.

WHAT'S *THE CAT* ABOUT?

Implicit in the iconic trade name, *Save the Cat!*, is the first lesson Snyder imparted to scriptwriters. "We have to like the guy we're following along," he explained. "The *Save the Cat!* moment is that moment when we meet the hero and he does something that makes us like him—such as saving a cat. It's remarkable how many times I've been in meetings at studios where executives say, 'Well, you know, it's a great script and everything, but I just don't like this guy.'" A sense of dissatisfaction occurs, according to Snyder, when an audience isn't given an excuse to take a liking to the protagonist. "You really need to put something in there that makes us want to root for him. Is that cheating? Is that not art? To me it's just good craft. It's just good storytelling."

Snyder resists referring to the method described in his books as a formula. "To me, this is just the essence of what makes good storytelling. I think the difference between how I wrote it out and told people about it and Aristotle's is this: I'm a slangy screenwriter." Snyder emphasizes that his recommendations can make the process of writing a salable script more comprehensible and systematic for working writers: "I'm a guy who's been

Sitting Down to Write

in the trenches writing screenplays for a long time and just sort of distilled it down into a way that would be easy to understand. They're the same dynamics that have made storytelling work forever."

THE LOGLINE'S IMPORTANCE

Snyder devoted a lot of his energy and much of the first section of *Save the Cat!* to teaching screenwriters how to craft a logline. "Your pitch is your headline," he stressed. "Write a bad headline for a newspaper story, and we won't read it. Or a misleading headline, or a blurry headline, or a confusing headline. We won't read the article. And that applies to all kinds of things. What's your first point of contact with somebody who isn't standing in your shoes?"

Using what might seem like an unorthodox and counterintuitive strategy, Snyder recommended that screenwriters compose their loglines before beginning to write their scripts. "Just by reworking that one sentence, the entire complexion of the story changes. If you can write a better logline for your story, you can deliver a better story," he said.

It's remarkable what comes out of that exercise, he added, when describing the four elements a truly effective logline must convey:

1. Irony
2. A compelling mental picture
3. Audience and production cost
4. A killer title

"What are you really trying to say?" Snyder asked. "What is the white-hot attraction of this particular idea? What does it boil down to at its essence? What's really cool about this? Figuring that out and then going on and exploiting it in the story really helps. It saves trees, by the way."

"BEAT IT OUT"

Using the "Blake Snyder Beat Sheet," writers can outline 15 points of transition and the exact moments at which they occur in every successful movie. "I think some people didn't believe me—that it could be that simple," he said. "The other reaction is: 'If it *is* that simple, I don't want to do it. If it *is* that simple, it means I will be stifled creatively.' No, you won't! You need these tools to free yourself. Everything I talk about is about a kind of empowerment for writers."

Snyder had a personal motivation for creating the checklist for his beat sheet. He admitted, "There were many scripts where I kind of ran out gas at page 50 and just couldn't finish." He urged the timid, "You can do so much more than you thought. You can be so much more. I think some writers—I was one—are sort of held back by not daring to dream big enough. This is a freeing thing, if I can tell you, when you're having problems at the midpoint of your story, to check certain requirements of it."

Save the Cat! Goes to the Movies, Snyder's second book, is an effort to address the skepticism of those who suspected the beat sheet and storyboard concepts defined in his first book were too simplistic. Snyder's knack for detecting the 10 basic patterns underlying all great movie scripts didn't immediately convince everyone of the value of his methods. "I love finding this stuff," he said. "The reason for the second book is because so many people said, 'Oh, it's a formula,' or 'Oh, it just works for Hollywood movies and big studio movies.' The second book is showing how the beat sheet works in all movies, including independent and experimental films like *Open Water*, which is almost documentary in its feel and yet follows the beats of the beat sheet minute per minute. I think that second book really helped clarify what I meant."

NETWORKING FOR SCREENWRITERS

Looking back on his early career, Snyder said, "I felt very isolated. It was me and my agent, and that was about it. I never really networked with other writers. And yet the thing that I learned most and fastest from was working with partners—working with people who were better than me, frankly."

In Spain, the U.K., and Canada—and across the U.S.—Snyder encouraged his workshop participants to form local *Cat!* groups and build on the networks they've established. He believed that adopting the jargon he employed and the methods he prescribed allows the members of the regional groups to understand and easily communicate with each other. *Cat!* groups ease writers into alliances Snyder hoped will help advance their careers. "My dream is to have these groups set up and, then, even help them market," he explained. "We send producers to some of these groups. We send managers and agents to these groups to hear what they're working on. We share resources. We pitch ideas back and forth to each other."

Ben Frahm, a middle school teacher who joined such a group, telephoned Snyder one day to announce he'd sold his first script, *Dr. Sensitive*, to Universal Studios for $300,000 upfront, against a total deal of half a million dollars. Snyder's reaction? "I'm more excited for Ben than I was ever excited for myself."

Snyder wanted screenwriters to understand that the Hollywood studios succeed because they deliver entertainment for the masses, and they do it using a time-honored method. "You don't have to reinvent the wheel to

Sitting Down to Write

be creative. You can be creative by putting a fresh spin on something you already know,'' he said. "That's what the job is."

IT'S ALL ABOUT STORYTELLING

"All stories are about transformation,'' Snyder reminded writers. His background made it easier for him to teach the concepts of catharsis and transformation. "I have had that transformative experience. I have been allowed to sort of have an Act Three in my life that I wasn't planning on."

Persistent in his search for life's hidden meaning, Snyder said, "For me personally, and for us as human beings, and I think for the heroes of all good stories, there's a point where the hero has a moment of clarity toward the end of the story, where he realizes what it has been about.'' He proposed, "That moment of clarity, for me, is touched by a higher power, touched by a sense of the divine. In movie after movie, story after story, the thing that gives us the chills, the thing that makes it work, is the subterranean story. It's the spiritual story."

When pressed to apply a character archetype to himself, something he frequently does with other people, Snyder laughed and said, "I'm the old soldier going back for one last mission—damaged, wounded, limping—but one last glorious mission."

Writing the TV Pilot

Three Rules for Doing It Right

by Chad Gervich

While the Writers Strike may have decimated 2007's pilot season, one thing it won't decimate is TV's continuing need for new show ideas. Now that the strike is over, networks and studios are looking for fresh shows and content. And fortunately, the market for spec pilots (pilots written without being first pitched and sold as ideas) has been surprisingly robust lately—with studios hungrier than usual to snatch up already-written scripts.

So as writers all across America work on their pilots, let's take a quick moment to discuss some of the vital elements that make pilots work.

First of all, let's answer this question, which a student in my "Writing the TV Pilot" class asked last month: What, exactly, is a pilot?

A pilot is most commonly thought of as the first episode of a television series—the first story in a series of many more stories. And while this is often the case, it's not entirely accurate.

The truth is: A pilot, whether in script form or actually produced, is a selling tool used to illustrate what the TV series is about and how it works. In other words, a pilot is designed to convince network or studio executives that this series a good investment of their money and airtime. Some pilots never even make it to air—they're simply used to get the series "picked up," then discarded.

When you begin looking at a pilot this way—as a selling tool, rather than just the first of many stories—you realize that pilots must accomplish certain things besides simply kicking off the series narratively. Thus, here are three important tips to think about as you craft your own TV pilots.

CHAD GERVICH (www.chadgervich.com) is a television producer, published author, and award-winning playwright. He has written, developed, or produced shows for Fox TV Studios, Paramount Television, NBC Studios, Warner Brothers, Fox Reality Channel, ABC Studios, E! Entertainment, and Twentieth Century Fox. Chad's book, *Small Screen, Big Picture: A Writer's Guide to the TV Business*, is currently available from www.mediabistro.com and Random House/Crown.

1. Pilots must prove your series has longevity.

TV series are designed to run not just for a few weeks, or even a few months. Successful TV series must run for years, which means your pilot needs to prove that this world can generate a nearly endless number of stories.

One way to do this is to base your series around a locale or occupation that organically generates stories. Cop and detective shows, like *Bones* or *CSI*, never run out of stories; as long as the world has crimes, these shows have tales to tell. After all, every time the door of a police station or detective agency opens, in walks a case—which is a story.

Soaps, like *Brothers & Sisters* or even *Heroes*, never run out of stories because they're filled with incredibly deep, rich, and complex relationships. It's easy for an executive to see—in a world where people are constantly lying, cheating, sleeping with and backstabbing each other—how these relationships will generate many years of interesting stories.

Whether you're writing a mystery show, like *NCIS*, or a character-driven dramedy, like *Grey's Anatomy*, it's your pilot's job to prove this series can generate an endless number of stories.

2. Pilots must illuminate how every episode of the series will work.

Although a pilot is kicking off a new series, meaning it works a bit differently than subsequent stories and episodes, it must also demonstrate how the series' regular episodes will work the same on a regular basis. In other words, they must help buyers (executives and producers) understand exactly what it is they're buying. Does each episode tell a single, close-ended mystery, like *Law & Order: SVU*? Or will each episode deal with a particular issue about married life or relationships, a la *'Til Death* or *Rules of Engagement*?

While a pilot is indeed the catalyst that sparks the rest of the series, it must also work just like every other episode of the series. If your doctors will heal one patient per episode, let them heal a patient in the pilot. If your squabbling couple must solve a marital problem each week, let them do so in the pilot.

This is often a difficult tightrope to walk. How can a pilot be both the beginning of a long-running saga as well as an example of a prototypical episode? This, unfortunately, is the delicate artform of writing a pilot, and one of the reasons it often takes writers years of working in and developing TV before they get a series on the air.

"Your pilot should introduce all of your main characters and set the tone for the series," says Aury Wallington, a TV writer who's written pilots for USA, ABC and Sony. "The pilot is all about getting an audience invested in what's going to happen over the next 22 weeks."

3. Pilots must (usually) show us how/if episodes are repeatable.

Repeatability is the bread and butter of traditional television. This is because relatively little money is made off the "first run" of a TV episode; the real money comes when a series is sold into syndication (reruns on local stations or cable channels). But in order to be repeatable, episodes must function in specific ways. The most repeatable episodes are "standalone," meaning they tell a singular, close-ended story in each episode. Each week, the cops of *K-Ville* receive, investigate, and solve a completely new mystery. It begins and ends all in one episode, making it easy for audiences to watch a single episode—whether it's the show's first run or a rerun—and still understand what's going on.

Similarly, Justin and Raja in *Aliens In America* deal each week with a new problem in their friendship, school, or family—and it's solved that same episode. Standalone episodes not only make a series more repeatable, they make it easier for audiences to pop in and watch just one episode at a time. (It's pretty difficult to simply bounce in and watch a single third-season episode of *Lost*.)

If your series has repeatable episodes, it's infinitely more sell-able, and you need to show this in your pilot. Let your detectives begin and close a mystery in the pilot. Let your bickering best friends deal with an issue and resolve it.

On the flip side, if your show is highly serialized or soapy, like *24* or *Cane*, with stories spanning many weeks or months, let us see how this works as well. Use your pilot to show how stories will play out over the course of an episode and then seduce us to come back the following week.

And always follow the rules in terms of length, grammar and submissions. "If you're lucky enough to have a producer or agent read your script, you don't want to be rejected just because it doesn't look right or is the wrong length or format," Wallington says. "Your pilot script also needs to conform to all the rules of any other TV script. If it's a drama, it should be 60 pages long; comedies should be 30 pages. Unless you're envisioning it specifically for a network like HBO or FX, you should double-check your dialogue to make sure it's appropriate for television."

Remember: selling a TV series is like selling anything else, from vacuum cleaners to used cars. You job is to show your buyer what they're buying and how it will continue to work. This is the true purpose of a pilot.

Sitting Down to Write

Writing the TV Spec Script

Break In Using Existing Shows

by Ellen Sandler

Here's a truth: There is only one way to get a job writing television—and no, it's not by getting the right agent. The way to get work is by having something fresh and wonderful that people get excited about.

It's just that simple.

Simple, but not easy.

Because it's common, television is often dismissed as insignificant— unworthy of respect and care. Because it's pervasive, it's voracious. Television needs material, and it reproduces like an amoeba, constantly driving and replicating itself to fill the continuing void. Television needs more, and it needs it now. That's where you come in. Your job as a writer is to supply it with content. This leads to fast, which leads to sloppy, which leads to formulaic, writing.

In order to write for TV, you must get a job. In order to get a job, you must have material to show that you can write. Usually, that will be a spec script.

WHAT IS A SPEC SCRIPT?

A television spec script is an unsolicited, original episode written for an established TV show. No money, no contract, no guarantees. In all likelihood, a spec script will never be sold nor produced. What it will be is *read*. That's what you write it for: to be read by as many people connected to show

---

ELLEN SANDLER (www.SandlerInk.com) received an Emmy nomination for her work as co-executive producer of "Everybody Loves Raymond." She has worked as a writer/producer for many other network television shows, including ABC's long-running series, "Coach." She has also created original series for numerous networks. This article reprinted with permission from *The TV Writer's Workbook: A Creative Approach to Television Scripts* (Delta Trade/Random House, 2007).

business as you can get to. Everyone counts. You never know who knows someone who knows someone.

A television spec script is different than a film spec script. You don't write a TV spec with the expectation of selling it to the show. It could happen, but what's much more likely, and therefore what we'll be talking about, is that you'll write a spec TV episode to prove that you can do the work. It's a writing sample—a portfolio piece. In film, people are looking for a script, but in TV they are looking for a *writer*.

WHY WRITE FOR TV?

The only reason to write a television episodic spec script is: money. When I teach, I usually draw a big $ on the whiteboard and everybody laughs. I suppose because that's what they were really thinking but were afraid to say. Or maybe they were even afraid to think it. Maybe they feel it's not a worthy reason to write. But the truth is that television is a commercial medium and you write it for money.

IS IT FORM OR FORMULA?

What writing for money means is that when you sit down to write, you have to follow the rules. By rules, I don't mean formula—*formula* is what makes a writer a hack, and leads to predictable, dull scripts that nobody wants to read past page eight. However, there is *form*—quite a different thing. Television scripts have a specific form, and you must follow it.

It doesn't matter if you think you know how to do it better or funnier than what's on the air. That's not your job when you're writing a spec script. You job is to do it exactly the way it's done and still be original. If you follow the rules without originality, your work will be okay but it will not distinguish itself as special.

Yes, you're writing for money, but you are not writing *only* for money. You must also put some art into your commercial product. It's very unlikely that you'll ever get to write for money if you don't put something of yourself into your script. The richest, most successful television writers I know have all written commercially savvy products from a personal point of view. Creative with the form? No. Creative with the content? Yes.

WHAT SHOW SHOULD YOU SPEC?

Write a show you love to watch. That, in my opinion, is the single most important factor in choosing a show to write. Don't write a spec of a show you don't like, even if someone in the industry has told you it's the hot show to write. When you get to pick, and your spec may be the only time

Stories to Avoid

When you do decide to sit down and write that glorious spec script, keep in mind these overused premises and steer clear of them.

Introducing an outside character
Writers may think they're showing how original they are, but what they're really showing is that they aren't excited enough by the show. A spec should show how you can color inside the lines and still make it fresh. In other words, that you can write for hire! And isn't that the point? The big exception here is for shows where the basic premise requires guest characters every week—medical shows have new patients, cop shows have new criminals and victims.

A famous guest star
It's called *stunt casting* and I know many shows do it, but it should be avoided in your spec; it says you're more interested in casting than in writing.

The past lover
Please don't write this as your spec script, especially if the ex-boy/girlfriend returns in a quirky, unexpected way. It seems like every third spec I read is a version of this story. It's just an overused idea.

The class reunion show
Besides being a much-used premise, which is reason enough to avoid it, anything involving the past history of your characters is shaky territory for a spec. It's really only appropriate for the show's creator to invent backstory, so leave the reunion show to him or her.

Trading places
I suggest you stay away from stories where the leads exchange roles. They can come across as contrived and gimmicky.

Trapped in an elevator/mountain cabin/bathroom, wherever
Dick Van Dyke got caught in a cabin in the snow and every sitcom since has done some version of this storyline. If you've got something that's fresh, okay—otherwise, come up with another idea.

More things to stay away from:
Animals and babies, flashbacks/fantasies/dream sequences, elaborate sets, exotic locations, and pop culture references.

you have that opportunity, by all means be picky. Only write a show that you relate to, a show you like to watch, with characters you care about. That is first and foremost—but it's not the only criterion.

Here are three other factors to keep in mind when choosing a show to write for.

1. The show must be on the air now

This is a rule. Don't write a "Friends" spec, even if you saw every episode and you have the greatest idea for a Rachel story ever. Anything that is off the air is an old show, even if reruns are playing every day.

In fact, any show that's been on the air more than five years is probably too old to write a spec for, even if it's not going off the air for a couple more seasons. If you're sending out an episode of an older show, the feeling is that you're not fresh, not current, not keeping up with the trends—and in TV, that is death.

2. It should be a hit

Here's why:

- A hit show is not likely to be canceled the day before you finish your spec.
- People who will be reading your spec will be familiar with the show and the characters.
- A hit is a hit because it works. A show that works will be easier to write and will make a much better sample.
- Hits are copied. There will be new shows like it on the air and those are shows that will be looking for staff. If you've written a spec of the show they've cloned, it will be an excellent sample to demonstrate how appropriate you would be for their show.

To be considered a "hit," a commercial network show should be in the top 25 to 30 on the list. Also consider critically acclaimed shows (think "Monk") that aren't necessarily a top-tier smash.

3. You have a connection

You went to acting school with someone in the cast; your roommate's buddy is an assistant editor on the show; your cousin knows a production assistant's life partner. If you have a genuine connection, no matter how minor, it could be a big help. For one thing, it will be easier to get scripts of the show to study. The most important advantage is the possibility of getting your spec read by a writer on the show and a chance for some professional feedback—and, who knows, maybe even a recommendation to that writer's agent or the showrunner. But don't expect that; just ask for feedback.

ELEMENTS OF A SPEC SCRIPT STORY
1. Your story must revolve around the central character

So how do you know which character is the central character? If their name is in the title ("My Name is Earl"), then *that's* how you know. If the name of the central character and the name of the actor playing the character are one and the same—"Everybody Loves Raymond"—then you *really* know.

What it means for a story to revolve around the central character is:

a. The story must have an emotional conflict for the central character.

b. The central character drives the action; that is, his choices make the plot progress.

c. The central character resolves the problem.

In other words, the story is told from the central character's point of view. It happens to him; and even more important, he makes it happen.

If your show has two characters in the title, such as "Two and Half Men," examine which one of the leads often drives the story. For a spec script, it's probably a good idea to follow that pattern.

With a show like "Desperate Housewives" or "Entourage," the title tells you that you have an ensemble show, meaning a group of characters that are equally important, or nearly so. In a show like this, episodes often revolve around a theme with storylines for various characters.

Shows with no character names in the title, such as *CSI* and *Law & Order*, are shows where the *procedure* is primary; however, they still have central characters. Do some research. Which character is in the most scenes and how many? Which character solves the case? Is it the same in every episode? If these factors shift to different characters in different episodes, you have a choice of which character to feature in your script.

2. Your story must use all of the regular supporting characters

The regular characters are the ones featured in the opening credits. They appear in every episode, and therefore, they all must be in your spec script. Rule out ideas that create solitary confinement for the central character—lost at sea, home alone, etc.

3. Your story must respect the premise of the show

This means that if, for example, your show is about a married man whose parents live across the street, you don't choose a story for your spec script in which he files for divorce or moves to Vancouver. Create a story that illustrates the basic elements of the show as they exist in the premise. Your spec script is not an opportunity to demonstrate how much better the show would be if it were different. Your spec script is your opportunity to demonstrate how close you can come to exactly what the show is about and still be original, which, incidentally, is a much more difficult task.

Queries and Synopses

Your First Contact with Power Players

by Chuck Sambuchino

Before a manager or producer will read your work, you have to give them a reason to do so. Simply put, that means pitching your work through a query and synopsis and piquing enough interest to force them into demanding the full script. After all, Hollywood is famous for moving slowly. But how much slower would it move if everybody were reading every page of every script? That's a lot of text to slog through!

To combat the sheer volume of scripts waiting to be read, agents and producers want to see short versions of stories to judge whether time will be well spent further considering the project. And that's where queries and synopses come in handy.

QUERIES

A query is a one-page, single-spaced letter that quickly tells who you are, what the work is, and why the work is appropriate for the market in question. Just as queries are used as the first means of contact for pitching magazine articles and novels, they work just the same for scripts.

A well-written query is broken down into three parts.

Part I: Your reason for contacting/script details

Before even looking at the few sentences describing your story, a producer wants to see two other things:

1. What is it? State the title, genre, and whether it's a full-length script or a shorter one. This is also a place to include your logline if you've boiled it

---

CHUCK SAMBUCHINO is the editor of *Screenwriter's & Playwright's Market*. He also edits *Guide to Literary Agents* (www.guidetoliteraryagents.com/blog) and oversaw the third edition of *Formatting & Submitting Your Manuscript*.

Sample Query Letter

Include all contact information— including phone and e-mail—as centered information at the top.

John Q. Writer
123 Main St.
Writerville, USA
(212)555-1234
johnqwriter@email.com

Date

Agent
JQA & Associates
678 Hollywood St.
Hollywood, CA 90210

Use proper greetings and last names.

Dear Mr./Ms. (Last Name):

Include a reason for contacting the reader.

My name is John Q. Writer and we crossed paths at the Writer's Digest Books Writers' Conference in Los Angeles in May 2008. After hearing the pitch for my feature-length thriller, *October Surprise*, you requested that I submit a query, synopsis and the first 10 pages of the script. All requested materials are enclosed. This is an exclusive submission, as you requested.

Try and keep the pitch to one paragraph.

U.S. Senator Michael Hargrove is breaking ranks with his own political party to endorse another candidate for President of the United States. At the national convention, he's treated like a rock star V.I.P.—that is, until, he's abducted by a fringe political group and given a grim ultimatum: Use your speech on live TV to sabotage and derail the presidential candidate you're now supporting, or your family back home will not live through the night.

Regarding your credentials, be concise and honest.

The script was co-written with my scriptwriting partner, Joe Aloysius. I am a produced playwright and award-winning journalist. Thank you for considering *October Surprise*. I will be happy to sign any release forms that you request. May I send the rest of the full screenplay?

Best,

John Q. Writer

down to one sentence. (If it's more several sentences, there isn't much of a point, seeing as how the multi-sentence elevator pitch is to follow.)

2. Why are you contacting this market/person in particular? There are thousands of individuals who receive scripts. Why have you chosen this person to review the material? Is it because you met them in person and they requested to see your work? Have they represented writers similar to yourself? Did you read that they were actively looking for zombie comedies? Spelling out your reason upfront shows that you've done your research, and that you're a professional.

Part II: The Elevator Pitch

If you wrote the first paragraph correctly, you've got their attention, so pitch away. Explain what your story is about in 3-6 sentences. The point here is to intrigue and pique, only. Don't get into nitty-gritty details of any kind. Hesitate using a whole lot of character names or backstory. Don't explain how it ends or who dies during the climax or that the hero's father betrays him in Act II. Introduce us to the main character and his situation, then get to the key part of the pitch: the conflict.

Try to include tidbits here and there that make your story unique. If it's about a cop nearing retirement, that's nothing new. But if the story is about a retiring cop considering a sex change operation in his bid to completely start over, while the police union is threatening to take away his pension should he do this—*then* you've got something different that readers may want to see.

Part III: The Wrap-Up

Your pitch is complete. The last paragraph is where you get to talk about yourself and your accomplishments. If the script has won any awards or been a finalist in prominent competitions, this is the place to say so. Mention your writing credentials and experience. Obviously, any paid screenwriting experience is most valuable, but feel free to include other tidbits such as if you're a magazine freelancer or a published novelist.

Sometimes, there won't be much to say at the end of a query letter because the writer has no credits, no contacts and nothing to brag about. As your mother would tell you: If you don't have anything nice to say, don't say anything at all. Keep the last section brief if you must, rather than going on and on about being an "active blogger" (whatever that amounts to) or having one poem published in your college literary magazine.

Following some information about yourself, it's time to wrap up the query and propose sending more material. A simple way to do this is by saying:

"The script is complete. May I send you the full screenplay or perhaps some pages?"

SYNOPSES

If an agent or producer is intrigued by the super-condensed version of your story (in the query), their next step is to see your whole tale front to back in the form of a synopsis. A synopsis is a condensed summary of the entire story that showcases the central conflict of the story and the interlocking chain of events set off by that conflict. Unlike a query, a synopsis is designed to tell the *full* story, meaning the ending is revealed. Don't be coy or hold back information.

The challenge lies in telling your complicated and amazing story simply and briskly. You must introduce the protagonist, the antagonist, the love interest and the hook—and that's just the beginning! When in doubt, stick to the plot. If the character starts out lost in the Yukon, say so—but don't waste time talking about how remote and desolate and hopeless the area is. Keep moving! If you're stuck, try this: Sit down with a 10-year-old and give yourself two minutes or less to explain the entire story. You'll be forced to keep it simple and keep it moving.

The reason you have so little time is that a good screenplay synopsis should run approximately two full pages, double-spaced. "Although writers may submit as long of a synopsis as they desire, ideally it should get to the point fairly quickly," says Margery Walshaw, script manager for Evatopia. "In a sense, this is the writer's first test to see if they can get their point across in a concise manner that is also engaging."

Do not intrude the narrative flow with authorial commentary, and do not let the underlying story framework show in your synopsis. Don't use phrases such as "At the climax of the conflict . . ." or "Act II begins with . . ." In short, do not let it read like a nonfiction outline. Your goal is to entrance with the story itself and not to break the spell by allowing the supporting scaffolding to show.

Concerning the format, use a header and include page numbers. Make sure that you capitalize the names of all major characters as they are introduced. Double space the text and make sure your writing is in the present tense: "Michael wakes up to find that his family is gone."

FOLLOWING DIRECTIONS

When you submit your work to an agent or producer, remember to submit exactly what's asked. Send the materials in the requested manner, as well. If you got a request to submit materials and you're afraid your solicited script is just going to get tossed in with 400 others in the slush pile, put "Requested Material" on the envelope. Then, in the query's first paragraph, quickly explain when the material was requested to back up your claim.

You've spent months or years (or even decades) on that script, and so it may be frustrating to jump through the hoops of the submission process—but it's important. Don't give readers an excuse to ignore your work. You must craft a killer query and synopsis before the script gets its big shot. Compose them well, and you're on your way to selling that screenplay.

Submitting Your Work

Best in Show

*Advice From Judges on Winning
Screenwriting Contests*

by Trai Cartwright

Screenwriting contests, they are a-changin':
Used to be, there were only a handful of different contests, and winning one scored you a small title and a smaller check, but little else for your trouble. Used to be, only story editors and junior executives or their assistants judged most contests, bringing with them limited expertise or interest in the outcome. Used to be, only dramatic or indie screenplays had any chance of winning.

But times, they have a-changed.

While there are still a suspiciously high number of contests that are at best unhelpful to a writer and at worst shameless scams, in the past decade a dynamic range of industry-minded and increasingly powerful contests have emerged. It's the Golden Era of Screenwriting Competitions and there's never been a better time to submit your scripts to (carefully researched) contests, and reap the rewards.

WHAT JUDGES LOOK FOR

One indicator that things have changed in the contest world is that the iron-fisted rulership of the coming-of-age/historical biography/family drama has ended. Now, any and every genre has a shot at taking the top slot. Why? Because contest-winning screenplays are no longer just calling cards to the industry. They are commercial enterprises that get attention and sometimes even get made.

This million-dollar cottage industry's mission is now about providing real assistance for new writers hacking their way into Hollywood, often by

TRAI CARTWRIGHT (website www.craftwrite.com) has judged more than a dozen screenplay contests; she is a writing consultant, film and theater producer and newly-minted MFA student.

sending out the best contest scripts all over Hollywood for consideration. You don't even have to win—placing in the quarter or semifinals of any of the top contests can be a springboard to getting your script read. These competitions now attract brand name players as their upper strata judges, and they facilitate launching the careers of new writers, sometimes by taking on those scripts themselves.

Once the best-kept secret in town, screenwriting contests are now fertile ground for high-stakes competition, with future power-scribes duking it out for real-money prizes and that crucial all-access industry pass. As a competitor, it's more important than ever to submit only your best work. What does it take to win or place in a contest? What exactly do contest judges look for? What excites them? What turns them off? What's a guaranteed pass? We've lined up a panel of contest judge superstars to find out.

Format

"I can tell in the first 10 pages if a script is not going to move on. A big giveaway is the formatting," says Chris Sablan, an agent at Original Artists.

Screenwriting format involves very particular margins, plus devices like transitions, parentheticals and capitalizations to help explain the action. Mastering this format is the first crucial step to escaping the first round cuts. "If the screenplay is poorly paginated or filled with typos, that's a sure sign of a nonprofessional script," says Caren Bohrman of The Bohrman Agency.

If the ultimate goal is to convince your readers that you're a professional-level writer waiting to be discovered, then proper formatting goes without saying. If you're uncertain about the format in your script, look at the article in this book (page 40), or buy some scriptwriting software.

Narrative

A properly written screenplay isn't just about knowing how to center the dialogue, or how to write a slugline. It's about narrative, as well. Narrative—or scene description—is the action of the screenplay; it tells us exactly what's happening on the screen. It is also the second most obvious indicator of a weak writer. "In scene description, remember to tell us only what is absolutely necessary to understand what's going on," says script doctor and screenwriter Lance Thompson. "Leave flowery description to prose writers."

Sablan couldn't agree more: "Writers think that by writing long and beautiful descriptions, that's going to make the script better. Maybe for books, but not for screenplays. The less the better. Readers tend to focus on dialogue and will scan through description."

The "rule" in screenwriting is that every page should be two-thirds white space. That means your narrative must be streamlined and brief, making room for plenty of dialogue. Once your script "looks" right and you're promoted to the second round, your story can really shine—or raise more red flags.

"Also, if the action is overwritten—for example, too much description, citing things that can't be filmed, or inserting camera directions—that's a good tipoff that the writer hasn't developed their craft to the professional level yet," says Bill Lundy, chairman emeritus of the Scriptwriter's Network.

Structure

A winning script at the Scriptwriter's Network's Hollywood Outreach Program is going to have "a compelling, well-structured story with interesting twists and turns," says Lundy. Judges want surprises; a predictable or derivative story is another reason to pass. Structure is about more than just three well-placed acts. It's the spine, and controls many of the crucial craft aspects of a script, such as the pacing and tone of your plot, and the interweaving of your story and character arcs.

"I think studying the technique of writing a screenplay is very important, and it's easy to see when one of those elements is off. With a properly structured screenplay, many of the other elements will fall into place, and be a much better read," says Eric Williams, president of Zero Gravity Management.

Not sure how to crack this complex concept? Examine your story in outline form, the consider these questions from Thompson: Does the story move forcefully toward a conclusion, or does it meander and take too many detours? Does the character have a clear goal? Does the conclusion of the story tell us not only whether the main character attained his goal, but also give us a deeper insight into the character?

Characters

There is as much riding on your characters as on your story, if not more. If a judge can't relate to your characters, she will fall out of your story—and halt its rise beyond the second round.

"Do I like and care about the characters? Do I feel like I am going on a journey that makes them better people by the end? How do they relate to the other characters and how do they help each other grow?" These are the questions Kat Blasband, director of development at Tapestry Films asks, plus one last one that might surprise contest entrants: "Is the character castable?"

According to Williams, unique, sharp characters attract cast. Actors look for interesting roles to play, so it's imperative that the characters and their dialogue really stand out.

Again, the goal of a winning script is to secure representation and/or to sell; why not write characters that attract great actors that help you in that task? But before you start reworking your hero just for Will Smith, keep in mind that great screenwriting means creating characters that work within your story.

Focus on some basic goals: Create a character that is someone we haven't seen before, and have him or her drive the action, so they're not merely reacting to events and circumstances.

"If the characters are not properly set up, the story won't move on. But if I find myself thinking about the characters once I've put the script down, that's a pretty sure bet the script is alive and something I'd like to take to the big screen," says Bohrman, who has found clients through the contests she judges, including trackingb.com, and the CINE Awards.

Dialogue

"I read scripts all year round and I can instantly tell if someone can write. One of the most important things is writing dialogue, writing dialogue that when you read it, it feels natural," says Mark Andrushko, co-founder of Scriptapalooza.

What makes for great dialogue? Thompson says to it should be "lean— not full of exposition or chit-chat." Lundy says to work for "dialogue that incorporates subtext and feels 'real' in the world of the story. Avoid overwrought or on-the-nose dialogue."

Blasband cites an even more delicate feat: "I love when after I've read a couple pages of a script, I no longer have to look to see which character is speaking. I just know it, because the characters each have their own distinct personalities in the dialogue."

FROM GOOD TO GREAT

Okay, so you've blasted through the first round by being a master of the screenwriting basics like format and narrative. The second round proved no challenge to your serious skills with structure, character and dialogue. Congratulations—your script has made it to the Quarter or Semifinals! But is it a winner?

Below are the secrets to that ever-elusive first place win, given away freely by the people who've handed out the top prize to hundreds of contest winners.

Concept

It's as simple as this: If the script is well written and it's commercial, then that will get the writer representation. It might even win a contest.

"I've read so many scripts that have a great idea and terrible execution or incredible writing on a script that could never be made into a movie. It needs to be a great idea," says Blasband, but "it also needs to be clean, preferably high concept, original and commercial."

This emphasis on commerciality might surprise contest writers, but it's a theme that came up repeatedly with our judges. This is a new twist in a game where the tent-pole picture or high concept film once had little traction against the coming of age or family drama. Not every contest has shifted gears to be more competitive in Hollywood, but knowing whether the contest you're submitting to has this objective tells you if you've targeted the right contest for your script.

In other words, having a "winning concept" is a matter of perspective. Check out a contest's winners over the last five years. If the scripts are all high concept, then know that this is the place for your globe-trotting bio-hazard thriller. If the winners were all gentle dramas, then you've found the best possible arena for your father and son separated-at-birth story.

Winning Scripts

I asked contest judges to share their candid thoughts on what separates the best of best from the rest of the pack. Here's what they had to say: "You need to hook your reader in the first 10 pages. You have to have a great story and great characters. Here is an easy explanation: If a script is a comedy, it should make me laugh. If it's a horror, it should make me scared and if it's a thriller, it should make me tense."

—Sablan

"The script I remember most had a main character who was torn between her greed and her native religion, but greed won out. The plot imaginatively supported this dilemma. The action was fast and the suspense built steadily. Every word of dialogue and description was necessary to the story—there was nothing wasted. This script was polished, professional and ready to shoot."

—Thompson

"This year's winner was a writer who knew his craft and was ready for the big leagues. Each winner in the Scriptwriter's Network twenty-year contest history has secured representation."

—Lundy

"Last year I found a script I was still thinking about three days later. The writing and dialogue was exceptional. The lead character jumped off the page and was easily relatable. I've gone back and read the screenplay maybe ten times."
—Williams

"I always say great writing floats to the top. Right from the start, you can tell the winning writer can write but it's more than that. It's the storytelling, the way he writes. You can't put it down."
—Andrushko

But, admittedly, every winning script needs to be more than the sum of its parts; it needs to be just a little bit magic.

With so much to gain as an entrant, there's no reason not to find the right contest for your script and take your shot. But before you press the Send button on the submission page, take these judges' advice. Knowing what they look for will help you write your best possible screenplay, and sidestep some of the obstacles to winning. They're waiting for you, and they don't just want to give you a trophy and a few dollars; they want to help start your career.

Screenwriting contests our panel has judged include: Scriptapaloooza, Final Draft Big Break, Carl Sautter Screenplay Competition, PAGE International Screenwriting, Hollywood Outreach Program, trackingb.com, CINE Awards, Blue Cat and ScriptShark.

Find a Script Manager

7 Steps to Landing Representation

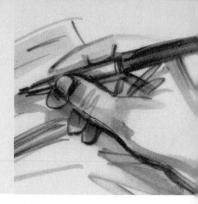

by Mike Kuciak

Writers call our office every day. They say all kinds of crazy things. It soon becomes obvious that most of these writers don't have a realistic view of what's needed to take the first steps toward becoming professional screenwriters. Many simply lack the experience to have a clear idea of what they should be doing. Some of the people who call are insane. Some are just kind of stupid.

There is nothing I can do to cure the insane and stupid, but I can do some thing for the inexperienced and unclear. Thus, I have crafted a step-by-step process of exactly what you should be doing if you want to acquire a literary manager to represent your screenwriting career. There are no guarantees. That's because there are no guarantees in Hollywood at all ... for anybody ... ever. However, following these steps will do a hell of a lot more for your career than calling companies out of the *Hollywood Creative Directory* and saying nutty things.

STEP ONE: WRITE TWO AWESOME SCRIPTS

File this one under "Well, duh." Way too many writers take their work into the world before it's ready. They're too excited or impatient to get into the game the right way. Let your craft develop and mature. Read as many scripts as possible. Write several scripts no one will ever read. Let yourself make mistakes. There's only one true way to learn the craft, and that's sweating over the white space. If you start submitting your work before it's ready to be considered at a professional level, you're just burning bridges for no good reason.

MICHAEL T. KUCIAK is vice president of acquisitions at management/production company AEI (*Joe Somebody, Life or Something Like It, The Truth About The Canal Street Brothel*). He spends every day chasing the perfect logline.

When I get calls and e-mails from writers pitching me their very first script, I roll my eyes. Could it be great? Sure, but those are one in a million. Don't submit a script just because your girlfriend thinks it's, like, totally awesome or you got a B+ on it in Screenwriting 101. Also, even if you've written several scripts before, don't pitch something until you've polished it. Athletes have to train for years and years before they even have a shot at the big leagues. The same goes for writers.

You should have at least two great scripts. Sometimes literary managers have to pass on an otherwise wonderful script. There are several reasons this could happen: They already have one just like it on their slate; they just took out a similar project and it didn't set up; the subject matter is something they don't like; that type of script is a tough sell; etc. If the script is a pass but the writing is great, the manager might ask to see something else you've written. But if the passed script is the only one that's polished to a professional level and all you have to send next are your unprofessional, unpolished scripts, you're shooting yourself in the foot. Back up your first great script with a second one for a knockout, one-two script read.

Make sure that you not only have two great scripts, but they are two feature-length scripts in the proper format. Do not try to sell yourself until the scripts are done. You're not only proving that you have a wonderful, commercial film idea; you're also trying to show the industry that you're a talented writer with the skill and craft to competently execute the idea into a fantastic screenplay.

Writers are sometimes confused because they read about scripts getting sold from a treatment or pitch. Many of the confused writers are just lazy and want to find out if they can become rich and famous just by having what they are certain is a whiz-bang idea, without having to go through all that damn hassle of learning to write and stuff. True, projects do sell on treatment or pitch, but rarely, and this typically occurs with professional writers who have proven to the industry that they can execute a good script from their ideas. I cannot repeat this enough: You are not only marketing the script, you are also marketing the writer.

STEP TWO: WRITE A FANTASTIC SYNOPSIS TO EACH SCRIPT

The synopsis should be one or two pages long. Include the title, logline and a description of the story and characters. Really fine-tune these things. Make 'em sing.

A synopsis is useful for offering the manager a next-step response to your script without having to request it yet. Meaning this: I sometimes get pitched loglines that sound interesting. I'll ask if there's a synopsis to read.

This way, I can not only scan the story to see if the project is worthwhile, I also get a chance to see a sample of the writer's craft before having to deal with a script on my desk. If the synopsis is this meandering wreck filled with typos and craziness, I know not to waste time on reading anything more by said writer. I'll just keep looking for scripts with similar loglines, hoping to find a writer who can realize a great idea into a professional screenplay.

STEP THREE: RESEARCH, ENTER AND PLACE WELL IN SCREENWRITING CONTESTS

You shouldn't have to call lit managers if they're calling you. The best way to make this connection happen is to place well in a reputable screenwriting contest.

Not all great scripts win contests, and not all scripts that win contests are great. However, a script that placed in the semifinals of the Nicholl (Oscars. org/awards/nicholl) has a far higher chance of being worth the limited reading time of literary managers than one which did not. Many companies closely watch the bigger contests for potential new clients. Contests are helpful for us because they tend to sift out most of the crap, a process requiring a massive amount of time, energy, patience and masochism. Most major contests also release their ranking scripts to interested companies. Thus, entering and doing well in contests helps you in two ways: a) building your résumé as a screenwriter, and b) marketing your script and writing abilities to literary managers.

I stress "place well" in reputable contests because I've read a lot of scripts that were, say, the third-place "winners" in Joeschmoscriptcontest.com, and they were all garbage. Which leads to your natural question: "How do I know which contests are worth my entry fees?" The only real answer is research. That subject is another kettle of fish, which I don't have the word count to get into here. Web sites and magazines such as this one are a valuable resource.

STEP FOUR: BUY AND RESEARCH A GUIDE TO LITERARY MANAGERS

You have written several scripts, at least two of which are awesome. You have entered and placed well in reputable contests. Yet, you're still unsigned. (No guarantees, remember?) The next best step is to get proactive and market yourself directly to literary managers.

There are several wonderful guides filled with contact information for literary agents and managers. Go buy one. Take the book home and flip through it. You'll see an alphabetical listing of lit reps, including their addresses, web sites, e-mails, names and phone numbers. At this critical juncture, you may feel the overwhelming desire to dive right in and just start calling around.

Should this urge strike, adhere to these guidelines:

a) Stop.

b) Put down the phone.

c) Walk away.

You've just saved yourself from becoming an annoying menace. "But then, how do I ... ?" you frantically splutter. Settle down. Here's how:

Carefully read through the listings. You're specifically looking for literary managers. Cross out all the agents. (Right now you're specifically looking for a lit manager who can later help you find an agent. If you don't get a manager, you can start chasing the agents themselves. However, a word of warning: If all the managers pass, that likely means you need more work on your craft or different scripts.) Cross out all the managers who don't represent screenwriters. You now have a narrowed-down list of literary managers who represent screenwriters. It's time to query them.

STEP FIVE: WRITE A SHORT, WONDERFUL QUERY AND SEND IT TO LIT MANAGERS

Reread these listings for their submission policies. There may also be a Web site for the companies. If so, go to the Web site and look around for the company's submission policies. If neither strategy tells you what you need to know, then and only then is it time to call.

Professionals in Hollywood who know each other tend to lead into conversations with a bit of chittychat. How are you? You just got back from vacation? Have you seen this or that movie? If there isn't already an established relationship, calls are short and directly to the point. When I pick up the phone and the person on the other end says: "Hey, man ... how ya doin'?" I instantly know he'll waste my time. Also, please understand that assistants usually answer the phone, and they frequently juggle multiple calls and tasks throughout the day. Asking how they're doing will earn you forced politeness for maybe five seconds. After that, you're begging for a dial tone.

If you want to convey that you are an industry professional ready to interact with other industry professionals, it's best to emulate this practice. In a situation where you need to call an office to find out the submission policy, here is the exact transcription of the conversation that should take place:

HARRIED ASSISTANT
XYZ Literary! How can I help you?

AWESOME SCREENWRITER
Hello. Are you accepting queries from new screenwriters?

HARRIED ASSISTANT
Yup, sure are!

AWESOME SCREENWRITER
Are there any submission guidelines?

To which Harried Assistant will say something like –

HARRIED ASSISTANT
You can e-mail a query to me at harriedassistant@xyzlit.com.

Or –

HARRIED ASSISTANT
Go to our web site at Xyzlit.com.

Or –

HARRIED ASSISTANT
Just snail mail queries to us, "Attention: Submissions."

If you don't hear multiple lines ringing and people screaming in the background, you could maybe ask –

AWESOME SCREENWRITER
Are you still at (read off the address)?

HARRIED ASSISTANT
Sure are!

And the most important part of this call: Say thanks ... and hang up immediately.

Here is a short sampling of things you should not say:

- "Is the head of XYZ Literary there?"
- "Guess what? I've just written a screenplay!"
- "Do you represent actors?"
- "This script will make you a million dollars!"
- "What's a query?"
- "How do you spell 'query?'"
- "Could you tell me how the industry works?"
- "I need to sell this immediately!"
- "So, you're an agent, huh?"

- "I'm calling all the way from (state other than California)!"
- "Do I really need to write a whole script?"
- "This is an incredible story about (and proceed to badly pitch it)."
- "I'm sending you the script."
- "This is the story of my life, and I have to play the lead role."

(All of these are real things said to me by real writers, by the way).

Once you have the proper submission guidelines, make sure you follow them. Every day scripts pour into our box from writers who are apparently just dumping their work in the mailbox and hoping for the best.

A BRIEF WORD ABOUT QUERY LETTERS

There are entire books and classes devoted to teaching writers how to craft successful query letters. Again, word count dictates the short version.

Do your homework and address the query to someone in the company. Queries that start out with "Dear Literary Manager" or "Dear Sir/Madam" are struggling for life right out of the womb. You are only sending these queries to the literary managers you have researched from your industry guide. You are only sending queries for excellent, polished and completed scripts in your possession.

You are only sending queries. Some particularly dense and/or impatient writers don't understand the query process and want to blow straight past it. They have no idea why they can't just send the script so I can immediately tear open the envelope, read it, love it, declare them geniuses and sign them by next week. Do not send a script to anyone who hasn't asked to see it, under any circumstances. If you feel the urge, save yourself the postage by printing up the script and throwing it in the trash yourself. The sight of your screenplay lying at the bottom of a wastebasket should quell this self-destructive urge and lead you to better activities.

Once you have sent the query, the best thing to do is absolutely nothing. Most offices get dozens of queries a day. Even with diligent, hard-working professionals working those stacks, it generally takes weeks and weeks to respond. E-mails are a bit faster, but even then it can be weeks before you hear back, if at all. There are plenty of constructive things to do to build your career in the meantime: researching companies and contests, sending out more queries, writing, etc. Keep track of when and where the query went, but otherwise the best thing to do is forget about it.

The worst thing you can do is pace around, stare at the phone, get impatient and call the company. "I sent a query letter three days ago and I haven't heard back! What the hell's going on?! If I don't get an answer immediately, I'll keep calling until ... Hello? Hello?!"

Submitting Your Work

All you're doing is getting your query instantly thrown in the trash and labeling yourself "inexperienced" at best, and "a nutjob" at worst.

STEP SIX: THANK THEM FOR PASSES OR SEND SYNOPSIS/ SCRIPTS ON REQUEST

Your query may generate several possible responses:

- A pass letter or e-mail. Your response: "Thank you for the consideration."
- A letter, e-mail or call from the office responding with a pass on that particular script, but interest in what else you may have. Your response: Offer a brief logline and description of *Awesome Script #2*. Follow their requests. Do not immediately send #2. Wait for them to ask for it. Both scripts might not be right for that company. Keep them in mind for later projects.
- A request to see a synopsis of the script. Your response: You already wrote a fantastic synopsis, so this is just a matter of giving the people what they ask for. Send it out with a smile.
- A request to see the script. Your response: Find out their submission policies and follow them.

Many companies (including our own) require a signed standard submission form with every script. This is a regular industry business practice. Some companies may ask for a synopsis. Always include a short, polite cover letter created with a word processor.

Keep track of the who's and when's of the script submission. As with the query letter, forget about it and go about your business for a while. Unlike a query, however, after about two months or so, you're within rights to follow up on the submission.

This call will be just as quick and direct as the submission guidelines call (assuming you made that, which isn't necessarily the case).

HARRIED ASSISTANT
XYZ Literary! How can I help you?

AWESOME SCREENWRITER
Hello. My name's Awesome Screenwriter. I'm calling to follow up on a screenplay called *Awesome Script #2*. Ms. XYZ requested I send it on 3/22, and I just wanted to see if she has had a chance to take a look yet.

HARRIED ASSISTANT
Can I get your name again and a number, please?

Spit out that name and number, be polite, say "thanks" and hang up the phone. It is imperative that, if you make this call, you are as friendly and professional as possible. The slightest hint of obnoxiousness or insanity sends up a red flag. Harried Assistant will likely report this red flag. When she reports to Ms. XYZ, you want her to say something like: "The dude who wrote *Awesome Script #2* called to check in." Ms. XYZ might reply: "Poor guy, I've been so rushed and busy ... remind me to take it on the plane with me to New York." Get on the phone with your impolite attitude, and the conversation will probably be more like: "That a**hole who wrote *Awesome Script #2* keeps calling." To which Ms. XYZ might well reply: "Boy, it's a good script, but life's too short. Dump it in the trash and tell him we passed."

STEP SEVEN: REPEAT UNTIL YOU SCORE REPRESENTATION

At this stage, if you have been polite, intelligent, friendly, professional, hard-working and talented, the stars may align and you'll get a call. Throughout all of these efforts, keep writing, writing and rewriting. Make sure you're always adding fresh titles to your growing slate and polishing your current scripts.

Remember: There are no guarantees. But if you follow this step-by-step process, there is a high likelihood you'll eventually find a literary manager who will take you on as a client.

Working with Representation

Agents, Managers & Lawyers

by Robin Mizell

You've probably heard that finding the right professional representation will give your script the best chance of someday being made into a feature film, a television episode, or perhaps a video game. Persuading a studio or production company executive to give you a moment of attention can be torture. The task is made more complicated by contentious perspectives of which category of representative you should enlist to help you: an agent, a manager, or an attorney specializing in entertainment law. The debate about which type is most ethical, helpful, accessible, and cost-effective has been going on for years. How much of your projected income can you afford to pay for representation? Can you afford not to?

Throw out all the rhetoric. Toss the hyperbole. Disregard slick branding. Forget the snide remarks of disgruntled competitors. Regardless of title—agent, manager, or attorney-at-law—the person's skill, intelligence, and industry connections are what really matter. The good, the bad, and the worthless exist in all three categories. The less desperate and clueless you are, the better your chances of avoiding a ruthless opportunist who knows more about loopholes in labor laws than how to close deals in the entertainment industry.

Learn exactly what these different kinds of professionals can do to help advance your career, as well as what they don't do, and you'll avoid unrealistic expectations and enjoy a much better relationship with the one, or several, you choose to advise you.

THE DIFFERENCES ARE NOT JUST SEMANTIC

It's not always possible to tell by the business name whether a person is

---

ROBIN MIZELL (robinmizell.com) is a literary agent and the founder of Robin Mizell Ltd., Literary Representation. She was formerly an editor for *Screenwriter's & Playwright's Market*.

a manager, agent, packager, producer, or some combination thereof. Learn what the terms *should* mean, but remember they're often used loosely and interchangeably.

Agents

Agents that do business in California, New York, and other states with laws similar to California's Labor Code Sections 1700-1701 (commonly referred to as the Talent Agency Act) must be licensed by the state and bonded before they can procure work for writers. The Talent Agency Act also limits a talent agent's commission fee to 10 percent of a client's gross income, although provisions in the law permit an agent to recover from clients certain expenses related to postage, courier services, etc.

California law prohibits agents from collecting registration fees from clients. It also strictly regulates "advance-fee" agents and stipulates that clients of "advance-fee" agents be informed in writing of their right to cancel and their right to a prompt refund of fees paid in advance if they don't receive the services promised. This is a basic measure to help writers avoid scammers.

Agents can collect larger fees from studios and production companies for packaging talent. Packaging involves attaching several elements—maybe a script, an actor, and a producer—to one deal and then selling it to a buyer.

Agents whose clients are members of professional guilds, such the Writers Guild of America, West (WGAW), are also bound by guild regulations related to agencies, which are negotiated by the Association of Talent Agents (ATA). Agents can become franchised by a guild and are then referred to as guild signatories. One of the most significant of guild regulations is the stipulation that agents may not own any of their clients' work, which means they can't also serve as producers. For more detailed explanations, see the ATA's Web site, www.agentassociation.comand the WGAW's Web site, www.wga.org

Managers

Managers working in California are not currently required to be licensed, as long as they can demonstrate they are not "procuring work" for their clients. They typically charge writers 15 to 20 percent for their services.

There are many types of managers, including personal managers, business managers, and literary managers. The roles sometimes overlap, so it's important to understand the business model of the individual who offers to represent you. Managers consider their clients to be under contract, whether the contract is a written or oral agreement. Make sure you fully understand, in advance, the terms of the contract to which you'll be held, including the provisions for terminating it.

Managers differ from agents in that they have more time to work with new clients and shepherd material. "If you're indeed a newbie, try targeting managers," says Candy Davis, a screenwriter and freelancer. "A manager is someone who makes herself available to new talent and helps develop and polish a script. She's just as picky as any agent, and yes, she gets a bigger percentage of your take—somewhere around 15 percent. To the writer living outside Tinseltown, she's worth it. Managers nurture new talent with deft coaching, high expectations and a kick in the pants where needed."

Lawyers

Lawyers in the entertainment field are the easiest types of writers' representatives to identify. As you probably already know, possessing the professional law degree, Juris Doctor, doesn't automatically authorize an individual to practice law. Each state in the U.S. requires professionals with law degrees to be members of the state bar in order to practice law. On the other hand, power of attorney can be granted to anyone, including a manager or an agent. If the term "attorney" is being used to imply an authority of which you're uncertain, then check the individual's credentials through the American Bar Association's Web site, www.abanet.org

Entertainment lawyers can charge hourly rates, flat fees for drafting or reviewing certain types of contracts, and percentages that are referred to as contingency fees. Some agents and managers have lawyers on staff or attorneys with whom they consult as needed. It's not unusual for an entertainment attorney to be able and willing to make the crucial connection between a scriptwriter and a studio or producer.

Because some experienced agents and managers review and negotiate hundreds of contracts, they can become just as adept as entertainment lawyers at interpreting rights agreements. Larger talent agencies and management companies often have in-house counsel; boutique businesses might engage a lawyer when needed. A scriptwriter who has an agent or manager can also pay for an entertainment attorney to conduct an independent review of a contract.

Know who your entertainment attorney's other clients are. Lawyers are not immune to conflicts of interest. In the event you're unhappy with your lawyer's services, you can dismiss him or her without difficulty.

WHICH ONE TO ENGAGE

Some agents, managers, and entertainment lawyers will agree to collaborate on the representation of a single scriptwriter. Others prefer to work independently to avoid inadvertent duplication of efforts. It would be unfortunate if two professionals representing the same writer unwittingly approached the same studio or producer separately to arrange a meeting. Clear and constant communication among the writer and his or her various representatives is imperative. Good relationships facilitate deals.

FLYING SOLO

Some studios are reluctant to arrange a sale or option agreement with a writer who isn't represented by an agent or a lawyer, just as judges are extremely cautious about allowing respondents or defendants represent themselves in court. To a production executive, it might not be worth the increased risk that an unrepresented writer will later claim a rights contract was confusing and unfair.

Furthermore, a glut of queries and submissions leaves everyone in the entertainment industry overworked. Studios contend with the heavy load by enabling agents and managers to act as gatekeepers, permitting only the most promising and commercially viable scripts through for their consideration.

PERSONALIZED CAREER DEVELOPMENT

You'll encounter claims that managers are hungrier for clients or that they devote more time to developing a writer's career and, therefore, are more willing to work with emerging talent. The same is said of agents who are new to the business, whether working independently or as junior associates at major talent agencies like the Creative Artists Agency, the William Morris Agency, and International Creative Management. Any writers' representative launching a new business will have more time for each client initially, before the business's client list expands.

The more working clients an agent, manager, or attorney has, the more money he or she can make. Naturally, you'd prefer undivided attention. That will happen only if your representative is a member of your family. If you can't swing such a beneficial arrangement, then find a representative who does a good job of balancing the client load, so you won't get lost in the crowd. If your phone calls or e-mail inquiries aren't answered promptly, if your questions are given short shrift, or if you don't feel a sense of partnership, then you won't be getting the service to which you're entitled.

You can certainly judge a business by the success of the clients it represents. A list of clients or their work is often published on an agency's or management company's website. If the information isn't provided, then don't hesitate to ask for it. Search the Web for any and all references to the business, as well as the individual manager or agent with whom you'll be dealing. Web sites devoted to exposing scams and frauds can help you avoid unnecessary expense and embarrassment, not to mention wasted time.

HOW DO YOU GET NOTICED?

You might meet script agents, managers, and entertainment lawyers at playwrights' or screenwriters' conferences or be introduced to them by other scriptwriters in your network of contacts. A personal meeting or introduction will help to distinguish you from other aspiring scriptwriters. If you don't already know someone who can recommend you to a representative, then start networking. Join a writers' group, post questions in an online forum devoted to the exchange of information among scriptwriters, apply for an internship, attend a workshop, or donate your time to a charity event at which professionals in the entertainment industry will be participating.

You'll still need to sell yourself with a query, samples of your work, and possibly a concise biography or resume. Although everything hinges on the quality and variety of your sample scripts, your query will reveal a great deal about you. Professional agents and managers deal with such a high volume of inquiries that they can spot a high-maintenance, self-absorbed prospective client after reading the first sentence of a query letter. No agent or manager wants to sign the infamous 20 percent who take up 80 percent of a workday, no matter how talented.

The more appealing you are as a prospective client, the more choice you'll have in terms of who represents you. Give yourself an advantage by knowing what genres agents and managers are seeking and which ones they tend to avoid. Each representative has peculiar tastes. It's not unusual for them to specialize by focusing on niches where their experience and industry connections are best put to use. Don't risk annoying someone who isn't looking for the types of scripts you've written.

Have several spec or sample scripts already written when you submit your query. The more scripts you have to show, the greater the chance something you're offering will fit the specific needs of a buyer. You'll demonstrate that you're versatile and that you're not just dabbling or testing the waters— you're in the scriptwriting business for the long haul.

Position yourself as a professional who is not only talented but available and easygoing. Write a polished, high-concept script with a solid story that's fresh and marketable. Know the business, network and query persistently, and you'll earn your success.

Pitch Perfect

How to Wow Producers in a Meeting

by Jonathan Koch and Robert Kosberg

Does the boardroom scare you? It shouldn't. Hollywood is looking for your script—you just have to know how to pitch it to them. Below are 12 dos and don'ts of pitch room etiquette. These tips will guide you in the conference room and give you the best possible chance of getting a producer to say yes.

THE DOS

Be on time

While obvious, it's still extremely important to be punctual. In Los Angeles, a five-mile journey might take you five and a half minutes, or it might take five and a half hours. Allow for extra time to get to your appointment. If you arrive early, run through your pitch, call to confirm other meetings, or grab a coffee. If you're running late, you must call the office. Let the assistant know that you'll be late and give her an approximate arrival time.

But please, do everything in your power to be on time. Remember that the producers and the execs with whom you're meeting are phenomenally busy. By being late, you risk messing with their schedules.

Sign the Studio Release Agreement

The Studio Release Agreement is a document that you might be asked to sign. Sign it. It's become somewhat of a standard in the industry, due to our hyper-litigious society. It states that you agree to not sue the company if it ends up producing a film or show that resembles yours.

Wait! Don't panic.

This article is excerpted from *Pitching Hollywood: How to Sell Your TV and Movie Ideas*, by **JONATHAN KOCH** and **ROBERT KOSBERG** with **TANYA MEURER NORMAN**. Used with permission of Quill Driver Books/Word Dancer Press.

Your knee-jerk response to a legally binding document like this is probably shock and horror. We don't blame you. The agreement is a necessary evil for the studios. Lawsuits are as expensive as they are annoying. They require vast amounts of time, effort, money and emotion. Nobody wants them. This document discourages such suits. If a company steals your idea, you can still sue. It's possible to sue anyone for anything, after all.

Be aware of current projects and past successes

Research the studios and production companies you'll be contacting. Know their past and current projects; learn what's slated for production in the near future. Use your research to illustrate how your idea fits into a particular company's format, goals and timing. Being able to discuss this demonstrates to an exec you're professional enough to have done the proper research, you feel your idea is a good fit for his company and that you aren't just shooting blind.

Be enthusiastic and confident

You believe in your idea. You know it's going to make everyone involved a boatload of cash. Make sure everyone in the room understands this by conveying an air of excitement about your project. If you aren't thrilled with it, how can they possibly be? Your enthusiasm will fuel theirs. It's infectious.

Maintain eye contact. Smile. Enjoy your story as you tell it.

Read the room

At the same time, gauge the energy level in the room. If everyone else is calm and quiet and low-key but you're jumping around the room, you could come off looking like a circus performer. If this is the case, you won't appear enthusiastic—just kind of creepy.

Again, maintain eye contact. Talk to these people, not at them. You're confiding in them, not pontificating to them. Notice their body language. Are they open and attentive, or are they only marginally aware of your existence?

Maybe they're tired or hungry. Maybe the biggest deal they ever landed just went belly-up. Maybe they just aren't in the mood. If they seem unreceptive, you might need to dial your pitch down.

Conversely, if they're rolling with laughter and are thoroughly entertained by your pitch, run with that. Take advantage of the high energy and give your idea the hard sell.

Allow for collaboration

As you begin to pitch, the execs will listen. At a certain point in your pitch, the execs will "get" the concept and see where the plot or show is going. Once they get it, they'll most likely stop listening and start working through the idea in their minds. They think about commercial viability, timing, demographics, their other shows, how they'll pitch your idea "up the ladder." That glazed look might not mean that they're bored. It could, in fact, be a very good thing.

They might start to throw out ideas of their own, tweaking your idea. Stress not. This is a good thing. If they're personally vested in the idea, their enthusiasm for it will grow. If they're enthusiastic, they'll try harder to sell the idea to their higher-ups.

They might ask you leading questions: And does the terrible antagonist die a horrific, bloody death? Should the girl dump him for her professor? They might put a great new spin on the idea.

Be willing to morph your plot a bit. This doesn't mean you should completely abandon your original idea. Just aim to be the easiest person in the room. Flexibility is always an asset. Be open to another's thoughts. You may even like the revised idea better.

Be brief

You may be sick of hearing this, but it bears repeating. Pitch, thank them and get out. This brevity will read: I respect your time. It'll also convey that you're busy and have other meetings (which, of course, you do). Any lingering or small talk could easily damage your chances for future meetings. Keep in mind that you're building relationships. Always leave the room on an up note.

THE DON'TS:

Don't panic

Yes, the execs to whom you're pitching could launch your career and lead you to wealth beyond your wildest dreams. Odds are they won't, but the thought that they could is a bit unnerving. Don't panic. Everyone in that room is in the business of making money. They want to succeed. They want your idea to be fantastic, so they can get rich and famous—or richer and more famous.

Sure, they might ask you some tough questions about your idea, playing devil's advocate, looking to ferret out major holes in your idea. Don't be alarmed by this. You've asked these same questions while preparing this pitch (and if you haven't, then get back to the drawing board). It's their place to pick your concept apart and look at it from every angle. View this

Submitting Your Work

kind of probing as a compliment. If your idea weren't intriguing, they would quickly thank you and dismiss you.

Don't rush

While it's important to keep your meeting as brief as possible, never rush your pitch. Nervous energy will often cause pitchers to move through the necessary information far too quickly. Vital points in the pitch might be glossed over or dropped completely. Suddenly, the pitch that you worked and reworked makes no sense. Additionally, the increased speed can make it tough for those listening to hear and understand all of your words.

Plan ahead for this. Time your pitch so that you'll feel comfortable with its natural length and not feel the need to hurry through it. Practicing the pitch in front of strangers (the waiter, your doctor, your kid's soccer coach) will be helpful. You'll be surprised by how receptive people are to hearing ideas for Hollywood. Take the edge off the fear before your meetings begin.

Don't talk your way out of a sale

If they love your idea and want to buy it, take yes for an answer. The sale ends when the customer says "yes." At that point, stop talking and get out of the room quickly. You never know what might change their minds, so go home. Celebrate.

We once sold a show but had made the mistake of bringing its talkative creator to the meeting with us. After a fantastic pitch and an immediate offer to buy the concept, our guest felt compelled to start chatting. He began to explain his reasons for creating the idea, a TV show that lampooned all court shows. He went on to state the reasons that court shows were so bad and deserving of ridicule. He went on and on and on.

After several minutes of this, the execs began to squirm. Their network was currently airing several of these shows, and they started to wonder if it as a good idea to make fun of their own shows. What had been a fabulous idea only moments before now seemed horrible. They backed out of the sale.

Don't leave anything in writing

When you leave the room, you want to be sure that all of the questions have been asked and answered. Be sure that you've covered all of the reasons the idea is fabulous. If an exec wants further information, he can contact you.

The last thing you'd want is for him to sit alone, reading over your idea. The energy in a live pitch brings a concept to life in a way that printed words on a page cannot. The exec could be thrilled with the idea, then go back and reread it before pitching it up the ladder and find it not nearly as exciting as he remembered.

Or perhaps, while reading it, he comes up with reasons the show or film might not work. If you're not there to work with him, answer his questions and explain away his concerns, the idea could be abandoned.

Having said that, you'll find that some buyers will ask for a one-page treatment. If you say you don't have one with you, some execs will request that you get one to him. In these instances, send it.

Don't become discouraged

You might pitch an idea for the first time and make a sale. You might pitch it 10 or 20 times before someone shows interest. In this business, it's easy to feel your confidence slipping away. This loss of confidence can only hurt your chances of a sale. If you have a solid, commercially viable, high-concept idea, and you have a concise, enthusiastic pitch, eventually, you'll find a buyer.

Playwriting: The Next Steps

From Networking to Staged Readings

by Chuck Sambuchino

So you're wrapping up the latest draft of that masterpiece and hiding a small smile every time you read it because the second act is pretty darn good. You're on your way—but you're also wondering what happens now. Now it's time to plug yourself into the playwriting community and educate yourself as to how and why things work the way they do.

NETWORK

As is true in many things, whom you know in the business is of much importance. A glowing recommendation from the right person may be enough to see your play set in the fall schedule two years from now. With that in mind, don't be a shut-in! Get out and network with actors, directors, producers and everyone else who loves plays or knows someone who has power.

Consider working or volunteering at a local hall. Get to know the staff and how a production functions. Familiarize yourself with all things theater. Sooner or later, there will be a good moment to mention that you, too, write plays. "When a play is over, the principals, for the most part, all come out from backstage to mingle with the audience. Strike up a conversation with them," says Clay Stafford, a playwright and screenwriter based in Nashville. "Tell them you are a playwright and you would like them to consider reading it for the purpose of producing it. You would be amazed how many doors in Los Angeles or Anytown, USA, open simply because you walk up to a stranger and say, 'I'm a writer and I've got something I'd like you to read. How should I go about getting that to you?'"

CHUCK SAMBUCHINO is the editor of *Screenwriter's & Playwright's Market*. He also edits *Guide to Literary Agents* (www.guidetoliteraryagents.com/blog) and oversaw the third edition of *Formatting & Submitting Your Manuscript*.

Even try acting in some small productions and see how it feels. The more you know about how actors operate when delving into a character and moving around onstage, the better you can craft a play with their likings in mind. If you get ridiculously lucky, you can bump into an angel or two—a wealthy arts lover who takes on passionate causes and bankrolls projects. Also, you may even be able to build a relationship with a theater that agrees to premiere all of your plays. But you can't do any of that if you're always at the computer.

JOIN A GROUP

If there is a writing group near you solely dedicated to playwrights, you're lucky, so don't pass up the opportunity to join and schmooze. When I got out of college, I saw a small notice in the alternative weekly paper about a playwriting contest. I submitted a play and it was chosen as a finalist by the Cincinnati Playwrights Initiative—a wonderful resource that I didn't even know existed because I was too lazy to even Google the words "Cincinnati" and "playwrights."

Soon after being named a finalist, I was heavily involved with the group, having numerous plays read and workshopped while helping others do the same with their plays. Joining the organization also plugged me into the city's pool of talent: actors and directors. Without my peers telling me whom to call or offering casting suggestions, I don't know what I would have done when trying to get a play off the ground.

There may not be a specific playwriting group, though, and that's all right, too. Look for a general writers group in the area. Though not ideal, you will still be surrounded by peers who can help offer their ideas on storytelling. It's a good first step to finding other playwrights in the area and seeing how they achieved successes. Referrals are born from this.

KNOW A PLAY'S THREE STAGES

A new play typically won't be produced right off the bat. A play gets born in stages—and that happens for a reason. Usually, a work isn't pristine until it's been read aloud by actors and altered appropriately by the writer who now has heard different perspectives on what works and what doesn't. Here are the three stages that a play takes en route to success.

1. The Staged Reading

This is the first step for a newborn play, and allows the writer to hear the work spoken by acting professionals. A staged reading involves actors reading parts aloud while sitting down, scripts in hand (usually behind music

Submitting Your Work

stands). Stage directions, character descriptions, and act introductions are also simply read aloud, usually by a "narrator" who is also sitting behind a music stand.

Since the play is new, a staged reading is an easy way to "work out the kinks" and see how dialogue plays live. Phrases and sections that once seemed to flow so well on the page may seem very awkward when spoken aloud or performed with a thick German accent. As the writer, you sit in the crowd and take notes. Since the reading will likely have a few rehearsals, you can also make notes at that time—and even tweak dialogue prior to the actual event.

Actors may ask for a little room to improvise and change dialogue slightly, and it's up to you as to how much slack they have, if any. Staged readings will have a director, and it's not uncommon for a playwright to also act as the director, as duties are minimal.

Readings are commonly performed in front of an audience. This is done for two reasons. First, the audience will chime in with compliments and comments following the performance, once again giving the playwright feedback on what worked and what did not. Perhaps more important than audience feedback is the chance for producers and power players to be seated in the crowd.

The whole process works like this: You call up a theater and explain that you would like to use the venue on an upcoming night for a staged reading and ask to rent the space for a reasonable fee. Once a date is agreed upon, you start to assemble a cast and rehearse. Also in that timeframe, you should contact producers and other individuals who choose what plays to produce for their respective theaters and groups. Invite them free of charge to come see the staged reading, giving them a short synopsis of what the play is about. The goal here is simple: Get them in the seats and let them see your genius work performed live. That way, if any producer is intrigued, they can contact you about producing the work in the future.

2. The Developmental Workshop

The second stage of a play's life process is neither a reading nor a production but rather something in the middle: a workshop. This stage involves putting on a loose performance of the play to further see how it will work during a real show. Costumes are worn, some scenes blocked out, some lighting used, etc. Actors may have memorized some dialogue, but they're typically walking around with their scripts (going "on book").

A workshop may have anywhere from three to a dozen rehearsals, and the goal is to take the play as far as it can go in that limited amount of time. Be prepared to help out in any way necessary. Just like a staged reading, the writer must work out a location, assemble a crew, and try to get producers in the seats.

3. The Production

The real deal, just like the performances you've seen at theaters. A full production means that everything is in place—costumes, props, memorized scripts, promotion, lighting and everything else. The playwright is likely paid, and hopefully you can get reviewers to see the play. A favorable review can serve as a stepping-stone to getting a larger, more prominent theater to also consider producing the work.

Think about it: If you were to query a theater in San Jose about producing the work, wouldn't it be nice to be able to say how the play was recently performed in Tulsa, got rave reviews, and sold out almost every night? That way, the producer considering your script knows that the material is both battle-tested and a draw for getting butts in the seats. And, just maybe, his best friend is an angel who will take interest in your work.

Submitting Your Work

Get Serious With Playwriting

Evaluating Submissions and Theaters

by Jacqueline McMahon

You've spent months developing your ideas into the perfect play. You have revised, proofread and edited into the wee hours of the morning. You formatted your play with the latest software, then headed for the business supply store with the cheapest photocopying prices. You saved copies of your script on disk, on your computer and now, on paper. There is nothing more to do.

Wait a minute! Writing the play was only just the beginning. Unless you know of opportunities that come knocking on the doors of writers, you must now address the business side of playwriting.

MARKETS

Playwrights have several choices for getting their work out to the public: contests, theaters, publishers and residencies.

Contests: The book you hold in your hands, combined with any search engine, will provide playwrights with an incredible number of appropriate contests—some that do not even charge a fee. Obviously, the more prestigious and well known the contest, the more competition one will have and the harder it will be to win or even place as a finalist. Winning a contest can provide many different results, including prize money, a reading or production and even publication.

Warning: Follow the contest guidelines exactly as specified. Many wonderful plays will never be considered because the author did not comply with the complete submission guidelines.

Theaters: Theaters are always looking for new material for upcoming

JACQUELINE MCMAHON runs a successful performing arts studio, "Slightly Off Broadway," with her best friend. See her Web site: www.slightlyoffbroadway.com. From 1998-2005, Jacqueline hosted Suite101's Performing and Writing Musical Theatre Web site. Today, she enjoys blogging at dramaquill.wordpress.com

productions. It is always best to inquire before sending a script. Market listings will specify whether to query, send a synopsis or the complete manuscript and whether the theater accepts unsolicited submissions or only those from agents. Other information available to writers might be rights, compensation (i.e., royalties) and the theater's response time if they're interested. Working with a theater allows playwrights a chance to form contacts in the field, which could lead to further productions.

Sometimes newer playwrights will choose the option of self-production. They must be prepared to provide the financing, assemble the cast and crew and publicize the play—but for some, this may be a necessary step to becoming a recognized playwright.

Publishers: Many writers dream of having their work available in published form made possible through a professional company. For playwrights, having their works available in the catalogues of publishers such as Samuel French not only means recognition but potential financial rewards as well. Drama departments and theatre groups can order copies and pay royalties when doing productions or they may also purchase copies for their script libraries. Either way, the playwright stands to make some money when his materials are used by these groups.

These publisher Web sites are a great place to start:

- www.samuelfrench.com
- www.bakersplays.com
- www.playscripts.com
- www.lillenas.com/drama
- www.meriwetherPublishing.com
- www.dramatists.com/index.asp
- www.brookpub.com

Concerning self-publishing, the innovative playwrights of today are forming their own publishing companies and selling their scripts through their Web sites. Offering both electronic scripts and hard copies online can be quite an instrumental way of marketing to a broad customer base.

Residencies: Established playwrights may apply for a variety of "playwright in residence" positions at colleges and universities. Benefits may include opportunities to lecture, a stipend, an atmosphere conducive to writing and being involved in the rehearsals of one's own work.

HOW TO FIND OUT WHAT'S IN DEMAND

With so many market opportunities, finding the right place for one's work can be a daunting task. No matter how one seeks out opportunities, one standard remains: Do not send anything that does not fit the guidelines.

Targeting a Market

With so many contests and theaters out there, where does a playwright begin when looking for a market? One play will not be a good fit everywhere; in fact, the more you research your options, the more tightly focused and shorter your list of markets will be. The good news is that markets will not only tell you exactly how to submit work, but they'll also tell you exactly what they're seeking.

For example, the Live Bait Theater is Chicago is upfront about their specifications: "We produce only new works by Chicago playwrights." Bingo—that's a key market for people in the region, but useless elsewhere. The Magic Theatre in San Francisco has an eye out for plays with "cutting-edge sociopolitical concerns." They are specific in their wants concerning subject and theme, but they will accept submissions from anyone anywhere.

If you're writing a play about a family that bravely escaped the Holocaust, look for theaters that seek works with Jewish themes. If your work has any multicultural aspect at all, for that matter—Latino themes, African-American themes, Native-American themes, etc.—then there are likely several theaters and contests that are specifically looking for works just like yours.

If you're writing something edgy, look for a local fringe festival that specializes in performing—you guessed it—edgy works. The first play I ever had professionally produced was a wacky comedy done through the local fringe festival. It was a perfect fit.

Identify what your play is. A comedy? Historical or contemporary? One-act or full length? Experimental? Deals with women's issues? Gay and lesbian themes? Mystery play? Has a Southern feel? Any or all of descriptive tidbits like these will help you target markets.

Contests, theaters and publishers will all provide playwrights with their specific requirements in this regard. (See this article's sidebar for more on targeting markets.)

It has been my experience that most contests do not accept musicals, plays for children, or scripts with large casts and elaborate sets. Their resources simply cannot support such productions. That means that writers of these types of works must diligently seek out compatible markets for such projects. Writers of plays for children, for example, will find publishers and producers in *Children's Writer's & Illustrator's Market*. Similar books exist for writers of other markets. There are publishers who specialize in genre publishing (such as musicals, works for youth and other specialized markets) and larger firms who publish a great variety of genres.

HOW DOES THE PLAYWRIGHT MAKE ENDS MEET?

Unfortunately, unless your name is synonymous with theater, it is unlikely that your playwriting income will provide you with the equivalent of a full-time job salary. Playwrights often supplement their income by writing articles for magazines and e-zines or with jobs in the field, like teaching courses in playwriting and drama or even directing the works of others.

The main sources of income will come from performance royalties, script sales, and contest prize money. But most playwrights will tell you that it isn't the monetary rewards that keep them writing—it's seeing their words come to life in the ultimate reward: a production.

ORGANIZATIONS OF INTEREST TO PLAYWRIGHTS

There are many benefits to joining a nationwide playwrights' organization, such as informative newsletters and/or magazines, contacts in the business, Web listings to promote and sell your work, workshops/seminars/retreats, a place to meet and connect with other playwrights, and online resources such as forums/listserves/chats/links/articles (many of which can be utilized by anyone, not just members).

The following groups are among the best to be involved with:

- Dramatists Guild: www.dramatistsguild.org
- Theatre Communications Group: www.tcg.org
- Professional Organization of Canadian Theatres: www.pact.ca
- International Centre for Women Playwrights: www.netspace.org/~icwp/index.html
- New Dramatists: www.newdramatists.org

Playwrights may also benefit from other writing organizations and Web resources. Although not a complete list, these are some of my favorites:

- National Association of Women Writers: www.naww.org
- Playwrights Union of Canada: www.puc.ca
- Virginia Commonwealth University's Playwriting Resource Page: www.vcu.edu/artweb/playwriting/resources.html

IS IT TIME FOR AN AGENT YET?

Many playwrights believe that an agent is necessary for a successful writing career. Playwriting, however, differs in one very significant way from other media of writing. For most playwrights, it is the prospect of a staged reading or production that entices them to continue with their craft; rather than the continual quest for publication sought after by writers of articles, short stories and novels.

New writers of any genre will find it difficult to obtain representation until they have developed somewhat of a proven track record in the field. After all, an agent is looking to make money from his/her relationship with a writer and newcomers have not yet established themselves as worthwhile risks.

Cleveland-based playwright Linda Eisenstein has defied the odds surrounding the necessity of an agent to achieve success. With more than 100 productions, a large number of readings and many of her works in print, she is proving that tenacity and self-promotion are viable tools to a playwright's success. In fact, Linda would have the same take on marketing and making contacts even if she did have an agent: "Even playwrights with agents need to do a great deal of their own marketing," she says.

So is it unnecessary for playwrights to have agents? Absolutely not! In fact, an agent can open doors to larger, more prestigious markets, deal with contract negotiations and recommend scripts to contacts many playwrights would otherwise not have.

When you're ready to get serious and tackle the business of playwriting, make sure you immerse yourself in how things work. Identifying the best markets for yourself—whether contests or theaters or community groups— is a key and difficult step in the process, so do it right. That way, you'll make enough money to not have to look for the absolute cheapest copy center in town.

From Page to Stage

Seeking Your Play Production

by Liza Lentini

For most of us, there was a time in our lives when we believed without question that a fairy flew into our bedrooms while we slept, lifted a baby tooth from under our pillow, and replaced it with legal tenure. As grown-ups, that now seems preposterous for so many rational reasons. Firstly, how did these fairies know where we lived? The status of our dentistry? Our patterns of sleep (including deepest hours)? And, most importantly, what would a fairy want with our gross, dead teeth anyway?

Most of us recall such simplistic idealism with a laugh and a head shake— and perhaps even a slight tinge of envy. As adults we have an obligation to *understand* the way the world works, to abide by the order of humanity, to respect the rules of give and take, work and play, addition and subtraction. The envy is thoroughly justified, as we simply must remain fully grounded in the real world in an effort to accomplish our all-important big girl/big boy goals. How great it would be to bottle that child-like innocence. How, in these difficult, ever-challenging times, could one replicate the purest, most absurd, rose-colored hopefulness of a child?

Just write a play.

Heck, why limit yourself to one? Write two; write three. If you're hooked on the high of completion, write more. But at some point in your playwriting post-coital afterglow, you will, I assure you, sit back and wonder, "When will someone produce these?" For the very (and I do mean very, very) lucky new writers, there's someone waiting in the wings for the final click of the "save" button. But for the rest of playwrights, an unexpected idealism rises

LIZA LENTINI's (www.lizalentini.com) plays have been performed at The Cherry Lane Theatre, PS122, The Women's Project, and The McGinn/Cazale Theatre, among others, garnering a multitude of honors and awards. She is the founder and creative director of Elephant Ensemble Theater, a charitable organization that brings performances to children in hospitals. Liza is currently writing a book called *How to Write a Play in 8 Weeks or Less*, which details her unique no nonsense method, the same she teaches in her NYC workshop.

which harkens back to our tooth fairy days: "When will someone want to sweep into my life and produce my play...and give me money for it?"

If you happen to be destined for a more realistic production path (that is, the "Why the heck is no one banging on my door?" path), there are things you need to do to assure your work will be artistically sound for opportunities you yourself will curate.

FORMAT YOUR WORK

Looks are everything. Well, this is not altogether true—it's what's *inside* your play that counts. But if your play isn't properly formatted, it's easy to spot the amateur in the room. Adam Greenfield, literary manager at Playwrights Horizons, knows exactly what he likes to see when your script arrives on his desk, and it includes a cover letter, résumé and synopsis: "A professional-seeming play submission will come bound (your choice of clips or brads). Your cover letter should be brief, fitting onto one page. Avoid using the cover letter to sell your play; instead, it should inform us of the play's history to date, and any relevant background information. A separate page should include your bio or a playwriting résumé. A separate page from that should include a brief (about 200 words) synopsis of the play; don't give us a moment-to-moment account, but rather a back-of-the-book overview. The cover letter, résumé and synopsis pages should be clipped to the front of the script."

There are several play formatting programs out there, and I'm sure they do the job just fine; however, I'm a firm believer in the old-fashioned way, where every single centered name and tabbed stage direction is typed by hand. Reason being, it forces you to re-live every little word, which is an invaluable experience.

READ IT, BABY

Whether you're putting on staged readings or developmental workshops, inviting audience feedback or not, the purpose is always to see what works and doesn't, which lines are clunkers, which character is under-played, which through-line doesn't make its way through. Those are the essential nuts and bolts, but even more important, it gives you a sense of what you want to say, what you want it to be, and how it all sounds out loud.

John Clinton Eisner is artistic director and co-founder of the Lark Play Development Center, a 15 year-old community of playwrights and artist collaborators committed to nurturing unheard voices and new ideas for the theater. "People are often unclear about what they mean when they speak of 'creative process' and 'play development,'" John says. "Both terms are frequently used negatively: in the first case describing a rambling or undisciplined approach to making a work of art, and in the second case implying a course of action by which producers seek to smooth out a play's rough edges for production by requiring a writer to compromise his or her work. I think of these ideas quite differently."

For Clinton Eisner, it's about a set of carefully considered steps in an artist-driven process to connect the ideas in a play to a whole work capable of engaging the audience the playwright has in mind. Play development is also connected to a playwright in the driver's seat making the play the kind of experience she or he has envisioned. "Another metaphor I like is of stones as stepping places across a river," he says. "A simple idea can be leapt like a small stream, but an ambitious idea requires a plan of attack to bring the initial vision into a form which it can be realized on stage. The struggle in defining these terms is about power. Is the artist in charge of the work being created, and at what point does collaboration—a hallmark of the theater—enter the picture?"

DATE YOUR DIRECTOR

This entire book could be devoted to accounts of the playwright/director relationship. With that, there would be stories of playwrights and their director holding hands, dancing through a field of daisies down the path of success. The other stories would tragically resemble a marriage of a few tamed Tennessee Williams characters, adding in some modern-day curse words and maybe even a lawsuit. A friend of mine recently came to me and said, "I found a director for my play…he's, well…he's very good and well-known…but he seems to hate the script."

My friend is well-known and very good at what he does, too. And the story made me enraged. I told him your director should be someone who treats you with respect, someone you can have a give and take with. That first meeting (and maybe the second and third) should be like a date—not literally, of course. (That, I promise you, I do not advise!) Only in the sense that this is a person who should have your best interests at heart. It's up to you, however, to know what your best interests are. You have to come into that meeting knowing what you are willing to change about your script, what you want out of the process. And, just like dating, if it looks like you two will never have staying power, give him/her a polite *sayonara* and move onto the next.

Andrew Goffman, writer and solo performer, agrees: "I think all good directors would have no problem working on a trial basis at first before anyone has to commit to anything. It's like a new relationship—first you go out to dinner, then the movies, and if it's still working out you go to the next level. Once that happens it gets more complicated. But if you are compatible, a lovely baby comes out that everybody loves—your show!"

STRAP YOUR BALONEY METER ON

At my college graduation, Carl Sagan very unscientifically advised us to strap on our baloney meter, a guard against insincerity and all-around balderdash. It's important for life, yes, but imperative for playwrights. Playwriting is different from every other medium because, for better and for worse, the writer is drawing a great, big target on their back and asking to be stabbed. That's every single person who witnesses your work: actors, directors, technical folk, grandmas-who-don't-get-it. I always tell my students, if you don't want your audience to find you and offer their opinion, don't write plays. Do absolutely anything else. Because people can't help it, you're sitting right there and they want to talk to you about what they've just seen.

It's your job to keep your baloney meter—your filter—so tightly secured that anything that doesn't complement your intentions and your process gets a gracious nod before it's thrown straight out the window of your existence. This applies to professional critics, too. Leonard Jacobs, editor of The Clyde Fitch Report (www.clydefitchreport.com), has been a New York theater critic for 20 years, covering Broadway, Off Broadway and Off-Off. He knows plays—and playwrights—and says: "Just as playwrights must discern between constructive and unhelpful criticism from directors, producers or dramaturgs, it's about extracting the information that seems well-founded and discarding the rest. But playwrights should make an effort to enter into dialogue with critics more. It needn't be public. But they should attempt to keep channels of communication open."

Leonard's solution in a nutshell: peace, love, and understanding. And I agree.

CULL YOUR CONTACTS

When I first got to New York City, I sat down with legendary Broadway producer Arthur Cantor and asked him how I could connect with other producers. He thought for a second, turned to me, and in the most matter-of-fact tone he gruffly pronounced, "Call them up!"

The creative side of playwriting is obvious, but the rest, I hate to say, is pure business. You can and should use all of your contacts to your best advantage. Support your fellow playwrights by going to their readings; create a community for yourself. Get to know their directors and find out who the new blood is.

If you think the world is small, the world of theater is infinitesimal. If you were interviewing for a regular old desk job, I'm guessing your best tactic for landing the position wouldn't include pitching fits and insulting people. The same goes for building your reputation in theater. You never know who knows who, and which intern is going to be the next star literary manager five years down the road. There is such a natural generosity in the theater, but it's also full of its own creative (and often difficult) animal species. Treat people wisely, and keep those that are good, smart, and talented close to home.

How do you meet people? Become a board member for an organization you really believe in, join an association or union, or, plainly, volunteer for your favorite theater company to be brought into the fold. As another theatrical Liza once proclaimed: "What good is sitting alone in your room?" E-mail is great, but allowing people to get to know you face-to-face and creating relationships is much, much better.

FIND A HOME

A playwriting home, that is. This can be a dingy little theater, a bright, open room, a basement, or your living room. And a home isn't a home without a family of like-minded individuals who care about you—and your work, so that you both always have a place to flourish. Even if you've had the greatest success, inevitably, your play will close some day. What then? How do you stay playwriting-minded in a world that, let's face it, isn't encouraging you to flaunt your creative side. I say, design your days so that flaunting is a must.

As with most true homes, they're not always storybook. They're better! At least that's what I found when I started working with Manhattan Repertory Theatre in 2006. The space itself is small—but it turned out to be the perfect venue for me to take risks and make mistakes. The dynamic duo who run the company, artistic director Ken Wolf and director of productions Jennifer Pierro, actually encourage risk-taking. I'm very fortunate to have a theater that supports my wackier works, but in 2006, I also decided to make a home of a different nature, in the form of a children's theater charity. It's called Elephant Ensemble Theater (www.elephanttheater.com), and we tour children's hospitals all around New York City bringing professional performances to sick kids. For me, it's a consistent reminder of why we perform—to change lives. I never wanted to write children's theater before our first tour, but when I see the effect our work has—right in front of us, on these kid's faces—it feels like home to me.

HAVE HEART

When I was just a wee lass, I met Irish playwright Miriam Gallagher, who told me ever-so-wisely, "Playwriting is not for the faint-hearted." I remember those words, so many years later, every time I want to throw in the theatrical towel. This is the reason I know playwriting is a calling; we develop plays for so many years in hopes they get produced, often earning little or no money while doing so, yet making tremendous sacrifices of time and energy. The trick is to appreciate it for exactly what it is, a life of building your craft doing something you love. There are no guarantees in this playwriting life, only the promise that, if it truly is something you're meant to be doing, you won't give up, no matter what.

Before playwright Eric H. Weinberger was a Drama Desk and Lucille Lortel Award nominee, he was writing his first play. A full-fledged grown-up at the time, he believed the world of playwriting would be a much easier road than it really was. "I wrote my first play for a well-known and respected actress. It is a one-woman play. I thought with her talent and fame, it would be fairly easy to get produced. I was wrong. There are so many people attempting to get plays produced and not everyone wants to do one-person ones despite the lesser costs. I found it very hard to get producers to read this first play or to come to the multiple readings we did of it. But we persisted with doing readings and finally, two producers of a non-profit theatre came forward and said they wanted to do it. They gave us a very fine production. After that, we did it Off-Broadway, but raising the money for it was a nightmare! In the end, I had to use a lot of my own money to make it happen."

So: Is it worth it? If it's your passion, then it's worth it without question. Despite Weinberger's travails, he wouldn't have it any other way. "It is very tough in many respects, but I love it in spite of the negative parts and know I wouldn't be happy unless I'm doing it," he says. "I love creating something and then seeing it come to life. I love my characters even if they are flawed. I love being able to work with so many brilliant, talented, creative people. It keeps me feeling young and alive and fulfilled. I love it if I can make audiences laugh or be moved or inspired in some way. I love applause!"

If that's not a great curtain line, I don't know what is.

Submitting Your Work

Know Your Avenues

Begin with Realistic Goals

by Chuck Sambuchino and Vanessa Wieland

If you're having trouble seeing your work come to life on the screen or the stage, perhaps the problem is as simple as aiming too high. Your first script doesn't have to wow Hollywood and generate Oscar buzz. Your first play probably won't win a Tony and make you oodles of money on Broadway. In any aspect of the writing business, scribes can always find happiness in knowing that one thing indeed leads to another. A play production at one location will greatly aid in getting another. Professional screenwriting credits, however small they are, will help show your skill and professionalism to key people.

There's no shame in setting realistic goals early on. Understandably, though, it can be confusing to a new writer when someone tells them to "simply start small and think local." That's why we've come up with several ways how new writers can jumpstart their career.

WRITE SHORT SCRIPTS

If you're stalling in the middle of a full-length work, look to shorter categories.

One-Act Plays

These plays range anywhere from 20 to 60 pages in length. One-acts are a good first step for a budding playwright, as the medium-sized length allows for things such as character arc, scene changes, and other aspects that are staples of a full-length work.

CHUCK SAMBUCHINO is the editor of *Screenwriter's & Playwright's Market*. He also edits *Guide to Literary Agents* (www.guidetoliteraryagents.com/blog) and oversaw the third edition of *Formatting & Submitting Your Manuscript*. **VANESSA WIELAND** is a staffer on the Writer's Digest Books editorial team.

10-Minute Plays

Just what it sounds like, 10-minute plays run 10 pages and have a minimal plot with a minimal cast. There are plenty of contests looking for scripts of this length, and several winners are usually chosen each time. The goal is to have a small group of actors play all roles in all the winning plays.

Short Screenplays

A lot of contests exist for short screenplays running fewer than 60 pages. You can find plenty of them in this book.

THE 48-HOUR FILM PROJECT

A godsend to writers across the country, this annual contest pits film crews in cities across America against one another. The concept is simple: Teams comprised of writers, directors, actors and crew members are given 48 hours to write, shoot and edit a short film. Guidelines are provided at the last moment before the 48 hours begin, so that scripts cannot be written before the weekend starts. Naturally, each team needs a writer (or a team of writers) to compose their short script—and that's where you come in.

So where can you find a list of participating cities? Check out the official Web site (www.48hourfilm.com), as new locations are being added every year while others drop out. The list of cities ranges from the big (Chicago, Los Angeles, Philadelphia) to the small (Fargo, N.D.; Asheville, N.C.; Portland, Maine). The contest is also international, with participating cities overseas including Paris, Geneva, Athens and many more.

"The 48-Hour Film Project is a great reason for writers to get off the couch and start shooting. It's an adrenaline rush," says Liz Langston, co-founder of the project.

WORKING IN SCHOOL

If you're taking classes at a school (rather than online courses), see if there's a television department where you can get involved. Look for news shows where you can write copy and stories. Perhaps you're taking night classes at a university that has multiple original shows filmed by students. Get involved any way you can and pen some scripts to show to cast members.

"To get started on a local level, you just need to write something and then find someone to make it, if you can't make it yourself," says Clay Stafford, a Nashville-based screenwriter and playwright. "Production departments at universities are always looking for good short scripts—say around 20 minutes. If I wanted to see my work produced and I wanted to build some

Online Script Warehouses

Script registries are Web sites where writers register their work to be viewed by prospective buyers. Sites such as InkTip and WriteSafe provide searchable databases allowing industry professionals to view thousands of loglines, synopses, treatments, and full scripts with the aim of purchasing the rights to create a play or film.

Registries are relatively new vehicles for marketing a script. The most obvious benefit is immediate accessibility to hundreds of industry professionals without having to query or find an agent. Once your script is uploaded to the site, anyone registered has immediate access to your work. If interested, they can then contact you to negotiate options or purchase your script. Another benefit: InkTip.com keeps records of the hits a logline or script has received. Knowing who is reading can be invaluable, and records are helpful in determining what captures attention versus what doesn't.

On the other hand, such Web sites create a risk of having work plagiarized or stolen and the creator receiving no credit—or money—for their efforts. WriteSafe.com cites this as the primary reason to register works with them. Not only does the work get presented to prospective buyers, the records showing when the work was created and who had access to viewing it offer some protection from theft. Yet proving intellectual property theft is neither easy, nor is it cheap, and ideas are not copyrightable. Anyone can look online, marvel at your concept, then put their own spin on the idea and turn it into a screenplay of their own.

Of course, like any warehouse, there is a lot to choose from—so will your script stand out? The advantage of a search engine is that the results are not only impartial, but tailored to the request. A search engine like InkTip's offers numerous methods for finding the right script: a simple title/author search, a keyword search, and an advanced search which pulls results based on up to 250 different options.

There is also the cost. Online registries make their money by being the middleman between you and potential buyers. Be sure that the service you're paying for will work for you and still be around in a few months' time. The ease of posting your work in one place may prove beneficial for getting you noticed but be sure that those wanting to buy are reputable. As always, be aware of potential frauds and predators. An online search brought up success stories—and a lot of warnings of shady behavior from "producers" who option scripts for little or no money.

According to InkTip President Jerrol LeBaron, the two common mistakes writers make when registering their works are: 1) writing loglines and synopses "that don't stand out," and 2) making typos and grammatical errors. "Experience has proven to [industry professionals] that writers who care about the professionalism of their work also care about structure, character, and have a much better understanding of development," he says.

- Filmtracker (www.filmtracker.com)
- The Hollywood Script Readers Digest (www.screenscripts.com)
- InkTip (www.InkTip.com)
- The Screenplayers (www.screenplayers.net)
- The Screenwriters Market (www.screenwritersmarket.com)
- WriteSafe (www.writesafe.com)

Submitting Your Work

credits for myself, this is probably the route that I would take. It costs the writer nothing but the paper the script is printed on and the phone call."

COMMUNITY THEATERS

Writers living in Smalltown, Idaho, for example, have a good chance of finding a community theater group in the area—probably called something such as "The Smalltown Players." Local community theaters and groups are everywhere—so use them! Take your new play and ask them if they would ever consider producing a work from a local writer. Your script should get a quick read, and if it's good, you're in business. Newspapers love headlines like "Regional Theater Group Produces Work by Local Playwright." If the media can get behind it, that means butts in the seats.

In the same vein, look at local high schools as market possibilities. If you've written a play, ask your alma mater to perform a premiere. They may be excited to produce the work of one of their own. Schools of any kind are a great place to seek staged readings of your work. Younger actors are hungry for new material to test their chops, and it wouldn't be hard to gather a half dozen college actors together to read through your play so you can hear the words out loud.

Whether it's a local high school or community group that produces your work, you probably won't make much money. Funds will be a problem, so consider passing on any upfront fees and instead ask for a portion of the money made from ticket sales—a.k.a. royalties. Eight percent is a safe bet.

Pitchfests

*A No-Bull Guide to
Succeeding at Conferences*

by Daniel Manus

The next five minutes could change your life."

That's the line that is so lovingly drilled into you before every pitchfest, right? Maybe if you accentuate *this* word instead of *that* one, maybe if you smile wider, maybe if you emphasize your second act, maybe, maybe, maybe. The "maybes" will drive you mad.

Here's the bottom line on pitchfests: They are big business. They are great networking events for the executives, great promotional outlets for advertisers, publishers and magazines and last, if not least, they are a chance for people on the outside of Hollywood to speak to someone on the inside. And just *maybe*, get their big break.

I have attended almost 20 pitchfests in the last few years in America and Canada. In five-minute intervals, that's 12 pitches an hour, three to four hour sessions, one to two sessions a day. All in all, I've probably listened to close to 1,500 pitches at these events. How many of the projects have I read? Maybe 80. How many did I really like? Maybe 10. How many did I option or decide to develop with the writer? Maybe four. Those are your odds.

Putting that aside, executives do *want* writers to come in and blow us away. We *are* looking for something great that we can bring back to our bosses and say, "Look what I found!" And we want your considerable money to be well spent. But we are a fickle bunch, and combined with the fact that we really don't enjoy waking up at 8 a.m. on a Saturday, there are a number of things that will immediately shut our window of interest.

I have seen the same mistakes made—the same rules broken—time after time. So I thought it was time writers knew the real score and were given the no-bullshit dos and don'ts to succeeding at a pitchfest. Executives love

---

DANIEL MANUS is producer and development exec with Clifford Werber Productions. He teaches at writers' conferences, and also instructs classes on pitching.

to discuss the best, the worst, and the most ridiculous. So here is a guide to make sure you are one of the first group.

ACT PROFESSIONAL

Here's a little secret that you may not be aware of. Depending on the vent, probably 70 percent of the time, you are pitching to an assistant—not an executive. Now, don't underestimate an assistant—they have their boss's ear and their opinion usually carries serious weight, but there is certainly no reason to be scared of them. Most are but a few years out of college, and some may even be attending their first pitchfest, too, and are just as nervous about what *they* are going to say—as you are. So, just be calm, cool and collected and have a conversation about your story. Be normal! We'd much rather talk to you like normal people about your story than hear a memorized speech or a sweaty, stuttering slur of words. It may sound oxymoronic, but be casually professional.

As for being normal, well … normal is a relative term. And it may sound horribly superficial, but you need to dress and act the part. You're not just selling your script—you're selling yourself. Basically, pitching is like speed dating. The first thing out of your mouth shouldn't be something horribly embarrassing or personal.

BEFORE YOU PITCH: THINGS TO AVOID

Executives are not only evaluating your story and your pitch—but whether or not we would hesitate putting you in a room with Studio Executives. And whether or not you are someone we are going to want to talk to and work with for the next 1-3 years of our lives. I can usually tell within the first minute if that's the case. So here are some tips to make sure you're not rejected before you even sit down.

1. Never put your hometown on your nametag unless you are from Los Angeles or New York. Sadly, there is a prejudice and elitist attitude many in LA have about the abilities of people who are from outside our little bubble. Many feel that if you are a serious screenwriter, you need to live in LA—so if you don't, perhaps you're not that serious about it. So, it may sound silly and insulting, but putting "Los Angeles" on your nametag will ensure that no one dismisses your talents before you get a chance to display them. As they say in the real estate business: location, location, location.

2. Do not wear a costume, and do not speak in your character's voice. You are not on an acting audition. If you have written a vampire script, do not wear a cape. If you have written a script about diving, do not wear a wetsuit. Stunts have been pulled before to sell a script, and sure—sometimes

What about Period Pieces?

Ah, the period piece. The eternal debate. Should you write it? Should you pitch it? Will it get bought? Probably not.

Here's the deal. If you are a first-time writer who has this great epic story inside of them to tell—then by all means—write it! Period dramas and epics are perfect for screenwriting competitions. They usually win because if you can do them well, they are very impressive. The problem is—*everyone* thinks they can do them well. And very few of the companies that attend pitchfests are looking for a $200-million trilogy epic or something that is set in the 1800s from a first time writer. These are the types of stories that are usually left to those with a proven and profitable track record. If 40 companies tell you they aren't looking for period pieces—why do you keep pitching them?

My advice is this: Write what is in you to write. When you finish your $100M period drama or sci-fi-fantasy epic, smile to yourself for a job well done…then put it in a drawer and write something you can sell. A horror, a thriller, a comedy, etc. Then, once you've sold that and everyone in town wants to know what else you have written, *that* is when you say, 'Well actually, I wrote this wonderful period piece…"

Do not write a "Hollywood Insider" story if you live in Nebraska. Or, quite frankly, even if you live in Hollywood. The Hollywood starlet who falls for the blue collar guy, the Hollywood star who must spend time in Middle America, any script based on Britney, Lindsay or Paris, the screenwriter who has writer's block until he meets a mysterious stranger, or the writer who gets sucked into his character's world. Two words—Been. Done. I don't want to sound like a coastal snob or an episode of *Studio 60*, but if you don't live and work in Hollywood—then you can't accurately portray it in a script. There's a lingo, a mind set and a speed to our conversations and those who don't live it, usually can't emulate it in a script.

---

they work—but more often than not, they don't. There was one man who bought out the entire 9:00-9:05 time slot for every company and pitched to the whole room at once. Probably cost him $800. Despite the auditory problems, it was a ballsy move. Sure, we all remember the story of what he did, but I doubt anyone recalls the story he was trying to sell.

3. Shorts or sandals = no service. Sure it's Saturday morning and the people to whom you are pitching may be in jeans and a T-shirt, but you should be dressed to impress. This doesn't mean a suit and tie, but it does mean no shorts and sandals. Don't make us think you're some schlub who had an extra 10 minutes in their day, so you decided to pitch a story. Make us think you're a professional writer in Los Angeles who just hasn't caught her big break yet. Dress like you're going to a meeting with a producer.

4. Don't huff or puff about your time. Fighting with the person pitching before or after you because he or she is taking up 30 seconds of *your* time, will only ensure that you won't get any of mine. We know that five minutes isn't much, and we want to hear your ideas. So, if we need an extra 30 or 60 seconds with someone else—don't get excited. You would want the same courtesy extended to you. There's no reason to get testy, not that we don't appreciate the drama.

WHEN YOU PITCH: THINGS TO AVOID

Okay—you've sat down, without incident, and you look and sound great. So, let's move on to your actual pitch.

5. Don't pitch to people who don't represent what you're writing. Do your research. Don't ask me what we are looking for. Go on IMDB and look at what we have done, whom we have worked with, and if there is a book of company profiles provided by the event, please do yourself a favor and read them.

Sure, sometimes a company is absent and you are sent to pitch to a company you have never heard of. If you get stuck with a "substitute" company that is not looking for what you have written, either say 'thank you, but I don't have that type of material' and then get back in line for another company (you should not be charged money for this), or ask the executive for advice on how your pitch sounds, or how it can be improved, or some other question you have wanted to ask. Good executives can and should evaluate your pitch and tell you how to improve it. Don't be afraid to ask.

6. This isn't Leno—don't use cue cards. I know many an executive who will dismiss a writer who reads word for word from a piece of paper. You need to know your story well enough to speak coherently about it for four minutes. If you don't know it well enough, who will?

Being prepared is half the battle. This doesn't mean you should memorize a four-and-a-half-minute spiel, because chances are the executive is going to jump in at some point and ask you a question. Some of us even do it on purpose—don't let it throw you. Have a couple prepared segues to get back to your story without letting us see that you are going through your whole pitch in your head trying to find your place like a broken bookmark.

If you still need to read from a page, then you're not ready to pitch your story yet. And under no circumstances should you give us your one-sheet and say, "It's all on there—read it and ask me any questions you might have." My question for you will be: Why are you trying to make me not like you?

Visual aids like an already cut trailer or a sketch drawing of your animated characters are okay. Otherwise, leave your props, toys, posters and dioramas at home.

7. Show emotion, but definitely not *too* much. Be excited about your story. If you're not, no one else will be—but don't pull a Tom Cruise and jump on the chairs. Let me put it this way: If you're stone-faced through the pitch, don't expect much more from the other side of the table. If you are being exciting and engaging, and you're still getting nothing from your exec, then he or she is probably like that normally and you shouldn't take it personally.

There's no crying in baseball—or pitching. Have you written a very personal story—your own autobiography perhaps—and you cry every time you pitch it? Then practice that pitch over and over until you no longer tear up. Showing some emotion is great, but bawling like a baby is embarrassing. Writing may be your therapy, but pitching isn't.

Be funny. If you have written the most hilarious comedy of the 21st Century, your pitch should make me laugh. If it doesn't, then either your script isn't funny—or you're doing something wrong.

8. Never pitch an unfinished project. This is to protect both of us. The point of a pitchfest is for me to ask for your script. If your response is "Well it's just in outline form right now, but I can finish it in about a month if you really like it," my response to you will be "Thank you for wasting the last 5 minutes of my life."

9. Don't insist on directing your script unless you can fully finance it yourself or you have an agent and a proven track record directing feature length Hollywood pictures. College shorts and that zombie movie you made with your buddies for $1,500 bucks don't count.

PUTTING YOUR BEST FOOT FORWARD

As I said, we will know within the first minute if we're into you and your story or not, so here is the info we need to get in that first 60 seconds; Your name, the title of your script, and any pertinent information about your background that will set you apart or give you a leg up such as if you have been produced or optioned before or won a prestigious contest, or have a hit YouTube video, or if you are already "in the business" in some way. Also your script's genre, the logline—the one or two sentences that will convince me you have a great hook and idea. And you can end with a couple comparison films, like saying my story is "THIS" meets "THAT," so we can place your script and pitch in a certain context.

You should mention some of the big set pieces or scenes that highlight your story during your pitch. Don't *just* tell us the broad strokes. Tell us what a few of the trailer moments in your script are. This is what's going to sell your script—if we can picture those glorious trailer moments. If it's a comedy, tell us a few of the funniest moments or scenes. If your comedy doesn't sound funny or your horror doesn't sound scary, why would we read it?

If you have told me your whole story all the way up to the big twist ending and I am so enthralled that I ask, "So—what happens?" don't tell me that I need to read the script to find out. Because I don't. If it's a great ending and a great idea, we will want to read the script anyway to make sure the writing matches the pitch. If you think you've got the greatest, most original twist ending—don't hide it from us!

Always bring a one-sheet. I don't care if the event tells you not to. If you don't have a one sheet with a synopsis and your contact information, how are we supposed to remember you or contact you? Ninety-Eight percent of the time, we will not give our contact info out. And even if we have cards, we will lie and tell you we don't. Why? Because somewhere along the way we had that *one* guy who bombarded us with e-mails and calls about every line of every script he wrote. It all comes back to being normal. So if you want us to get back to you or even remember you after hearing 60 pitches, you need to give us a one-sheet.

Be confident—but not pushy. It is definitely okay to ask if we would like a one-sheet. It is not okay to ask five times if we want to read your script or insist that you could just sneak it to me under the table. We will not take your script at the table. This is for a few reasons, the most important of which is that we cannot take and read scripts from everyone, and it would seem too obvious if we took one or two others but not yours. Plus, often after reading the one-sheet, we can tell what type of writer you are—which is why it's always important to have an impressive one-sheet.

If after you leave the room you run into one of the execs you pitched earlier that day, act *normal*. Say something you would normally say in conversation. Like "Hello." Don't mention the script you pitched, or the script you didn't get to pitch and you also don't have to be overly gracious or complimentary. And if you're next to them at a urinal… probably best not to say anything at all. There is an unwritten rule—no pitching in the bathroom.

Again, contacting a producer is like dating. If we actually gave you our card and asked for the script—wait two days and then send it. If I get home from the event and your script is already in my mailbox…I start to worry. If you did not get a card, but you gave us a one sheet—let us contact you.

If we don't get back to you within two or three weeks, you can consider it a pass. Not all execs will e-mail you either way. If we do e-mail you and tell you it's a pass, but say "If you have any other projects, feel free to let me know"— then please do. Don't e-mail us 26 loglines five minutes later, but mention that you would love a chance to send a few loglines of other projects in the future. Mine the relationship like a field of delicate flowers. No mowing.

To conclude, pitchfests are not for first time writers who have just completed their scripts two days prior. Pitchfests are for those writers who have written, edited, polished, re-read, and pitched their project to anyone who will listen. We should not be the first person you talk to about your project. You will just be wasting your time and ours. And that's against the rules.

Script Manager Secrets

The Inside Scoop From Reps

by E.L. Collins

It's no secret—Hollywood is a tough place to make a name for yourself. The same can be said of New York City, where hundreds of struggling screenwriters and playwrights vie for the attention of what seems like a handful of agents and producers. So, what can launch your script to the top? The following eight managers and agents offer their professional opinions, along with some advice, on how to navigate the often intimidating worlds of television, theatre and film.

Below we have gathered advice from the people you need to know—managers and representatives. Listen to what they have to say.

MARC MANUS

Marc is a script manager and the founder of Manus Entertainment in Hollywood.

What are you looking for when a writer talks to you in person or contacts you via a query?

Personally, I look for some sense of concept and marketing—is the person hitting the commercial side of my brain? Or is the person boring me with unnecessary details about how the main character changes because of a tragedy? If the person's loglines seem to encapsulate a really good movie idea, I will usually ask to read a sample. A person's background can help, as well. I will lend weight to someone who claims to have a background in writing (journalism, advertising, etc.) or someone who has gone to film school.

Assuming the writer makes it past the query stage and I've read a good sample from the person, it's time to meet. When I sit down (or chat via

E.L. COLLINS is a Virginia-based freelance writer.

phone) with a writer, I am essentially looking for someone that I am not afraid to put in a room with executives and producers. That person should be articulate and energetic. I've actually passed on representing people who come across as lethargic or argumentative. Life is too short.

Best advice or tips for newer writers?

It's not enough to simply generate a feature or TV idea, write the script and be done with it. You have to think about the business—how it grows, where it's moving. Think about your idea as intellectual property and not just a movie or television show ... platforming is important. And legacy. Will your idea stand the test of time? It's important to understand what moves human beings and how to effectively communicate that in your story.

GARRETT HICKS

Garrett is a script manager and literary agent. He founded Will Entertainment.

As a rep, you want to find a writer with a great writing sample(s) to pass around town, but how do you handle a writing sample that would be defined as "fan fiction"? If a friend of yours called you up and said "My friend has a script-will you read it?" You say yes, but the script is actually for *A Bug's Life 2*. How do you handle that? Even if you read it and it's good, can you pass material like that around town?

I recently had someone approach me with exactly that scenario (it wasn't *A Bug's Life*, but it was a sequel script to a produced property). For my thinking, it's not even useful as a sample. In TV writing, of course, it's always wise to have a spec script for a produced show, but for film or for publishing, it's not the best use of time or talent.

We know what the textbook definition is between a manager and an agent in Hollywood. That said, do you feel like contacting a manager is the best route for newer writers? Are agents just too busy?

I don't know if agents are too busy, but my gut sense is that managers see themselves as more hands-on nurturers of talent and so might be better for new writers. Every circumstance is unique and it depends on a number of factors: not all managers want to be creative executives for their clients, some writers don't need creative assistance from their representatives, etc.

MARGERY WALSHAW

Margery is the founder of Evatopia, a management company.

What genres and categories are you looking for right now concerning film?

Comedy is particularly hard to write and as a result, we find very little that stands out above the crowd. We would love to see more well written and smart comedies. We also enjoy strong character dramas that offer actors roles that are new and challenging.

Best advice concerning a topic we haven't covered?

I work with three writers who live in Europe. (I spend a lot of time in the UK working with publishers and broadcasters abroad.) What I like about their writing is that it takes me to another place and is told in a voice unique to what we typically hear in the States every day. I encourage writers to be true to their life's experiences and tell stories that may be off the beaten track. There's no point in copying what's already out there.

BRUCE BARTLETT

Bruce is a literary agent at Above the Line Agency.

What does it take to break in?

You have to be "good in a room." Established writers—or even new writers—who are up for a writing assignment are all going to be at about the same level of skill and talent based on a writing sample, a produced film, etc. You need to be able to convince a producer of your vision of how *The Last Samurai III* should go. If you can't infuse the people in the meeting with your enthusiasm and vision for that particular project, then you are not going to get the job.

What's the most common mistake new writers make?

New writers just don't understand that less is more when it comes to telling a film story.

RIMA BAUER GREER

Rima is the president and founder of Above the Line Agency.

Do you feel that the quality of film writing is suffering these days in favor of special effects?

I think movies in a lot of ways have actually gotten better, but I also think there's a trend to the lowest common denominator to sell the most tickets these days. That has had a deleterious effect on story versus special effects. But again, write the best script you can first. You don't have any control over any other aspect of the film anyway.

Perspectives

Should a writer try to capitalize on trends for you to consider them?

By the time a writer gets material to market, the market has passed him or her by.

JASON DRAVIS

Jason is a partner at the Monteiro Rose Dravis Agency.

What qualities in a script most grab your attention?

I want an engaging script with well-rounded characters and a story that is unique. I have read many scripts that were well written, but with a story that we all have seen many times. A fresh voice is what grabs my attention the most, and it's one of the hardest things to capture.

How long should authors give agents to sell their script?

Until the agent no longer believes in it. I have witnessed scripts sold in two days or eight years. It's always about finding the right filmmaker in which to entrust a story.

JOYCE KETAY

Joyce Ketay opened her agency in 1978.

What personality traits or habits help writers break into the business?

Theatre is a different business than film or television. Personality traits are not that important. What does help, though, are connections. Assisting a well-established writer is a very good idea. If you are brand new to the business and haven't graduated NYU, Julliard or Yale, it could help to intern at a theatre, producing office or even at an agency. Be nice to all assistants—they are the directors, producers and artistic directors of the future and they have long memories.

What is the most nitpicky thing you care about when reviewing submissions?

Blind submissions to an agent are useless. Inquiry letters are almost as useless. I have only asked for one play from a blind inquiry letter and that was because I was already fascinated by the subject matter. One play in 25 years—this is why connections are important. If someone I respect calls me and says you must read this play, I will read it.

WENDI NIAD

Wendi opened her own management company in 1997.

What qualities in a script most grab your attention?

I look for character development. There's nothing like opening a script and immediately being hooked into a character, getting invested in him/her and following what you hope to be a beautiful arc.

What personality traits or habits help writers break into the business?

A writer who is successful in this business is, first and foremost, a writer—someone who writes and writes and rewrites and writes some more. If you've got the material and the ideas, then you also need to be someone who is outgoing, personable, eager to please and who has a thick skin and knows how to read people. You need to be able to give the executives what they want even when they themselves have no clue what they want—which is quite often! The executives need to know that you're fun and easy to work with and that you get it and can deliver the goods. They need to know you don't have any problem writing and rewriting and then being rewritten by someone else. Someone who is going to spend a development meeting arguing about why you disagree with the executive's notes is not going to be working with that executive for long.

What is the most nitpicky thing you care about when reviewing submissions?

Granted everyone makes mistakes, but when I'm given a query letter that has obvious misspellings and grammatical errors, and spells my name wrong, why would I request a script from that person? More often than you'd like to hear about, we get scripts that have the name of a character that's been changed from a previous draft sprinkled throughout, confusing us as to who the "new" character is. It becomes tedious to read. You become so focused and angry about the lack of professionalism that it colors your reading.

What themes/genres never go out of style?

Horror that can be made cheaply is popular, and quality thrillers and high-concept comedies will always be viable genres. You will always find trends depending on what is doing well at the box office. The mistake is attempting to chase the trends. The key is to try to be ahead of the curve. Adaptations seem to be popping up all over the place. Talk a little about the pros and cons of writing and selling them versus original material.

Ken Sherman

A Script Manager Talks About Killer Writing Samples

by Chuck Sambuchino

I t was in Paris, observing French director Claude Sautet shoot a film, that script agent Ken Sherman officially fell in love with writing and movies.

"I observed the making of a Sautet film standing behind the director the entire shooting," says Sherman, whose company, Ken Sherman & Associates, works out of Beverly Hills. "I also went to movies every day and came back (to Los Angeles) after two years living in Paris—half of that time was spent extensively traveling."

Sherman, a Los Angeles native and University of California-Berkeley psychology graduate, returned from his adventures in Europe and started his career in film and television as a reader for Columbia Pictures. After less than a year reading screenplays, he interviewed at the William Morris Agency and was accepted into a training program the next day. Thus began his foray into the world of agenting.

It wasn't until a few years later, in the early 1980s, however, that Sherman would open his own agency. "I found space and opened my first literary agency where I am today. After two years, The (Robby) Lantz Office in New York bought my company. I worked in their L.A. office for four years. I kept my space here—the first office space—and reopened my agency in 1989. I decided it was time to be on my own again and that's what I've been doing ever since. I really like it. I find the independence and the ability to choose clients and projects much more satisfying than servicing a list of existing clients for other people."

Nowadays, Sherman's agency handles approximately 35 clients; he makes contact with most of his new writers through referrals, and he handles just about every topic you can think of in nonfiction, fiction and scripts. But no

---

CHUCK SAMBUCHINO is the editor of *Screenwriter's & Playwright's Market*. He also edits *Guide to Literary Agents* (www.guidetoliteraryagents.com/blog) and oversaw the third edition of *Formatting & Submitting Your Manuscript*.

matter where a new writer comes from, what Sherman's looking for hasn't changed throughout his years as an agent: "It's about passion. If writers don't feel obsessed about what they're writing, it won't come through on the paper. It's the basic adage to write what you know—better yet, right about what you know."

When a writer is composing his first screenplay, should he aim to write something perceived as trendy, marketable or salable? Or should he just write the best he can, even if the script will likely be unproducable?

What I'm looking for, and what every producer, studio, network and agent I know is looking for, is a killer writing sample—meaning something that we can send out in one day to 30 producers and have them say, "This may not be exactly the story I'm looking for, but I need to know this writer." And hopefully, each one of them will call me back and say, "We want the story. We want to option the material or purchase it outright." But most important is that they want to know the writer and meet with the writer and talk about other projects because the writer has a unique voice.

You just finished reading a book that'll make a great television series or movie. How does a work like that get optioned?

One of my internationally known book authors recently had his book on the *New York Times* bestseller list for a couple of months. There was a real flurry of interest in it. Finally, someone who really, really felt passionate about the story and was a proven producer called an executive at one of the movie studios and said, "I want to do this." The head of the studio called me to check if the rights were available because he wanted to make an offer—and he did. The offer of an option is for two things. First, the option guarantees the exclusive rights to the producer for a certain amount of time—in this case, 18 months. Nobody else can have the rights to that story during those 18 months. In that time, the producer can have a screenplay or teleplay developed. Second, the producer can then decide if they want to pay the purchase price and fully own the rights to the book.

Does some work get optioned more than once?

Yes. I have a client whose first book became an Oprah's Book Club book after it was published. We then had it under contract to Dreamworks, attached to a specific writer-director. The one-year option expired and we've just set it up with one of last year's Oscar-nominated producers. Sometimes a project will have many, many homes before it's actually produced. And there's no guarantee that anything will be produced even if the rights have been purchased.

In addition to working with television writers, screenwriters and book writers, you also deal with buying and selling life rights. How does that work?

Here's an example: I was sitting in my office one day and a TV/movie producer I know called me. He said, "I've spoken to a lady and the fireman who saved her life during the Oklahoma City bombing. Would you mind handling the life rights—the option and purchase price and contract for them?" I then negotiated for both (individuals). Their life rights were optioned and then the purchase price for the exclusive use of their stories for the TV movie *Oklahoma City: A Survivor's Story* was exercised.

If a writer wishes to see his idea on the big screen, is it more practical to write a good book and get it optioned into a film, rather than try to sell an original screenplay?

It depends in which form the author writes best. If the writer is a great screenwriter, I would hope they'd attack the story and characters as a screenplay, because, traditionally, screenplays take less time to write. I want to preface this by saying that there are no rules or answers to any of these questions. What I'm suggesting today are just a few ideas of a few ways things can happen for individuals—but everybody needs to find their own way in their own time. One prominent client wrote eight screenplays before things finally clicked.

Does an author get the first crack at writing an adapted screenplay of his own novel?

If the author is seriously interested in adapting his or her own book into a screenplay, I highly suggest they write a spec screenplay (or one based on their book) while they're waiting for the book to be published. That way, they can show the studio or the network or whomever is optioning the material that they can deliver the goods.

Do you pay any attention to what studios are buying?

I don't worry too much about that. I prefer to try and find really first-rate material that stands on it own. And even though it may be a genre that's a bit out of favor at the moment—maybe something that was hot three or five years ago for some reason—we can reignite interest with a solid screenplay or book. One thing I've noticed is that many executives in this business are very happy not to take a risk on anything. They're very happy to go along with what other people say, which is why sometimes you can get an auction going with multiple bids on the same project. You say, "Well so-and-so just made an offer on it," or "Such-and-such studio wants it." And they think that if another studio wants it, it must be something good. Of course it is…

Kind of like the business phrase "Don't sell the steak, sell the sizzle"?

Sometimes you can sell the sizzle, but more importantly, the material really has to stand on its own. Because don't forget that even with a TV movie, a producer or writer is with the project for a good six months to a year, if not more. A producer needs the passion to stay with the project and to be able to sell it, because they're constantly selling and reselling the material to new people who join the project.

Let's say someone writes a great script. You read it and love it. Before you sign a contract, is it important that the writer has other screenplays waiting in the wings?

That's ideal. Again, as I've said before, I'm looking for that killer writing sample: a screenplay I can send to anybody anywhere anytime and have them sit up and say, "Wow, this is a serious and professional writer." And more often than not, I won't take on clients without knowing that there are three or four or five good pitches behind them if they're to go into a meeting, and ideally another one or two screenplays that are polished and ready to be sent out.

What else should writers know about dealing with Hollywood agents?

I think (writers) should keep in mind that it's a collaborative effort between the writer and the agent. We work as a team. I've found that my reputation is only as good as the quality of writing I send from my office. Therefore the author should do everything they can to help themselves and help me get the material into perfect form so that people will sit up and say, "Yes, we want to be in business with this writer."

Perspectives

Hollywood Hotshots

Successful Writers on the Writing Process

by Brian A. Klems and Chuck Sambuchino

MARC CHERRY

Credentials: A self-described "crazed 'Simpsons' fan," Cherry reached A-list status in 2004 when his show, "Desperate Housewives," became a megahit. But even before he watched "Housewives" climb to the top of the Nielsen ratings, he'd been a player on the TV circuit since the late 1980s, serving three years as a staff writer on "The Golden Girls" and its short-lived spin-off, "The Golden Palace."

Marc Cherry

How did you get your start in TV writing?

Writing came out of my acting career not going well. One day, my best friend and I were watching a particularly bad episode of "ALF," and we realized we could do a better job. We moved up to L.A. and started writing our first spec scripts. Three months later we had an agent. It took a year and four months from the time we wrote our first script to getting our first TV writing job, a sitcom called "Homeroom." Six months later, we got jobs on "The Golden Girls" for seasons 5, 6 and 7.

How did you come up with the idea for "Desperate Housewives"?

It came from a conversation with my mother. She confessed that there were times she didn't enjoy raising my sisters and me. This was shocking to me because I always thought she had the life she wanted and that she was happy. To understand that a woman can get the life she wants and still be desperately unhappy, that was a revelation to me. Suddenly I thought, Why don't I write

BRIAN A. KLEMS is the online community editor of *Writer's Digest*. **CHUCK SAMBUCHINO** is the editor of *Screenwriter's & Playwright's Market*.

about women who got what they want—the iconic life of wife and mother—and still they aren't happy. That's something that hadn't been done.

Walk us through the writing process for "Desperate Housewives."

Oh, it's so ugly. Unlike most hour-long shows, we write it more like a sitcom—it's group written. There are generally four storylines for the four major women and one involving the mystery part of the show, We divvy up the storylines—one to one writer, one to another—so the whole staff will be working. In about three to four days, we'll have a first draft. Then we provide notes and give the writers a chance to improve on their scenes. Then we start to polish. The whole process takes about two weeks.

What's more important: plot and storylines or character development?

It depends. If you're writing a pilot, it's all about the characters—how you sell it and whether or not people want to engage, they have to be invested in them. That being said, I think that it's much easier if you have strong stories to make sure the characters have something that they're fighting for. Character is always easier to expound upon if you've got a good story. It's all about finding a story that serves the characters well. On our show, the stories are dictated by the characters. If they're great stories then the characters really pop.

What's the most common thing you see new screenwriters doing wrong?

They don't give an honest appraisal of their own work. It's so important for writers to read good screenplays, and the really good work of other people. I shudder to think of all the other people in writing classes at colleges who kind of just compare their work to the other people around them and go, "Well, my stuff is better than his." You need to aim higher. That's why I spent a lot of time reading Woody Allen and Aaron Sorkin. That's how you teach yourself. See how the good stuff looks on the page.

Someone has just finished a first script and is trying to sell it— what's the most important thing she should know before sending her work out to Hollywood?

It's really easy to get a rep as a bad writer by sending out something that people don't like. Give your stuff to people whose opinions you respect and try to get them to read it first. Don't just be good—be great. I think all writers need to teach themselves the act of writing or how to express what they have to say about humanity and what they've learned living on this planet.

What advice can you offer for new scriptwriters looking to break into television?

Have something to say. It's hard to say this to young people, especially, but go through life and try to make sense of it. What do you understand about relationships? What do you understand about love? Some writers say, "I want to write about a detective," but is there an idea expressed in it that's really fabulous? That's why many of the recent sitcoms have been annoying—people think of these funny situations but there's no theme resonating with it.

Anything else scriptwriters should know?

Writing is an up-and-down business. One minute you can be hot, and one minute you're not. I went three years without even getting an interview for a staff job. Then, all of a sudden, in 2004 I was the executive producer of "Desperate Housewives." The great thing about being a writer is that you can make your own way. It's all about you. You can write yourself out of trouble.

DIANA OSSANA

Credentials: Ossana's writing life took off in the early 1990s when her friend, bestselling Western author Larry McMurtry, was staying at her home after open heart surgery and composing his next work. Ossana began by transcribing McMurtry's notes, but the two quickly formed a writing collaboration—a partnership that peaked in March 2006 when the pair stood onstage together at the 78th

Diana Ossana

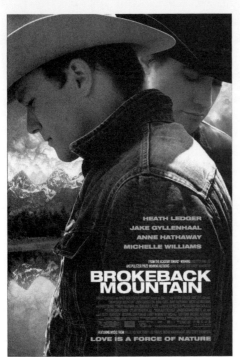

Annual Academy Awards to collect their best adapted screenplay Oscar for *Brokeback Mountain*. Ossana and McMurtry dominated the awards circuit that year, collecting writing accolades from the Hollywood Foreign Press, the British Academy of Film and Television Arts, and the Writers Guild of America. Now, with offers flowing in, Ossana's busy working on new projects and fielding offers.

You've been writing, as you once said, since you could read. How did you come to have such a passion?

I wrote mostly poetry and little short stories and some essays. I started writing poetry, of course, when I was a child. I had a diary. It just sort of became a natural offshoot of reading. I was a voracious reader as a child, and still am. So the thing that really inspired me to write was reading.

How do you work with Larry on a project—what's the writing process?

When Larry writes with me, he writes in a much more skeletal fashion. He's very methodical. He gets up first thing in the morning and writes five pages and limits himself in that way—the theory being that you don't let the well run dry. He types the pages on a manual typewriter, then I enter those pages into my computer and begin to work on them, add to them and move forward on the project.

How do your writing styles complement each other?

Larry has said that I, with screenplays, have a very strong sense of structure. Because of the way Larry's always written on a typewriter, he writes a draft and then a draft and then a draft. He's very linear—very A to Z. I, on the other hand, am adaptable. I can take a script and imagine scenes in different positions. He feels my strengths are structure and the internal lives of the characters.

What's the most common thing you see new screenwriters doing wrong?

I think they overexplain. Unless your script is a parable or something that's not realistic, you shouldn't try to make it too profound or affecting or sentimental. A lot of new screenwriters don't write the way people talk. And often, what's not said is just as important as what is said.

What's the most important thing writers should know before sending their work out to Hollywood?

Get an agent. That's critical. When you send a script out cold to folks, it's a rare thing that they'll read it. It's very important to get an agent who believes in you and whom you trust.

You've written screenplays, teleplays and novels—how is the writing process different for each?

Fiction writing is probably less confining and less constricting because you can let your story go wherever it will. Scripts are very much about structure and limitation and following specific timelines. The nice thing is that they complement one another. If you write fiction, which takes a different kind of mind, writing scripts is a way to take a break from one and go to the other.

What makes a script salable in Hollywood?

People and executives in Hollywood have a notion of what's good and what people will want, but over and over and over what's been proven is: Audiences love good stories with strong characters. If you believe in something and you have a passion for it, don't give up. Be relentless. Sometimes passion will get you much further than talent, although talent is important.

Has *Brokeback Mountain* opened more doors for you?

What's interesting is that Larry and I have always had a lot of people coming to us, wanting us to do projects for them. And in that regard, there's just more of it. We didn't have an agent or a manager for seven years. After we wrote *Brokeback Mountain*, we let our agents and managers go, and we pretty much did it on our own. We didn't get agents or managers again until after *Brokeback* was filmed. People just came to us. I mean, Tom Hanks called us directly.

LARRY COHEN

Credentials: A Hollywood writer for more than four decades, Cohen's written for both television and film, and has directed several of his own scripts. Recently, he's seen three of his thrillers—*Phone Booth*, *Cellular* and *Captivity*—hit the big screen. Cohen studied film at the City College of New York and gained prominence in the 1970s by writing and directing *Black*

Caesar and *Hell up in Harlem*, while his TV career has ranged from "The Fugitive" to "NYPD Blue."

When did you first know you wanted to write for television and film?

I was about 8 or 9 years old and already I was writing my own comic books as a hobby. I'd write and create a 64-page comic book. It was like a storyboard for a movie. By the time I was 13, I'd done many of these and was ready to start writing for movies or television.

How did you get your start in the industry?

At first, I sold things that didn't get produced. The first thing produced was an original teleplay based on characters in Ed McBain's 87th Precinct novels that had just come on the market at that time. I had to lie about my age so I could sign the contract because I wasn't 18.

What's your writing routine?

I just write in my spare time. I don't have any particular regimen. When I sit down to work, it takes me about five minutes, and I just blank out and get into the script. I'm gone until I finish working.

You're a big Alfred Hitchcock fan. How has his work impacted your writing (and directing) throughout the years?

I was always very impressed by the meticulous care he had in setting up his suspense. Like in *North by Northwest* when Cary Grant is going to be chased by that plane in the cornfields. Before you have the chase, there's a long sequence of him getting off the bus and waiting on an empty road. Some people come by; they get out of the car; a bus picks somebody up. A lot of things happen to build up to the big action sequence.

Today a character walks in and everything explodes. There's no time for getting the audience into the situation. To me, it all flattens out and nothing impresses you anymore because you've just seen so much. There's a reason or intelligence behind what Hitch did. Often, I ask myself, "What would Hitchcock have done with this situation? How would he have handled the scene?"

Perspectives

What's the most common thing you see new screenwriters doing wrong?

Everything seems to be the same. You always feel like you've seen the movie before. It's a formula. Screenwriting isn't taught so much as it's felt. It's just something called talent, and talent is stifled because suddenly talent is told it has to adhere to certain rules and regulations.

You wrote mainly for television when you started. Recently, it's more film and spec scripts. Why the switch?

I don't like to talk about what I'm writing before I do it. I don't like the rigid outlines [used by TV writing staffs], and I don't like to have all the elements worked out ahead of time—it takes all the fun out of writing the script if I know what's going to happen before I start writing.

What's your advice for dealing with rejection?

I've almost never had a script that wasn't turned down before it was bought. I've had scripts that were rejected for seven years that were bought and made into good movies.

I don't take it to heart when material gets turned down because it always happens the same way. Most of the producers and studio executives have all gone out and taken these writing courses to learn what to look for in a script and they're getting all the wrong criteria. Any time you write something really good, you're going to get turned down. If it's good, it's got to be original—and if it's original, it'll probably be turned down.

ZAK PENN

Credentials: A highly in-demand film scribe, Penn has found work on several highbrow comic book adaptations in recent years, including *X2*, *Elektra* and *X-Men: The Last Stand*. A trained playwright, he left the theater scene to look for work in Hollywood and found quick success by selling his script for *Last Action Hero*. He's formed his own production company (Zak Penn's Company, fittingly) and taken to directing some of his own low-budget films, such as *Incident at Loch Ness*.

Zak Penn

When did you start writing?

I started writing stories when I was 7 or 8 and then wrote my first play when I was in fourth grade. For a long time, I wrote plays. I went to Yale summer school to learn playwriting and wrote a bunch of plays while I was in college. When I graduated college, I immediately started writing screenplays.

Perspectives

Why did you transition from playwriting to film?

In college, I'd always been a big movie buff. I remember thinking that a lot of the plays I was seeing and even some I was writing were trying to be movies or TV shows. They were trying to use the mediums of television and film because theater felt like a second-class art form at the time. It felt like people were constantly borrowing techniques from film and television because the stage was limiting.

Was selling the *Last Action Hero* script a launching pad for your career?

Yes, it was. It was one of the first scripts we wrote—my writing partner, at the time, and I. I was very lucky, in that I came to Hollywood to be a writer and an actor and to be a director, hopefully—and the writing just took off. Within a year, we'd written *Last Action Hero*. That kind of dictated the paths of our careers.

What's the most common thing you see new screenwriters doing wrong?

Not properly formatting their scripts or following normal conventions. The biggest problems I find over and over again are real structural problems and storytelling problems on a fundamental level—where things that are set up don't pay off, characters don't have a full arc or the story isn't even told in three acts.

You collaborated on the third X-Men movie, *X-Men: The Last Stand*, with Simon Kinberg (*Mr. & Mrs. Smith*). How did that process work?

We did everything. The first draft—he came to my office and we just sat down splitting scenes and sections, pitching stuff out. We did everything we had to do to get it done. At one point, we had to get a draft done in a week. It was like trial by fire. I've had a lot of writing partnerships that had different ways that they worked. This was one where we tried every different way.

Perspectives

When you write original screenplays, do you start with the characters or the storyline?

I usually start with the concept—what the idea for the movie is. There are times when I have a character in mind while I write, but I write more story-driven. Story becomes the focal point for me. I'll come up with what I think is a good idea for story and then ask if the character I've come up with is the right one for the work.

Do you have a writing routine?

Now, my writing routine is whenever I can. I have children so it's difficult. The times I used to write were early in the morning and late at night—but those times aren't available anymore with three children. I go to the office every day and do work. I have a lot of other projects going on. I'll go months at a time without writing anything and then write an entire script in a couple of weeks.

What makes a script salable in Hollywood?

For the vast majority of people, it's not just about selling a script but actually making a career out of screenwriting—that's the goal. Scripts that can't sell on the open market can open doors and get you writing assignments immediately and serve as a sample for your writing career. That's a lesson worth taking to heart. If you write a fantastic thriller or sword-and-sorcery epic, when they need a writer for one of those things, you're going to be the guy they call.

What advice do you have for aspiring writers?

If you have any kind of writer's block, sit down and read some screenplays. I liked being a script reader because it inspired me. I would read these scripts and say, "Wait, I can do better than this! I won't make these mistakes."

ANDREA BERLOFF

Credentials: A rising star in the biz, her big break came when her feature script, *World Trade Center,* was bought and made into a film helmed by Oscar-winning director Oliver Stone (*Platoon*). With the film recently hitting the big screens and three new film projects in different stages of development, Berloff's career is off and running.

How did you get your start in screenwriting?

I got lucky. I had no agent and knew very few people in the business. I gave a spec script (*Harry and Caresse*) to an assistant at New Line. She passed it on, and within a week, it was optioned and is now in production. I

A TRUE STORY OF COURAGE AND SURVIVAL

WORLD TRADE CENTER

COMING SOON

then hooked up with agents and a manager, and my career grew from there.

What was the first script you wrote? Did you ever get it produced?

The first script I wrote was *Liberty*, a comedy about an amateur dart tournament. It didn't sell at the time, but people liked it, which encouraged me to keep writing. Only recently has it been optioned.

What's your advice for writers starting out in the business?

Write, write, write! And then write some more! People seem to get hung up on finding an agent, as if that will suddenly make them a writer. An agent won't make your dreams come true. Your talent and perseverance will. No one is born knowing how to write a screenplay. It takes practice and hard work. If your first script doesn't sell, write another one—and then another one. The cream really does rise to the top.

Do you have a writing routine?

I try to eat a good breakfast, exercise, then get to work by 10 a.m. It's a good day if I can get 4 to 5 hours of writing accomplished. If the words aren't flowing, I'll often stop and either take a walk to clear my head or else read someone else's work for inspiration.

What's more important to you when you write: the plot and storyline or the characters?

The characters. If you create a complex, intriguing character, watching him stand in line can be a great time (á la *Annie Hall*). Events, or plot points, are interesting to an audience only if it's invested in the characters participating in the event. For example, if we hear about a car crash, it hardly registers a blip on our consciousness. But when we read a newspaper article about a really kind kindergarten teacher who's on his way to his own wedding when killed by a drunk driver, we're shocked into thinking about that situation. How will his kindergarten students deal with the trauma of his death? We

Perspectives

wonder about his fiancée. How will she cope? Will she ever find love again? Will she seek revenge? The revenge-seeking fiancée could be the start of an action movie (see *Kill Bill*). It all starts with the character.

Can you walk us through the writing process of *World Trade Center*?

After optioning the rights to the story, producers Debra Hill, Michael Shamberg and Stacey Sher heard pitches from writers in the spring of 2004. After I was hired, I met with John McLoughlin, Will Jimeno and their families (the people on whom the film is based). From day one, the families were involved in figuring out how best to tell their story. One of the first questions I asked them: "Why do you want to make a movie out of your very personal experience?" They were very clear: To pay homage to the dozens of rescuers who risked their lives so that John and Will might live. With that positive message in mind, I got to work. I spent the rest of that summer creating an extremely detailed, 50-page outline. After tweaking it with the producers, I wrote the first draft of the screenplay in five weeks.

Did the *World Trade Center* script come together quickly, or was it a lengthy process of rewriting and more rewriting?

Again, I got lucky. The film was green-lit by Paramount off of the first draft. After Oliver Stone came aboard, then the rewriting began. Under his direction, I reworked the script over a six-week period prior to the start of production.

Perspectives

James V. Simpson

A Nicholl Finalist Talks His First Big Sale

by John Robert Marlow

In November 2006, screenwriter Jay Simpson quickly became known around the offices of Hollywood. His spec script, *Armored*, became an Academy Nicholl Fellowships finalist and sold the same week after a bidding war. (*Armored* was released on Sept. 18, 2009.) Now hard at work on other assignments and specs, Jay sat down to talk about how a script gets sold, how to snag representation, and a whole lot more.

How did you break in—and what role did the Nicholl play in that?

When you get that first big sale or that first big production, everyone wants to believe in the overnight rags-to-riches success story. But in my case, "breaking in" was more like "creeping in slowly and methodically over a long period of time."

The reality is, I'd been developing some projects with two of *Armored*'s producers before entering that script in the Academy's 2006 Nicholl Fellowships competition. They'd originally sought me out because I placed with a different script in the 2004 competition.

How did the deal go down—what events led up to the sale?

My rep and the producers developed a specific strategy and timeline for taking the script out. Their timeline happened to coincide with the end of the 2006 Nicholl competition. *Armored* went out on a Friday, and we started by slipping it to a few people my rep had great relationships with.

By Monday, we had two competing offers—and one of those included an attachment with Robert DeNiro. We also learned on Monday that a competing script with the same name was going out from a writer with a

---

JOHN ROBERT MARLOW is an Academy-honored screenwriter, script consultant, novelist and editor. John's online Self Editing Blog (http://selfeditingblog.com/) provides useful tips for screenwriters and book authors. His *Lonely Keyboard* website (http://lonelykeyboard.com/) contains extreme-length interviews with working screenwriters.

solid track record and a recent, high-profile, seven-figure sale. Over the next few days, territories were divided and more offers came in.

In the book world, "territories" are often countries. Here you mean...

Territories are essentially studios. Ideally, you want your project taken into the studios by producers who have the best possible relationships with those studios.

So you're basically placing the script with competing producers—who then present the script to whatever studio they have a preexisting deal or very strong relationship with.

Exactly. A producer can typically go to any studio, but some producers have better relationships with some studios than they do with others. The idea is to give each producer or production company an exclusive opportunity to take the script into a particular studio. For example, we let Imagine take the script into Universal. No other producer was allowed to take it to Universal, which meant that Imagine had Universal as its "territory." They also wanted Paramount, because they have a strong relationship there as well. We let them share Paramount with another production company—which also had a strong relationship at Paramount.

The Sony "territory" was given to two production companies, Buckaroo [now Star Road] and Screen Gems. Sometimes you go with a single producer for each territory, and sometimes you don't. It all depends on the relationships the production companies have with the studios.

And then what happened?

Then when I learned that *Armored* was a Nicholl finalist script, part of our pitch became that *Armored* was going to be a Nicholl Fellowships winner. Of course we had no way of knowing whether it would win or not, but that approach enabled us to juice up our pitch and create a sense of exclusivity and urgency by allowing people to read a "future Nicholl Fellowships winner" before the results were actually known.

The two original bidders combined their resources and came back with a huge offer. Then at the last moment, three other competing offers—Star Road [then called Buckaroo], Screen Gems, and Sony—combined to outbid everyone else. In the end, it wasn't just the money being offered that swayed my decision; it was the people involved and their commitment to getting the movie produced. On a Friday, exactly one week after *Armored* went out, I closed the deal with Sony, Star Road, and Screen Gems. The same day the finalists were publicly announced, *Variety* announced the sale of *Armored* to Star Road, Screen Gems, and Sony. That was a great day for me. I sent a copy of *Variety* to my mother. She wept when she read my name in it.

Because I was a finalist, I got to participate in Nicholl Week, where I met the amazing group of finalists selected by the Nicholl Committee. I also got to meet the wonderfully supportive committee members and Greg Beal, who runs the competition. It's because of potential secondary benefits like this that I recommend the Nicholl as the only contest worth entering; it's the only one that can—potentially—create opportunities for entrants other than the winners.

What does it feel like when the moment you've dreamed of for so long finally arrives?

Armored was a true fairy tale sale. There were about three days where I was glued to my phone and didn't sleep at all. Because it was the object of a bidding war, several big offers came in. Each one brought a new wave of mixed emotions.

My father had recently passed, so my thoughts were often about him, wishing he'd lived a few months longer, so that he could have seen my first sale. Luckily I had good people on my team, so I had excellent advice to inform my decision-making.

What happens next—after a writer accepts The Big Offer?

After the "big deal," you're in high demand. Everyone in town wants to meet you and work with you. The same thing happens at a higher level when your movie goes into production. You've proven that you have the ability to do the impossible by selling a spec and/or getting a movie into production.

There's a saying that success follows success, and I think that holds true for everything we're talking about here. If you find success with the Nicholl, it attracts interest. If you find success with a script sale, you attract still more interest. If you find success with assignments and getting projects produced, you attract even more interest.

It's nice to cross that line from chasing to being the one who's chased. You just can't let it go to your head. Never forget that you are a success because of the work you did—and if that success is to continue, you'll need to work your ass off every day.

Many writers believe that when you sell a script, you quit your job the same day. Others suspect they might starve before a check arrives. What does it really mean when you sell a script for $400,000?

There are a few months of contract tweaking, followed by a few months for the process to run its course before your check is cut. Your first payment usually comes about three to six months after the deal is accepted. Depending

Perspectives

on your situation, you may need to quit your job just so you can take your victory lap and meet with all the people who want to meet with you. In these meetings, you'll get a lot of offers for assignments—and chasing assignments is a full-time job if it's done right.

To get the maximum benefit from selling a script, you really need to be in a position to dedicate all of your time to your career, even if you haven't yet received your check from the studio. In my case, there were guarantees of progress to production, and financial penalties—rewards for me—if the studio did not begin production within a year of buying the script. Within a month we had a director attached, and shortly after that we were narrowing down casting choices and going out to talent.

The whole process moved very fast, and my experience was the fairy tale. In most cases, even scripts that are bought never see the light of day. I was very lucky.

Is there anything you wish you'd known when you started out?

It's easy to get caught up in the whirlwind. In my case, the whirlwind was intense because I was selling a spec that was then rushed into production. That almost never happens. I wish I could go back and tell myself to not become as emotionally invested in the process as I was. The lesson I learned the hard way is that once you sell a script, your job is no longer about telling a story; it is about creating a product that can be packaged and sold to an audience.

How do you approach writing—do you have particular habits or working environments that you find helpful?

I did have strict routines before selling *Armored*, and those routines became an albatross around my neck when I turned professional. When you're chasing assignments and going to meetings that fit into a producer or studio exec's schedule, your own schedule has to be flexible enough to allow you to write multiple projects at all hours of the day.

It's been said that nothing is more common than unsuccessful people with talent. So other than the obvious—an abundance of talent—what do you believe makes you different from other writers?

Honestly, I don't think I am any different from other writers. Whoever said success is ten percent inspiration and ninety percent perspiration was right. I've never been afraid of work, and I refuse to let setbacks define me. Writing can be brutally tough on your ego if you let it. Whenever I've been knocked down, I've always been able to pick myself up and get back in the fight. I think if you can do that, you will eventually find success.

What goes through your head when you sit down to write—what are you thinking?

Mostly how much I hate writing. Seriously. Writing is lonely and frustrating. If you can find happiness doing anything else, I suggest you do that instead, because writing is not for the frail-hearted.

When I'm not thinking about how much I would rather be doing something—anything—else, I'm deep in imagination land, watching my movie unfold before my eyes as I transcribe it onto my computer. I need to be able to see my story unfold in a cinematic manner before my mind's eye, or else I feel I'm not writing a movie. If I can't see it, I can't write it. Not all stories are movies, and I don't waste time writing non-movies in script format.

What are the most important things for a writer to know?

The make-or-break decisions happen before you type FADE IN. Designing a story that will attract buyers and talent is as much an art form as the actual writing of the story. Writing is rewriting—but the real work, the important work, is done before you ever start writing.

What gets your attention and makes a script stand out from the crowd?

The concept. Most writers obsess over execution. Execution is important to a point, in that it needs to exploit the concept and clearly convey it in an interesting and entertaining way. But if you don't start with a concept—a "hook"—that grabs someone's attention at first blush, you're stacking the odds against your own success.

What makes you think a script will be a chore to read, and is there anything you find particularly lacking in today's scripts?

You can tell in the first page if the script will be a chore to read. A lot of scripts I read simply don't start where the story begins. I think those writers either don't know what their story is really about, so they aren't sure where to start it—or they realize their story is not really interesting on its own, so they try to distract from the mundane story with creative visuals and structure. It never works.

What are some of the mistakes you see writers make—with their scripts or in their approach to people or the industry?

A lot of writers invest thousands of hours studying and improving their craft, but virtually no time learning about the business or developing a network with people in the business.

What are the most important things writers need to know about "the business"?

Too many writers labor under the illusion that if they write it, buyers will come. They type FADE OUT—then have no idea what to do next. But if you want to work in the film business, you need to be a professional, and that means understanding the business in which you wish to work.

It's a ridiculously small industry. Every aspiring writer should have a general idea of who works where, and who buys the kind of product they're writing. It's also a good idea to understand the reality and the mechanics of the way the business works, to inform your story choices before you write and to prepare you for making informed choices when approaching buyers and dealing with the development and production process.

Aside from the script itself, what says to people in the business— "Hey, I want to work with this writer?"

That's it. It's all about the project and/or the writer's ability to deliver a good product. Being able to take notes and collaborate with creatives is a bonus, but not a requisite. Those things will help keep you on a project, but in terms of selling a script, the only thing that matters is the story.

What says, "I *don't* want to work with this writer?"

Resistance to notes and being antagonistic toward others involved in the project.

You may be the wrong guy to ask—but what are the odds of selling a spec, as opposed to getting work off a spec that doesn't sell?

The odds of selling a spec are small, and the odds of getting work without selling a spec are even smaller. The people competing for assignments are people with sold specs and/or produced movies under their belts.

There's a widespread perception that a big part of making it in Hollywood is "who you know." How true is that—and how does "who you know" stack up against "what you know" or "how good you are"?

Who you know is crucial. Going back to my earlier comments, knowing the producers who championed *Armored* was vitally important. Knowing my manager and having his tireless support was crucial to my success. Having connections with producers and studio execs gets you on the short list for assignments, because once you're recognized as someone they want to work with, buyers will continue to offer you assignments. Of course, it all begins with the ability to deliver a good product. How good you are is extremely important—as is your ability to impress others and develop a network. But it all stems from your work.

How does a new guy or gal make contacts?

Everyone knows someone. Everyone went to school with someone who went to school with someone who works in the industry. There's no shortage of information on the Internet. I'm not a great social engineer, and I managed to develop a network of fans in L.A. while I was in Vancouver, Canada. If I can do it, anyone can do it.

It's been said that there are three crucial elements to breaking in: talent, access, and timing. Can you rate their relative importance— or would you alter the equation to include other elements?

I think success is primarily a function of having the right script in the right place at the right time. Part of that has to do with talent, part of it has to do with access—but most of it has to do with timing. The frustrating and demoralizing part of this business is that the biggest factor in your success is entirely out of your control. It's also a little humbling to accept that your success or failure has little to do with your talent.

What are the chances of making it in this business without a good rep?

There are many roads to success. Most of them involve a good rep. All involve the writer as relentless self-promoter.

Any tips on this relentless self promotion?

When someone asks you to do an interview, you say yes. Seriously, it takes an entrepreneurial mindset to be a writer. You need to constantly be developing a network of potential reps and buyers, and constantly promoting new and better products that you are prolifically producing.

Agent vs. manager—which is best, or does a writer need both?

It's often easier for a new writer to approach a manager than it is to approach an agent. Managers are often more willing to take on unproven clients. Agents tend to want clients with some proven value that can be marketed. A new writer first needs a good manager; managers develop careers. You then need a good agent; agents create networks and deals. Finally, you need a good lawyer, because lawyers negotiate deals. There's a large amount of overlap with all of them.

    When your career reaches the level of a David Koepp, you no longer need a manager. When your career reaches the level of William Goldman, you no longer need a manager or an agent. But when you're starting out, you need all three.

Thoughts on manager-producers?

I found it very beneficial to have another voice of support in the room during the development and production stages. It also saved me 10% of the sale price, because a manager doesn't collect a commission when being paid as a producer by the studio.

What makes a good rep, and what are some of the things that tell you you're dealing with a keeper?

A good rep shares your vision for your career, and remains in constant contact with you in order to be putting you out for assignments and tracking your progress in writing original material. Good reps act like partners who are equally invested in your success. Average reps act like they work for you, only working when you direct them to. A bad rep acts like you work for them, expecting you to do all their legwork for them.

What are some signs of a bad rep—things to watch out for? The legwork bit you don't find out about until it's too late.

1) A stable of clients that's too large to be properly serviced. 2) A stable of clients that have been with the rep for a long time, but have had no work or sales in that time. 3) A rep who doesn't return your calls and can't get your work into the hands of people who like it. 4) An inability to get clients up for assignments or even into "meet and greet" meetings with producers and studio execs.

Big agency vs. boutique vs. small agency: what's your take, pro and con?

For me, what matters isn't the size of the agency; it's their ability to get movies made. A lot of the big agencies can't get movies made because they don't rep the kinds of people who can be packaged to get a movie made. I think the writer should make sure they're with a company that can not only get work for clients—but also get clients' work produced.

Care to name names when it comes to effective agencies with the ability to package?

Endeavor, CAA, and WMA are the only powerhouses left in Hollywood. Other agencies can help you get work, but these three are the only ones with the juice to package and push projects into production.

What about sending scripts out to producers? Many writers have qualms about that.

I think most of the pitfalls are associated with blindly approaching producers. If a writer does the appropriate due diligence, most potential pitfalls will be eliminated. Developing and maintaining relationships with producers is essential to launching and sustaining a career. The sooner you start building those relationships, the better. Having a rep is a shortcut for your due diligence, as you tend to rely on their experience and access to filter the people you work with.

How important are loglines, pitch-sheets, and treatments?

Their importance cannot be overstated. The logline is the cornerstone of your pitch. The ability to pitch is crucial for success. The ability to write treatments is essential when chasing assignments—and assignments are the bread and butter of the working writer, easily accounting for over 90 percent of the work.

Many writers believe it's all on the page: Once the script is in the right hands, the writing will sell itself. In your opinion, how important is it to be "good in a room," and to be able to pitch the work in person?

When selling a spec, it really is all on the page and a matter of getting it into the right hands at the right time. When trying to land an assignment, you absolutely need to be able to work a room and pitch not only your take, but also yourself as a writer who is interesting, reliable, creative, and someone people want to work with.

For the writer, how important is it to read scripts—good, bad, or indifferent—as opposed to watching movies?

Reading scripts and watching movies are both very important for aspiring writers, but it's more important to deconstruct scripts and movies to understand how and why they succeed or fail.

Artistically or commercially?

Both. Movies are a commercial art form, and I believe that commercial and artistic success are intrinsically linked.

What do you see as the pros and cons of television vs. feature work?

Television work offers employment security; feature work allows you to be the master of your own destiny.

Should writers want to direct or produce—and if so, why?

Most writers do not have the detachment or skill sets needed to direct or produce.

What industry trends do you see that writers should be aware of right now?

We are entering an era of big movies. Currently that's dominated by comic book adaptations, but there is an increasing appetite for original big movies.

Any tips for those looking to follow in your footsteps?

Don't take no for an answer.

And of course, the eternal question: How does a writer get repped?

Start with a concept that feels like a movie, and could not be done as anything but a movie. A concept that has a unique and appealing hook that is solidly rooted in a specific genre, and that elevates and twists that genre in a new and interesting way. Then write a script that fully exploits your concept, and relentlessly promote it.

Can you cite any examples of this in films readers might be familiar with?

I remember reading an interview with the writers of *Wedding Crashers*, who said they had great difficulty with their first drafts. The ending didn't feel right, and they didn't know how to fix it. They tried everything, but it wasn't until they went back to their core concept that they realized what the problem was. Their story was about a guy who crashes weddings, so naturally the ending had to involve him crashing a wedding. So by exploiting the concept, they were able to find the way to fix their story.

I know my answer sounds like the same old tripe we've all heard before, but it really is that simple. I've never had a problem getting representation, so I've never understood why writers find it so difficult. I suppose those writers who can't interest people in their work are those who don't believe their concepts are the most important part of their story. They probably believe execution is everything—but you can't pitch execution, and you can't put execution in a query letter.

Is there any one thing you took away from the development process that might help new writers in crafting a script that appeals to buyers?

The importance of creating moments, as opposed to just writing scenes. Producers and directors are always looking for moments—powerful and dramatic moments that crystallize plot, character, and theme. When writing, think in terms of moments and not scenes—and your script will "feel" more like a movie, and be more appealing to buyers.

These "moments"—can you point to a few top-end examples on film?

People naturally communicate moments. When we tell people about our past, we tell them about the moments that crystallize our emotional experience. We instinctively edit out the mundane details and focus on the emotional moments. We do the same thing when we describe a movie to someone who hasn't seen it.

A scene is capable of advancing the plot. A scene can also advance the character's arc. A moment advances the audience's emotional experience. Look at movies like *The Dark Knight* and *Iron Man*. Both deliver emotional moments on a regular basis—and that was enough to sustain audience interest and leave viewers satisfied, despite the flaws.

The "scenes" are easily forgotten. We don't care about the bullet reconstruction scene, because it's emotionally flat. No one is going to recommend that movie to friends because of the great bullet reconstruction scene. They will recommend it because of the great "moment" where [spoiler warning] Gordon is shot, or the great "moment" where Dent and Rachel know they're going to die.

Iron Man is interesting because they turned what would have been a flat scene—building the third-generation suit—into a series of funny moments by treating the trial-and-error as gags. A lesser writer and director would have treated them as scenes, without an emotional experience for the audience.

Can you point to a few films that have "scenes" instead of "moments"—and suffer because of it?

That is hard to do because scenes are the first things cut from a movie. They're easier to find in scripts than in movies. Most mystery films tend to have more scenes than moments, resulting in intellectual puzzles rather than emotional experiences for the audience.

Last question: Any suggested resources for writers?

Chris Lockhart's *The Inside Pitch* DVD.

Take Away the "No's"

Think Like a Producer and Sell Your Script

by Trai Cartwright

The foremost priority of writers is to write what's in their heart, right? Obeying the muse is paramount, and no one would have writers shun or shirk their inspiration. No one, that is, except a Hollywood producer.

In Hollywood, different muses call for a different sort of obedience. Generally coming in the guise of a power-suited agent, a jeans-and-cashmere-sweater-clad producer, or even a backwards baseball cap-wearing director, they are beholden to the muse of the bottom line. That's because it's the bottom line that ensures a green light to make their movie—your movie.

What does this have to do with you? Isn't the budget their problem? Yes and no. A little production-sensitive script polishing by the writer could be the difference between a yes and a fast pass. Think of screenwriting as 90 percent inspiration and 10 percent consideration.

A producer I know calls it, "Taking Away the No's." He has an uncanny knack for predicting what details in a script will give his targeted investor, director or agent a reason to pass. He also knows that if he can circumvent those "no's" via some savvy tweaking, then he'll have a better chance of getting ahead. Those no's can be obvious to spot—a cameo by President Obama, for example—but others are seated in the subconscious. Understanding the filter through which a producer, director or agent reads a script will help you identify all the potential no's in your script. Below are ten standard problem "pass points" in a screenplay—and suggestions for how to Take Away the No's!

TRAI CARTWRIGHT (website www.craftwrite.com) is a fifteen-year veteran development executive and film & theater producer, a writing consultant and newly-minted MFA student.

NO #1: THE TITLE

A great title can get you read; a weak, awkward or "B Movie" title can guarantee an instant "no" by producers and future theater-goers.

Name your film *Rogue Nazi Killers* and you're stalled at the gate. Sure, it tells us exactly what the movie's about, that it's going to be bloody and edgy, but it's not tasteful or clever—and therefore, we assume your screenplay won't be, either. But a title like *Inglourious Basterds*, while still lacking taste, does invite fun—and the misspelling is a great touch. It gets the brain churning right away about just what that sort of adventure we're in for. *Man Versus Woman* might be appropriate for a gender war romantic comedy, but again, it's not particularly clever and it's definitely not cute. In fact, it's off-putting and vague. But *The Ugly Truth* is indeed clever; it insinuates that it's an equal opportunity gender war, and invites the audience in on the joke.

Have a look at your title: Is it catchy but not campy? Intriguing but not too vague? Indicative of the subject matter without being on-the-nose (although *Star Trek* might have an argument for on-the-nose titling)? Is it appropriate for the genre? A good title is the best possible introduction to your film; make sure yours is working as hard as it can for you.

NO #2: LOCATION

This is another rather simple tweak that many writers may not have even considered while writing their script, but it's guaranteed the producer will. *30 Days of Night*, a movie about a vampire attack on an Alaskan village during the month when the sun doesn't rise has a very good reason to shoot in the snow, at night, in Alaska. Otherwise, that set-up would be the kiss of death.

Location and setting should be a part of the writer's thinking process. Finding the right place and time can best complicate the hero's journey, but most of the time, it can and will be fudged due to budgetary concerns. A writer can circumvent these issues. For example, John Hughes specifically wrote *The Breakfast Club* as a small film ideal for his directorial debut. It had one location (a school library—any school library) and was set at the ideal time to get a film crew in to shoot unobstructed (on the weekend when no one's around).

Granted, few movies can plant themselves in a single location for the duration and tell their story effectively, but that doesn't mean there can't be consideration for the resources it takes to build sets or travel from place to place. Would it alter your story too much to shoot zombies after the mall closes instead of during that height of the Memorial Day Sale-a-thon? Would it compromise anything to have your characters confront in a town car with tinted windows as opposed to a convertible Porsche? Does the 18th-Century film about courtly manners absolutely have to place each new scene in a new part of a filigreed palace?

Have a good hard look at the locations in your script. You don't want a producer to say "no" just because your settings break the bank.

NO #3: TALENT

Most movies ultimately get made for one of two reasons: star vehicle or commercial appeal. Or, to put it bluntly, Oscar bait or tent-pole pic. If your film falls somewhere in the middle, this is where great roles for actors can help take away the no's. If you've got a vibrant, dynamic protagonist (and a keen antagonist doesn't hurt), you're halfway to having talent attachments—actors with track records at the box office who might convince the moneymen that their investment is sure to be returned.

Does your film have a strong lead role? Is the main character something new for your genre? Just because it's an action film doesn't mean he has to be a two-dimensional tough guy. Just because it's a drama doesn't mean she has to be weepy and sorrowful. Just because it's a horror doesn't mean she can't bring real pathos to the role. Ditto the villain, the romantic interest, even sidekicks and secondary characters. The more life you bring to their lives, the better chance you'll light up a producer or agent with talent possibilities.

NO #4: KIDS AND DOGS

You know the old adage: "Never work with kids or dogs." What you may not know is that it was a producer who said that. The easiest way to go over budget is to cast a monkey. The second easiest way? Cast a child. After all, kids can only work a set number of hours each day, and animals don't always perform on cue.

If your story is about a kid who is kidnapped and saved by a little dog named Benji, then by all means, go forth. But if your film has a single scene in which a team of heavily armed bad guys flee a bank robbery and run right through a mob of grade school tourists, guns blazing —you just added days to the production and money to the budget. Would it be as effective if they ran through a gaggle of jogging mothers with unseen babies in strollers?

This category is a more minor "no," and may not a deal breaker, but it's one that could compound the lean toward a pass.

NO #5: KNOW YOUR SCOPE

If you've got a story about two best friends on a road trip across the sunny

Southwest in which they make few stops and speak to a few people, chances are you've got yourself a low-budget film. This is a doable film, even if you write a climax that involves Thelma and Louise being chased down by an FBI task force and their helicopters, and driving their vintage convertible off a cliff.

Now, if you've got a film that takes place in outer space in mostly zero-G conditions, featuring an attack by an army of fully-articulated aliens in an armada of ships that are translucent like jellyfish and move like them, too, you've just joined the $150 million club.

In between these two extremes are lots of variations with variables that can be finessed for a reasonable, viable scope for your film. If you've got a one-room drama, you can make that room as elaborate as you want. If you've got an intercontinental thriller, you'd be wise to set much of it indoors so a sound stage can be employed rather than asking the whole production to actually travel to Rome, Siberia, Topeka and Cozumel.

Scope also includes concepts like scene count, interiors vs. exteriors, heavy weather, cast size and set pieces. A lower-budgeted film tends to have fewer scenes: this generally equates to fewer locations and fewer company moves. Low budget films tend to have smaller casts of more developed characters; big budget films splurge with lots of extras (sometimes computer-generated!). Low budget films tend to take place mostly indoors, or outside during daylight hours (no lights to rent); big budget movies don't even think about this. Big budget movies have towns covered in snow, or hurricanes, or even just romantic rain showers during which the lovers share their first kiss; lower-budgeted movies don't try to dictate weather.

Knowing the scope of your film is not just knowing what budget range your film falls in to, but also adjusting production elements to be most appropriate for your film's context. A conscientiously created world doesn't give the producer, director or agent a budgetary reason to say no.

NO #6: ACTION SEQUENCES

Not every movie has action in it, so if your script doesn't feature this particular piece of filmmaking, skip to #7. The rest of you, be advised that action sequences are another tricky area where a producer can say no.

A great action sequence features some or all of the following: an original backdrop, like the catacombs under Paris, or a candy factory; maybe a fun, innovative vehicle; a very personal, mano-a-mano fight; and finally, a surprising weapon—what's laying around and how can it be most interestingly applied?

The key to writing great action choreography is pacing, surprise, stakes and climax. Study the pros to see how they do it, because it's important.

Perspectives

In fact, a couple of great action sequences can actually buy you "yes's"— reprieves from "no's" elsewhere in the script.

NO #7: GENRE

Yes, horror sells. It is the perennial seller in Hollywood. Comedy sells in phases, but hysterically funny is always marketable. Would you believe that really smart also sells well? But what if you aren't a rocket scientist with a terrifying tale about a ravenous space monster, or a clone of Judd Apatow (or Adam Sandler. Or Christopher Guest. Or whoever's in vogue at the moment)? What does genre have to do with you?

Demonstrating that you've mastered your genre's rules shows the producer that you've got a strong grasp of screenwriting craft, a key component to getting a "yes." Genre is, after all, structure, tone and theme all in one.

So have you mastered your genre's rules? Do the beats fall where they are supposed to? Is your tone consistent, and appropriate to your genre? If you've written an action film but it's got multiple multi-page talking head scenes and only two major action sequences, you've missed your target. If you've written a drama about a raging flu epidemic, but it's packed with pratfalls and one-liners, you're way off base. A producer can forgive weak dialogue or a poorly-drawn villain, but he can't forgive a story whose very underpinnings aren't solidly built. Do your homework and read a screenwriting how-to book; take a class or join a group of savvy writers.

NO #8: DERIVATIVE/TRENDY

It's only natural that this category follows genre. If your script reads like something the producer or agent just saw in the theater, it's a "no." If it's trying to capitalize on the flash-fire of a new box office success (for example, 2008 was *Cloverfield*; 2009 is *District 9*), just remember that it takes between 18 months and two years to go from script to theater; if your script is too trendy, it's already dated by the time it hits the producer's desk.

As for trends making bigger waves, that's fair game. It's okay to jump on the vampire bandwagon, but you've got to find a unique twist. It's also fine to write the 10,000th romantic comedy, but you've got to ground it in a fun new set-up. The point is that every idea to be had has already been had; you can write anything you want, but if you don't find what's original and fresh about the subject matter, you'll get a "no."

If your script isn't following a trend at all, but rather is your contribution to, for example, the coming-of-age genre, the same rules still apply: Hollywood does not want to see one more crazy night in Vegas/after prom/ while-the-hubbies-are-away comedy when everything goes awry, true love is discovered and friendships are forged in fire. Bring us your talent, your voice, your heart—but please don't bring us another unsung WWII hero or *Saw*-like psychopath. At least not until it's in vogue again.

NO #9: RIGHTS TO MATERIAL

This is a very simple one. Don't adapt and try to sell something you don't have the rights to. Don't try to sell something when you're battling with your co-writer over credit. Don't try to sell something that is just your slightly altered spin on someone else's idea. Don't try to sell something that isn't legally yours. Not only will this get you a big fat "no," but it will get you a big fat lawsuit, too.

NO #10: MARKETING

If the bottom line is a fickle muse, then the marketing muse is haranguing harridan. If she can't see your film's poster or tagline, she's going to force a "no."

You don't have to be a marketing pro to be sensitive to how important marketing is to Hollywood. It's the interface through which they make back their money; if they can't figure out how to market a film, they won't make it. This is the biggest, most resolute "no" of all.

This brings us full circle to the title: Is there a hook in your concept, a location or world to showcase, a relationship to exploit, a villain to supersize? Even the lowest-budget film starring the least-known actors has something unique about it that will entice an audience. Make sure that something unique gets the attention on the page it deserves. One memorable visual, one pithy catchphrase, one original conceit that makes the brain fizz with expectation—that's all your producer is asking for. If you build it, they will come (the tagline of *Field of Dreams*). The Navy pilots in *Top Gun*. Jack and Rose on the bow of the *Titanic*. Darth Vadar.

Help your producer, your director, your agent help you: Deliver a screenplay that has eliminated the traps and tripwires that make his job tough. You don't have to change your writing, your concept, your genre or anything of major thematic import. Thinking like a producer when you write can help you deliver a more professional, producible product. Take away a few "no's," and he'll be more inclined to give you that golden, glorious "yes."

Get Ahead of the Pack

7 Overlooked Elements of Scriptwriting

by Dr. Philip Zwerling

We writers create full-bodied characters, sizzling plots, and dazzling dialogue—but that doesn't quite do it. Too often we overlook some details that can either enhance our scripts or protect our livelihoods. There are at least seven such elements we need to be thinking about: creating the world of the script, specificity, stage directions, the author's legal rights, realism and beyond, plagiarism, and script revision.

1. CREATING THE WORLD OF THE SCRIPT

I do not intend to blaspheme, but I offer this metaphor: As a writer, you are a god. Like a god, you create the world of the script. Will the story be set in the jungles of Congo or the jungles of Manhattan? Like a god, you create the people of this world. Will they be male or female, old or young, good or bad? Like a god, you then disrupt this world by introducing a snake in the form of jealousy, violence, conflict, desire, need, etc. And then like a god, you somehow resolve the mess you have created and end with your Adam (or Eve) having completed a journey from ignorance to knowledge. We become writers to create, to be like the gods.

So, do a godlike job. Make your created world (your set) intriguing. When I first began teaching scriptwriting at colleges, I got a lot of plays set in dorms or frat houses with the characters sitting around drinking beer and discussing their love life. Why, I asked my students, do you choose to create such a boring world? Well, they said, we thought we were supposed to write what we know.

PHILIP ZWERLING is assistant professor of English and Creative Writing at the University of Texas Pan American and a published and produced playwright.

I told them: "Don't write what you know. Use their imaginations to write what you don't know." And things got more interesting. The power of the *Star Trek* movies is that they take us where no one has been. In his play *Angels in America*, Tony Kushner takes us to Antarctica. Shakespeare set his plays in Italy, France, Denmark, and Scotland though he himself never set foot outside England. When you create a world, make it interesting.

2. SPECIFICITY

Good writing is specific. It takes the reader or viewer into a world so rich with detail that they can see, touch and taste it. Bad writing loses us in a murky, undifferentiated limbo.

Scriptwriters need to be specific about setting and characters. If you set your script in an apartment, you need tell us what country, state, and city, and part of that city the apartment is in. Northern California is so different from the south that residents have debated for a hundred years sawing the state in two at the Tehachapis. And a Los Angeles apartment in Brentwood looks a lot different than in Echo Park. I once overheard a director ask a playwright who had set her play in a bar what buildings were on either side of that tavern. She hadn't thought about that. It does make a difference.

After you've decided your character's age and gender, you need to think about their hopes and fears, their morals and goals. As one writing teacher told me: "You need to know your characters so well that you could tell me what I would find if I looked under their beds."

Every detail builds the given circumstances of the script. If your character is 6'2'' tall, he cannot be a jockey. If she is a high school dropout, she will not use the word "oxymoron" in her speech. You will not use all of these details in your script but knowing the details will keep your writing true.

Sometimes writers choose not to name a character or the city where they live hoping that a lack of specifics will make their story more universal. The irony is that a specific character is more universal than one without details because they become a flesh and blood person for us rather than an intellectual construct.

3. STAGE DIRECTIONS

Stage directions are the descriptions of characters and setting you write at the beginning of each act and scene. You want to write them. You're attached to them. You feel they are part of your craft. Just remember, however, that stage and film directors will regularly disregard them and that they are free to do so, so don't put too much time into them.

Screenwriters sell their scripts and lose all control over changes, interpretations, and revisions. Don't bother writing in camera angles because a film director will make all of those choices for herself. Playwrights keep control of the dialogue of their scripts but directors are free to ignore their written stage directions.

My rule of thumb: Use stage directions to describe actions so a reader can follow the plot. Don't tell a reader information what will be gleaned from the script (i.e., "Teddy was a big man with a big heart." Better that we should see Teddy do something that shows us he has a big heart). And don't give such detailed stage directions that it limits actors and directors in producing your work. Playwright Eugene O'Neill was famous for his pages and pages of stage directions as well as for his record-setting four Pulitzer Prizes for drama. In his *Moon for the Misbegotten*, he describes key character Josie as "so overgrown for a woman that she is almost a freak." Happily, actresses of all sizes have brought Josie to life on the stage and screen.

4. YOUR LEGAL RIGHTS

You only have rights if you know and exercise them.

Several years ago, I read about a play being produced in Chicago with the same title as a play I had written ten years earlier. Both plays were titled "Dr. Sex". Both plays were about the sex research of Dr. Alfred Kinsey. I thought: *Plagiarism. Lawsuit.* But as I looked into it, I saw that the resemblance between the two plays ended there. The Chicago play was a musical; mine was a drama. Their protagonist was Kinsey himself; mine was one of his (fictional) grad students. All they shared was a title and, as a lawyer informed me, play and film titles cannot be copyrighted. No harm, no foul.

But creative ideas need to be protected. Sometimes great minds really do think alike and sometimes they just "borrow" material without credit or pay. For that eventuality we have copyright law. For just $45 dollars online you can register your script (or multiple unpublished scripts by a single author) with the United States Copyright Office. Yes, people seal a script in an envelope and mail it to themselves to get a dated post mark but this does not act the same as an official copyright.

If your script is to be produced on stage or film, you need legal representation and a binding contract. Every right you surrender (creative control, overseas distribution, exclusive use, second printing) should be monetarily compensated. The Dramatists Guild and the Screenwriters Guild exist to protect playwrights and screenwriters respectively.

5. REALISM AND BEYOND

Structurally there are three kinds of scripts:

Linear: the plot unfolds chronologically (the classical structure of drama seen in 95% of all plays and movies).

Nonlinear: the plot moves backwards and forwards in time (movies like *Babel* and *Pulp Fiction*).

Circular: the plot ends where it began and there is usually very little action (Absurdist plays like Beckett's *Endgame* and *Waiting for Godot*).

Within these three structures, the writer has many choices as to style in addition to the most common structure, realism. In realism, things happen according to the laws of nature (people do not fly, animals do not talk, etc.). But by "realism," I mean "stage realism" or "heightened realism," which is simply real life with all of the boring bits left out. How else would we create a conflict, build tension, pack in the action, and resolve the conflict all in 120 minutes?

Alternatives to realism include naturalism, absurdism, surrealism, futurism, constructivism, minimalism, magical realism, and many more. A writer should be aware of these options and how our art developed over time. But most importantly, a writer should remember that, as in architecture, dramatic form follows function. After you decide that your idea is a movie and not a play or a novel you must decide how best to tell that story. A movie like *Memento* or a play like *Betrayal* shows us that stories do not have to progress chronologically. Their form serves the story. Never choose a form for mere novelty.

6. PLAGIARISM

Students turn in research papers containing plot summaries and critiques they've plagiarized off the Internet. Politicians plagiarize other politicians' speeches. Journalists invent quotes and statistics. Even scriptwriters, whose job it is to make things up, plagiarize. In 2004, English writer Bryony Lavery's play *Frozen* was nominated for a Tony Award for best play of the year. It was about a psychiatrist confronting a serial killer. Then charges surfaced that the play plagiarized whole paragraphs from an earlier New Yorker article and a book about a very similar psychiatrist and serial killer. In the end, no lawsuits were filed and Lavery apologized for her "naiveté."

My message to you: Don't be naive. Plagiarism is intellectual theft and easily avoided. Get permission and credit the original author. You can turn a novel into a film or a short story into a play but you have to obtain the rights to that material (usually for a fee) unless the material is in the public domain. One reason Shakespeare is reprised in film and on stage so frequently (over 40 film versions of *Hamlet* alone) is that he was not only a good writer but he has also been dead for 400 years and his plays are in the public domain. They're free to reproduce.

News stories are usually fair game. Peter Shaffer wrote *Equus*, the prize-

Perspectives

winning-play-turned-movie after reading a brief notice about a teenage boy charged with blinding horses in a stable. Shaffer added characters, religious and sexual themes, and made the story his own. John Guare based his award-winning play (also turned into a movie) *Six Degrees of Separation on* the real-life story of David Hampton, who went to prison for scamming people by pretending to be the son of Sidney Portier. Hampton sued Guare for a cut of the script's profits but lost.

When in doubt, ask permission and share credit.

7. REVISING YOUR PLAY

Someone very smart said. "Writing is rewriting." I didn't say it first, but I write it on the board at least once every semester. I tell students Ernest Hemingway rewrote the final paragraph of *A Farewell to Arms* 26 times before he was satisfied with it. Are they going to cut corners because they're better than Hemingway?

The fact is writers, like everyone else, tend to be lazy. We also tend to like what we write. Our spouses and our friends often like what we write. But writers only succeed from a burning desire to always write better. You have to be prepared to rewrite your scenes 26 times also.

I like the word revision better than rewriting. *Re-vision* means seeing again. To see your script again after it's written, ask yourself these 10 questions:

1) What is the best thing in my script? Start with the positives.

2) In 25 words or fewer, what is my script about? If you need more than 25 words, you have a problem.

3) Is it clear who the main character is? Remember the poem, "Humpty Dumpty?" Who is the main character of that poem? Not Humpty. It's "all the King's horses and all the king's men" because *they're* the ones who do something. Also, stick to just one main character.

4) Does the dialogue fit the characters as you have created them?

5) Does the main character go on a journey from ignorance to knowledge?

6) Is the main conflict clear, strong, believable, and interesting?

7) What is the message of your play? I know: "If you want to send a message, call Western Union." But we all believe in certain things. Are your values, what you want an audience to receive, in your play?

8) Are there confusing or unbelievable moments in the script?

9) Is the script theatrical? Is there a compelling reason it is a play or screenplay rather than a short story or novel?

10) What do you not like about the script? How can you fix that?

Contracts and Rights

Making Sense of Copyright and Lingoese

by Robin Mizell

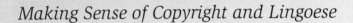

I f you're an aspiring scriptwriter who has yet to meet the requirements for joining a guild or other professional writers' association, you can attempt to break into the business by speculating. By drafting an original script, you will have a means of attracting the interest of an agent, manager, or producer. Before you begin writing a spec script, however, you must understand the provisions of copyright, defamation, and privacy laws—both to protect your investment in your work and to avoid infringing on the rights of others.

COPYRIGHT

Story ideas, basic plots, concepts, facts, and information commonly known cannot be protected by copyright. That said, the expression of your story or idea in a fixed form such as your script, book, or film—including any original, well-defined character that is part of your work product—*is* subject to copyright. As soon as the tangible work is created, it becomes the property of the author. The copyright notice does not need to appear on the work for copyright law to apply.

Until you agree to sell your script, you possess the copyright. When you enter into a purchase agreement with a buyer—once the expressed terms of the contractual agreement are met, the ownership of the script is transferred to the purchaser, and the copyright is transferred along with the script. This gives the purchaser the ability to modify the script, sometimes extensively, to suit a project. Often, this means another writer will eventually be hired to revise portions of your work.

ROBIN MIZELL (robinmizell.com) is a literary agent and the founder of Robin Mizell Ltd., Literary Representation. She was formerly an editor for *Screenwriter's & Playwright's Market*.

Registration is not required for copyright law to cover your script. However, the relatively minor cost of registering your script with the U.S. Copyright Office in Washington, D.C., does help you to establish ownership as of a specific date. You can save money by using the electronic registration option at www.copyright.gov. It's possible to register your work at any time during the decades of copyright's duration. However, if you wait to do so after being accused of copyright infringement, you will no longer be entitled to the full extent of the law's provisions. For a similar fee, you can record ownership and the date of your script's creation by registering it with the Writers Guild of America Registration Office, even if you are not a guild member.

It's important to understand that any dramatic work you create in the regular course of your employment is considered the property of your employer. Absent a contractual agreement to the contrary, your employer legally becomes the work's author as well as the copyright holder. The same is true of a commissioned script you are under contract to write, otherwise known as work-for-hire. The company or individual that commissioned the work holds the copyright.

You might find yourself inspired by material to which you do not possess the copyright, such as a song, book, poem or video recording. In order to use even small excerpts from the work of others in your script, you must incorporate the required attribution and the material must be in the public domain, out-of-copyright, or licensed appropriately. Some versions of the Creative Commons license permit derivative works under certain conditions. It's also possible to use portions of another person's material, with specifications, if you obtain authorization from the copyright holder, although it can sometimes be an expensive proposition. Whenever you are given permission to use someone else's material, be extremely careful to retain documentation of the licensing, authorization and all correspondence that will protect you in the event of future claims of infringement. You must also correctly acknowledge the originator of the material to avoid allegations of plagiarism.

DEFAMATION AND PRIVACY LAWS

It's common to base a script on the lives of real people, actual events, or your own experiences. Even when a story is fictionalized, if the individual on whom you based one of your characters can be identified, you can be accused of defamation or invasion of privacy. Obtaining a written release from the person whose story you intend to use offers you only partial protection. You must be extremely cautious about portraying falsely or in an unflattering manner any character based on a real person, living or deceased. You should also think twice about revealing intimate personal details the average person would consider private.

Any works you create based on real circumstances, individuals, or events require the added protection of an errors and omissions (E&O) policy to insure you against any resulting claims by injured parties. The studio or purchaser that acquires your script should provide this coverage, and the specific clause requiring the E&O insurance policy must be included in the purchase agreement.

SUBMISSION AGREEMENTS

A detailed discussion of copyright could make you hesitate to pitch a mere idea or concept to a producer or agent for consideration. If your idea isn't protected by copyright, then how can you prevent someone from taking it without compensating you? Perhaps the best solution is to submit a complete treatment or a draft of your script, which is covered by copyright.

Some producers will ask you to sign a submission agreement that, for your protection, should include a clause specifying your material will not be used unless you are compensated. Unfortunately, the submission agreement will also spell out the very real possibility that a similar treatment or script might be submitted by another writer. Ultimately, the safest course of action is to deal only with established studios and producers whose honorable reputations are known to you, your agent, or your attorney.

Professional Associations

These associations' websites are excellent sources of information about industry standards and minimum compensation for scriptwriters in various markets.

- **Writers Guild of America, West**, www.wga.org
- **Writers Guild of America, East**, www.wgaeast.org
- **Screenwriters Federation of America**, www.screenwritersfederation.org
- **American Screenwriters Association**, www.asascreenwriters.com
- **The Dramatists Guild of America,** www.dramatistsguild.com
- **Writers Guild of Canada**, www.writersguildofcanada.com
- **The Writers' Guild of Great Britain**, www.writersguild.org.uk

Perspectives

CONTRACTS: OPTION AGREEMENTS FOR SPEC SCRIPTS

A producer is usually not in a position to set up a project immediately upon entering negotiations to purchase your script. Instead, the producer is likely to pay a relatively small amount of money in exchange for the option to purchase the script in the future. Optioning a script takes it off the market for a specified length of time, usually one or two years, after which the producer must exercise the option to proceed with a purchase agreement or lose the contractual right to do so. Option prices are applicable to, or in other words, deductible from, the purchase price—something of a rent-to-own strategy. Producers sometimes attempt to option scripts for free.

The Writers Guild Agreement prohibits a producer from submitting a script to studios or other buyers for consideration unless there is a written agreement with the scriptwriter. This protects Guild members from the occasional unscrupulous producer who would shop a script around during ongoing negotiations for an option rather than after the option has been purchased.

RIGHTS

As the creator of an original script, copyright law establishes your rights of reproduction, adaptation, and public distribution, performance, and display. You can separate these rights and sell them individually or in groups. You can also negotiate to retain some of them. Although your agent and attorney should guide the process, it doesn't hurt to know they will often be able to negotiate for you to reserve these and other specific rights to your work:

- Novelization and other types of publication
- Radio and live television performance
- Stage production
- Sequels or series
- Merchandising

COLLABORATION AGREEMENTS

After you've experienced one contract negotiation, you'll have a better perspective of the potential pitfalls of collaborating with another writer on a spec script. If you decide to work with another writer, each of you will need to agree to the terms of any option or purchase agreement. It's best to have a written agreement with the other writer before work on the script begins.

A collaboration agreement should specify what percentage of the material is owned by each writer; otherwise, it will be assumed each person is entitled to 50 percent ownership and compensation. The writers' collaboration agreement should also include the minimum acceptable terms for the sale of the script and for any subsequent writing assignments. Collaboration complicates the sale of a script, especially when one of the writers is also a producer or when the writers' contributions to the work are unequal.

CONTRACTS: WORK-FOR-HIRE

When you are commissioned to write a script, you will sign an agreement to provide your writing services, almost always exclusively, to the studio or buyer to which you are under contract. You will be given a contractual deadline for submitting your first draft and often the right to perform a single rewrite as well. A bonus payment may be stipulated if you receive a writing credit. You can also be hired to revise another scriptwriter's work, in which case you might, in certain circumstances, be entitled to a writing credit and the related bonus.

Under work-for-hire agreements, you are likely to be paid half at the beginning of a project and the balance upon completion of it. The Writers Guild Agreement establishes industry minimum standards for scriptwriters' financial compensation. If you are engaged as a writer with a television series production and are considered indispensable, it's possible to negotiate a percentage of profits. More often, the producer is looked upon as a vital component of the production, while the writer is viewed as replaceable. It's a competitive business.

Perspectives

Nancy Gall-Clayton

An Up-and-Coming Playwright Speaks Out

by Chuck Sambuchino

Nancy Gall-Clayton is a quintessential example of an up-and-coming playwright—neither uber-popular nor utterly unknown. Her 14 years in the playwriting world have given her the chance to do it all—write commissioned works, see her full-length works produced, pen plenty of 10-minute plays, get paid four figures for a world premiere, and more.

A staple in the Louisville playwriting community, Gall-Clayton's first play came to life simply by chance. "My first play was a finalist for the Heideman Prize at Actors Theatre of Louisville. I had no idea what I'd done right, but with recognition like that, I decided playwriting was easy and took up my pen again," she says. Surprised and buoyed by her first success, she quickly penned a second play, only to realize it wasn't nearly as good as the first. That second play ended up in the shredder instead of onstage, but the fate of her sophomore work wasn't really important. What *was* important was that this new medium allowed Gall-Clayton to write about complicated subjects where she had a passionate opinion. "Members of the audience may not agree with my take on genetic engineering, sweet potato pie, or interfaith marriage, but if I do my job right, the audience will think about the issue and probably in a new way," she says.

During the past decade, more than 40 of Gall-Clayton's works have come to life on the stage, and several of said works were produced in numerous locations. Now battle-tested and wise in the ways of stage plays, Gall-Clayton is a great resource for fellow playwrights who are trying to get produced and build a portfolio.

CHUCK SAMBUCHINO is the editor of *Screenwriter's & Playwright's Market*. He also edits *Guide to Literary Agents* (www. guidetoliteraryagents.com/blog) and oversaw the third edition of *Formatting & Submitting Your Manuscript*.

Nancy, why write plays? What draws you to playwriting?

It's harder to get poetry and fiction published, and then if you do reach print, you will probably be read once—and only once—by the subscribers of one literary journal. If you are unknown and write a book, it's difficult to have it published, and then if it is published, it's difficult to have it reviewed, and then if it is reviewed but not enthusiastically, it's difficult to sell it. A well-written play can and will reach many stages and many people over time.

I am drawn to playwriting because theater is collaborative. I create the characters and the plot, and I write the words, but the director, actors and designers bring their expertise and experience to the play. Playwriting is different from all other writing. The story is told exclusively in dialogue and exclusively in the present tense. If these criteria are not met, the result is not a play, at least not in any traditional sense. I love the challenge of telling a story in dialogue and the fact that each time it is presented, it's as if the story is unfolding afresh.

You have memberships in some writing and playwriting groups. What do these groups offer for a writer?

I belong to a few groups, each of which serves a different purpose in my literary life. I have a sense of camaraderie with other writers, playwrights, and artists and a feeling that we understand one another better than non-artists.

At some point, every serious playwright needs to join the Dramatists Guild of America. Regardless of your level of success, the guild has lots to offer, including free contract templates and legal advice as well as a bimonthly publication where you can publicize your latest shows and awards and a directory of theaters, competitions, residencies, and other opps for playwrights.

You seem to tap into a lot of your own life and its themes when writing plays—such as being a mother, being involved in social justice themes, being Jewish. Do you feel this allows you to dig deeper into subjects?

I start with what I know and what concerns me and interests me, but I don't feel I'm going deeper or less deep when I go beyond the immediate. I disagree with the idea "Write only what you know." It's exciting to explore.

When you sit down to flesh out a character, what are some steps you take?

With full-length plays, I create timelines of major events (9/11, JFK assassination, Katrina, etc.) and personal events in the characters' lives (father died, dropped out of college, met future spouse). This work is tedious at times, but just as we are influenced by the events large and small around us, so are our characters. If I'm stuck, I go back to the timeline (it's not static, I work on it off and on while creating the play) to help me figure out who the character really is and how they would respond, act, and so on. I also make sure no two characters are alike or nearly alike, from speech to views.

I saw one of your plays at a staged reading and it was a series of monologues, which are not an easy thing to write. What's your advice for composing a monologue?

I recommend holding off on writing monologues . . . On the other hand, I think it's very helpful to write monologues for characters in plays when these monologues are strictly for you the writer to gain insight. For example, imagine your character is walking toward you across a field. She has something in her hand. When she finally gets to you, she says, "There's something you need to know." Write the rest of her speech to you.

After you're done, what is your rewriting process like?

I'm never done. I have plays in print that I'm rewriting. If a play is produced or read nearby, I go to every performance with a notepad. I sit in the back and watch when people get restless. I listen intently. I try to make lines actor- and director-proof, meaning the dialogue does it all. No one can misunderstand or misinterpret.

Looking at your accomplishments, you have a large amount of 10-minute plays in your repertoire. What draws you to this form?

I work full time and have the usual busy life everyone else has. It takes me at least a year to write a full-length and two years if it's based on a historical person or time. A 10-minute play should have all the same elements of a full-length, so writing them keeps me in practice. I can respond to all sorts of things going on in the world—and then be done with it. Also, it was *Special Delivery*, a 10-minute play, that was a finalist at Actors Theatre of Louisville for their annual contest that draws as many as 2,500 entries. If a theater like Actors is interested in 10-minute plays, so am I. A literary manager visited a playwriting workshop I was in this winter and indicated that the 10-minute play competition allows the theater to "meet" writers they may want to know better.

When you sit down to write a 10-minute play, what are your goals?

My goals for a 10-minute play are the same as my goals for any play. For a first attempt at a 10-minute play, I recommend three characters as well as times within the play that allow for each combination—these two, those two, and all three. All of us act differently depending on who is around.

1. Decide what the main character really, really wants—it can be serious or silly: to work up the courage to propose, to quit a job to paint, to dye one's hair, to get his teenager to mow the grass.

2. Now figure out what obstacles the protagonist is facing—someone else has just proposed to her on a billboard, no less; you support yourself, so you gotta work; your children will think you've gone nuts if you become a redhead; there has never been a way to motivate your teen to do anything.

3. Who's the third character? Someone else with a stake one way or another: the intended bride or groom, the boss or your painting instructor; the clerk who will sell you the dye; the teen's other parent.

4. Place these people anywhere but the living room, and keep it simple. No scene changes, no fancy props. Think of places where interesting things happen that also allow movement.

5. Don't write with the ending in mind. Put these people together and get into each of their heads as you write. About the bottom of page nine, draw things to a close. When a play is done, it's really done.

When you write a full-length drama, are you shooting for a particular length? Or do you just write?

I think "full length" but not necessarily X number of pages. I think mine range from 90 to 110 pages. I don't worry about details until the first draft is done, and I don't do huge amounts of revision while I'm working since the ending or the decisions a character makes may change as I write.

You have all of your scripts available online on your website to order for a nominal fee. Would you suggest others do it?

I'm in eight or 10 anthologies, and I do hear from people who saw an excerpt or a monologue and want the whole play. Usually, these are students or people auditioning for a part, and they like using material that's not being done by half the competition. I do license productions at very modest fees. I even offer a rebate if they send me flyers about a show I license them to perform. I'm not interesting in posting whole scripts on the web, but I love hearing from people who are interested in my work.

In a circumstance where a theater or group contacts you and wants to do a play, how do you negotiate price and royalties?

I have set rates for most work. I expect more for a premiere because many competitions don't want work that has been performed. For a full-length,

I always want a written contract, though I use a very short one-pager from the Dramatists Guild if I am able to supply it.

How loose are you with your text? Do you allow actors some slack in changing the pace and wording to suit them?

I am not loose at all. No one has the right to change a word of my script without my permission. However, if it's a new play and I am at the rehearsal, I love hearing ideas from the actors and director, and I often agree, but it's strictly my call. Some years ago, I had a $1,000 prize for a full-length play that was produced and changed radically. I wasn't happy and realized as I was sitting there cringing at the premiere that we had not entered a contract. Something about that $1,000 check blinded me temporarily, but no more.

What's the most times you've had to submit a play to various markets before it was awarded or picked up?

I'm not at home with my records, so I can't swear to a number, but I've had way over 40 submissions on a few plays.

Talk to me about how a play gets produced. You finish a full-length work and it's polished. Now what?

After at least one informal reading and usually two, I put it on the list to market. When a play is brand new, I'm very particular about where to send it since so many competitions and theaters want to do premieres. I definitely spend a lot of time marketing. I learn about opportunities from the International Centre for Women Playwrights, from Dramatists Guild's *Resource Directory*, from the TCG publication *Dramatist's Sourcebook*, from Googling at times if I have a play that seems to fit a very specific market, and from playwright friends who see an opp that seems right for me.

I also submit to theaters that have produced or read me before. They obviously already like my work, and I've had second experiences because of that.

Do you have any relationships with theaters where they agree to debut some of your work?

Yes, several. My relationships are local and were built around them not just knowing my work, but knowing me. I'm not a hothead and I play well with others. In a collaborative venture like theater, there is no room for prima donnas, and theaters appreciate having someone involved who wants to be a team player.

Do you enter a lot of contests? What are some guidelines you adhere to when doing so?

I do not pay submission fees. I'm with the Guild on this.

I follow the guidelines very, very carefully and follow them precisely. I make sure my play fits their solicitation. I try to submit at least a little before the deadline. I make sure everything I send looks professional. I never send postage-paid envelope for return of a rejected script. It's too much work for the theater or they'll overlook it or by the time they think of it, the postage rates will have gone up. Or the post office will mangle it and it can't be sent out again. And of course, in my case, I will have revised the play before it is returned.

I don't mark my calendar up awaiting a response. Some never reply. I've got 50 + scripts in circulation, and it's highly unlikely I will remember what I sent to whom. The acceptance by a theater in the Northwest last spring truly puzzled me. It turns out they accepted my 2004 submission in 2008 without even mentioning the name of the play in the acceptance letter. A friend in the area eyeballed the theater, and I decided to (say no).

Do you still find yourself having to be a huge marketer and advocate for your work?

Yes. Even friends with agents find they are their own best advocate.

Thinking over all you've said so far, let's say you sit down with a writer who says they have a good story, but are unsure if a play is the correct medium for it. You say, "You've got to ask yourself some questions before you know if it's a play." He asks, "What questions?" You say:

First and foremost: Is there conflict? A mentor of mine says, "Nothing is more boring on stage than nice people being nice to each other.''

How much time is covered? The longer the time period covered in a play, the harder it is to write well. The story of someone's life, no matter how engaging, should—if on stage—focus on one moment in that person's life.

How many issues are there? Plays work best when they focus on one issue or question or problem.

Is there a main character in this story? The best plays focus on one central character and that character's desire and the roadblocks to that desire.

In your mind's eye, do you need "close ups" of your characters' faces or quick costume changes or many scene changes? Stage plays aren't the best vehicle for stories that need these things.

Richard Hatem

*An Established TV Writer Looks Back
at His Road to Success*

by Chuck Sambuchino

Ask Richard Hatem about the first script he ever wrote, and the seasoned TV writer can't help but smile. "I was 16, a junior—it was March of 1983—and the first script I wrote was for 'The A-Team' " he says. The thought of being a teenager, sitting at home, and working on his mother's *IBM Selectric* typewriter is more than enough to get Hatem nostalgic and excited. A huge fan of Stephen J. Cannell shows such as "The Greatest American Hero," he fell in love with TV storytelling at a young age—gravitating toward material that was both exciting and smart. For Hatem, the plan at that age was simple: 1) Sell spec script. 2) Drop out of high school in East Los Angeles to join the writing staff of "The A-Team." 3) Move into cool apartment in Los Feliz. 4) Get girls.

Unfortunately, his spec script didn't sell—but Hatem was not deterred. As high school progressed, he pumped out more scripts—*a lot* more—for a dozen different shows. None of those additional episodes ever opened any doors, but they did teach him a lot about writing.

Now, Hatem is an experienced writing pro in Hollywood, passing on his knowledge to young scribes who also want to tell stories on the screen. Along with some screenwriting work, he's gathered an impressive number of TV writing credits—both as a writer and as a showrunner. He's even formed his own production company: Summerland Entertainment. And he's still in love with storytelling that challenges the minds of audience members, but entertains them at the same time.

Hatem sat down to talk with *Screenwriter's & Playwright's Market* about what it takes to make it as a writer out west. Here's what he said.

CHUCK SAMBUCHINO is the editor of *Screenwriter's & Playwright's Market*. He also edits *Guide to Literary Agents* (www.guidetoliteraryagents.com/blog) and oversaw the third edition of *Formatting & Submitting Your Manuscript*.

What was your first job in LA? How did you enter the entertainment business?

Well, my first *normal* job was busing tables at a public golf course dining room called Almansor Court in Alhambra. I waited tables there and at a place in Pasadena called Dodsworth that isn't there anymore, and then I spent years serving ribs at Tony Roma's. Plus, I did stand-up comedy and ended up teaching Comedy Traffic School for five years. So these were sort of "post-college, trying-to-survive" jobs while I tried to sell scripts.

Your first major credit was a "story by" credit on *Under Siege 2: Dark Territory*. Were you commissioned to pen this script?

Under Siege 2: Dark Territory (*US2DT*) started out as a spec feature that Matt Reeves and I wrote in 1990, a couple years after college. (Matt and I became friends at USC film school.)

We wanted to write a big action movie, which they tell you never to do in film school. In film school, they really encourage you to write personal, idiosyncratic scripts that represent an original viewpoint and voice. Unfortunately, almost no one in film school, at age 19, has that. We were all a bunch of film and TV geeks that wanted to be Martin Scorsese or the Coen Brothers. We all wanted to be like the people we loved, so most of what we did was imitative, which is exactly appropriate—not only for that stage in our creative development, but also for the medium in question. It's much more valuable in the long run for a writer to be able to write a classically structured action movie or romantic comedy than to try to be the next Charlie Kaufman.

Anyway, Matt and I were hanging around in a video store trying to come up with an idea of something to write and we were talking about how great *Die Hard* was. And it was like, "Wouldn't it be fun to write a movie like that? What if it was like . . . '*Die Hard* on a Train'?" So we decided to do that. And here's the thing; it wasn't cynical and we didn't think we were slumming or selling-out. We honestly thought—and still think—that *Die Hard* is a remarkably well-written, well-made movie. We were setting the bar high for ourselves in trying to build a machine that worked as well as *Die Hard*. So we did what all smart screenwriters *should* do—we took apart *Die Hard* the way a young inventor takes apart a toaster. We rented the video and paused after every scene and wrote down what the scene was and what it accomplished in terms of the over-all storytelling. And then we tried to write equivalent story and character beats in our own movie. I learned more about writing in the four months it took us to write *Dark Territory* than in my entire time at USC Film School.

We tried to sell *Dark Territory* in January of 1991—the week the first

Gulf War started. It didn't sell. We did a few rewrites, and sent it out again under a different title and with our names replaced by pseudonyms so it would get a fresh read at all the same places. By then, a producer named Gary Goldstein was attached and he'd just had big success with *Under Siege* at Warner Bros. He saw an opportunity to present the script to WB as a possible sequel, and with that in mind, they bought it. It was an incredibly, impossibly lucky thing to have happen. Selling a script is one thing, but having a studio seriously want to make that film is another.

That's the hardest part of screenwriting—the realization that writing is only half of it. You have to be lucky and have a lot of things happen that you have *absolutely no control over*. You can write a fantastic script, but selling it is a crapshoot—always.

You didn't have another produced writing credit until your screenplay for *The Mothman Prophecies* seven years later. What did the experience of *US2DT* teach you about writing for Hollywood?

First, a few things I learned: Starting your writing career as half of a writing team, as I did (because *US2DT* was written by Matt Reeves and me) only really benefits you if you stay in that partnership. Soon after we sold the script, Matt began his feature directing career and I went back to writing alone, which is always how I'd done it before. But I had to establish myself all over again as a single writer, so a lot of the momentum from that first sale was blunted. It was like reaching the crest of Everest and then getting knocked halfway back down. Another thing I learned is that success is success, and work is work, and a credit is a credit—even if it's a sequel to a Steven Seagal movie. When Matt and I wrote that movie, we wanted Harrison Ford to star in it; we thought we had this classic underdog hero. The one thing we *didn't* want the movie to be was a sort of Arnold-Schwarzenegger-style thing where the poster would describe it as, you know, "Twelve terrorists pick the wrong train to hijack," where the hero is just picking them off one by one and never breaking a sweat. Which is, of course, exactly what it turned into. *Exactly*. Was it disappointing creatively? Sure. But it took me to the next step and I still get residual checks, so I'm not complaining. I've always figured it was up to me to determine the level of the stuff I write.

The year that *Under Siege 2: Dark Territory* came out—1995—I went out with another crime-thriller spec called *Truth or Consequences* that didn't sell. But that script, in a truly bizarre and fantastic coincidence, got me a shot to pitch a feature version of "The A-Team" that Universal was hot to make back then. So I got to pitch to my hero, Stephen J. Cannell, and I got the job. But—no big surprise by now, right?—the movie didn't get made. That was 12 years ago and, since then, at least five other writers have written five other versions and it still hasn't been made. And every one of those writers, including me, was very well paid to write those un-filmed drafts, so that's how most screenwriters make their living in between actual screen credits.

In 1997, I got it into my head to write a movie about paranormal phenomena. In another brilliantly well-timed coincidence, I happened across a book called *The Mothman Prophecies*, which captured exactly the sort of paranormal phenomena experiences I was interested in. I optioned the book myself for $2,500 and spent the summer and fall of 1997 writing a highly fictionalized spec script based on it. The script went out in November to every major studio in town. And it didn't sell. But what felt like failure at the time turned out to be another incredible stroke of luck. Because in January of 1998, it did sell, for a relatively small price, to Lakeshore Entertainment, a small, self-financed company that didn't buy dozens of scripts a year. They only bought one or two—*but they always made them*. It took a couple years to get all the elements into place—director, star—but once they did, they made the movie.

When I wrote *The Mothman Prophecies*, it was very unexpected because to the level I was known, I was known as an action writer. And changing genres is a big deal in movies and TV. Again, it's like starting your career over. So I couldn't just hope someone asked me to write a paranormal thriller. I had to spec one out (more on that later). And once it sold, paranormal thrillers were all I got offered. The final other big thing I learned is that, for most writers, there is no one big moment of success where you wake up one morning and you've "made it."

Finally, in the 12 months before *Mothman* came out, my TV career started.

Exactly. After *Mothman*, the floodgates started to open. You were writing for "Miracles," "Tru Calling," "The Insider." You were co-creator and showrunner in some instances. How did this happen so well so quickly?

The script for *Mothman* is what led to my first TV experience, which was the show "Miracles." Spyglass Entertainment and Touchstone TV (Now ABC TV Studios) contacted me because they had a feature film script that they felt might be the basis for a good TV show. The script was by a wonderful writer named Michael Petroni called "Miracles." It was sort of a romantic drama with supernatural overtones, about a young seminarian investigating miracles and sort of finding his own faith along the way. When I met with Megan Wolpert (Spyglass) and Suzanne Patmore (Touchstone), they told me that they'd like to take the idea of a young priest who investigates miracles and turn it into a sort of "spiritual *X-Files*." Our first meeting lasted three hours and I would say 95% of what the show turned out to be was developed in that meeting that day.

A quick word about TV development. There are *hundreds* of meetings just like this one taking place in offices all around town every day. The likelihood that any one of these conversations turns into a TV show you might ever see is very small. TV development is like any other elimination sport—you start with a very crowded field, and it keeps thinning out until just a few are left standing. Those are the shows that make it to the air—and then those start dropping like flies when no one watches. So any show you see on TV for more than a year is really like a lottery winner or an Olympic Gold medalist—maybe not in terms of quality, but certainly in terms of luck and odds.

So, over the summer and fall of 2001, I wrote the pilot for "Miracles" with a ton of help and direction from Spyglass and Touchstone, all in the hopes that ABC will like the script enough to actually film a pilot. Luckily—and this is not *nearly* always the case—Spyglass and Touchstone had a very clear idea of what ABC wanted, so we could tailor our script to their needs. (There's a much longer discussion here about how studios sell shows to networks, but suffice to say it really helps when the studio knows what the network wants. It helps even more if the *network* knows what the network wants.)

In January of 2002—the month *Mothman* came out in theaters—ABC decides to shoot the "Miracles" pilot. And they have this guy they want to direct it, a guy they love, the co-creator of "Felicity," which was a big hit for Touchstone. And they run his name past me to see if it's okay with me. It's Matt Reeves. My best friend who wrote *US2DT* with me. It was the single best, luckiest thing that's ever happened in my career. (Are you noticing how many times I've used the word "lucky" when describing my career success? Good.) So 15 years after Matt and I toiled away on our Super 8 film projects at USC and dreamed the impossible dream that maybe one day we'd have a career in Hollywood, here we are shooting a $3 million pilot with a real crew and a real cast and real free snacks. It was the greatest thing ever. Oh, and one other thing: It came out great.

Tell us about the transition from writer to showrunner. Is that a natural step all writers should be prepared for? What *weren't* you prepared for?

To the extent that I was a creator/showrunner of "Miracles," which was a *very* brief amount of time, I knew early on how I *didn't* want to do things. For instance, the people who work for you, various department heads and writers—they all kind of half-expect you to be a real jerk because most of them have worked for jerks in the past. So if you're not a jerk, they're ridiculously grateful and you end up getting great work from them. Someone told me early on that the way to get respect as a first-time showrunner was to walk onto the set the first day and fire someone. What bullshit. To me, that would be a display of massive insecurity. Some showrunners like to create a sense of competition among their writing staff so that everyone is trying to out-do or outmaneuver the other guy. Again, I think this is a huge mistake. I don't think most writers do their best work scared. I know I don't.

To be honest, I've always found the stress of working for someone else to be far greater than the stress of being the boss, because at least when you're the boss you know what you want, so you can just do it. Working for someone else, there's always a degree of guess work—"Is this what they want? Is *that* what they want? Am I doing this right?" And a lot of talented writers aren't particularly skilled at communicating to other writers what they want. Often it's because they don't *know* what they want until they're rewriting your script. It's only when the pages are running through *their* typewriter that they discover what it is they want, and by then it's very easy for them to think "Ah, I'm the *only* person in the world who can write this show. My staff sucks." However, if you know exactly what you want at the story breaking stage or the outline stage, you can equip the writer with everything they need to turn in work that's going to please you.

One thing some people don't understand well is how much concern a writer should give whether a pilot is for FX, or HBO, or Disney the networks, or . . .? Can you give some advice on learning what networks air what shows and how that will come in handy during pitch time?

If you're doing face-to-face pitching and you have an agent, you can reasonably expect your agent to have a sense of what the various networks might be looking for. Even better, if you are working with a production company that has some TV credits, they, too, should know the landscape and can help strategize. But really, the best advice is simply this: Pitch everywhere. Pitch your show to the networks, to the cable channels—just pitch it everywhere, because you never know who might love it.

Let's say you're talking to someone who is trying to break in, and has some spec scripts ready. They say to you "I'm thinking about

writing an original, but I don't think it'll really matter much." What do you say?

Right now is a very good time to have an original spec TV pilot. It's always been a good way of demonstrating your own voice, but now, much more than any time I've been in the business, spec TV pilots are actually selling. There are a lot of networks, cable and otherwise, looking for signature shows to distinguish their "brand," so there's a greater openness to considering new concepts from unknown writers.

How do you decide if an idea you have is best fit for TV versus the big screen?

Here's a stupid but honest answer: Some ideas just *feel* like movies, whereas others *feel* like TV shows. If an idea is "event-based," it's probably a movie. For instance, "Someone is trying to kill the president," or "One day, a monster comes out of the water in New York harbor and starts stomping around." You're examining one incident in great detail, so that feels like a movie. However, an idea that is more about characters and settings probably feels more like a TV show. For example, "Three competitive brothers open a private golf course in Beverly Hills," or "A neurotic, control-freak New Yorker inherits a small-town newspaper in Nevada." These are "characters in a setting" ideas and they can be explored from many angles over a long period of time. Character-based movies like "The Odd Couple" make great TV shows. Same thing with "setting-based" movies like "M*A*S*H."

I've heard that composing bibles early on is a waste of time. True?

Yeah, I'd say this is true. If you're pitching a new series or writing a spec pilot, it's good to have general idea about where the show might go, but it's probably not important to write out a detailed bible or even detailed episode ideas. The time will come for that sort of work after the pilot has been sold. (Often, it's after the pilot has been shot and you want to make sure the network has every reason to pick up the show to series.)

What other advice can you throw writers on anything we've missed?

If you want to write for movies and television, you should move to Los Angeles. Take classes at UCLA Extension, AFI, USC and get to know the people. (This is that "networking" thing you've heard about.) Chances are you'll meet people who work at small production companies—or even large agencies—and they will have ideas and advice about how to get your script into the right hands. More important, the people you meet are your peers. They are struggling right along with you. Some of the people you meet in the first few months you live here will turn into lifelong friends. Short of that, they will be the future writers/producers/executives/agents/studio chiefs you'll be working with for the balance of your career.

Most new writers on network and/or cable shows are former writer's assistants. A writer's assistant is someone who takes notes in the writer's room on any given series. They usually get this job as a promotion from office assistant in the production company that produces the show. Or sometimes they start as the personal assistant to one of the writer-producers. The reason these people get promoted onto a writing staff is because they are a familiar face to all the current writers, so they don't frighten or threaten them as much. They're already a member of the family.

I happily and confidently urge you to keep pushing forward and never give up. There are plenty of people warning you about long odds and low pay and lack of respect and sleazy producers. So gently set all that good advice aside and remind yourself of one persistent, undeniable little fact: *Every night, somewhere in Hollywood, a new writer is celebrating their first big sale. Every. Single. Night.*

But Will It Get Produced?

Don't Write With Red Carpets in Mind

by Chuck Sambuchino

I f you want to be a screenwriter, you must love writing. When it comes down to it, that's all you're guaranteed—time sitting down cranking out scenes and getting paid for it. If your ultimate goal is something other than to make a living writing scripts, then you may be in trouble. Below you will find four classic bad ideas that novice script scribes may think about as they begin their voyage to screenwriter superstardom. Avoid them like the Blob—or Keyser Soze.

BAD IDEA NO. 1: WRITE FOR A TREND

At a recent writers' conference in Los Angeles, a panel of script managers sat down to answer audience questions on screenwriting. Invariably, an attendee stood up and asked about "what's hot," bringing up the topic of trends. Wisely, instead of answering the question, the script managers refused to expound on the topic, saying that writers shouldn't write to trends.

The reasoning behind this is two-fold. First, a writer will likely be too late to capitalize on an existing trend. At the time of the conference, the latest Indiana Jones film was released, stirring up much interest in adventure-type films with treasures and hidden places. But there was no point in trying to follow the trend, because Hollywood was flooded by Indiana Jones rip-offs well before the film hit theaters.

In an absolute best-case scenario, a film may hit theaters two years after a writer starts writing the script. That takes into consideration everything at every stage going perfect. But, more than likely, it will be several years

CHUCK SAMBUCHINO is the editor of *Screenwriter's & Playwright's Market*. He also edits *Guide to Literary Agents* (www.guidetoliteraryagents.com/blog) and oversaw the third edition of *Formatting & Submitting Your Manuscript*.

from writing to fruition, thereby ruining any chance screenwriters have to capitalize on a trend.

The second reason to avoid trends is because a writer's best writing will show up where the writer is passionate. If vampire flicks are hot right now and you try to craft tale about the undead, but you don't really know or care about the subject matter, then your best work will not land on the page.

To be fair, trends may come into play for you down the road. If you have an agent and you inquire one day as to what studios are looking for, he may say "a space opera fantasy." At that point, you'll be ahead of the trend, and may be able to talk your way into a writing (or rewriting) assignment for a space opera fantasy that's in development somewhere. Perhaps you have a completed script around that you could rewrite and see if excellence develops. If it does, give it to your agent to make some rounds.

BAD IDEA NO. 2: COMPROMISE YOUR QUALITY FOR SALABILITY

Yes, ideally you want to write something that will sell and land you a hefty paycheck. But the truth is: post-strike boom aside, spec scripts are a tough sell. Studios have already spent oodles of money acquiring all kinds of properties that are now in development. It's in their best interest to get those projects moving, not buy something completely new that has no built-in fan base.

The goal is to write to your passions and create a writing sample so astounding that power players of the film business will want you to work on other projects. The spec script you write serves as a wonderful way to get your foot in the door and land you assignments. Like manager Ken Sherman of Ken Sherman Associates says: "What I'm looking for, and what every producer, studio, network and agent I know is looking for, is a killer writing sample—meaning something that we can send out in one day to 30 producers and have them say 'This may not be exactly the story I'm looking for, but I need to know this writer.' (That way), they will meet with the writer and talk about other projects because that writer has a unique voice."

Screenwriter Zak Penn, scribe of *X-Men 3: The Last Stand* and *The Incredible Hulk*, says a great example of how to break into the business correctly was his friend, Marc Hyman. According to Penn, Hyman wrote a spec script that was an animation comedy starring fish. The script was extremely funny, but at the same time, would be a difficult project to produce and turn a profit on. The fish project never materialized, but producers knew Hyman's name and his humor skills because his script proved he was a formidable writer. Years later, when an animation comedy called *Osmosis*

Jones was materializing, the studio needed a funny writer who could deal with animation. They called Hyman.

Mission accomplished.

BAD IDEA NO. 3: GET REALLY UPSET IF YOUR WORK ISN'T PRODUCED

If you're like me (i.e., if you're a writer with a heartbeat), you love bylines. Getting an assignment is a jolt. Writing the piece is fun. Getting my check in the mail is awesome. And lastly, seeing my work in print gives me the final thrill, as well as something else: closure. The process I just described is how a typical magazine writing assignment goes. If a magazine contracts and purchases an article from me, they will print it somewhere, many more times than not. If a writer sells a novel, it, too, will likely see the light of day, as the publishing house has paid you for it and they want to put the content in print and use it. It's in this regard that screenwriting stands alone. In Hollywood, much more material is written and optioned and passed around town than will ever come to life. There's so much money flying around, that it's hardly uncommon to see a studio pay $1 million for a dynamite new script and $250,000 for a rewrite of another, with neither project ever hitting the big screen.

It all adds up to this: If you want to be a career screenwriter, you must enjoy the actual duty of screenwriting. We all picture our stories on the big screen, envisioning ourselves looking smashingly handsome (or stunning glamorous) at a red carpet premiere. But that's not likely to happen. There will be meetings, assignments, and nice paychecks, but production is another monster altogether. If the thought of your work never coming to life sounds maddening, then you'll definitely want to write a lot of magazine articles on the side to scratch that itch.

BAD IDEA NO. 4: JUST WRITE ONE SCREENPLAY

Don't put all your eggs in one basket. Agents all say the same thing: They represent careers, not projects. A manager may not even send you out to a pitch meeting until you have several projects up your sleeve. Having multiple scripts in your arsenal allows you to be more valuable, and shows that you're a dedicated writer who actually does what they should—writes!

Perspectives

Hollywood Pet Peeves

Avoid These Peeves and Get Your Work Read

by Chuck Sambuchino

Here's a secret many writers don't know about managers and producers. When they tackle the slush pile (much like when readers review entries in a writing contest), they are flooded with hundreds, sometimes thousands, of submissions. With such an overwhelming volume of potential scripts to consider, producers are looking for reasons *not* to choose a particular script. They're looking for any sign of weakness in your writing or professionalism that will justify rejecting your work and making their huge stack of scripts decrease by one. That's why your work must be as perfect as it can be. And before an agent even reads your work, you've got to do something more important: Avoid Hollywood pet peeves.

There's a scene in the television show "Arrested Development" where the character Tobias Funke, an aspiring actor, starts packaging his headshot to send out to different casting directors in Hollywood. Each headshot is placed in a decorative bag filled with glitter, candy and a note saying, "I know where you live, ha ha." We then see a casting director struggling to open one of these glittery bags, then looking at the headshot and telling herself aloud never to hire Tobias Funke. This is a quintessential example of an amateur implementing gimmicks to get their work noticed—and remember, gimmicks and "cute" don't work. In fact, they're huge Hollywood pet peeves.

Glitter and unfunny notes aren't the only dislikes in the movie world—there's plenty more. Keep your work concise and professional to help avoid annoying possible representatives for your work. Below you'll find a series of tips and need-to-know facts that will help your work get a fair read by the people in power. Study them well.

CHUCK SAMBUCHINO is the editor of *Screenwriter's & Playwright's Market*. He also edits *Guide to Literary Agents* (www.guidetoliteraryagents.com/blog) and oversaw the third edition of *Formatting & Submitting Your Manuscript*.

REGARDING SUBMISSIONS

- Any type of misspelling or gross formatting error will make an agent grimace, and likely reject your query.
- No matter how much you want to woo a specific manager or production company, never submit a work to a market that doesn't accept the genre in question—you're just showing you can't follow directions (and wasting postage).
- Don't embellish your accomplishments; that just leads to a very awkward moment later when you have to explain yourself. If you get caught in a lie, it's likely people will start to wonder what else you were untruthful about.
- Don't mention ideas for your movie's poster design or possible casting. If you have suggestions, let that conversation happen naturally down the road. Likely, such decisions will be out of your hands, and offering your input too soon (or even at all) makes you look amateurish. This brings up another point: Know when to work your tail off, and when to step away and let other people operate.
- Single-space your query letters.
- Managers and agents may assist with rewriting suggestions, but they're not there to act as the world's editors. If your query or pitch has a sentence such as "Act III needs a little tweaking," then you should never have pitched in the first place.
- Don't submit a query that's written in the voice of your lead character.
- Don't submit your query in script format.
- Make sure you always provide what's asked of you.

REGARDING APPEARANCE

- Avoid letterhead or logos on your work. Remember: Always avoid "cute."
- Keep things short (e.g., query letters should be one page). You may go long because you feel that your plot can't properly be condensed into just one or two paragraphs. This leads to a larger problem: If you can't summarize your work with a short explanation or a concise logline, then the manager won't be able to summarize the work when talking to production companies who may consider the project. You put him at a disadvantage in selling your work.
- Format your materials and always use a standard font.
- Use no graphics or art (or worse: Clip Art).
- Take dates off your script and don't say that this is "Draft 5."

REGARDING THE SCRIPT

- Don't mention who you think should play a character in the role, and don't include pictures of actors.
- Don't turn in a super long script. Especially with spec scripts, less is more. Aim for approximately 110 pages.
- Don't awkwardly staple or bind your script together. The standard format of two brads is chosen because it's easy for readers, and easy to undo should copies be needed.
- Beware including music cues in your work. Yes, Queen's "Bohemian Rhapsody" would really be great in that scene you're writing, but a director will have a much better sense of movie music.

ON ETIQUETTE

- Act with humility always, whether when writing your query or speaking with a producer in person. If you can show someone that you deeply respect their time, you've shown them that you're a professional and courteous writer, which ups your value as a potential client.
- Don't write an exec and tell her she's an idiot for not signing you. Let's say someone sends you a form rejection letter and you've got an inkling that they gave your script a quick read let alone any true consideration at all. You're frustrated. Sending an angry letter giving your candid thoughts is not the answer. The letter isn't likely to make someone change their submission review procedures, and a worse scenario is that person contacting fellow professionals and warning them against taking you on as a client.
- Mentioning how much money your project will make is a big no-no. Writers, many of which are very proud of their work, will often compare their script to a current blockbuster. It's best to not even joke about these cliches.
- Don't say your family members or writing group liked your work. Their opinion, though kind, means nothing to agents. And because professionals think that writers should know these opinions are worthless, they'll look down on writers who mention such statements.
- Take no chances when addressing a person whose gender is ambiguous (e.g., Pat or Alex). Call up the studio and ask the person who picks up whether Pat/Alex is male or female.
- Don't demand a cameo (or worse—a starring role) in your script should it get produced. You're a writer, so write.

ON CONTACTING

- Though it's been said before, it bears repeating: Personalize your queries.
- If you receive a rejection letter, you likely won't get any personal feedback on your work. If this happens, don't contact that manager after a rejection and ask her for feedback, or a specific reason as to why you received only a generic rejection letter. I know you're thinking that you're entitled to a reason as to why your work was rejected (and perhaps you are), but reps are too busy to give personal feedback to everyone. Instead of contacting the agent, get feedback from where it would logically come—peers in a writing group.
- Never ask an agent if she charges fees. Use Internet forums, blogs and this book to weed out inappropriate agencies before pitching, then you'll know you're dealing with someone legitimate.
- Don't refer to yourself as "a screenwriter." That's obvious, no?
- Don't submit your script with two additional scripts for your proposed sequels.

ON FOLLOWING UP AND MOVING ON

- Beware calling without a request. I know this is tempting because you may actually get a live person on the end of the phone, but it provides for a massively awkward situation with agents as they're requested to explain why they haven't gotten back to you yet. The last thing an agent wants is to have that awkward moment on the phone.
- If a representative takes you on, make sure you don't clamor for an unrealistic payday. If you've done your homework, you should know what a logical payout for a script/series will be.
- Don't be a blowhard. Your work will get rewritten and some of your ideas may be stolen. Such is the nature of Hollywood. Kicking and screaming will do no good.

Navigating Hollywood requires a careful balance of what to do and what not to do, but the basics will always be the same: Be professional, write well and always follow directions. Avoid the pet peeves and ensure that your work ends up in the hands of a big-time power player, not a recycle bin.

Agents & Managers

This section contains agents and managers who represent feature film scripts, television scripts and theatrical stage plays. Many of the script agents listed here are signatories to the Writers Guild of America (WGA) Artists' Manager Basic Agreement. They have paid a membership fee and agree to abide by the WGA's standard code of behavior.

It's a good idea to register your script before sending it out, and the WGA offers a registration service to members and nonmembers alike. Membership in the WGA is earned through the accumulation of professional credits and carries a number of significant benefits.

A few of the listings in this section are actually management companies. The role of managers is quickly changing in Hollywood. Actors and the occasional writer were once the only ones to use them. Now many managers are actually selling scripts to producers.

Like literary agents, some script agencies ask that clients pay for some or all of the office fees accrued when sending out scripts. Always have a clear understanding of any fee an agent asks you to pay.

SUBHEADS

Each listing is broken down into subheads to make locating specific information easier. In the first section, you'll find contact information for each agency. You'll also learn if the agent is a WGA signatory or a member of any other professional organizations. Other information provided indicates the agency's size, its willingness to work with a new or unpublished writer, and a percentage breakdown of the general types of scripts the agency will consider.

Member Agents: Agencies comprised of more than one agent list member agents and their individual specialties to help you determine the person to whom you should send your query letter.

Represents: In this section, agents specify what type of scripts they represent. Make sure you query only agents who represent the type of material you write.

> ⚏ Look for the key icon to quickly learn an agent's areas of specialization. In this portion of the listing, agents mention the specific subject areas they're currently seeking, as well as those subject areas they do not consider.

How to Contact: Most agents open to submissions prefer an initial query letter that briefly describes your work. Script agents usually discard material sent without a SASE. In this section, agents also mention if they accept queries by fax or e-mail; if they consider simultaneous submissions; and how they prefer to solicit new clients.

Recent Sales: Reflecting the different ways scriptwriters work, agents list scripts optioned or sold and scripting assignments procured for clients. The film industry is sometimes secretive about sales, but you may be able to get a list of clients or other references upon request—especially if the agency is interested in representing your work.

Terms: Most agents' commissions range from 10-15 percent, and WGA signatories may not earn more than 10 percent from WGA members.

Writers' Conferences: A great way to meet an agent is at a writers' conference. Here agents list the conferences they usually attend. For more information about a specific conference, check the Conferences section starting on page 315.

Tips: In this section, agents offer advice and additional instructions for writers seeking representation.

Quick Reference Icons

At the beginning of some listings, you will find one or more of the following symbols:

N   Agency new to this edition

   Canadian agency

   International agency

◯   Agency actively seeking clients

   Agency seeking both new and established writers

   Agency seeking mostly established writers through referrals

◎   Agency specializing in certain types of work

⊘   Agency not currently seeking new clients

Find a pull-out bookmark with a key to symbols on the inside cover of this book.

SPECIAL INDEXES

Agents Specialties Index: This index (page 399) organizes agencies according to the subjects they are interested in receiving. This index should help you compose a list of agents specializing in your areas. Cross-referencing categories and concentrating on agents interested in two or more aspects of your manuscript might increase your chances of success.

Agents Index: This index (page 408) provides a list of agents' names in alphabetical order along with the name of the agency for which they work. Find the name of the person you would like to contact, and then check the agency listing.

General Index: This index (page 414) lists all agencies, theaters, production companies, contests and conferences appearing in the book.

3R Entertainment Group

Blackwood Talent Management, 8306 Wilshire Boulevard, Suite 1724, Beverly Hills CA 90211. (310)295-0111. Fax: (310)295-0110. E-mail: horacio@ blackwoodcompany.com, raquel@blackwoodcompany.com. Website: www. blackwoodcompany.com/.

Represents movie, movie scripts, feature film.

How to Contact Query with SASE. Submit logline with query letter.

⊕ A&B PERSONAL MANAGEMENT LTD

162-168 Regent St., Suite 330 Linen Hall, London England W1B 5TD United Kingdom. (44)(207)434-4262. Fax: (44)(207)038-3699. E-mail: billellis@aandb. co.uk. **Contact:** R.W. Ellis.

Represents Nonfiction books, novels, episodic drama, movie, TV, movie scripts, feature film, sitcom, stage plays.

How to Contact Submit by mail with SAE. Write before submitting synopsis.

Terms Fee only for reading full length mss.

◙ ABOVE THE LINE AGENCY

468 N. Camden Drive, #200, Beverly Hills CA 90210. (310)859-6115. Fax: (310)859-6119. Website: www.abovethelineagency.com. **Contact:** Bruce Bartlett; Rima Bauer Greer, owner. Signatory of WGA. Represents 35 clients. 10% of clients are new/unpublished writers. Currently handles: movie scripts 100%.

- Prior to opening her agency, Ms. Greer served as president of Writers & Artists Agency.

Represents Movie scripts, feature film. **Considers these script areas:** cartoon.

⚿ "We are rarely accepting new clients."

How to Contact This agency accepts clients through our web program.

Terms Agent receives 10% commission on domestic sales. Agent receives 10% commission on foreign sales.

Recent Sales *The Great Cookie Wars*, by Greg Taylor and Jim Strain (Fox); *Velveteen Rabbit*, by Greg Taylor (Disney); *Wing and a Prayer*, by David Engelbach and John Wolff (Franchise).

◙ ABRAMS ARTISTS AGENCY

Theatrical and Literary Agency, 275 Seventh Ave., 26th Floor, New York NY 10001. E-mail: vincent.devito@abramsart.com. Website: www.abramsartists.com/.

Represents Stage plays, screenplays, books. **Considers these script areas:** action, biography, comedy, contemporary, detective, ethnic, experimental, family, fantasy, feminist, gay, glitz, historical, horror, juvenile, mainstream, multicultural, multimedia, mystery, psychic, regional, religious, romantic comedy, romantic drama, science, sports, teen, thriller, western.

⚬ This agency specializes in musicals and stage plays.

How to Contact Query with SASE. Prefers to read materials exclusively. Referrals needed for new materials. *No unsolicited mss.* No e-mail or fax queries.

◉ AEI: ATCHITY EDITORIAL/ENTERTAINMENT INTERNATIONAL, INC. MOTION PICTURE PRODUCTION & LITERARY MANAGEMENT

9601 Wilshire Blvd., Box #1202, Beverly Hills CA 90210. (323)932-0407. Fax: (323)932-0321. E-mail: submissions@aeionline.com. Website: www.aeionline. com. **Contact:** Jennifer Pope. Other memberships include Producers Guild of America. Represents 65 clients. 50% of clients are new/unpublished writers. Currently handles: nonfiction books 25%, novels 25%, juvenile books 5%, movie scripts 40%, TV scripts 5%.

Member Agents Ken Atchity (books and film); Chi-Li Wong (TV and film); Brenna Lui (books); Mike Kuciak (films and TV); Greg F. Dix (uplifting stories, inspirational, faith-based work).

Represents Nonfiction books, novels, juvenile, animation, miniseries, websites, games for dramatic exploitation. **Considers these nonfiction areas:** animals, biography, business, computers, current affairs, ethnic, government, health, history, how to, humor, memoirs, military, money, nature, popular culture, psychology, religion, science, self help, translation, true crime, women's. **Considers these fiction areas:** adventure, confession, detective, ethnic, family, fantasy, historical, horror, humor, juvenile, literary, mainstream, mystery, religious, science, thriller, western, young, African-American, ethnic, psychic/supernatural. **Considers these script areas:** action, biography, cartoon, comedy, contemporary, detective, fantasy, horror, juvenile, mainstream, mystery, psychic, religious, romantic comedy, teen, thriller.

⚬ "We've developed the niche of focusing on storytellers instead of 'projects' or 'writers,' and helping them tell their stories (whether fiction or nonfiction) for all possible markets (book, film, Web, etc.)." Actively seeking young adult novels, nonfiction, mom lit, minority lit, action screenplays, broad comedy screenplays. Does not want to receive poetry, children's books or photo books.

How to Contact "E-mail and snail mail queries for novels, nonfiction book proposals, screenplays, and treatments should consist of a compelling and businesslike letter giving us a brief overview of your story, the audience for which it is intended—and a one-sentence pitch. Be sure to include your return address, and a telephone number with your letter and SASE." Accepts simultaneous submissions. Responds in 3-6 weeks to queries. Responds in 8-10 weeks to mss.

Obtains most new clients through recommendations from others, solicitations, conferences, referrals from our books, Web site.

Terms Agent receives 15% commission on domestic sales. Agent receives 30% commission on foreign sales. Offers written contract, binding for 1 year; 30-day notice must be given to terminate contract. Agency charges for misc. expenses, but costs not to exceed $500 from any publication advance, with the balance recoupable from other gross proceeds.

Recent Sales Sold 10 titles and 5 scripts in the last year. *Demon Keeper*, by Royce Buckingham (Putnam/Fox 2000); *Dark Gold*, by David Angsten (Thomas Dunne); *Arm Bone Flute*, by Alaya Johnson (Agate).

Writers Conferences Santa Barbara Writers' Conference; Midwest Literary Festival; Pacific Northwest Writers' Conference.

Tips "Respect what we do as story merchants, and treat us, from the beginning, as business partners who can help you build the creative life of your dreams. Find out who we are and know what we like and believe in even before you approach us. It's all on our Web site. Most of all, think outside the box and take an entrepreneurial approach to both your career and your relationship with us."

⊕ THE AGENCY, LTD.

24 Pottery Lane, Holland Park, London England W11 4LZ United Kingdom. E-mail: info@theagency.co.uk. Website: www.theagency.co.uk. Currently handles: movie scripts, TV scripts, stage plays, other Radio Scripts.

Member Agents Partners: Stephen Durbridge, Leah Schmidt, Julia Kreitman, Bethan Evans, Norman North, and Anna Cameron. Directors: Hilary Delamere and Katie Haines Associates: Nick Quinn, Faye Webber, Fay Davies, Ian Benson, and Jago Irwin. Hilary Delamere represents children's authors and illustrators.

Represents Juvenile, movie, TV, movie scripts, feature film.

How to Contact All unsolicited mss returned unopened.

⊕ AIM

Associated International Management, Fairfax House, Fulwood Place, London England WC1V 6HU United Kingdom. (44)(207)831-9709. Fax: (44)(207)242-0810. E-mail: email@aimagents.com. Website: www.aimagents.com/. Other memberships include Personal Managers Association.

Member Agents Derek Webster, Stephen Gittins, and Lisa-Marie Assenheim.

How to Contact Query with CV, photo and SAE to the address above.

Recent Sales Other clients include David Bartlett, Peter Cregeen, John Davies, Ken Russell, Carol Wilks.

ANCHORAGE PRESS PLAYS

617 Baxter Ave., Louisville KY 40204-1105. (502)583-2288. Fax: (502)583-2288. E-mail: applays@bellsouth.net. Website: www.applays.com. **Contact:** Marilee Hebert Miller, publisher. PO Box 2901, Louisville, KY 40201-2901

Represents Stage plays, for children and young people.

How to Contact Submit review sheet, SASE. Submit complete ms.

⊕ ANCO ENTERTAINMENT THEATER PRODUCTIONS

Zijperstraat 41, Alkmaar 1823 CX The Netherlands. 072 - 520 82 56. Fax: 072 - 520 82 58. E-mail: info@toneelwerken.nl. Website: www.toneelwerken.nl/.

⊕ DARLEY ANDERSON LITERARY, TV & FILM AGENCY

Estelle House, 11 Eustace Rd., London England SW6 1JB United Kingdom. (44) (207)385-6652. Fax: (44)(207)386-5571. E-mail: enquiries@darleyanderson. com. Website: www.darleyanderson.com. **Contact:** Darley Anderson (Crime and Thrillers); Julia Churchill (Children's Books); Lucie Whitehouse (Women's Fiction); Zoe King (Nonfiction).

Represents Sitcom. **Considers these nonfiction areas:** animals, biography, child, cooking, memoirs, popular culture, religion, self help, sports, finance, children's nonfiction. **Considers these fiction areas:** adventure, confession, erotica, ethnic, family, fantasy, gay, historical, horror, juvenile, mainstream, mystery, picture books, regional, religious, romance, science, sports, thriller, young adult, women's 'chick lit'. **Considers these script areas:** action, biography, cartoon, comedy, contemporary, detective, ethnic, family, glitz, psychic.

How to Contact Submit synopsis. Send query letter with SAE. Accepts query letters by phone. Submit first 3 chapters.

ANONYMOUS CONTENT

588 Broadway, Suite 308, New York NY 10012. (212)925-0055. Fax: (212)925-5030. E-mail: info@anonymouscontent.com. Website: www.anonymouscontent.com/. Los Angeles Office: 3532 Hayden Ave., Culver City, CA 90232, (310)558-3667/ (310)558-4212 fax; London Office: 7 / 8 Bourlet Close, London, UK W1W 7BW (44)(207)927-9400 / (44)(207)927-9401 fax. Currently handles: movie scripts, TV scripts, multimedia, other Commercials, Music Videos, Web.

Member Agents Paul Muniz and Lisa Sabatino - East Coast; David Wagner - Midwest; Michael Di Girolamo - West; Dave Morrison - Commercials.

Represents Movie scripts, feature film, TV scripts, TV movie of the week.

How to Contact Query with SASE.

🌐 A.P. WATT, LTD

20 John St., London England WC1N 2DR United Kingdom. (020) 7405 6774. Fax: (020) 7831 2154. E-mail: apw@apwatt.co.uk. Website: www.apwatt.co.uk. **Contact:** Caradoc King, Derek Johns, Georgia Garrett (Literary Fiction, General Nonfiction, Narrative Nonfiction and Children's Authors); Linda Shaughnessy (Translation Rights, Literary Estates); Natasha Fairweather (Nonfiction, Young Novelists); Christine Glover, Rob Kraitt (Scripts, Screenplays and Playwrighting); Teresa Nicholls (foreign rights).

Represents Nonfiction books, TV, movie scripts, feature film, TV movie, stage plays. **Considers these fiction areas:** juvenile, literary, commercial.

   ⚷ No poetry considered.

How to Contact Send query letter.

🌐 AURA-PONT

Veslaøský ostrov 62, Podoli 147 00 Praha 4 Czech Republic. E-mail: aura-pont@ aura-pont.cz. Website: www.aura-pont.cz/en/.

Member Agents Petra Markova, head of the Theatre Department; Zuzana Jezkova, foreign rights; Anna Pychova, foreign rights; Jitka Sloupova, literary manager; Michal Kotrous, literary manager, distribution of texts and archive.

   ⚷ The agency represents dramatists, writers, and translators.

🌐 AUTHOR LITERARY AGENTS

Novels, thrillers, faction, nonfiction, graphic novels, and children's books, and graphic and illustrated media edutainment concepts (home 15%, overseas/ translations 20%, advertising/sales promotion one-third). Pitches to publishers and producers., 53 Talbot Rd., Highgate, London England N64QX United Kingdom. (44)(208)341-0442. Fax: (44)(208)341-0442. E-mail: agile@authors. co.uk. **Contact:** John Havergal. Estab. 1997.

Represents **Considers these nonfiction areas:** agriculture horticulture, animals, anthropology, art, biography, business, child, computers, cooking, education, history, humor, language, music, nature, psychology, religion, science, sociology, true crime, Crafts & Hobbies, Film. **Considers these fiction areas:** adventure, confession, detective, experimental, family, fantasy, historical, juvenile, literary, literary, mainstream, mystery, picture books, religious, romance, science, thriller, young. **Considers these script areas:** action, biography, cartoon, contemporary, detective, experimental, family.

How to Contact Send first chapter, scene or section, and graphics samples (if any), plus a half to one page plot or topic outline. Query with SASE.

☑ BASKOW AGENCY

2948 E. Russell Road, Las Vegas NV 89120. (702)733-7818. Fax: (702)733-2052. E-mail: jaki@baskow.com; info@baskow.com. Website: www.baskow.com. **Contact:** Jaki Baskow. Represents 8 clients. 40% of clients are new/unpublished writers. Currently handles: nonfiction books 5%, novels 5%, movie scripts 20%, TV scripts 70%.

Member Agents Jaki Baskow (true life stories and comedies).

Represents Episodic drama, movie scripts, feature film, TV movie of the week, sitcom, documentary, variety show, miniseries. **Considers these script areas:** action, biography, comedy, contemporary, family, glitz, mystery, religious, romantic comedy, romantic drama, science, juvenile only, thriller.

- Actively seeking unique scripts, all-American true stories, kids' projects, and movies of the week. Looking for light, comedic and family-oriented work. Does not want to receive scripts with heavy violence or scripts that require animation.

How to Contact Query with SASE. Submit outline, proposal, treatments. Responds in 1 month to queries. Responds in 60 days to mss. Obtains most new clients through recommendations from others.

Terms Agent receives 10% commission on domestic sales. Agent receives 10% commission on foreign sales. Offers written contract.

Recent Sales *Dying to be Young*, by Eric Katlan (Nightengale Books); *Malpractice*, by Larry Leirketen (Blakely); *Angel of Death* (CBS). Other clients include Cheryl Anderson, Camisole Prods, Michael Store.

☑ BEACON ARTISTS AGENCY, INC.

120 E. 56th St., Suite 540, New York NY 10022. (212)736-6630. Fax: (212)868-1052. **Contact:** Patricia McLaughlin. Member of AAR. Represents 20-25 clients.

Represents Episodic drama, movie, TV movie, stage plays. **Considers these script areas:** mainstream.

- "We are not seeking new clients at this time. We handle playwrights and screenwriters, as well as some TV and the occasional book. We are a small agency with very personal service."

Terms Agent receives 10% commission on domestic sales. Agent receives 15-20% commission on foreign sales. Offers written contract, binding for 2-3 years (renewable). Client pays own legal fees and any extraordinary office costs.

BENDERSPINK

110 South Fairfax Ave, Suite 350, Los Angeles CA 90036. E-mail: info@benderspink.com. Website: www.benderspink.com/.

Represents TV, movie scripts, feature film, TV movie.

○━ "Our company's focus is on 'breaking' new talent and constantly discovering, creating and developing unique and interesting material." Actively seeking writers with a distinct voice.

How to Contact Submit synopsis, query.

Recent Sales *Just Friends* (2005).

☑ BICOASTAL TALENT

210 North Pass Ave., Suite 204, Burbank CA 91505. (818)845-0150. Fax: (818)845-0152. E-mail: literary@bicoastaltalent.com. Website: www.bicoastaltalent.com/.

Member Agents Liz and Greta Hanley.

○━ Writers of feature-length screenplays should submit queries only. The agency does not represent authors of self-published or unpublished manuscripts, treatments, concepts, or TV pilots.

How to Contact Query with a list of completed screenplays with title, genre, and a one-paragraph pitch (4-8 lines). Should have a minimum of 3 completed screenplays available upon request.

⊕ ☺ ALAN BRODIE REPRESENTATION LTD.

Fairgate House, 78 New Oxford St., Sixth Floor, London England WC1A 1HB United Kingdom. E-mail: info@alanbrodie.com. Website: www.alanbrodie.com. Other memberships include PMA. 10% of clients are new/unpublished writers.

Member Agents Alan Brodie; Sarah McNair; Lisa Foster.

○━ Does not want to receive fiction, nonfiction or poetry.

How to Contact Submit a letter and CV in the first instance together with a letter of recommendation from an industry professional. North American writers accepted only in exceptional circumstances. Responds if interested. Obtains most new clients through recommendations from others.

Terms Charges clients for photocopying.

Recent Sales See agency's website for clients and sales.

Tips "Biographical details can be helpful. Generally only playwrights whose work has been performed will be considered, provided they come recommended by an industry professional. Please be aware that all submissions are treated as strictly confidential. Be advised: From time to time, two writers will come up with very similar ideas; this is the nature of the business and is purely coincidence. In submitting your material to us you are relying on our professional integrity."

MARCUS BRYAN & ASSOCIATES INC. LITERARY AGENCY

1500 Skokie Blvd., Suite 310, Northbrook IL 60068. (847)412-9394. Fax: (847)413-9396. E-mail: mba3308@aol.com. Website: marcusbryan.com/. Signatory of WGA.

- "We are always happy to take query letters from screenwriters as well as Book Authors. We pride ourselves in trying our best to help new writers as well as those of you that have been writing for years. Everyone needs a little help now and then."

KELVIN C. BULGER AND ASSOCIATES

4540 W. Washington Blvd., Suite 101, Chicago IL 60624. (312)218-1943. E-mail: kcbwoi@aol.com. Website: bulgerandassociates.biz/profile.html. **Contact:** Kelvin Bulger. Signatory of WGA. Represents 25 clients. 90% of clients are new/unpublished writers. Currently handles: movie scripts 75%, TV scripts 25%.

Represents Movie scripts, feature film, TV movie of the week, documentary, syndicated material. **Considers these script areas:** action, cartoon, comedy, contemporary, ethnic, family, religious.

How to Contact Query with SASE. Submit 1-page logline, 1-page plot synopsis (beginning/middle/end), first 10 pages of screenplay. Accepts simultaneous submissions. Responds in 3 weeks to queries. Responds in 2 months to mss. Obtains most new clients through recommendations from others, solicitations.

Terms Agent receives 10% commission on domestic sales. Agent receives 10% commission on foreign sales. Offers written contract, binding for 6-12 months.

Recent Sales *Severed Ties*, by David Johnson (Maverick Entertainment).

Tips "Proofread before submitting to an agent. We only reply to letters of inquiry if a SASE is enclosed."

CAPEL & LAND LTD

29 Wardour St., London England W1D 6PS United Kingdom. (44)(207)734-2414. Fax: (44)(207)734-8101. E-mail: georgina@capelland.co.uk. Website: www.capelland.com. **Contact:** Director: Georgina Capel (Literary); Director: Anita Land (TV/Radio); Joscelyn Evans (Television and Radio, Corporate); Phillipa Brewster, Abi Fellows, Rosie Apponyi (Literary).

Represents Nonfiction books, movie, TV, movie scripts, feature film. **Considers these nonfiction areas:** biography, history. **Considers these fiction areas:** literary, general.

How to Contact Submit synopsis, 3 sample chapters. Query letter with SAE.

Recent Sales Clients include Kohn Bew, Matthew Dennison, Julie Burchill, Andrew Greig, Eammon Holmes, Liz Jones, Dr. Tristam Hunt, Stella Rimington, Jeremy Paxman, Fay Weldon and Greg Woolf.

CASAROTTO RAMSAY & ASSOCIATES LIMITED

Waverley House, 7-12 Noel Street, London W1F 8GQ United Kingdom. E-mail: info@casarotto.co.uk. Website: www.casarotto.co.uk/.
Member Agents Jenne Casarotto, (Film and TV, Represents Writers and Directors); Tom Erhardt (Theatrical); Mel Kenyon (Theatrical); Ruth Arnaud (Amateurs and Stock Rights); Kirsty Coombs (Stage Directors).
Represents Movie scripts, feature film, TV scripts, theatrical stage play, stage plays, radio scripts.
How to Contact Query with SASE.

CATALYST AGENCY

12400 Wilshire Blvd., Los Angeles CA 90025. (818)597-8335. Fax: (818)597-1443. E-mail: dogtownharvey@gmail.com. Website: www.catalystagency.com/.
Contact: Harvey E. Harrison.
Represents TV, movie scripts, feature film, animation, Video and New Media.
Tips "We do not accept or review query or literary material except by known referral. We seek to see compelling online video such as that at Burning Shorts. www. burningshorts.com."

⊘ CEDAR GROVE AGENCY ENTERTAINMENT

P.O. Box 1692, Issaquah WA 98027-0068. (425)837-1687. Fax: (425)391-7907. E-mail: cedargroveagency@msn.com. **Contact:** Samantha Powers. Other memberships include Cinema Seattle. Represents 7 clients. 100% of clients are new/unpublished writers. Currently handles: movie scripts 90%, TV scripts 10%.

 • Prior to becoming an agent, Ms. Taylor worked for Morgan Stanley Dean Witter.

Member Agents Amy Taylor, senior vice president of motion picture division; Samantha Powers, executive vice president of motion picture division.
Represents Movie scripts, feature film, TV movie of the week, sitcom. **Considers these script areas:** action, biography, comedy, detective, family, juvenile, mystery, romantic comedy, science, sports, thriller, western.

 • "Cedar Grove Agency Entertainment was formed in the Pacific Northwest to take advantage of the rich and diverse culture, as well as the many writers who reside there." Does not want to receive period pieces, horror writing, children's scripts dealing with illness, or scripts dealing with excessive substance abuse.

How to Contact Submit 1-page synopsis via mail with SASE or via e-mail (no attachments). No phone calls, please. Responds in 10 days to queries. Responds in 2 months to mss. Obtains most new clients through referrals, website.

Terms Agent receives 10% commission on domestic sales. Offers written contract, binding for 6-12 months; 30-day notice must be given to terminate contract.

Tips "We focus on finding that rare gem, the undiscovered, multi-talented writer, no matter where they live. Write, write, write! Find time every day to write. Network with other writers when possible, and write what you know. Learn the craft through books. Read scripts of your favorite movies. Enjoy what you write!"

⚫ THE CHARACTERS TALENT AGENCY

8 Elm St., Toronto ON M5G 1G7 Canada. (416)964-8522. Fax: (416)964-6349. E-mail: clib5@aol.com. Website: www.thecharacters.com. **Contact:** Carl Liberman. Other memberships include Signatory of WGC. Represents 1,000 clients (writers, actors, directors). 5% of clients are new/unpublished writers. Currently handles: movie scripts 50%, TV scripts 50%.

• Before becoming an agent, Mr. Liberman was an advertising executive, writer and actor.

Member Agents Brent Jordan Sherman (film/TV writers and directors); Ben Silverman (writers).

Represents Movie scripts, feature film, TV scripts, TV movie of the week, episodic drama, sitcom, animation, documentary, miniseries, soap opera, syndicated material. **Considers these script areas:** action, biography, cartoon, comedy, contemporary, detective, erotica (no porn), ethnic, family, fantasy, feminist, gay, glitz, historical, horror, juvenile, mainstream, mystery, psychic, romantic comedy, romantic drama, science, sports, teen, thriller, western.

☞ Actively seeking romantic comedy features, comedy features, family comedy features, and strong female leads in thrillers (MOW/features). Does not want to receive stage plays.

How to Contact Query with SASE. include a 1-page synopsis Accepts simultaneous submissions. Responds in 2 days to queries if by e-mail; to queries. 60 days to ms if query is accepted. Obtains most new clients through recommendations from others.

Terms Agent receives 10% commission on domestic sales. Agent receives 10% commission on foreign sales. No written contract.

Recent Sales *Ada*, by Ronalda Jones (Milagro Films); *13th Apostle*, by Paul Margolis (Stallion Films); *Drake Diamond: Exorcist for Hire*, by Arne Olsen (Montecito Pictures); *Grounded in Eire*, by Ralph Keefer (Amaze Film & TV).

Tips "To reach or get information about each individual agent, please call for an e-mail address. All agents are based in Toronto, except one in Vancouver."

◪ CIRCLE OF CONFUSION

Fax: (212)572-8304 or (212)975-7748. E-mail: queries@circleofconfusion.com. Website: www.circleofconfusion.com.
Represents Movie. **Considers these script areas:** action, fantasy, horror, science, thriller.

 ⚬ This agency specializes in comic books, video games and screenplays (science fiction, action, fantasy, thrillers, urban, horror).

How to Contact Submit query and brief synopsis via e-mail. Obtains most new clients through recommendations from others, writing contests, queries.

Terms Agent receives 10% commission on domestic sales. Agent receives 10% commission on foreign sales. Offers written contract, binding for 1 year.

Recent Sales Movie/TV MOW script(s) optioned/sold: *The Matrix,* by Wachowski Brothers (Warner Brothers); *Reign of Fire,* by Chabot/Peterka (Dreamworks); *Mr. & Mrs. Smith,* by Simon Kinberg.

Tips "We look for writing that shows a unique voice, especially one which puts a fresh spin on commercial Hollywood genres."

COLLECTIVE, THE

9100 Wilshire Blvd., 700W, Beverly Hills CA 90212. (310)288-8181. Fax: (310)888-1555. Website: www.thecollective-la.com/. Currently handles: movie scripts, TV scripts, other Music.

Member Agents Jeff Golenberg; Michael Green; Sam Maydew; Aaron Ray.

Represents Movie, TV, movie scripts, feature film.

COMMUNICATIONS AND ENTERTAINMENT, INC.

4201 N. Ocean Blvd., #303-C, Boca Raton FL 33431-5359. (561)391-9575. Fax: (561)391-7922. E-mail: jlbearde@bellsouth.net. **Contact:** James L. Bearden. Represents 10 clients. 50% of clients are new/unpublished writers. Currently handles: novels 10%, juvenile books 5%, movie scripts 40%, TV scripts 40%.

 • Prior to opening his agency, Mr. Bearden worked as a producer/director and an entertainment attorney.

Member Agents James Bearden (TV, film).

Represents Novels, juvenile, movie, TV, syndicated material. **Considers these nonfiction areas:** history, music, film. **Considers these fiction areas:** adventure, comic, fantasy, historical, mainstream, science, thriller.

How to Contact For scripts, query with SASE. For books, query with outline/proposal or send entire ms. Responds in 1 month to queries. Responds in 3 months to mss. Obtains most new clients through recommendations from others.

Terms Agent receives 10% commission on domestic sales. Agent receives 5% commission on foreign sales. Offers written contract.

Tips "Be patient."

ⓤ THE CORE GROUP TALENT AGENCY, INC.

89 Bloor St. W., Suite 300, Toronto ON M5S 1M1 Canada. (416)955-0819. Fax: (416)955-0825. E-mail: literary@coregroupta.com; info@coregroupta.com. Website: www.coregroupta.com. **Contact:** Charles Northcote, literary agent/co-owner. Other memberships include WGC. Represents 60 clients. 10% of clients are new/unpublished writers. Currently handles: movie scripts 25%, TV scripts 25%, stage plays 50%.

Represents Movie scripts, feature film, TV scripts, TV movie of the week, episodic drama, sitcom, animation, documentary, miniseries, soap opera, stage plays. **Considers these script areas:** action, biography, cartoon, comedy, contemporary, detective, erotica, ethnic, experimental, family, fantasy, feminist, gay, glitz, historical, horror, juvenile, mainstream, multicultural, mystery, psychic, regional, romantic comedy, romantic drama, sports, teen, thriller, western.

○▄ Seeks previously-produced writers with Canadian status. Does not want queries from international writers without Canadian status.

How to Contact Query with SASE. Responds in 1 week to queries.

Terms Agent receives 10% commission on domestic sales. Offers written contract, binding for 1 year; 60-day notice must be given to terminate contract.

ⓤ CREATIVE ARTISTS AGENCY

CAA, 2000 Avenue of the Stars, Los Angeles CA 90067. (424)288-2000. Fax: (424)288-2900. Website: www.caa.com/. Other offices in New York, Nashville, London, Beijing, St. Louis, Calgary, Stockholm

⊕ CREATIVE MEDIA MANAGEMENT

Ealing Studios, Ealing Green, 3b Walpole Court, London England W5 5EP United Kingdom. (44)(208)584-5363. Fax: (44)(208)566-5554. E-mail: enquiries@creativemediamanagement.com. Website: www.creativemediamanagement.com/. **Contact:** Paul Usher. Currently handles: movie scripts, TV scripts, other Radio Scripts.

• With a scriptwriter for a father and an agent and film producer for a mother, perhaps it was inevitable that Jacqui would end up in the 'business.' She produced many award-winning commercials and had her own music library company prior to becoming an agent in 1992 when she joined KCPM. She was joint-managing director when she left to start Creative Media Management.

Member Agents Writers' submissions should be made to Paul Usher.

Represents Episodic drama, movie, TV, movie scripts, feature film, sitcom, Radio.

How to Contact Query with SASE.

⊕ CREATIVE REPRESENTATION

274 Brunswick St., 2nd Floor, Fitzroy VIC 3065 Australia. E-mail: agents@ creativerep.com.au. Website: www.creativerep.com.au. P.O. Box 108
Member Agents Jacinta Waters; Helen Townshend; Katherine Dodd.
Represents Movie, TV, stage plays.
How to Contact Query with SASE.
Recent Sales Clients include Tim Robertson, Adam Richard, Paul McCarthy, Alan Hopgood, Ryan Shelton, Richard Marsland, Lech Maciewicz, Edward White.

⊕ CAMERON CRESWELL

61 Marlborough St., Surry Hills NSW 2010 Australia. E-mail: info@ cameronsmanagement.com.au. Website: www.cameronsmanagement.com.au/. Currently handles: nonfiction books, movie scripts, TV scripts, stage plays.
Member Agents Jane Cameron; Sadie Chrestman; Sue Muggleton; Anthony Blair; Sophie Hamley.
Represents Nonfiction books, novels, juvenile books, TV scripts, stage plays.
Considers these nonfiction areas: health, history, memoirs, psychology, sex, sociology, spirituality, sports, travel.
How to Contact E-mail submissions only. Check website first. Responds in 1 year to mss.
Recent Sales Clients include Craig Pearce, Don Watson, David Williamson, Bob Ellis, John Alsop, Pip Karmel.

CRITERION GROUP, INC.

4842 Sylmar Avenue, Sherman Oaks CA 91423. (818)995-1485. E-mail: info@ criterion-group.com. Website: www.criterion-group.com/. **Contact:** Susan Wright; Julie Fitzgerald. Signatory of WGA.
Represents Movie, movie scripts, feature film, theatrical stage play, stage plays.
How to Contact Query with SASE. All unsolicited mss returned unopened.
Recent Sales Clients include Charles Daniels, Proctor/Hirsch, Mark Reese, Dave Richards.

⊕ THE DENCH ARNOLD AGENCY

10 Newburgh St., London England W1F 7RN United Kingdom. 020 7437-4551. Fax: 020 7439-1355. E-mail: contact@den06harnold.com. Website: www.dencharnold. co.uk. **Contact:** Elizabeth Dench, Michelle Arnold, Matthew Dench, Fiona Grant, Louise Jordan.
Represents Nonfiction books, movie, TV.
How to Contact Query with SASE. Submit author bio, Sample of work for scripts. SAE.

Recent Sales Other clients include Joe Ainsworth, Jan Bauer, Maurice Bessman, Karen Brown, Peter Chelsom & Adrian Dunbar, Greg Cruttwell, Eric Deacon, Matthew Faulk & Mark Skeet, Lucy Flannery, Ellis Freeman, Ted Gannon, Robert Golden, Henrique Goldman, Steve Gough, Jeff Gross, Robert Hammond, Malcolm Kohll, Anna Kythreotis, Sarah Lambert, Paul Makin, Kevin Malony, Grant Morris, Matthew Newman, Omid Nooshin, Phil O'Shea, Dave Simpson, Roger Tucker, Alan Whiting, Kate Wood, Heather Dixon, Nick Stevens, Luke Watson, Anthony Alleyne, Peter Briggs, Jim Davies, Tiffany Freisberg, Mark Anthony Galluzzo, Liam Gavin, Jo Ho, Julian Kemp, Seth Linder, Dominic MacDonald, Steve McAteer, Bob McCabe & Rob Churchill, Abigail Abban-Mensah, Katie Newman, Junior Rhone.

DIVERSE TALENT GROUP

9911 Pico Blvd.,, Suite 350W, Los Angeles CA 90035. (310)201-6565. Fax: (310)201-6572. Website: www.diversetalentgroup.com/.
- ☞ This selective agency specializes in talent and literary representation. Query with a referral.

⊕ DRAMA, AGENCE

24, rue Feydeau, Paris 75002 France. E-mail: dramaparis@dramaparis.com. Website: www.dramaparis.com.
Member Agents Suzanne Sarquier (dramaparis@dramaparis.com); Maxime Kottmann, Assistant (m.kottmann@dramaparis.com); Caroline Babuty (c.babuty@dramaparis.com); Elisabeth Sémon(e.semon@dramaparis.com).
Represents Theatrical stage play, stage plays.
Terms Charges administrative fee.

▣ DRAMATIC PUBLISHING

311 Washington St., Woodstock IL 60098. (815)338-7170 (international). Fax: (815)338-8981. E-mail: submissionseditor@dpcplays.com. Website: www. dramaticpublishing.com. **Contact:** Linda Habjan. Currently handles: textbooks 2%, stage plays 98%.
Represents stage plays.
- ☞ This agency specializes in a full range of stage plays, musicals, adaptations and instructional books about theater.

How to Contact Query with SASE. Submit complete ms, SASE. Reports in 4-6 months to mss.

DRAMATISTS PLAY SERVICE, INC.

440 Park Avenue South, New York New York 10016. (212)683-8960. Fax: (212)213-1539. E-mail: postmaster@dramatists.com. Website: www.dramatists.com.
Member Agents Stephen Sultan, President (sultan@dramatists.com); Bobbi Masters, Assistant (masters@dramatists.com); Tamra Feifer, Director of Operations (feifer@dramatists.com).
Represents Stage plays.
How to Contact Query with SASE.
Recent Sales Clients represented include *August: Osage County* by Tracy Letts; *Rabbit Hole* by David Lindsay-Abaire; *Doubt, A Parable* by John Patrick Shanley; *I Am My Own Wife*, by Doug Wright.

⊕ BRYAN DREW, LTD

Quadrant House, 80-82 Regent St., London England W1B 5AU United Kingdom. (44)(207)437-2293. Fax: (44)(207)437-0561. E-mail: bryan@bryandrewltd.com. Website: www.bryandrewltd.com. **Contact:** Literary Manager: Bryan Drew.
Represents Nonfiction books, movie, TV, movie scripts, feature film. **Considers these nonfiction areas:** biography.
How to Contact Query with SASE. Submit synopsis, 2-3 sample chapters, query letter with SAE/IRC.

ENERGY ENTERTAINMENT

999 N. Doheny Dr., #711, Los Angeles CA 90069. (310)274-3440. Fax: info@ energyentertainment.net. Website: www.energyentertainment.net/.
- Prior to their current positions, Brooklyn Weaver worked at Endeavor, Adam Marshall worked for Brillstein-Grey Entertainment, and Jake Wagner was in series production at MTV.
- ⚟ "Energy has two divisions: a management division comprised of writers and actors - and a production division. This agency specializes in discovering new edgy screenwriters."

How to Contact All unsolicited mss returned unopened. Query only!
Recent Sales *The Low Dweller*, by Brad Ingelsby.

☑ THE E S AGENCY

6612 Pacheco Way, Citrus Heights CA 95610. (916)723-2794. Fax: (916)723-2796.
Contact: Ed Silver, president. Signatory of WGA. Represents 50-75 clients. 70% of clients are new/unpublished writers. Currently handles: nonfiction books 50%, novels 25%, movie scripts 25%.

- Prior to becoming an agent, Mr. Silver was an entertainment business manager.

Represents nonfiction books, novels, movie scripts, feature film, TV movie of the week. **Considers these fiction areas:** adventure, detective, erotica, experimental, historical, humor, literary, mainstream, mystery, thriller, young. **Considers these script areas:** action, comedy, contemporary, detective, erotica, ethnic, experimental, family, mainstream, mystery, romantic comedy, romantic drama, sports, thriller.

⟐ This agency specializes in theatrical screenplays, MOW, and miniseries. Actively seeking anything unique and original. Does not want to receive horror, sci-fi, mob, or Vietnam stories.

How to Contact Query with SASE. Send a one-page pitch. If the pitch is liked, they will ask for a beat sheet and then coverage before requesting the full script. Accepts simultaneous submissions. Obtains most new clients through recommendations from others, Queries from WGA agency list.

Terms Agent receives 15% commission on domestic sales. Agent receives 20% commission on foreign sales. Agent receives 10% commission on film sales. Offers written contract; 30-day notice must be given to terminate contract.

◪ EVATOPIA, INC.

8447 Wilshire Blvd., Ste. 401, Beverly Hills CA 90211. E-mail: submissions@ evatopia.com. Website: www.evatopia.com. **Contact.** Margery Walshaw. **Represents** 15 clients. 85% of clients are new/unpublished writers. Currently handles: movie scripts 100%.

- Prior to becoming an agent, Ms. Walshaw was a writer and publicist for the entertainment industry.

Member Agents Mary Kay (story development); Stacy Glenn (story development); Jamie Davis (story assistant); Jill Jones (story editor).

Represents Movie. **Considers these script areas:** action, biography, cartoon, comedy, contemporary, detective, ethnic, family, fantasy, historical, horror, juvenile, mainstream, mystery, psychic, romantic comedy, romantic drama, science, sports, teen, thriller.

⟐ "We specialize in promoting and developing the careers of first-time screenwriters. All of our staff members have strong writing and entertainment backgrounds, making us sympathetic to the needs of our clients." Actively seeking dedicated and hard-working writers.

How to Contact Submit via online submission form. Accepts simultaneous submissions. Responds in 3 weeks to queries. Responds in 4 weeks to mss. Obtains most new clients through recommendations from others, solicitations.

Terms Agent receives 15% commission on domestic sales. Agent receives 15% commission on foreign sales. Offers written contract, binding for up to 2 years;

Agents & Managers

30-day notice must be given to terminate contract.

Tips "Remember that you only have one chance to make that important first impression. Make your loglines original and your synopses concise. The secret to a screenwriter's success is creating an original story and telling it in a manner that we haven't heard before."

LAURENCE FITCH, LTD.

Mezzanine, Quadrant House, 80-82 Regent St., London England W1B 5AU United Kingdom. (44)(207)734-9911. Fax: (44)(207)734-0044. E-mail: information@ laurencefitch.com. Website: www.laurencefitch.com. **Contact:** Brendan Davis, director.

Represents Considers these script areas: juvenile, mainstream.

How to Contact Submit proposal package, synopsis, query letter with SAE, sample chapters & 3 sample scenes/screens.

Recent Sales Clients include Dave Freeman, Ray Cooney, Walter Greenwood, Ronald Gow, Edward Taylor, John Graham.

⊕ JILL FOSTER, LTD

9 Barb Mews, Brook Green, London England W6 7PA United Kingdom. (44) (207)602-1263. Fax: (44)(207)602-9336. E-mail: agents@jflagency.com. Website: www.jflagency.com. **Contact:** Jill Foster, Alison Finch, Simon Williamson, Dominic Lord, Gary Wild.

Represents Movie, TV.

   ⊶ No books, poetry or short stories considered.

How to Contact Include query letter with submission.

FOURSIGHT ENTERTAINMENT

8840 Wilshire Blvd., 2nd Floor, Beverly Hills CA 90211. (310)358-3150. E-mail: info@foursight.com. Website: www.foursight.com/.

Member Agents Jeremy Bell; George Heller; Michael Lasker; Brent Lilley.

   ⊶ Foursight Entertainment is a management/production company comprised of writers, directors, and actors with a concentration on young professionals and new voices. Based in Los Angeles, Foursight represents filmmakers, properties, and talent in motion pictures and television.

How to Contact Submit queries by e-mail.

◉ SAMUEL FRENCH, INC.

45 W. 25th St., New York NY 10010-2751. (212)206-8990. Fax: (212)206-1429. E-mail: info@samuelfrench.com. Website: www.samuelfrench.com. **Contact:** Lawrence Harbison, senior editor. Member of AAR.

Member Agents Leon Embry.

Represents Theatrical stage play, musicals. **Considers these script areas:** comedy, contemporary, detective, ethnic, fantasy, horror, mystery, thriller.

   ⚬ This agency specializes in publishing plays which it also licenses for production.

How to Contact Query via online form. Does not accept unsolicited submissions. Accepts simultaneous submissions. Responds immediately to queries. Responds in 2-8 months to mss.

Terms Agent receives variable commission on domestic sales.

Recent Sales This agency prefers not to share information on specific sales.

◉ THE GAGE GROUP

14724 Ventura Blvd., Suite 505, Sherman Oaks CA 91403. (818)905-3800. Fax: (818)905-3322. Signatory of WGA. Other memberships include DGA.

Member Agents Jonathan Westover (feature, television); Joshua Orenstein (TV).

Represents Movie, TV, movie scripts, feature film, theatrical stage play.

   ⚬ Considers all script subject areas.

How to Contact Snail mail queries preferred. Accepts simultaneous submissions. Responds in 1 month to queries. Responds in 1 month to mss.

Terms Agent receives 10% commission on domestic sales. Agent receives 10% commission on foreign sales. This agency charges clients for photocopying.

Recent Sales This agency prefers not to share information on specific sales.

GARY-PAUL AGENCY, THE

1549 Main St., Stratford CT 06615. (203)345-6167. E-mail: info@thegarypaulagency. com. Website: www.thegarypaulagency.com/. Signatory of WGA.

How to Contact Query with SASE.

◉ NOEL GAY

19, Denmark St., London England WC2H 8NA United Kingdom. (44)(207)836-3941. E-mail: info@noelgay.com. Website: www.noelgay.com.

Member Agents Alex Armitage, CEO; Nick Ranceford-Hadley, Managing Director; Jane Compton, Assistant Agent; Jessica Williamson, Assistant Agent; Claire King, Agent.

➠ Noel Gay has a long established reputation as a leading theatrical management company in the West End. It managed the hugely successful *Me And My Girl* at the Adelphi Theatre and supervised more than a dozen other productions of the show around the world.

How to Contact Query with SASE.

⊕ ERIC GLASS, LTD

25 Ladbroke Crescent, London England W11 1PS United Kingdom. (44)(207)229-9500. Fax: (44)(207)229-6220. E-mail: eglassltd@aol.com. **Contact:** Janet Glass. **Represents** Nonfiction books, movie, TV, radio scripts.

➠ Does not want to receive short stories, poetry, or children's titles.

How to Contact Query letter with SAE. Send the entire ms, if requested.
Recent Sales Clients include Herbert Appleman, Henry Fleet and Alan Melville.

⊘ GRAHAM AGENCY

311 W. 43rd St., New York NY 10036. Fax: (212)489-7731. E-mail: grahamacynyc@aol.com. **Contact:** Earl Graham. Represents 40 clients. 30% of clients are new/unpublished writers.
Represents theatrical stage play, musicals.

➠ This agency specializes in playwrights. "We're interested in commercial material of quality. Does not want to receive one-acts or material for children."

How to Contact Query with SASE. Responds in 3 months to queries. Responds in 6 weeks to mss. "We are not seeking new clients at this time." Obtains most new clients through recommendations from others, solicitations.
Terms Agent receives 10% commission on film sales.
Recent Sales This agency prefers not to share information on specific sales.
Tips "Write a concise, intelligent letter giving the gist of what you are offering."

GRUENBERG FILM

Blankenburger Chaussee 84, Berlin D-13125 Germany. E-mail: info@gruenbergfilm.de. Website: www.gruenbergfilm.com/.
Represents Movie, movie scripts, feature film. **Considers these script areas:** action, adventure, horror, mystery, action comedy, thriller.

➠ "While concentrating on producing films, the agency manages a few writers and has sold scripts to production companies." Actively seeking script and project synopses

How to Contact Query with SASE. Send loglines and synopses first.

Recent Sales Movie/TV MOW script(s) optioned/sold: In 2006 the agency sold *A Girl Named Freedom*, written by Ed Dawson, to an Irish production company; negotiations for the option to Castle Stalker, renewed in December 2007.

🌐 THE ROD HALL AGENCY

6th Floor, Fairgate House, 78 New Oxford St., London England WC1A 1HB United Kingdom. (44)(207)079-7987. Fax: (44)(845)638-4094. E-mail: office@ rodhallagency.com. Website: www.rodhallagency.com. **Contact:** Company Director: Charlotte Mann; Tanya Tillet (Submissions, Amateur & Play Leasings, Foreign Rights, General Inquiries); Emily Hayward (Film, TV & Theatre).

- Charlotte Mann has worked extensively in theatre, while Tanya Tillet's experience lies in film & TV development & production. Emily Hayward studied drama before working as an agent at both PFD and Sheil Land Associates.
- ⚬ Film, theatre, and television. No writing partnerships or soap writers considered. Does not represent print authors except for existing clients.

How to Contact Currently not accepting submissions. Submit outline, author bio, CV. Send query with SAE.

Recent Sales Clients include Hassan Abdulrazzak, Lydia Adetunji, Yousaf Ali Khan, Samina Baig, Simon Beaufoy, Simon Bennett, Alecky Blythe, Oliver Bosman, Harriet Braun, Jeremy Brock, Sean Buckley, Jane Carter Woodrow, Suzette Coon, Nick Cohen, Marco Crivellari, Loughlin Deegan, David Dipper, Clare Duffy, Matthew Dunster, Janet Eisenstein, Ben Ellis, Jane Elson, Susan Everett, Tom Farrelly, Robert Farquhar, Brian Fillis, Josh Freedman Berthoud, and more.

🌐 DAVID HIGHAM ASSOCIATES LTD

5-8 Lower John St., Golden Square, London England W1F 9HA United Kingdom. (44)(207)434-5900. Fax: (44)(207)437-1072. E-mail: dha@davidhigham.co.uk. Website: www.davidhigham.co.uk. **Contact:** Anthony Goff, Alice Williams, Bruce Hunter, Lizzy Kremer, Veronique Baxter (Fiction, Nonfiction, Children); Caroline Walsh (Fiction, Children, Illustrators); Georgia Glover, Georgia Ruffhead, Nicky Lund (Script Writing & Drama); Ania Corless (Translation).

Represents Nonfiction books, movie, TV, movie scripts, feature film. **Considers these fiction areas:** juvenile, adult.

- ⚬ Actively seeking good commercial and literary fiction, and general nonfiction.

How to Contact Submit outline, synopsis, 3 sample chapters, author bio. Send query letter with SAE. No e-mail submissions.

Recent Sales Clients include Chinua Achebe, J.M. Coetzee, Roald Dahl, Anne

Fine, F. Scott Fitzgerald, James Herbert, John le Carre, Penelope Lively, Mervyn Peake, Alice Sebold, Gertrude Stein and Alice Walker.

◎ HOHMAN MAYBANK LIEB

9229 Sunset Blvd., Suite 700, Los Angeles CA 90069. (310)274-4600. Fax: (310)274-4741. E-mail: info@hmllit.com. Website: www.hmllit.com/.
Member Agents Bob Hohman; Bayard Maybank; Devra Lieb; Trish Connery; Andy Tunnicliffe.
Represents Movie, TV, movie scripts, feature film.
○┅ This agency specializes in representing screenwriters.
How to Contact Send queries only with a strong referral.
Tips "Query with a referral."

⊕ ◎ AMANDA HOWARD ASSOCIATES LTD.

AHA, 21 Berwick Street, London W1F 0PZ United Kingdom. (44)(207)287-9277. Fax: (44)(207)287-7785. E-mail: mail@amandahowardassociates.co.uk. Website: www.amandahowardassociates.co.uk.
Member Agents Amanda Fitzalan Howard; Kate Haldane; Mark Price; Kirsten Wright; Darren Rugg; Chloe Brayfield.
○┅ Popular non-fiction, humour, manuals, and memoir. "The agency will not take on a new client who resides outside the UK and Ireland. It does not represent poetry."
How to Contact Submit outline, synopsis, author bio, SASE. Do not sent full manuscript. Recommendation from known professional preferred.
Recent Sales Clients include Niall Ashdown, Julie Balloo, Michael Begley, Simon Blackwell, Andrew Collins, Trevor Dann, Susie Donkin, Rufus Jones, Stuart Maconie, Phelim McDermott, Charlotte McDougall, Jim Miller, Iain Pattinson, David Quantick, Carrie Quinlan, Jan Ravens, Tom Robinson, Catherine Shepherd, Adam Smith, Justin Spear, Adam Tandy, John Tiffney, Jonny Trunk.

HUDSON AGENCY

3 Travis Lane, Montrose NY 10548. (914)739-4668. Website: www.hudsonagency.net. Signatory of WGA. Represents 20 clients. Currently handles: movie scripts 100%.
Member Agents Sue Giordano (Partner/Producer); Pat Giordano (Partner/Producer); Kelly Olenik (Creative).
Represents Movie scripts, feature film, TV movie, animation, miniseries. **Considers these script areas:** action, cartoon, comedy, contemporary, detective, family, fantasy, juvenile, mystery, romantic comedy, romantic drama, teen, western.
○┅ "Originally launched as a motion picture agency, we quickly expanded

into television and developed a strong talent base of children's television writers. Feeling a responsibility to influence the world in a beneficial way through entertainment, and with over a thousand contacts in the business, we have earned the reputation of being hard working, pleasantly persistent agents who follow through."

How to Contact Query with SASE. Accepts simultaneous submissions. Obtains most new clients through recommendations from others.

Terms Agent receives 10% commission on domestic sales. Agent receives 10% commission on foreign sales.

INNOVATIVE ARTISTS

1505 Tenth Street, Santa Monica CA 90401. (310)656-0400. E-mail: literary@iala. com. Website: www.innovativeartists.com. **Contact:** Scott Harris. Signatory of WGA.

Represents Movie, movie scripts, feature film. **Considers these script areas:** romantic comedy, thriller.

⚬⌐ Innovative Artists does not accept unsolicited material.

How to Contact Snail mail queries preferred.

🌐 INTERNATIONAL ARTISTES LTD.

4th Floor, Holborn Hall, 193-197 High Holborn, London England WC1V 7BD United Kingdom. (44)(207)025-0600. Fax: (44)(207)404-9865. E-mail: reception@ internationalartistes.com. Website: http://intart.co.uk/. Currently handles: stage plays.

Member Agents Malcolm Browning; Michael Cronin; Phil Dale, assisted by Lucy Saunders; Emma Engers; Laurie Mansfield, assisted by Keely Gilbert; Michèle Milburn, assisted by Tara Lynch; Robert Voice, assisted by Nicola Hobbs; Mandy Ward, assisted by Kirsty Lloyd-Jones.

Represents Movie, TV, movie scripts, feature film, theatrical stage play, stage plays.

How to Contact Query with SASE.

INTERNATIONAL ARTS ENTERTAINMENT

8899 Beverly Blvd., Suite 800, Los Angeles CA 90048. (310)550-6760. Fax: (310)550-8839. Website: www.internationalartsentertainment.com/. **Contact:** Alan Greenspan.

KAPLAN STAHLER GUMER BRAUN AGENCY

KSGB Agency, 8383 Wilshire Blvd., Suite 923, Beverly Hills CA 90211. (323)653-4483. Fax: (323)653-4506. E-mail: info@kaplanstahler.com. Website: www.ksgbagency.com/.

- Mitchell Kaplan got his start in the William Morris Agency mailroom along with agency co-founder Elliot Stahler.

Member Agents Mitchell Kaplan; Elliot Stahler; Robert Gumer; Alan Braun; Bradley Stewart Glenn; Gordon Hvolka; Sean Zeid; Dino Carlaftes; Zac Simmons.

Represents Movie, TV, movie scripts, feature film, reality TV.

How to Contact Query with SASE.

⊕ MICHELLE KASS ASSOCIATES

85 Charing Cross Road, London England WC2H 0AA United Kingdom. (44)(207)439-1624. Fax: (44)(207)734-3394. E-mail: office@michellekass.co.uk.

Contact: Michelle Kass.

Represents Movie.

How to Contact All unsolicited mss returned unopened. Contact by phone before submitting mss.

⊘ CHARLENE KAY AGENCY

901 Beaudry St., Suite 6, St.Jean/Richelieu QC J3A 1C6 Canada. E-mail: lmchakay@hotmail.com. **Contact:** Louise Meyers, director of development. Signatory of WGA. Other memberships include BMI. 50% of clients are new/unpublished writers. Currently handles: movie scripts 50%, TV scripts 50%.

- Prior to opening her agency, Ms. Kay was a screenwriter.

Member Agents Louise Meyers.

Represents Episodic drama, TV, movie scripts, feature film, TV movie of the week, sitcom. **Considers these script areas:** action, biography, family, fantasy, psychic, romantic comedy, romantic drama, science.

- ⊶ "This agency specializes in teleplays and screenplays." "We seek stories that are out of the ordinary, something we don't see too often. A well-written and well-constructed script is important." Does not want to receive thrillers, barbaric/erotic films, novels, books or mss.

How to Contact Query with SASE. Submit outline/proposal only. Unsolicited scripts will not be read. Does not return materials. Rejected mss are shredded. Responds in 6 weeks to queries, approximately 10 weeks to mss.

Terms Agent receives 10% commission on domestic sales. Agent receives 10% commission on foreign sales. Offers written contract, binding for 1 year.

Recent Sales Movies in post production: *Sheriff of Contention*; in pre-production: *Cass*. Two other working titles movies and TV series in the works.

Tips "This agency is on the WGA lists, and query letters arrive by the dozens every week. As our present clients understand, success comes with patience. A sale rarely happens overnight, especially when you are dealing with totally unknown writers. We are not impressed by the credentials of a writer, amateur or professional, or by his/her pitching techniques, but by his/her story ideas and ability to build a well-crafted script."

⊕ KUBLER AUCKLAND MANAGEMENT
KAM, PO Box 1064, Double Bay NSW 1360 Australia. E-mail: Sydney@ KublerAuckland.com. Website: www.kublerauckland.com. Alternate address: PO Box 1062, Milton, Qld 4064
Represents Theatrical stage play, stage plays. **Considers these fiction areas:** plays.
o↝ The agency represents playwrights throughout Australia.
How to Contact Do not send queries from North America.
Recent Sales Clients include Buck Buckingham, Adam Couper, Stephen Davis, Philip Dean, Rowan Ellis Michael, Margery Forde, Michael Futcher, Helen Howard, Elise Greig, Marjean Holden, Sally McKenzie, Danny Murphy, Matthew Ryan, Kien Shorey, Sven Swenson.

⊘ THE CANDACE LAKE AGENCY
10677 Somma Way, Los Angeles CA 90077. (310)476-3883. Fax: (310)476-0203. E-mail: candace@lakeliterary.com. **Contact:** Candace Lake. Other memberships include Signatory of WGA, DGA. 50% of clients are new/unpublished writers. Currently handles: movie scripts 80%, TV scripts 20%.
Member Agents Candace Lake, president; Ryan Lewis, agent.
Represents Novels, episodic drama, movie scripts, feature film, TV movie of the week. **Considers these script areas:** action, comedy, contemporary, detective, fantasy, historical, horror, mainstream, mystery, psychic, romantic comedy, romantic drama, science, teen, thriller.
o↝ This agency specializes in screenplay and teleplay writers.
How to Contact *No unsolicited material.* Obtains most new clients through recommendations from others.
Terms Agent receives 10% commission on domestic sales. Agent receives 10% commission on foreign sales. Offers written contract, binding for 2 years.

◖ THE LANTZ OFFICE
247 West 87th Street, 24G, New York NY 10024. (646)546-5104. Fax: (212)787-0723. E-mail: rlantz@lantzoffice.com; tlo@lantzoffice.com. Website: www.lantzoffice.com. **Contact:** Robert Lantz. Member of AAR.
Represents Movie, movie scripts, feature film, theatrical stage play.

How to Contact *The Lantz Office LLC is not seeking and will not accept new clients.* Obtains most new clients through recommendations from others.

Terms Agent receives 10% commission on domestic sales. Agent receives 10% commission on foreign sales.

Tips "This is a very selective agency."

⊕ MIKE LEIGH ASSOCIATES

37 Marylebone Lane, London England W1U 2NW United Kingdom. Website: www.mikeleighassoc.com.

Represents TV, TV movie, radio scripts, commercials.

How to Contact Query through online form.

Recent Sales Clients include Neil Cole, Iain Coyle, Dominik Diamond, Chas Early, Paolo Hewitt, Dominic Holland, Marianne Levy, Neil Sean, Paul Simper, Dave Skinner, Richard Thomson, Christos Tolera, Phil Whelans.

JACK LENNY ASSOCIATES

9454 Wilshire Blvd., Suite 600, Beverly Hills CA 90212. (310)271-2174. Signatory of WGA.

Represents Movie scripts, feature film.

How to Contact This is a very selective representative company that should only be queried through a referral, or if your work was solicited.

Terms Agent receives 10% commission on domestic sales. Agent receives 10% commission on foreign sales.

MICHAEL LEWIS & ASSOCIATES

2506 Fifth St., Suite 100, Santa Monica CA 90405. (310)399-1999. E-mail: lewislitagency@gmail.com. Signatory of WGA.

Represents TV scripts, movie scripts, feature film.

THE MANAGEMENT CO.

1337 Ocean Ave., Suite F, Santa Monica CA 90401. **Contact:** Tom Klassen. Represents 18 clients.

- Prior to starting his agency, Mr. Klassen was an agent with International Creative Management (ICM).

Member Agents Tom Klassen; Steve Gamber; Helene Taber; Paul Davis.

Represents TV, movie scripts, feature film, (scripts), Internet scripts, computer game scripts.

- ⊶ Actively seeking studio-quality, action-drama scripts and really good comedies. Does not want to receive horror scripts.

How to Contact Submit e-queries only with the e-mail subject line saying Query: (Title) Responds in 2-3 weeks to queries. Obtains most new clients through recommendations from others, conferences.

Terms Agent receives 10% commission on domestic sales. Agent receives 10% commission on foreign sales. Offers written contract, binding for 2 years.

Recent Sales Sold 14 scripts in the past year.

Writers Conferences Sundance Film Festival; film festivals in New York, Telluride, Atlanta, Chicago, Austin, Minnesota.

Tips "We only accept e-mail queries. Send only what is requested. If you have a 1-2 page synopsis, say so and we may request it, but do not send it with the initial query. We only respond if interested. Be sure to send your phone number(s) as we generally call if interested. We rarely take on non-referred material, but have done very well with those we have taken on."

⊕ ANDREW MANN, LTD

1 Old Compton St., London England W1D 5JA United Kingdom. (44)(207)734-4751. Fax: (44)(207)287-9264. E-mail: louise@manuscript.co.uk. Website: www.andrewmann.co.uk. **Contact:** Louise Burns.

Represents Nonfiction books, movie, TV, movie scripts, feature film, radio plays. **Considers these fiction areas:** juvenile, young adult.

⊶ No poetry considered.

How to Contact Submit 1-page synopsis, first 50 pages double-spaced, SAE. Prefers hard copy submissions, but will review a brief synopsis by e-mail. No attachments.

⊕ ◲ MARJACQ SCRIPTS, LTD

34 Devonshire Place, London England W1G 6JW United Kingdom. (44)(207)935-9499. Fax: (44)(207)935-9115. E-mail: philip@marjacq.com; luke@marjacq.com. Website: www.marjacq.com. **Contact:** Philip Patterson (literary); Luke Speed (film). Represents 80 clients. 40% of clients are new/unpublished writers. Currently handles: nonfiction books 10%, novels 40%, juvenile books 5%, movie scripts 20%, TV scripts 25%.

• Prior to becoming an agent, Mr. Patterson was a film, TV and theatre agent at Curtis Brown and sold rights at HarperCollins; Mr. Speed worked in film production with Civilian Content and worked at Saatchi and Saatchi.

Member Agents Philip Patterson, literary agent; Luke Speed, film/TV agent.

⊶ "We are a young and vibrant agency always looking for clients. We handle all rights—print publishing, film, TV, radio, translation and intellectual property." Actively seeking quality fiction, nonfiction, children's books and young adult books. Does not want to receive plays, poetry or short stories.

How to Contact Submit outline, synopsis, 3 sample chapters, bio, covering letter, SASE. .Do not bother with fancy bindings and folders. Keep synopses, bio and covering letter short. Accepts simultaneous submissions. Responds in 3 days to queries. Responds in 4-6 weeks to mss. Obtains most new clients through recommendations from others, solicitations, conferences.

Terms Agent receives 10% commission on domestic sales. Agent receives 20% commission on foreign sales. Offers written contract. Charges for bank fees for money transfers.

Recent Sales *Second Time Round*, by Sophie King (Hodder & Stoughton); 3-book deal for Stuart McBride (HarperCollins UK); 3-book deal for Catrin Collier (Orion Books); 2-book deal for Jack Sheffield (Transworld); 2-book deal for John Connor (Orion Books). Other clients include Katerine John, Rosie Goodwin, R.D. Wingfield, Christopher Goffard, Guilio Leont, Ben Pastor, James Follett, George Markstein, Richard Lambert, Michael Taylor, Pat Mills, Graham Oakley, Richard Craze, Ros Jay, Richard Asplin, Stewart Hennessey, Claes Johansen, David Clayton.

Tips "Keep trying! If one agent rejects you, that is his/her opinion. Perseverance and self-belief are important. Listening to constructive criticism is good, but be warned, few agents will give you advice. We just don't have the time. Be aware of what is being published. If you show awareness of what others writers are doing in your field/genre, you might be able to see how your book fits in and why an editor/agent might be interested in taking it on. Take care with your submissions. Research the agency and pay attention to presentation. Join writers groups. Sharing your work is a good way to get constructive criticism. If you know anyone in the industry, use your contacts. A personal recommendation will get more notice than cold calling."

⊘ THE MARTON AGENCY, INC.

One Union Square W., Suite 815, New York NY 10003-3303. Fax: (212)691-9061. E-mail: info@martonagency.com. Website: www.martonagency.com. **Contact:** Tonda Marton. Member of AAR.

Member Agents Tonda Marton; Anne Reingold.

  ⟜ This agency specializes in foreign-language licensing.

⊕ MBA LITERARY AGENTS, LTD

62 Grafton Way, London England W1T 5DW United Kingdom. (44)(207)387-2076. Fax: (44)(207)387-2042. Website: www.mbalit.co.uk. **Contact:** Managing Dir. & Lit. Agent: Diana Tyler; Dir.: John Richard Parker (Fiction/Nonfiction, Science Fiction & Fantasy); Dir.: Meg Davis (Scriptwriters/Authors all genres); Dir.: Laura Longrigg (Fiction/Nonfiction); David Riding & Jean Kitson (Film, TV, Theatre, Radio Scripts).

Represents Movie, broadcast scripts. **Considers these nonfiction areas:** biography, history, memoirs, popular culture, self help, travel. **Considers these fiction areas:** fantasy, literary, science, Commercial.

How to Contact Submit proposal package, 3 sample chapters, Query letter, SAE.

Recent Sales *The Tenderness of Wolves*, by Stef Penney; *Warprize,* by Elizabeth Vaughan; *Hideous Absinthe*, by Jad Adams; *A Fete Worse than Death*, by Iain Aitch. Other clients include Robert Jones, Nick Angel, Dr. Mark Atkinson, Anila Baig, Rob Bailey, Ed Hurst, Christopher Hurst, Christopher Bird, Vivienne Bolton, Audrey & Sophie Boss, Martin Buckley, Debbie Cash, Vic Darkwood, Sarah Ash, Michael Cobley, Murray Davis, Alan Dunn & Stef Penney.

◪ THE STUART M. MILLER CO.

11684 Ventura Blvd., #225, Studio City CA 91604-2699. (818)506-6067. Fax: (818)506-4079. E-mail: smmco@aol.com. **Contact:** Stuart Miller. Other memberships include Signatory of WGA, DGA. Currently handles: movie scripts 50%, books 50%.

Represents Nonfiction books, novels, movie. **Considers these nonfiction areas:** biography, computers, current affairs, government, health, history, how to, memoirs, military, self help, true crime. **Considers these fiction areas:** adventure, detective, historical, literary, mainstream, mystery, science, sports, thriller. **Considers these script areas:** action, biography, cartoon, comedy, contemporary, detective, family, historical, mainstream, multimedia, mystery, romantic comedy, romantic drama, science, sports, teen, thriller.

How to Contact For screenplays, query via e-mail, narrative outline (2-3 pages). For books, e-mail narrative outline (5-10 pages). Accepts simultaneous submissions. "If requests full screenplay or mss, requires reasonable exclusivity period." Responds in 5 days to queries, 4-6 weeks to screenplays and mss.

Terms Offers written contract, binding for 2 years. Agent receives 10% commission on screenplay and screenwriting deals; 15% commission on sales to publishers, motion picture/TV rights sales for books and other non-screenplay literary properties.

Recent Sales This agency prefers not to share information on specific sales.

Tips "Always include an e-mail address or dedicated (meaning, not on the same line as your telephone) fax number with query letters. Agents are incredibly busy, make it easy to respond."

MKS & ASSOCIATES

8675 W. Washington Blvd., Suite 203, Culver City CA 90232. (310)838-1200. Fax: (310)838-1245. Website: www.mksagency.com/.

◉ MONTEIRO ROSE DRAVIS AGENCY, INC.

4370 Tujunga Ave., Suite 145, Studio City CA 91604. (818)501-1177. Fax: (818)501-1194. E-mail: monrose@monteiro-rose.com. Website: www.monteiro-rose.com. **Contact:** Candy Monteiro. Signatory of WGA. Represents 50 clients. Currently handles: movie scripts 40%, TV scripts 20%, other 40% animation.

Member Agents Candace Monteiro; Fredda Rose; Milissa Brockish; Jason Dravis.

Represents Episodic drama, movie scripts, feature film, TV movie of the week, animation. **Considers these script areas:** action, cartoon, comedy, contemporary, detective, ethnic, family, historical, juvenile, mainstream, mystery, psychic, romantic comedy, romantic drama, science, teen, thriller.

> ⚷ "The Monteiro Rose Agency represents live action and animation writers for children's television, features, home video, and interactive markets, and has done so for more than 15 years. We invite you to contact us and discuss your needs. We would be happy to work with you to select the best scriptwriters for your projects from our multi-talented, award-winning list of clients."

How to Contact Query with SASE. Responds in 1 week to queries. Responds in 2 months to mss. Obtains most new clients through recommendations from others, solicitations.

Terms Agent receives 10% commission on domestic sales. Offers written contract, binding for 2 years; 3-month notice must be given to terminate contract. Charges for photocopying.

Recent Sales This agency prefers not to share information on specific sales.

Tips "We prefer to receive inquiries by e-mail, although snail mail is OK with a SASE. We do not return manuscripts. We suggest that all feature manuscripts be no longer than 120 pages."

⊕ WILLIAM MORRIS AGENCY (UK), LTD

Centrepoint Tower, 103 Oxford St., London England WC1A 1DD United Kingdom. (44)(207)534-6800. Fax: (44)(207)534-6900. Website: www.wma.com. **Contact:** CEO: Jim Wiatt; Chairman: Norman Brokaw.

Represents Nonfiction books, novels, movie, TV.

How to Contact Query with SASE. Submit synopsis, up to 50 sample pages.

NATURAL TALENT, INC.

3331 Ocean Park Blvd., Suite 203, Santa Monica CA 90405. (310)450-4945. E-mail: info@naturaltalentinc.com. Website: http://naturaltalentinc.com/. **Contact:** Will Swift. Signatory of WGA.

Represents Animation, comics, video games. **Considers these script areas:** cartoon.

☞ Specializing in the consultation and representation of creative talent and intellectual properties in the converging markets of animation, comics, and video games.

◎ NIAD MANAGEMENT

15030 Ventura Blvd., Bldg. 19 #860, Sherman Oaks CA 91403. (818)774-0051. Fax: (818)774-1740. E-mail: queries@niadmanagement.com. Website: www. niadmanagement.com. Represents 20 clients. Currently handles: novels 1%, movie scripts 99%.

Represents Movie, movie scripts, feature film, TV movie, miniseries, stage plays. **Considers these nonfiction areas:** biography. **Considers these fiction areas:** psychic, adventure, detective, family, literary, mainstream, multicultural, mystery, romance, thriller. **Considers these script areas:** action, biography, comedy, contemporary, detective, ethnic, family, historical, horror, mainstream, multicultural, mystery, psychic, romantic comedy, romantic drama, sports, teen, thriller.

How to Contact Query with SASE. Responds to queries only if interested, Accepts simultaneous submissions. Responds in 1 week to queries. Responds in 3 months to mss. Obtains most new clients through recommendations from others.

Terms Offers written contract, binding for 1 year; 30-day notice must be given to terminate contract. Agent receives 15% commission on all gross monies received.

◎ OMNIQUEST ENTERTAINMENT

1416 N. La Brae Ave., Hollywood CA 90028. Fax: (303)802-1633. E-mail: info@ omniquestmedia.com. Website: www.omniquestmedia.com. **Contact:** Michael Kaliski. Currently handles: novels 10%, juvenile books 5%, movie scripts 40%, TV scripts 20%, multimedia 10%, stage plays 15%.

Member Agents Michael Kaliski.

Represents Considers these script areas: action, biography, comedy, contemporary, detective, experimental, family, fantasy, historical, mainstream, multimedia, mystery, psychic, romantic comedy, romantic drama, science, thriller.

☞ Does not accept unsolicited material at this time.

How to Contact Obtains most new clients through recommendations from others.

Terms Agent receives 15% commission on domestic sales. Agent receives 15% commission on foreign sales. Offers written contract.

Recent Sales This agency prefers not to share information on specific sales.

ORIGINAL ARTISTS

9465 Wilshire Blvd., Suite 324, Beverly Hills CA 90212. (310-)275-6765. Fax: (310)275-6725. E-mail: matt@original-artists.com. Website: www.original-artists. com/. **Contact:** Matt Leipzig; Jordan Bayer. Signatory of WGA.

- Mr. Bayer began his career at the William Morris Agency. Mr. Leipzig broke into the entertainment industry at New Horizons Pictures.

Represents Movie, TV.

- ๑ Original Artists writer clients have sold over 100 spec screenplays and pitches and dozens of television pilots.

PARADIGM TALENT AND LITERARY AGENCY

360 N. Crescent Drive, Beverly Hills 90210. (310)288-8000. Fax: (310)288-2000. Website: www.paradigmla.com.

Member Agents Lydia Wills, others.

Represents Movie, TV, movie scripts, feature film, theatrical stage play, stage plays.

- ๑ Paradigm Talent and Literary Agency is an Los-Angeles-based talent agency with an additional office in New York City. The firm acquired Writers & Artists Group International in 2004. The acquisition of WAGI added both talent and agents to Paradigm's roster, bolstering its New York office with legit agents, representing playwrights and theatre directors.

How to Contact Query with SASE.

Recent Sales *Outside In*, by Courtney Thorne-Smith (Broadway); *What Pets Eat*, by Marion Nestle and Malden Nesheim (Harcourt).

PTI TALENT AGENCY

14724 Ventura Blvd., Penthouse Suite, Sherman Oaks CA 91403. (818)386-1310. Fax: (818)386-1311. Website: www.ptitalentagency.com/. **Contact:** Sheryl Abrams.

QUALITA DELL' ARTE

6303 Owensmouth Ave., 10th Floor, Woodland Hills CA 91367. 818-598-8073. Signatory of WGA.

How to Contact Letter of inquiry required.

⊘ THE QUILLCO AGENCY

3104 W. Cumberland Court, Westlake Village CA 91362. (805)495-8436. Fax: (805)373-9868. **Contact:** Sandy Mackey. Signatory of WGA. Represents 7 clients.

Represents Movie scripts, feature film, TV movie, animation, documentary.

How to Contact Prefers to read materials exclusively. Will only consider references from people known to it.

Terms Agent receives 10% commission on domestic sales. Agent receives 10% commission on foreign sales.

Recent Sales This agency prefers not to share information about specific sales.

⊕ RCW

14 Dean St., London England W1D 3RS United Kingdom. (44)(207)437-4188. E-mail: malcolm.rasala@realcreatives.com. Website: www.realcreatives.com. **Contact:** Malcolm Rasala, Mark Maco.

Represents Episodic drama, technology, science & general entertainment scripts. **Considers these nonfiction areas:** medicine, psychology, science, technology, new media, IT. **Considers these fiction areas:** , Considers all fiction.

How to Contact Query via e-mail through website.

READ. A LITERARY & TALENT AGENCY

8033 Sunset Blvd., Suite 937, Los Angeles CA 90046. (323)876-2800. E-mail: melissa@readagency.net. **Contact:** Melissa Read. Signatory of WGA.

REBEL ENTERTAINMENT PARTNERS, INC.

5700 Wilshire Blvd., Suite 456, Los Angeles CA 90036. (323)935-1700. Fax: (323)932-9901. E-mail: inquiry@reptalent.com. Website: www.reptalent.com/. Signatory of WGA.

Member Agents Philip Irven; Seth Lawrence; Jason Egenberg; David Olsen.

> ⊶ "For over 35 years, Rebel Entertainment Partners or REP (formerly Abrams-Rubaloff & Lawrence) has built a solid reputation as a high quality, top-of-the-line talent agency. REP currently focuses on the representation of hosts and celebrities, as well as a multitude of directors, producers, and production companies specializing in non-scripted programming such as Talk, Game, News, Late-Night and Reality Television."

How to Contact "We recommend you send a query letter, rather than submitting an unsolicited script. It should be concise, outlining relevant credentials and briefly describing the nature of the work."

◼ ⊕ REISLER, AGENCE

Reisler Talent, P.O. Box 55067 csp Fairmount, Montreal Quebec H2T 3E2 Canada. (514)843-4551. Fax: (866)906-6106. Website: www.reisler.ca/. Other memberships include WGC.

Member Agents Mollye Reisler, Tania Giampetrone.

Represents Movie, TV, animation, stage plays, commercials.

⚬⇁ "We are dedicated to the local and international entertainment industry, and represent approximately 45 Anglophone and Francophone artists. Our performers are union affiliated (ACTRA, UDA, CAEA, SAG, AFTRA, WGC) and highly trained, with primarily theatre, on-camera and vocal training. We represent a very diverse group of actors, ranging in age (from late teens to seniors), ethnicity, looks and skills. Many of our artists take on more than one trade, either combining acting/writing, acting/directing, or acting/writing and directing. Our professionalism is second to none. We have built relationships with some of the leading production companies, networks, advertising companies, theatres, artistic directors and casting directors in town and abroad. Reisler Talent services film, television, theatre, animation and local, national and commercial markets. As one of Canada's first talent agencies, Reisler Talent has been part of a number of success stories. We have brought many actors to winning or being nominated for Genie Awards, MECCA Awards, Masques Awards, Quebec Drama Festival Awards, The Governor General Award and Le Prix d'Excellence des Arts et de la Culture. Reisler Talent is an important part of today's entertainment industry, and plans to service it for many years to come."

How to Contact Query with SASE.

Recent Sales Clients include Don Druick, Mark Blutman.

RESULT TALENT GROUP

RTG, 468 N. Camden Drive, Suite 300J, Beverly Hills CA 90210. (310)601-3186. Fax: (310)388-3121. E-mail: newfaces@rtgtalent.com; info@rtgtalent.com. Website: www.rtgtalent.com. **Contact:** Darren VanCleave, darren@rtgtalent.com.

Represents Movie, TV, movie scripts, feature film.

⚬⇁ "**RTG** specializes in the representation of actors, screenwriters and directors. We look for outstanding talent that has not reached its full potential due to the exclusive nature of the Hollywood system or has fallen through the cracks of a business that is often more interested in the heat on talent, instead of the actual talent. In addition, **RTG**'s has a special division of authentic southern and southwestern talent- **The Texas Connection Division**, that provides outstanding, authentic southern talent- both men and women, for projects with a southern, western, or cowboy theme. The RTG management team has successfully managed Fortune 500 Companies, private enterprises, and careers of professionals for over 25 years." "**RTG** also understands that the Entertainment Industry is pushing toward vertical integration and the one stop shopping concept. In order to accommodate the needs of our industry we operate nine synergistic divisions: Talent (actors &

directors); Feature and Television; Literary; Commercial Modeling; Theater; Creative (Photographers, stylists, hair & makeup artists); Production; The Texas Connection; Fluent Spanish Division."

⊕ RGM ASSOCIATES

Robyn Gardiner Management, "After five years acting purely as a theatrical agency, RGM expanded and developed a highly successful literary department, creating the first agency in Australia with a serious commitment to actors, voice over artists, corporate presenters, writers and directors.", 64-76 Kippax Street, Level 2, Suite 202, Surry Hills NSW 2010 Australia. E-mail: info@rgm.com.au. Website: www.rgm.com.au/. **Contact:** Dayne Kelly. Estab. 1982.

Represents Theatrical stage play, stage plays.

- ⊶ "RGM Artist Group is one of Australia's leading theatrical management agencies, representing a number of great plays which are available for amateur and professional production. At rgm.com.au you can read a synopsis of each play, find out cast size and gender divisions, and learn about the playwrights."

How to Contact All unsolicited mss returned unopened.

Recent Sales Clients include Hilary Bell, Paul Brown, Matt Cameron, Raimondo Cortese, Wesley Enoch, Louise Fox, Jonathan Gavin, Alma De Groen, Trudy Hellier, Ned Manning, Suzie Miller, Justin Monjo, Tee O'Neill, Debra Oswald, Suneeta Peres da Costa, Andrew Upton, Alana Valentine, Catherine Zimdahl.

⊕ THE LISA RICHARDS AGENCY

"Originally established as a theatrical agency, Lisa Richards now provides representation for actors, comedians, voice-over artists, authors & playwrights, directors, designers and presenters.", 108 Upper Leeson St., Dublin 4 Republic of Ireland Ireland. (03)(531)637-5000. Fax: (03)531)667-1256. E-mail: info@ lisarichards.ie. Website: www.lisarichards.ie. **Contact:** Chairman: Alan Cook; Managing Director: Miranda Pheifer, Fergus Cronin, Patrick Sutton; Actors' Agents: Lisa Cook, Richard Cook, Jonathan Shankey, Lorraine Cummins: Comedy Agents: Caroline Lee, Christine Dwyer; Literary Agent: Faith O'Grady; Voice Overs & Corp. Bookings: Eavan Kenny. Estab. 1989.

Represents Movie, TV, broadcast. **Considers these nonfiction areas:** biography, current affairs, history, memoirs, popular culture, travel, politics. **Considers these script areas:** comedy, general scipts.

How to Contact Submit proposal package, synopsis, 2-3 sample chapters, query letter with SAE.

Recent Sales Clients include Denise Deegan, Arlene Hunt, Roisin Ingle, Declan Lynch, Jennifer McCann, Sarah O'Brien, Kevin Rafter.

◑ MICHAEL D. ROBINS & ASSOCIATES

23241 Ventura Blvd., #300, Woodland Hills CA 91364. (818)343-1755. Fax: (818)343-7355. E-mail: mdr2@msn.com. **Contact:** Michael D. Robins. Signatory of WGA. Other memberships include DGA.

- Prior to opening his agency, Mr. Robins was a literary agent at a mid-sized agency.

Represents Nonfiction books, novels, episodic drama, movie, TV, movie scripts, feature film, TV movie, animation, miniseries, stage plays.

How to Contact Query with SASE. Accepts simultaneous submissions. Obtains most new clients through recommendations from others.

Terms Agent receives 10% commission on domestic sales. Agent receives 10% commission on foreign sales. Offers written contract.

Recent Sales This agency prefers not to share information about specific sales.

MAGGIE ROIPHE AGENCY

1721 S. Garth Ave., Los Angeles CA 90035-4303. (310)876-1562. Signatory of WGA. Represents 25 clients.

- Maggie Roiphe graduated from Oberlin College.

Represents Movie, movie scripts, feature film. **Considers these script areas:** action, comedy, horror, romantic comedy, thriller.

- ⟜ Actively seeking high concept comedies, urban comedies, thrillers especially psychological thrillers, action, horror, a really good romantic comedy. Other things of importance include originality. Strong concept, characters and dialogue. The writing cannot be not oblivious to the marketplace.

How to Contact This agency likes writers who contact through a referral.

BRANT ROSE AGENCY

Represents writers, directors, & producers for film & TV, 6671 Sunset Blvd., Suite 1584-B, Los Angeles CA 90028. (323)460-6464. Signatory of WGA.

- Brant Rose began his career as an agent at UTA in 1994. Before that, he worked at Procter & Gamble in brand management. He graduated from Dartmouth College.

Represents Movie, TV.

How to Contact Query with SASE.

THE ROTHMAN AGENCY

9465 Wilshire Blvd. Ste 840, Beverly Hills CA 90212. (310)247-9898. Fax: (310)247-9888. E-mail: reception@rothmanagency.com.

⊕ ⊘ SAYLE SCREEN, LTD

11 Jubilee Place, London England SW3 3TD United Kingdom. (44)(207)823-3883. Fax: (44)(207)823-3363. E-mail: info@saylescreen.com. Website: www. saylescreen.com. Represents 100+ clients. 5% of clients are new/unpublished writers. Currently handles: movie scripts 50%, TV scripts 50%.

Member Agents Toby Moorcroft; Jane Villiers; Matthew Bates.

Represents Episodic drama, movie, TV, sitcom. **Considers these script areas:** action, comedy, contemporary, detective, ethnic, experimental, fantasy, horror, mainstream, mystery, psychic, romantic comedy, romantic drama, teen, thriller.

　　⊶ Actively seeking writers, directors, and producers for film, TV, stage, & new media.

How to Contact "We only accept submissions by post. Please send a showreel or script with a CV and covering letter. We do carefully consider every submission made to us, but unfortunately we will only respond to submissions we wish to take further and we are not able to return material sent to us." Responds in 2-3 months to queries. Responds in 2-3 months to mss. Obtains most new clients through recommendations from others.

Terms Agent receives 10% commission on domestic sales. Agent receives 15% commission on foreign sales. Offers written contract; 1-month notice must be given to terminate contract.

Recent Sales *The Curious Incident of the Dog in The Nighttime*, by Mark Haddon (Warner Brothers); *Night Watch*, by Sarah Waters (BBC); *Dog Called Gorki*, by Josie Doder (Xingu); *Dreamer*, by David Hilton (Rocket/Silver Creek).

⊕ THE SHARLAND ORGANISATION

The Manor House, Manor Street, Raunds Northamptonshire NN9 6JW United Kingdom. E-mail: tso@btconnect.com. Website: www.sharlandorganisation. co.uk/. **Contact:** Mike Sharland, Alice Sharland.

　　• Before becoming an agent, Mike Sharland started in the film industry and became a writer on more than 600 TV shows. He is a past chair of the Writers Guild of Great Britain.

Represents Movie, TV, movie scripts, feature film, soap opera, theatrical stage play, stage plays, radio scripts.

How to Contact Query with SASE.

Recent Sales Other clients include David Conville; David Gooderson; Brian McAvera; Anthony Marriott; Alistair Foot; Mike Coleman.

⊕ SHEIL LAND ASSOCIATES, LTD

52 Doughty St., London England WC1N 2LS United Kingdom. (44)(207)405-9351. Fax: (44)(207)831-2127. E-mail: info@sheilland.co.uk. Website: www.

sheilland.co.uk. **Contact:** Sonia Land, Vivien Green, Ben Mason, Emily Hayward (Film Theatre & TV); Sophie Janson (Film, Theatre & TV); Gaia Banks (Foreign Rights).

Represents Movie, broadcast scripts. **Considers these nonfiction areas:** biography, cooking, gardening, history, humor, military, travel, politics. **Considers these fiction areas:** detective, literary, romance, thriller, drama.

o⌐ No science fiction, fantasy, children's or poetry considered.

How to Contact Submit proposal package, synopsis, 2-3 sample chapters, author bio, SAE.

Recent Sales Other clients include Peter Ackroyd, Hugh Bicheno, Melvyn Bragg, David Cohen, Anna del Conte, Seamus Dean, Bonnie Greer, Susan Hill, Richard Holmes, HRH The Prince of Wales, Mark Irving, Richard Mabey.

◙ KEN SHERMAN & ASSOCIATES

9507 Santa Monica Blvd., Beverly Hills CA 90210. (310)273-8840. Fax: (310)271-2875. **Contact:** Ken Sherman. Other memberships include BAFTA, PEN International; signatory of WGA, DGA. Represents approximately 35 clients. 10% of clients are new/unpublished writers.

- Prior to opening his agency, Mr. Sherman was with The William Morris Agency, The Lantz Office and Paul Kohner, Inc. He has taught The Business of Writing For Film and Television and The Book Worlds at UCLA and USC. He is currently a commissioner of arts and cultural affairs in the city of West Hollywood, and is on the international advisory board of the Christopher Isherwood Foundation.

Represents Nonfiction books, novels, movie, TV, not episodic drama, teleplays, life rights, film/TV rights to books. **Considers these nonfiction areas:** agriculture horticulture, Americana, crafts, interior, New Age, young, animals, anthropology, art, biography, business, child, computers, cooking, current affairs, education, ethnic, gardening, gay, government, health, history, how to, humor, language, memoirs, military, money, multicultural, music, nature, philosophy, photography, popular culture, psychology, recreation, regional, religion, science, self help, sex, sociology, software, spirituality, sports, film, translation, travel, true crime, womens, creative nonfiction. **Considers these fiction areas:** glitz, New Age, psychic, adventure, comic, confession, detective, erotica, ethnic, experimental, family, fantasy, feminist, gay, gothic, hi lo, historical, horror, humor, literary, mainstream, military, multicultural, multimedia, mystery, occult, picture books, plays, poetry, poetry trans, regional, religious, romance, science, short, spiritual, sports, thriller, translation, western, young. **Considers these script areas:** action, biography, cartoon, comedy, contemporary, detective, erotica, ethnic, experimental, family, fantasy, feminist, gay, glitz, historical, horror, mainstream, multicultural, multimedia, mystery, psychic, regional, religious, romantic comedy, romantic drama, science, sports, teen, thriller, western.

How to Contact Contact by referral only. Reports in approximately 1 month to mss. Obtains most new clients through recommendations from others.

Terms Agent receives 15% commission on domestic sales. Agent receives 15% commission on foreign sales. Agent receives 10-15% commission on film sales. Offers written contract. Charges clients for reasonable office expenses (postage, photocopying, etc.).

Recent Sales Sold more than 20 scripts in the last year. *Back Roads*, by Tawni O'Dell (Dreamworks); *Priscilla Salyers Story*, produced by Andrea Baynes (ABC); *Toys of Glass*, by Martin Booth (ABC/Saban Entertainment); *Brazil*, by John Updike (film rights to Glaucia Carmagos); *Fifth Sacred Thing*, by Starhawk (Bantam); *Questions From Dad*, by Dwight Twilly (Tuttle); *Snow Falling on Cedars*, by David Guterson (Universal Pictures); *The Witches of Eastwick-The Musical*, by John Updike (Cameron Macintosh, Ltd.).

Writers Conferences Maui Writers' Conference; Squaw Valley Writers' Workshop; Santa Barbara Writers' Conference; Screenwriting Conference in Santa Fe; Aspen Summer Words Literary Festival.

BLAIR SILVER & COMPANY LLC

PO Box 3188, Manhattan Beach CA 90266. (310)546-4669. E-mail: blairsilver@ aol.com. Website: www.blairsilver.com/.

Represents Movie, TV, multimedia, video games.

➤ This agency reps Actors, Animators, Athletes, Comedians, Directors, Models, Multimedia Artists, Music Professionals, Producers, Screenwriters, Television Writers and Video Game Professionals.

How to Contact Query with a referral.

THE SUSAN SMITH COMPANY

1344 N. Wetherly Drive, Los Angeles CA 90069. (310)276-4224. E-mail: susan@ susansmithco.com. Website: www.susansmithco.com. Signatory of WGA.

⊕ MICHELINE STEINBERG ASSOCIATES

104 Great Portland St., London England W1W 6PE United Kingdom. (44) (207)631-1310. Fax: (44)(207)631-1146. E-mail: info@steinplays.com. Website: www.steinplays.com/. Currently handles: movie scripts, TV scripts, stage plays, other Radio Scripts.

Represents Movie, TV, movie scripts, feature film, animation, theatrical stage play, stage plays, radio scripts. **Considers these script areas:** action, biography, cartoon, comedy, contemporary, detective, erotica, ethnic, experimental, family, fantasy, feminist, gay, glitz, historical, horror, juvenile, mainstream, multicultural, mystery, psychic, regional, religious, romantic comedy, romantic drama, science, sports, teen, thriller, western.

⚬ The agency represents writers and writer-directors for stage, television, film, radio, and animation.

How to Contact Query via e-mail first.

⚫ SUITE A MANAGEMENT TALENT & LITERARY AGENCY

120 El Camino Drive, Suite 202, Beverly Hills CA 90212. (310)278-0801. Fax: (310)278-0807. E-mail: suite-a@juno.com. **Contact:** Lloyd Robinson. Other memberships include Signatory of WGA, DGA, A.F.T.R.A. Represents 76 clients. 10% of clients are new/unpublished writers. Currently handles: novels 15%, movie scripts 40%, TV scripts 40%, stage plays 5%.

• Prior to becoming an agent, Mr. Robinson worked as a manager.

Member Agents Lloyd Robinson (adaptation of books and plays for development as features or TV MOW).

Represents Episodic drama, movie scripts, feature film, TV movie of the week, documentary, variety show, miniseries, stage plays, CD-ROM. **Considers these script areas:** action, cartoon, comedy, contemporary, detective, erotica, ethnic, experimental, family, fantasy, mainstream, mystery, psychic, religious, romantic comedy, romantic drama, science, sports, teen, thriller, western.

⚬ "We represent screenwriters, playwrights, novelists, producers and directors."

How to Contact Submit synopsis, outline/proposal, logline. Obtains most new clients through recommendations from others.

Terms Agent receives 10% commission on domestic sales. Agent receives 10% commission on foreign sales. Offers written contract, binding for minimum 1 year. Charges clients for photocopying, messenger, FedEx, postage.

Recent Sales This agency prefers not to share information on specific sales or client names.

Tips "We are a talent agency specializing in the copyright business. Fifty percent of our clients generate copyright (screenwriters, playwrights and novelists). Fifty percent of our clients service copyright (producers and directors). We represent produced, published, and/or WGA writers who are eligible for staff TV positions, as well as novelists and playwrights whose works may be adapted for film or TV."

⚫ TALENT SOURCE

1711 Dean Forest Road, Suite H, Savannah GA 31408. Website: www.talentsource. com/literary.html. **Contact:** Michael L. Shortt. Signatory of WGA. 35% of clients are new/unpublished writers. Currently handles: movie scripts 85%, TV scripts 15%.

- Prior to becoming an agent, Mr. Shortt was a TV program producer/ director.

Represents Movie scripts, feature film, TV movie of the week. **Considers these script areas:** comedy, contemporary, detective, erotica, family, juvenile, mainstream, romantic comedy, romantic drama, teen.

- ⟳ Actively seeking character-driven stories (e.g., *Sling Blade* or *Sex, Lies, and Videotape*). Does not want to receive science fiction or scripts with big budget special effects.

How to Contact Send a cover letter (query) with SASE, synopsis. Reports on queries in 10-12 weeks. Obtains most new clients through recommendations from others.

Terms Agent receives 10% commission on domestic sales. Agent receives 15% commission on foreign sales. Offers written contract.

Recent Sales This agency prefers not to share information on specific sales.

Tips "See the literary button on our website for complete submissions details. No exceptions."

⊕ THE TENNYSON AGENCY

10 Cleveland Ave., London England SW20 9EW United Kingdom. (208)543-5939. E-mail: submissions@tenagy.co.uk. Website: www.tenagy.co.uk. **Contact:** Christopher Oxford (Film, Theatre & TV scripts); Adam Sheldon (Arts & Humanities); Jane Hutchinson.

Represents Drama and screenwriting. **Considers these nonfiction areas:** arts & humanities.

- ⟳ Does not want to receive poetry, short stories, science fiction, fantasy or children's titles.

How to Contact Submit proposal package, synopsis, author bio, details of any previously published work.SAE

Recent Sales *Billy's Day Out,* by Anthony Mann; *Helen's Story*, by Ken Ross; *Lighthouse*, by Graeme Scarfe; *The Hammer*, by Johnathan Holloway. Other clients include Vivienne Allen, Tony Bagley, Kristina Bedford, Alastair Cording, Caroline Coxon, Iain Grant, Philip Hurd-Wood, Joanna Leigh, Steve MacGregor, John Ryan, Walter Saunders, Diane Speakman, Diana Ward, and the estate of Julian Howell.

🌐 JULIA TYRRELL MANAGEMENT, LTD.

57 Greenham Road, London N10 1LN United Kingdom. (44)208)374-0575. E-mail: julia@jtmanagement.co.uk. Website: www.jtmanagement.co.uk. **Contact:** Abigail Hedderwick.

- Following a career as a dancer, Julia Tyrrell started at Noel Gay Organization as an assistant to literary agent Pauline Asper and production secretary for Noel Gay Theatre. After 10 years at Hamilton Asper, she joined MacFarlane Chard Associates before starting her own agency.

Represents Movie, TV, movie scripts, feature film, TV movie, theatrical stage play, stage plays, radio.

How to Contact Query with SASE. Submit sample chapters, SASE.

🗗 UNITED TALENT AGENCY, INC.

UTA, 9560 Wilshire Blvd., Suite 500, Beverly Hills CA 90212-2401. (310)273-6700. Fax: (310)247-1111. Website: www.unitedtalent.com/. Signatory of WGA.

Represents Nonfiction books, novels, movie, TV, movie scripts, feature film, animation, stage plays, video games, commercials.

How to Contact All unsolicited mss returned unopened.

Tips "This agency operates exclusively by referral."

WASHINGTON SQUARE ARTS & FILMS

310 Bowery, 2nd Floor, New York NY 10012. (212)253-0333. Fax: (212)253-0330. E-mail: production@wsfilms.com. Website: www.washingtonsquarearts.com.

Represents TV, movie scripts, feature film, documentary, theatrical stage play, miniseries, stage plays, musicals.

How to Contact Query only. Do not send unsolicited work.

Recent Sales *Adrift in Manhattan, Sweet Flame, Old Joy, and Love Ludlow.* Other clients include Johanna Baldwin, Richard Gray, Chris Jeffries, Dacid Bar Katz, Suzanne Maynard Miller, Kelly Younger.

🗗 PEREGRINE WHITTLESEY AGENCY

279 Central Park W., New York NY 10024. (212)787-1802. Fax: (212)787-4985. E-mail: pwwagy@aol.com. **Contact:** Peregrine Whittlesey. Signatory of WGA. Represents 30 clients. 50% of clients are new/unpublished writers. Currently handles: movie scripts 1%, stage plays 99%.

- This agency specializes in playwrights who also write for screen and TV.

How to Contact Query with SASE. Prefers to read materials exclusively. Responds in 1 week to queries. Responds in 1 month to mss. Obtains most new clients through recommendations from others.

Terms Agent receives 10% commission on domestic sales. Agent receives 15%

commission on foreign sales. Offers written contract, binding for 2 years.

Recent Sales Sold 20 scripts in the last year. Scripts sold to Actors Theatre of Loiusville's Human Festival, South Coast Repertory, Stratford Festival, Ontario Canad, Alabama Shakespeare Festival, ACT Seattle, Seattle Rep, Arena Stage, City Theatre Pittsburgh, Repertorio Espanol and producers in England, Germany and Spain.

② WILL ENTERTAINMENT

1228 Romulus Drive, Glendale CA 91205. (818) 246-4850. E-mail: info@ willentertainment.com. Website: www.willentertainment.com. **Contact:** Garrett Hicks. Represents 23 clients. 30% of clients are new/unpublished writers. Currently handles: juvenile books 30%, movie scripts 30%, TV scripts 40%.

- Prior to becoming a literary and script manager, Mr. Hicks was a development executive for Disney Animation.

Represents Juvenile, movie, TV, movie scripts, feature film. **Considers these script areas:** action, cartoon, comedy, fantasy, juvenile, mainstream, romantic comedy, teen.

- ⚬⇥ Specializes in children's book authors and illustrators, especially those crossing over from film, TV and animation. Juvenile, picture books and young adult.

How to Contact Query by e-mail to info@willentertainment.com. Accepts simultaneous submissions. Responds in 4-6 weeks to queries and mss. Obtains most new clients through recommendations from others.

Terms Agent receives 15% commission on domestic sales. Agent receives 15% commission on foreign sales. Offers written contract; 60-day notice must be given to terminate contract.

Recent Sales Sold 2 titles and sold 5 scripts in the last year. *Hot Sour Salty Sweet*, by Sherri Smith (Delacorte); *Flygirl*, by Sherri Smith (Putnam); *Patty Dolan is Dead*, by Patrick O'Connor (FP Prods/Disney); *Hopeville*, TV pilot by Howard Nemetz (Fox).

Tips "Mr. Hicks is a manager."

⦸ WRITERS' PRODUCTIONS LITERARY AGENCY

P.O. Box 630, Westport CT 06881-0630. (203)227-8199. E-mail: dlm67@mac.com. **Contact:** David L. Meth. Currently handles: novels 40%, other 60% drama.

- ⚬⇥ "We are not accepting new clients at this time."

How to Contact Contact by e-mail, if your work was asked for. Obtains most new clients through recommendations from others.

Terms Agent receives 15% commission on domestic sales. Agent receives 25% commission on foreign sales. Offers written contract. Charges clients for land-line transmissions.

Tips "We are not taking on new clients."

Contests

The contests and awards listed in this section are arranged by alphabetical order.

New contests and awards are announced in various writer's publications nearly every day. However, many lose their funding or fold—and sponsoring magazines go out of business just as often. We have contacted the organizations whose contests and awards are listed here with the understanding that they are valid through 2010. **Contact names**, **entry fees**, and **deadlines** have been highlighted and set in bold type for your convenience.

To make sure you have all the information you need about a particular contest, always send a SASE to the contact person in the listing before entering a contest. The listings in this section are brief, and many contests have lengthy, specific rules and requirements that we could not include in our limited space. Often a specific entry form must accompany your submission.

When you receive a set of guidelines, you will see that some contests are not applicable to all writers. The writer's age, previous publication, geographic location, and length of the work are common matters of eligibility. Read the requirements carefully to ensure you don't enter a contest for which you are not qualified. You should also be aware that every year, more and more contests are charging entry fees.

Winning a contest or award can launch a successful writing career. The power players in Hollywood often look at who's placing well in contests around town and around the country.

20/20 SCREENWRITING CONTEST

3639 Malibu Vista Drive, Malibu CA 90265. (310)454-0971. Fax: (310)573-3868. E-mail: 2020contest@screenbrokers.com. Website: www.2020contest.com. "Send in the first 20 pages of your scripts for the first round and then go from there." Electronic submissions accepted. **Deadline: June 20. Charges $20 basic, $40 expanded feedback.** Prize: "You will win a WGA-signatory, veteran agency representation. In addition, winners will also receive either a pass to the next Screenwriters' Expo, or a four DVDs from past Expo speakers." All genres; 20-page excerpt from script.

ACTORS' CHOICE AWARDS

The Screenwriting Conference in Santa Fe, PO Box 29762, Santa Fe NM 87592. (866)424-1501. Fax: (505)424-8207. E-mail: writeon@scsfe.com. **Deadline: May 15. Charges $25.** Prize: All 5 winners receive free admission to the PAGEawards screenwriting competition. In addition, scripts are forwarded to producers attending Producers seminar. All genres.

⚅ ALBERTA PLAYWRITING COMPETITION

Alberta Playwrights' Network, 2633 Hochwald Ave. SW, Calgary AB T3E 7K2 Canada. (403)269-8564. Fax: (403)265-6773. Offered annually for unproduced plays with full-length and Discovery categories. Discovery is open only to previously unproduced playwrights. Open only to residents of Alberta. **Deadline: March 31. Charges $40 fee (Canadian).** Prize: Full length: $3,500 (Canadian); Discovery: $1,500 (Canadian); plus a written critique, workshop of winning play, and possible reading of winning plays at a Showcase Conference.

AMERICAN GEM SHORT CONTEST

FilmMakers Magazine, American Gem Short Screenplay Contest, P.O. Box 4678, Mission Viejo CA 92690. Contest is held annually. Short scripts only. **Deadline: April 30; late deadline: June 15. Charges $29-$59.**

ANNUAL INTERNATIONAL ONE-PAGE PLAY COMPETITION

Lamia Ink!, P.O. Box 202, Prince Street Station, New York NY 10012. **Contact:** Cortland Jessup, founder/artistic director. Offered annually for previously published or unpublished 1-page plays. Acquires the rights to publish in our magazine and to be read or performed at the prize awarding festival. "We will publish and award prizes annually, but may not in every year hold a public performance of the finalist plays. In years without a live performance festival we will award prizes via mail and list all finalists on website." Playwright retains copyright. There are 3 rounds of judging with invited judges that change from year to year. There are up to 12 judges for finalists round. Guidelines available online. The competition is a short-form theatrical exercise created to nurture aspiring writers, challenge established writers and encourage a wide range of experimentation. **Deadline: March 15. Charges $2/play; $5/3 plays (maximum).** Prize: $200 for the winner; all finalists will be published.

Tips "Send SASE for guidelines or download them from the website."

ANNUAL NATIONAL PLAYWRITING COMPETITION

Wichita State University, School of Performing Arts, 1845 Fairmount, Wichita KS 67260-0153. (316)978-3360. Fax: (316)978-3202. E-mail: bret.jones@wichita.edu. **Contact:** Bret Jones, Director of Theatre. Offered annually for full-length plays (minimum of 90 minutes playing time), or 2-3 short plays on related themes (minimum of 90 minutes playing time). Open to all undergraduate and graduate students enrolled at any college or university in the US (indicate school affiliation). **Deadline: March 15.** Prize: Production by the Wichita State University Theatre. Winner announced April 15. No plays returned after February 15.

ANNUAL ONE-ACT PLAYWRITING CONTEST

TADA!, 15 W. 28th St., 3rd Floor, New York NY 10001. (212)252-1619, ext. 17. Fax: (212)252-8763. E-mail: jgreer@tadatheater.com. Website: www.tadatheater. com. **Contact:** Joanna Greer, associate artistic director. Offered annually to encourage playwrights to develop new plays for teen and family audiences. Call or e-mail for guidelines. **Deadline: January 31, 2010.** Prize: Cash award and staged readings.

ARIZONA SCREENPLAY SEARCH

Phoenix Film Foundation, 1700 N. Seventh Ave., Suite 250, Phoenix AZ 85007. (602)955-6444. This contest is actually multiple contests in one. One contest only accepts scripts where the plot happens in the state. The other contest is open to all plots. Charges fee varies by year. Prize: Cash prizes offered.

BIG BEAR LAKE SCREENWRITING COMPETITION

P.O. Box 1981, Big Bear Lake CA 92315-1981. (909)866-3433. E-mail: BigBearFilmFest@aol.com. **Deadline: April 1. Charges $40.** Prize: No confirmed money prizes, but winners receive software and their script submitted to studios.

THE BRITISH SHORT SCREENPLAY COMPETITION

c/o Pinewood Film Studios, Pinewood Road, Iver Heath, Buckinghamshire SL0 0NH United Kingdom. E-mail: info@kaosfilms.co.uk. Website: www.kaosfilms. co.uk/rules/. The British Short Screenplay Competition is open to writers of any nationality from any country. The entered screenplay must not have been previously optioned, sold or produced. Screenplays must be written in English language. The screenplay must be no less than five-minutes and no more than fifteen minutes screen time. Charges 25-35 British pounds. All genres.

BUNTVILLE CREW'S AWARD BLUE

Buntville Crew, 118 N. Railroad Ave., Buckley IL 60918-0445. E-mail: buntville@ yahoo.fr. **Contact:** Steven Packard, artistic dir. "Presented annually for the best unpublished/unproduced play script under 15 pages, written by a student enrolled in any Illinois high school. Submit 1 copy of the script in standard play format, a brief biography, and a SASE (scripts will not be returned). Include name, address, telephone number, age, and name of school." **Deadline: May 31.** Prize: Cash prize and possible productions in Buckley and/or New York City. panel selected by the theater.

BUNTVILLE CREW'S PRIX HORS PAIR

Buntville Crew, 118 N. Railroad Ave., Buckley IL 60918-0445. E-mail: buntville@ yahoo.fr. Website: www.buntville@yahoo.com. **Contact:** Steven Packard, artistic dir. "Annual award for unpublished/unproduced play script under 15 pages. Plays may be in English, French, German, or Spanish (no translations, no adaptations). Submit 1 copy of the script in standard play format, a résumé, and a SASE (scripts will not be returned). Include name, address, and telephone number." **Deadline: May 31. Charges $8.** Prize: $200 and possible production in Buckley and/or New York City. Panel selected by the theater.

CALIFORNIA YOUNG PLAYWRIGHTS CONTEST

Playwrights Project, 2356 Moore St., #204, San Diego CA 92110-3019. (619)239-8222. Fax: (619)239-8225. E-mail: write@playwrightsproject.org. Website: www. playwrightsproject.org. **Contact:** Cecelia Kouma, managing director. "Offered annually for previously unpublished plays by young writers to stimulate young people to create dramatic works, and to nurture promising writers. Scripts must be a minimum of 10 standard typewritten pages; send 2 copies. Scripts will *not* be returned. If requested, entrants receive detailed evaluation letter. Writers must be California residents under age 19 as of the deadline date. Guidelines available online." **Deadline: June 1.** Prize: Professional production of 3-5 winning plays at a professional theatre in San Diego, plus royalty.

CHRISTIAN SCREENWRITE

P.O. Box 447, Bloomfield NJ 07003. (201)306-5093. E-mail: info@ christianscreenwrite.com. Website: www.christianscreenwrite.com. Contemporary Christian screenplays only. The contest is "looking for films that spread the messages and principles and Christianity." **Deadline: July 2009-September 2009. Charges $40.** Prize: Cash prizes offered for top three winners.

CINEQUEST FILM FESTIVAL SCREENPLAY COMPETITION

Cinequest Film Festival, 22 N. Almaden Ave., San Jose CA 95110. (408)295-3378(FEST). Fax: (408)995-5713. E-mail: info@cinequest.org. All genres and lengths of screenplays (up to 125 pages) are accepted, from low-budget Indie dramas to mega-money flicks. Charges $35-40. Prize: Multiple prizes, with a $5,000 grand prize. Winning scripts will be passed on to moviemakers.

CITA SKETCH WRITING AND PLAY CONTEST

Christians in Theatre Arts, P.O. Box 26471, Greenville SC 29616. (864)679-1898. E-mail: admin@cita.org. Website: www.cita.org. "Annual sketch contest for CITA members: to encourage excellence in theatrical sketch writing, focusing on material created to minister in worship services, evangelistic outreach, street theatre, or educational, amateur, or professional theatre performance. Sketches must in some way reflect Christian truth, values, or questions. Sketches may be presentational, slice-of-life, monologue, mime, or any combination of forms. Prize winners of Drama and Comedy categories will receive a plaque at a general session of the CITA National Conference in June. See website for guidelines. Annual play contest: The goal of this competition is to encourage CITA playwrights by providing the competition winner with exposure and connection with organizations related to CITA which may then consider it for further development and/or production." **Deadline: February 1. Charges $10/entry for sketch contest; $20/entry for play contest.** Prize: Staged readings/productions of these works may also be a part of the conference at the discretion of the judges. Works may be published in the CITA magazine, *Christianity and Theatre*, with the author's permission. All further production rights will be reserved by the author.

COE COLLEGE PLAYWRITING FESTIVAL

Coe College, 1220 First Ave. NE, Cedar Rapids IA 52402-5092. (319)399-8624. Fax: (319)399-8557. E-mail: swolvert@coe.edu. **Contact:** Susan Wolverton. Estab. 1993. "Offered biennially for unpublished work to provide a venue for new works for the stage. We are interested in full-length productions, not one-acts or musicals. There are no specific criteria although a current resume and synopsis is requested. Open to any writer." **Deadline: November 1, even years.** Notification: January 15, odd years. Prize: $500, plus 1-week residency as guest artist with airfare, room and board provided.

⊕ CREATIVE WORLD AWARDS (CWA) SCREENWRITING COMPETITION

International screenwriting contests, PO Box 10699, Marina del Rey CA 90295. E-mail: info@creativeworldawards.com; submissions@creativeworldawards. com. **Contact:** Marlene Neubauer/Heather Waters. "Creative World Awards (CWA) has quickly become among the most sought after international screenwriting contests in the industry! This competition has secured an unprecedented amount of commitments from A-list companies—all of which have agreed to give first looks to the 2009 top finalists. Also, be sure to check out the website for ongoing, one-of-a-kind educational features! Over $16,000 in cash prizes awarded! Enter today at www.creativeworldawards.com." All screenplays must be in English, between 90-120 pages and in standard spec screenplay format. See website's Basic FAQ page for more detailed information. Feature length screenplays only. Short screenplays are not accepted. **Deadline: July 21, 2009** (this has been extended). **Charges $45-65.** Prize: One Grand Winner, 4 Category Winners - Over $16,000 in cash and prizes awarded.

DAYTON PLAYHOUSE FUTUREFEST

The Dayton Playhouse, 1301 E. Siebenthaler Ave., Dayton OH 45414-5357. (937)424-8477. **Contact:** Amy Brown, executive director. Three plays selected for full productions, three for staged readings at July FutureFest weekend. The six authors will be given travel and lodging to attend the festival. Professionally adjudicated. Guidelines online. **Deadline: October 31.** Prize: $1,000.

DC SHORTS SCREENWRITING COMPETITION

DC Shorts Film Festival, 1317 F Street, NW, Ste 920, Washington DC 20004. (202)393-4266. **Contact:** Jon Gann. DC Shorts is proud to present a different kind of screenwriting competition. A panel of judges consisting of filmmakers, screenwriters and critics will review and provide condensed coverage (feedback) for scripts of 15 pages or less. A set of finalists (no more than 7) will be selected to be featured during the festival weekend, which the screenwriters are invited to attend, and cast a live reading of the script from a bank of actors and directors. The live readings will be performed in front of an audience, who will vote on their favorite. These votes, along with the scores of the judges, will determine a competition winner. Prize: One script will receive $1,000 up front, plus a $1,000 upon completion of the final film. The final film is guaranteed entry into DC Shorts 2010.

DUBUQUE FINE ARTS PLAYERS ANNUAL ONE-ACT PLAY CONTEST

Dubuque Fine Arts Players, 1686 Lawndale, Dubuque IA 52001. E-mail: gary. arms@clarke.edu. **Contact:** Gary Arms. "We select 3 one-act plays each year. We award cash prizes of up to $600 for a winning entry. We produce the winning plays in August. Offered annually for unpublished and unproduced work. Guidelines and application form for SASE." **Deadline: January 31. Charges $10.** Prize: 1st Place: $600; 2nd Place: $300; 3rd Place: $200. Five groups who read all the plays; each play is read at least twice. Plays that score high enough enter the second round. The top 10 plays are read by a panel consisting of 3 directors and 2 other final judges.

ESSENTIAL THEATRE PLAYWRITING AWARD

The Essential Theatre, 1414 Foxhall Lane, #10, Atlanta GA 30316. (404)212-0815. E-mail: pmhardy@aol.com. **Contact:** Peter Hardy. "Offered annually for unproduced, full-length plays by Georgia resident writers. No limitations as to style or subject matter." **Deadline: April 23**. Prize: $600 and full production.

⊕ THE LOUIS ESSON PRIZE FOR DRAMA

Victorian Premier's Literary Awards, State Government of Victoria, State Library of Victoria, 328 Swanston St. C, Melbourne VIC 3000 Australia. (61)(3)8664-7277. E-mail: pla@slv.vic.gov.au. Website: www.slv.vic.gov.au/pla. **Contact:** Project Officer. "Annual prize for theatre or radio scripts produced between May 1 and April 30. The State Library of Victoria reserves the right to place a copy of all nominated works in its collection. Further copyright remains with the author. Authors must be Australian citizens or permanent residents." **Deadline: Usually May each year.** Prize: AUD $15,000.
Tips "For guidelines and nomination forms please visit our website."

FADE IN AWARDS

287 S. Robertson Blvd., #467, Beverly Hills CA 90211. (310)275-0287. "The Fade In Awards were established in 1996 to assist talented new writers and writer/directors in getting recognized within the Hollywood community in order to begin a career as a working filmmaker." Prize: Cash prizes offered, and industry exposure to agents, producers, and executives. Open to any writer worldwide. Seven categories and two formats to choose from.

Tips "You can enter the contest online or mail in a submission."

FEATURE LENGTH SCREENPLAY COMPETITION

Austin Film Festival, 1801 Salina St., Austin TX 78702. (512)478-4795. Fax: (512)478-6205. E-mail: alex@austinfilmfestival.com. Offered annually for unproduced screenplays. The Austin Film Festival is looking for quality screenplays which will be read by industry professionals. This year AFF will be providing 'Readers Notes' to all Second Rounders (top 10%) and higher for no additional charge. Two main categories: Drama Category and Comedy Category. Two optional Award Categories (additional entry of $20 per category); Latitude Productions Award and Sci-Fi Award. For guidelines for SASE or call (800)310-3378. The writer must hold the rights when submitted; work must be original and not under option. The screenplay must be feature length and in industry standard format. **Deadline: May 15 (early); June 1 (late). Charges $40/early entry; $50/late entry.** Prize: $5,000 in Comedy and Drama; $2,500 for Latitude Productions Award and Sci-Fi Award.

FESTIVAL OF NEW AMERICAN PLAYS

Firehouse Theatre Project, 1609 W. Broad St., Richmond VA 23220. (804)355-2001. E-mail: info@firehousetheatre.org. Website: www.firehousetheatre.org. **Contact:** Carol Piersol, artistic director. "Annual contest designed to support new and emerging American playwrights. Scripts must be full-length and previously unpublished/unproduced. (Readings are acceptable if no admission was charged.) Submissions should be mailed in standard manuscript form. This means no disks, no emails. All author information must be on a title page separate from the body of the manuscript and no reference to the author is permitted in the body of the script. Scripts must be accompanied by a letter of recommendation from a theater company or individual familiar with your work. Letters of recommendation do not need to be specific to the play submitted; they may be general recommendations of the playwright's work. All letters must be received with the script, not under separate cover. Scripts received without a letter will not be considered. Due to the volume of mail, manuscripts cannot be returned. All American playwrights welcome to submit their work." **Deadline: June 30 postmark.** Prize: 1st Place: $1,000 and a staged reading; 2nd Place: $500 and a staged reading. All plays are initially read by a panel of individuals with experience in playwriting and literature. Previous judges have included Lloyd Rose (former *Washington Post* theatre critic), Bill Patton (frequent Firehouse director), Richard Toscan (dean of the Virginia Commonwealth University School for the Arts), and Israel Horovitz (playwright). All finalists are asked to sign a contract with the Firehouse Theatre Project that guarantees performance rights for the staged reading in January and printed credit for Firehouse Theatre Project if the play is produced/published in the future.

FILMMAKERS INTERNATIONAL SCREENWRITING AWARDS

P.O. 4678, Mission Viejo CA 92690. E-mail: info@filmmakers.com. Website: www.filmmakers.com. **Deadline: May 31; late deadline: June 30. Charges $49-$69.**

FIREHOUSE THEATRE PROJECT NEW PLAY COMPETITION

The Firehouse Theatre Project, 1609 W. Broad St., Richmond VA 23220. (804)355-2001. **Contact:** Literary Manager FTP. Calls for previously unpublished full-length works with non-musical and non-children's themes. Submissions must be in standard play format. Scripts should be accompanied by a letter of recommendation from a company or individual familiar with your work. Submissions must be unpublished. Visit website for complete submission guidelines. "We're receptive to unusual, but well-wrought works." Acquires the right to produce the winning scripts in a staged reading for the FTP Festival of New American Plays. Following the Festival production dates, all rights are relinquished to the author. Open to US residents only. **Deadline: June 30.** Prize: 1st Prize: $1,000; 2nd Prize: $500 a committee selected by the executive board of the Firehouse Theatre Project.

JOHN GASSNER MEMORIAL PLAYWRITING COMPETITION

New England Theatre Conference, 215 Knob Hill Dr., Hamden CT 06158. Fax: (203)288-5938. E-mail: mail@netconline.org. "We annually seek unpublished full-length plays and scripts. Open to all. Playwrights living outside New England may participate." **Deadline: April 15. Charges $10 fee.** Prize: 1st Place: $1,000; 2nd Place: $500.

GOTHAM SCREEN FILM FESTIVAL AND SCREENPLAY CONTEST

603 W. 115th St., Suite 384, New York NY 10025. E-mail: info@gothamscreen.com. "Submit via Withoutabox account or download form at Website. The contest is open to anyone. Feature length screenplays should be properly formatted and have an approximate length of 80-120 pages. On the cover page, please put the title, the writer's name(s) and the contact details." **Deadline: September. Charges $35-50.** Prize: $2,500. In addition, excerpts from selected contest entries will be performed live by professional actors at a staged reading during the festival. Drama, comedy, adventure, horror, thriller/suspense, family, romantic comedy, documentary. **Tips** "Include an e-mail address to be notified."

☑ GOVERNOR GENERAL'S LITERARY AWARD FOR DRAMA

Canada Council for the Arts, 350 Albert St., P.O. Box 1047, Ottawa ON K1P 5V8 Canada. (613)566-4414, ext. 5573. Fax: (613)566-4410. "Offered for the best English-language and the best French-language work of drama by a Canadian. Publishers submit titles for consideration." **Deadline: March 15, June 1, or August 7, depending on the book's publication date.** Prize: Each laureate receives $25,000; nonwinning finalists receive $1,000.

AURAND HARRIS MEMORIAL PLAYWRITING AWARD

The New England Theatre Conference, Inc., 215 Knob Hill Dr., Hamden CT 06518. Fax: (203)288-5938. E-mail: mail@netconline.org. "Offered annually for an unpublished full-length play for young audiences. Guidelines available online or for SASE. 'No phone calls, please.' Open to all." **Deadline: May 1. Charges $10 fee.** Prize: 1st Place: $1,000; 2nd Place: $500.

HENRICO THEATRE COMPANY ONE-ACT PLAYWRITING COMPETITION

Henrico Recreation & Parks, P.O. Box 27032, Richmond VA 23273. (804)501-5138. Fax: (804)501-5284. E-mail: per22@co.henrico.va.us. **Contact:** Amy A. Perdue. "Offered annually for previously unpublished or unproduced plays or musicals to produce new dramatic works in one-act form. Scripts with small casts and simpler sets given preference. Controversial themes and excessive language should be avoided." **Deadline: July 1.** Prize: $300; Runner-Up: $200. Winning entries may be produced; videotape sent to author.

HOLIDAY SCREENPLAY CONTEST

P.O. Box 450, Boulder CO 80306. (303)629-3072. E-mail: Cherubfilm@aol.com. Website: www.HolidayScreenplayContest.com. "Scripts must be centered on a holiday. The screenplay must be centered around one Holiday (New Year's Day, President's Day, Valentine's Day, St. Patrick's Day, April Fool's Day, Easter, 4th of July, Halloween, Thanksgiving, Hanukkah, Christmas, Kwanzaa, or any other world holiday you would like to feature). This contest is limited to the first 400 entries." Screenplays must be in English. Screenplays must not have been previously optioned, produced, or purchased prior to submission. Multiple submissions are accepted but each submission requires a separate online entry and separate fee. Screenplays must be between 90 - 125 pages. **Deadline: November. Charges $30.** Prize: Up to $500.

Contests

HORROR SCREENPLAY CONTEST

Cherub Productions, P.O. Box 540, Boulder Co 80306. (303)629-3072. E-mail: Cherubfilm@aol.com. "This contest is looking for horror scripts." This contest is limited to the first 600 entries. Screenplays must be between 90 - 125 pages. **Charges $35.** Prize: More than $5000 in cash and prizes.

INTERNATIONAL FAMILY FILM FESTIVAL (IFFF)

4531 Empire Ave., #200, Burbank CA 91505. (661)257-3131. Fax: (818)847-1184. E-mail: info@iffilmfest.org. "IFFF advocates, promotes and encourages excellence in films produced for a general audience by emerging screenwriters, filmmakers and studios worldwide. "Friz Award" for Lifetime Achievement in Animation, Lifetime Achievement in Film, IFFF "Spirit" Award, IFFF Directors Gold Award, Top Applause Award. " Short screenplays and feature screenplays reviewed. Features should be fewer than 120 pages, and shorts should be fewer than 45 pages. With entry form, you will need to include a 50-word synopsis as well as character descriptions. **Deadline: January. Charges $30 (short); $60 (full).** Drama, comedy, animation, sci-fi/fantasy, musical.

KUMU KAHUA/UHM THEATRE DEPARTMENT PLAYWRITING CONTEST

Kumu Kahua Theatre, Inc./University of Hawaii at Manoa, Dept. of Theatre and Dance, 46 Merchant St., Honolulu HI 96813. (808)536-4222. Fax: (808)536-4226. E-mail: kumakahuatheatre@hawaiiantel.net. Website: www.kumukahua.com. **Contact:** Harry Wong III, artistic director. Offered annually for unpublished work to honor full-length and short plays. Guidelines available every September. First 2 categories open to residents and nonresidents. For Hawaii Prize, plays must be set in Hawaii or deal with some aspect of the Hawaiian experience. For Pacific Rim prize, plays must deal with the Pacific Islands, Pacific Rim, or Pacific/Asian-American experience—short plays only considered in 3rd category. **Deadline: January 2.** Prize: Hawaii: $600; Pacific Rim: $450; Resident: $250.

L.A. DESIGNERS' THEATRE-COMMISSIONS

L.A. Designers' Theatre, P.O. Box 1883, Studio City CA 91614-0883. (323)650-9600 or (323)654-2700 T.D.D. Fax: (323)654-3210. E-mail: ladesigners@juno.com. **Contact:** Richard Niederberg, artistic director. Estab. 1970. "Quarterly contest to promote new work and push it onto the conveyor belt to filmed or videotaped entertainment. All submissions must be registered with copyright office and be unpublished. Material will not be returned. Do not submit anything that will not fit in a #10 envelope. No rules, guidelines, fees, or entry forms. Just present an idea that can be commissioned into a full work. Proposals for uncompleted works are encouraged. Unpopular political, religious, social, or other themes are encouraged; 'street' language and nudity are acceptable. Open to any writer." **Deadline: March 15, June 15, September 15, December 15.** Prize: Production or publication of the work in the Los Angeles market. We only want 'first refusal.'

LAS VEGAS INTERNATIONAL FILM FESTIVAL SCREENPLAY COMPETITION

Las Vegas International Film Festival, 10300 W. Charleston Blvd., Las Vegas NV 89135. (502)371-8037. E-mail: info@lvfilmfest.com. Website: www.lvfilmfest.com/Filmmakers/Screenplay_Competition.aspx. "This annual screenplay competition was created to help aspiring screenwriters break into the entertainment industry as well as to support emerging new talent." Scripts may be submitted via hardcopy or electronic file. Scripts should be no longer than 180 pages. **Charges $30.** Prize: Cash prizes are awarded to the First, Second, and Third place winners.

MAXIM MAZUMDAR NEW PLAY COMPETITION

Alleyway Theatre, 1 Curtain Up Alley, Buffalo NY 14202. (716)852-2600. Fax: (716)852-2266. E-mail: newplays@alleyway.com. **Contact:** Literary Manager. Estab. 1989. "Annual competition. Full Length: Not less than 90 minutes, no more than 10 performers. One-Act: Less than 20 minutes, no more than 6 performers. Musicals must be accompanied by audio CD. Finalists announced October 1; winners announced November 1. Playwrights may submit work directly. There is no entry form. Writers may submit once in each category, but pay only 1 fee. Please specify if submission is to be included in competition. Alleyway Theatre must receive first production credit in subsequent printings and productions." **Deadline: July 1. Charges $25.** Prize: Full length: $400, production; One-act: $100, production.

MCKNIGHT ADVANCEMENT GRANT

The Playwrights' Center, 2301 Franklin Ave. E., Minneapolis MN 55406-1099. (612)332-7481, ext. 10. Fax: (612)332-6037. Estab. 1981. Offered annually for either published or unpublished playwrights to recognize those whose work demonstrates exceptional artistic merit and potential and whose primary residence is in the state of Minnesota. The grants are intended to significantly advance recipients' art and careers, and can be used to support a wide variety of expenses. Applications available mid-October. Guidelines for SASE. Additional funds of up to $2,000 are available for workshops and readings. The Playwrights' Center evaluates each application and forwards finalists to a panel of 3 judges from the national theater community. Applicant must have been a citizen 'or permanent resident of the US and a legal resident of the state of Minnesota since July 1, 2009. (Residency must be maintained during fellowship year.) Applicant must have had a minimum of 1 work fully produced by a professional theater at the time of application. **Deadline: February 3.** Prize: $25,000 which can be used to support a wide variety of expenses, including writing time, artistic costs of residency at a theater or arts organization, travel and study, production, or presentation.

MCLAREN MEMORIAL COMEDY PLAY WRITING COMPETITION

Midland Community Theatre, 2000 W. Wadley, Midland TX 79705. (432)682-2544. Fax: (432)682-6136. Estab. 1990. "Offered annually in 2 divisions: one-act and full-length. All entries must be comedies for adults, teens, or children; musical comedies are *not* accepted. Work must have never been professionally produced or published. See website for competition guidelines and required entry form." **Deadline: Jan1-Feb28. Charges $20/script.** Prize: $400 for winning full-length play; $200 for winning one-act play; staged readings for full length finalist.

MEXICO INTERNATIONAL FILM FESTIVAL SCREENPLAY COMPETITION

Mexico International Film Festival, 20058 Ventura Blvd., Suite 123, Woodland Hills CA 91364. E-mail: info@mexicofilmfestival.com. **Charges $30.** Awards are based solely on overall merits of the screenplays.

MONTEREY SCREENPLAY COMPETITION

Monterey County Film Commission, 801 Lighthouse Ave, Suite 104, Monterey CA 93940. (831)646-0910. Fax: (831) 655-9250. E-mail: info@filmmonterey.org. Feature scripts must be between 90 and 120 pages. A completed and signed Entry Form and Entry Fee must accompany each submission. The act of signing and submitting the form constitutes acceptance without reservation of all rules and requirements of the Monterey Screenplay Competition and all decisions rendered by its judges. **Deadline: May 19. July 31. Charges $40-$50.**

MOVIE SCRIPT CONTEST (FEATURE & SHORT)

P.O. Box 6336, Burbank CA 91510-6336. Fax: (818)688-3990. E-mail: info@ moviescriptcontest.com. **Contact:** Jason Zimmatore, Contest Coordinator. To discover & promote new writing talent. **Deadline: July 31.** Prize: $1,000 for 1st Place Short Script Winner. Golden Brad Trophey and promotion for 1st through

3rd place Winners in our feature contest, and the top 10 loglines are read by our producer partners.

MUSICAL STAIRS

West Coast Ensemble, P.O. Box 38728, Los Angeles CA 90038. (818)786-1900. Fax: (818)786-1905. **Contact:** Les Hanson. Offered annually for unpublished writers to nurture, support, and encourage musical creators. Permission to present the musical is granted if work is selected as finalist. **Deadline: June 30.** Prize: $500 and presentation of musical.

NANTUCKET FILM FESTIVAL SCREENPLAY COMPETITION

Nantucket Film Festival, 1633 Broadway, suite 15-333, New York NY 10019. (212)708-1278. Fax: (212)708-7490. E-mail: info@nantucketfilmfestival.org. Screenplays must be standard feature film length (90-130 pages) and standard U.S. format only. **Charges $50.**

NATIONAL CHILDREN'S THEATRE FESTIVAL

Actors' Playhouse at the Miracle Theatre, 280 Miracle Mile, Coral Gables FL 33134. (305)444-9293, ext. 615. Fax: (305)444-4181. E-mail: maulding@actorsplayhouse. org. **Contact:** Earl Maulding. Offered annually for unpublished musicals for young audiences. Target age is 4-12. Script length should be 45-60 minutes. Maximum of 8 actors to play any number of roles. Prefer settings which lend themselves to simplified scenery. Bilingual (English/Spanish) scripts are welcomed. Call or visit website for guidelines. Open to any writer. **Deadline: April 1. Charges $10 fee.** Prize: $500 and full production.

Tips "Travel and lodging during the festival based on availability."

NATIONAL TEN-MINUTE PLAY CONTEST

Actors Theatre of Louisville, 316 W. Main St., Louisville KY 40202-4218. (502)584-1265. Offered annually for previously (professionally) unproduced 10-minute plays (10 pages or less). "Entries must *not* have had an Equity production." One submission/playwright. Scripts are not returned. Please write or call for submission guidelines. Open to US residents. **Deadline: November 1 (postmarked).** Prize: $1,000.

NEVADA FILM OFFICE SCREENWRITER'S COMPETITION

555 E. Washington Ave., Ste. 5400, Las Vegas NV 89101. 1-877-NEV-FILM. "At

least 75% of the locations in the script must be filmable in Nevada." **Deadline: August 30. Charges $25 for pdf submission or $50 for hardcopy.**

NEW AMERICAN COMEDY WORKSHOP

Ukiah Players Theatre, 1041 Low Gap Rd., Ukiah CA 95482. (707)462-9226. Fax: (707)462-1790. E-mail: info@ukiahplayerstheatre.org. **Contact:** Nathan O. Bell, exec. dir. "Offered every 2 years to playwrights seeking to develop their unproduced, full-length comedies into funnier, stronger scripts. Two scripts will be chosen for staged readings; 1 of these may be chosen for full production. Guidelines for SASE are online." **Deadline: November 30 of odd-numbered years.** Prize: Playwrights chosen for readings will receive a $25 royalty/performance. The playwright chosen for full production will receive a $50 royalty/performance, travel (up to $500) to Ukiah for development workshop/rehearsal, lodging, and per diem.

NEW JERSEY SHORT FILM SCREENPLAY COMPETITION

New Jersey State Short Film Festival / Cape May Film Society, PO 595, Cape May NJ 08204. (609)823-9159. Fax: (609) 884-6700. E-mail: info@njstatefilmfestival. com. **Contact:** chair. "The initial emphasis on short films speaks to an avenue ignored by most screenplay competitions, which tend to favor features. Who is eligible: all New Jersey residents; students at New Jersey colleges; anyone else who uses New Jersey as the principal setting for the script." Short scripts should be 12 pages or fewer. (1) Entry form—Can be downloaded from the festival's website closer to submission schedule . Copy must be included with preview DVD. (2) DVD. Both case and tape must be labeled with the title, running time and contact information. (3) Optional: Still from film (photograph or jpeg file). (4) Optional: Promotional material. Notification: Filmmakers will be notified via e-mail. Films must be received, fee paid, no later than October 2, 2009 to be accepted for screening. "To encourage and reward New Jersey film writers." **Deadline: Aug. 15-$10 (early); Sept. 15-$15 (reg.); Oct. 2-$25 (late).** Prize: Grand prize: Manuscript made into a movie.
Tips "Can submit electronically."

NEW VOICE SERIES

Remembrance Through the Performing Arts, P.O. Box 162446, Austin TX 78716. E-mail: RemPerArts@aol.com. **Contact:** Rosalyn Rosen, artistic director. Offered annually to find talented American playwrights who are in the early stages of script development. We develop plays on the page, provide staged readings, work in progress productions, then produce our most developed 'production ready' during our mainstage season. Playwrights must query through e-mail only. Send bio and brief synopsis. Open to Texas playwrights only. **Deadline: Ongoing.**

DON AND GEE NICHOLL FELLOWSHIPS IN SCREENWRITING

Academy of Motion Picture Arts & Sciences, 1313 N. Vine St., Hollywood CA 90028-8107. (310)247-3010. E-mail: nicholl@oscars.org. Website: www.oscars. org/nicholl. Estab. 1985. "Offered annually for unproduced screenplays to identify talented new screenwriters. Open to writers who have not earned more than $5,000 writing for films or TV." **Deadline: May 1. Charges $30 fee.** Prize: Up to five $30,000 fellowships awarded each year.

ONE ACT MARATHON

Attic Theatre Ensemble, 5429 W. Washington Blvd., Los Angeles CA 90016-1112. (323)525-0600. E-mail: info@attictheatre.org. **Contact:** Literary Manager. "Offered annually for unpublished and unproduced work. Scripts should be intended for mature audiences. Length should not exceed 40 minutes. Guidelines for SASE or online." **Deadline: December 31.** Prize: 1st Place: $300; 2nd Place: $100.

ONE-ACT PLAY CONTEST

Tennessee Williams/New Orleans Literary Festival, 938 Lafayette St., Suite 328, New Orleans LA 70113. (504)581-1144. E-mail: info@tennesseewilliams.net. Website: www.tennesseewilliams.net. **Contact:** Paul J. Willis. "Annual contest for an unpublished play." "The One-Act Play Competition is an opportunity for playwrights to see their work fully produced before a large audience during one of the largest literary festivals in the nation, and for the festival to showcase undiscovered talent." **Deadline: December 1. Charges $15.** Prize: $1,000 and a staged reading at the festival. The play will also be fully produced at the following year's festival. The Tennessee Williams/New Orleans Literary Festival reserves the right to publish. an anonymous expert panel.
Tips "Guidelines and entry forms can be found on the website, or send a SASE."

ONE IN TEN SCREENPLAY CONTEST

Cherub Productions, P.O. Box 540, Boulder CO 80306. E-mail: Cherubfilm@ aol.com. Website: www.OneInTenScreenplayContest.com. Scripts that provide a positive portrayal of gays and lesbians. "A requirement of the competition is that at least one of the primary characters in the screenplay be gay or lesbian (bisexual, transgender, questioning, and the like) and that gay and lesbian characters must be portrayed positively. All writers are encouraged to enter!" **Deadline: September 1. Charges $45.** Prize: $1,000.

PAGE INTERNATIONAL SCREENWRITING AWARDS, THE

7510 Sunset Blvd., #610, Hollywood CA 90046-3408. E-mail: info@pageawards. com. **Contact:** Zoe Simmons, contest coor. "Annual competition to discover the most talented new screenwriters from across the country and around the world. Each year, awards are presented to 31 screenwriters in 10 different genre categories. Guidelines and entry forms are available online. Open to all writers over 18 years of age who have not previously earned more than $25,000 writing for film and/ or television." Adaptations of books, plays, or other source material written by another author are not eligible under any circumstances; nor are scripts adapted from books, plays, or other source material written by you if your source material has been sold, produced, or is currently under option to any third party. Scripts adapted from your own self-published books, plays, or other source material are eligible if you have retained all rights to your work. **Jan. 15 (early); March 1 (regular); April 1 (late). Charges Entry fees: $39 (early); $49 (regular); -$59 (late).** Prize: Over $50,000 in cash and prizes, including a $25,000 Grand Prize, plus Gold, Silver, and Bronze Prizes in all 10 categories. Most importantly, the award-winning writers receive extensive publicity and industry exposure. action/ adventure, comedy, drama, family, historical, sci-fi/fantasy, thriller/horror, short film script, TV drama pilot, and TV sitcom pilot. The contest is judged by Hollywood professionals, including industry script readers, consultants, agents, managers, producers, and development executives.

THE PAGE INTERNATIONAL SCREENWRITING AWARDS

The PAGE Awards Committee, 7510 Sunset Blvd., #610, Hollywood CA 90046-3408. E-mail: info@PAGEawards.com. **Contact:** Zoe Simmons, contest coordinator. Annual competition to discover the most talented new screenwriters from across the country and around the world. "Each year, awards are presented to 31 screenwriters in 10 different categories: action/adventure, comedy, drama, family film, historical film, science fiction/fantasy, thriller/horror, short film script, TV drama pilot, and TV sitcom pilot. Guidelines and entry forms are online. The contest is open to all writers 18 years of age and older who have not previously earned more than $25,000 writing for film and/or television. Please visit contest Web site for a complete list of rules and regulations." **Deadline: January 15 (early); March 1 (regular); April 1 (late). Charges $39 (early); $49 (regular); $59 (late).** Prize: Over $50,000 in cash and prizes, including a $10,000 grand prize, plus gold, silver, and bronze prizes in all 10 categories. Most importantly, the award-winning writers receive extensive publicity and industry exposure.

Judging is done entirely by Hollywood professionals, including industry script readers, consultants, agents, managers, producers, and development executives. Entrants retain all rights to their work.

THE PEN IS A MIGHTY SWORD

The Virtual Theatre Project, 1901 Rosalia Rd., Los Angeles CA 90027. (877)787-8036. Fax: (323)660-5097. E-mail: pen_sword2008@yahoo.com. **Contact:** Whit Andrews. "Annual contest open to unproduced plays written specifically for the stage. Contest opens January 1, 2010. Plays should be bold, compelling, and passionate. Guidelines for SASE or online." **Deadline: June 30. Charges $10.** Prize: 1st Place: $2,000 and staged reading; 2nd Place: $1,000 and a staged reading; 3rd Place: $500 and a reading. In addition, up to 7 honorable mentions receive $100 each. Judged by a panel of professional writers, directors, and producers.

ROBERT J. PICKERING AWARD FOR PLAYWRIGHTING EXCELLENCE

Coldwater Community Theater, c/o 89 Division, Coldwater MI 49036. (517)279-7963. Fax: (517)279-8095. **Contact:** J. Richard Colbeck, committee chairperson. Estab. 1982. Contest to encourage playwrights to submit their work and to present a previously unproduced play in full production. Must be previously unproduced monetarily. Submit script with SASE. "We reserve the right to produce winning script." **Deadline: December 31.** Prize: 1st Place: $300; 2nd Place: $100; 3rd Place: $50.

PILGRIM PROJECT GRANTS

156 Fifth, #400, New York NY 10010. (212)627-2288. Fax: (212)627-2184. E-mail: davida@firstthings.com. **Contact:** Davida Goldman. "Grants for a reading, workshop production, or full production of plays that deal with questions of moral significance." **Deadline: Ongoing.** Prize: Grants of $1,000-7,000.

⚎ PRAXIS FALL SCREENWRITING COMPETITION

Praxis Centre for Screenwriters, 515 W. Hastings St., Suite 3120, Vancouver BC V6B 5K3 Canada. (778)782-7880. Fax: (778)782-7882. E-mail: praxis@sfu. ca. "We are looking for feature film scripts of any genre. Each writer remains anonymous to the jury until a short list has been identified. Must be Canadian citizens or landed immigrants." **Deadline: 06/27/2009. Charges $75.**

RHODE ISLAND INTERNATIONAL FILM FESTIVAL FEATURE SCREENPLAY COMPETITION

P.O. Box 162, Newport RI 02840. (401)861-4445. Fax: (401)861-7590. E-mail: adams@film-festival.org. Website: www.film-festival.org/enterascreenplay.php. "This contest for the festival looks for feature length scripts." Scripts not to exceed 130 pages. "The purpose of the contest is to promote, embolden and cultivate screenwriters in their quest for opportunities in the industry." **Deadline: July 5.** All genres.

Tips "Screenplays will be judged on creativity, innovation, vision, originality and the use of language. The key element is that of communication and how it complements and is transformed by the language of film."

RHODE ISLAND INTERNATIONAL FILM FESTIVAL SHORT SCREENPLAY COMPETITION

PO Box 162, Newport RI (401)861-4445. Fax: (401)490-6735. E-mail: adams@film-festival.org. Website: www.film-festival.org/enterascreenplay.php. "This second contest for the festival looks for short and feature length scripts." "The purpose of the contest is to promote, embolden and cultivate screenwriters in their quest for opportunities within the industry."

RICHARD RODGERS AWARDS IN MUSICAL THEATER

American Academy of Arts and Letters, 633 W. 155th St., New York NY 10032-7599. (212)368-5900. Fax: (212)491-4615. Website: www.artsandletters.org. **Contact:** Jane E. Bolster. Estab. 1978. "The Richard Rodgers Awards subsidize full productions, studio productions, and staged readings by nonprofit theaters in New York City of works by composers and writers who are not already established in the field of musical theater. Authors must be citizens or permanent residents of the US. Guidelines and application for SASE or online." **Deadline: November 1.**

SCREENWRITING EXPO SCREENPLAY COMPETITION

6404 Hollywood Blvd., Ste 415, Los Angeles CA 90028. (323)957-1405. Fax: (323)957-1406. E-mail: contests@screenwritingexpo.com. **Contact:** Pasha McKenley, contest coordinator. "Writers must be at least 18 years old and have not earned more than $8,000 for writing services in film or television. Submitted screenplays must be the unproduced, unoptioned, and wholly original work of the writer(s). There must be no dispute about the ownership of submitted screenplays or the writers' right to submit screenplay. Submitted teleplays will adhere to the industry "spec script" practice of being a derivative work based on a pre-existing television series, however submitted teleplays must contain original story and dialogue. For teleplays, any characters created by the writer(s) must be wholly original work. Pilots for unproduced television shows or episodes of an unproduced series will not be accepted." **Deadline: multiple deadlines. Charges $45-65.** Prize: $20,000 grand prize, a trip to LA for the Expo, and four genre prizes totaling $10,000. Action-Adventure, Thriller, Sci-Fi, Comedy, Family, Animation, Low Budget Indie, Horror, Fantasy.

SCRIPTAPALOOZA SCREENPLAY COMPETITION

Writers Guild of America west Registry and sponsored by Write Brothers, Inc., 7775 Sunset Blvd., PMB #200, Hollywood CA 90046. (323)654-5809. E-mail: info@scriptapalooza.com. Estab. 1998. "Annual competition for unpublished scripts from any genre. Open to any writer, 18 or older. Submit one copy of a 90- to 130-page screenplay. Body pages must be numbered, and scripts must be in industry-standard format. All entered scripts will be read and judged by more than 90 production companies." **Early Deadline: January 7; Deadline: March 5; Late Deadline: April 15. Charges $40 (early); $45 (regular deadline); $50 (late).** Prize: 1st Place: $10,000 and software package from Write Brothers, Inc.; 2nd Place, 3rd Place, and 10 Runners-Up: Software package from Write Brothers, Inc. The top 100 scripts will be considered by over 90 production companies.

SCRIPTAPALOOZA TELEVISION WRITING COMPETITION

7775 Sunset Blvd., PMB #200, Hollywood CA 90046. (323)654-5809. E-mail: info@scriptapalooza.com. "Biannual competition accepting entries in 4 categories: reality shows, sitcoms, original pilots, and 1-hour dramas. There are more than 25 producers, agents, and managers reading the winning scripts. Two past winners won Emmys because of Scriptapalooza and 1 past entrant now writes for Comedy Central." **Deadline: October 15 and April 15. Charges $40.** Prize: 1st Place: $500; 2nd Place: $200; 3rd Place: $100 (in each category).

"SET IN PHILADELPHIA" SCREENWRITING COMPETITION

Greater Philadelphia Film Office, 100 S. Broad Street, Suite 600, Philadelphia PA 19110. (215)686-2668. Fax: (215)686-3659. E-mail: sip@film.org. Website: www.film.org. Screenplays must be set primarily in the Greater Philadelphia area (includes the surrounding counties). All genres and storytelling approaches are acceptable. Screenplays must be between 85-130 pages in length. There are different awards, such as an award for the best script for writers under 25, as well as the best script for a regional writer. See the Web site for full details. **Charges $45-65.** Prize: $10,000 grand prize, with other prizes offered.

🌐 SHRIEKFEST HORROR/SCI-FI FILM FESTIVAL & SCREENPLAY COMPETITION

PO Box 920444, Sylmar CA 91392. E-mail: shriekfest@aol.com. Website: www. shriekfest.com. **Contact:** Denise Gossett/Todd Beeson. "No, we don't use loglines anywhere, we keep your script private." We accept award winning screenplays, no restrictions as long as it's in the horror/thriller or scifi/fantasy genres. We accept shorts and features. No specific lengths. "Our awards are to help screenwriters move their script up the ladder and hopefully have it made into a film. Our winners take that win and parlay it into agents, film deals, and options." **Deadline: May 22 and June 30. Charges $25-55.** Prize: Trophies, product awards, usually cash. Our awards are updated all year long as sponsors step onboard. The winners go home with lots of stuff. The contest is open to any writer, all ages, we have an under 18 category too. And we are an international contest. We have at least 15-20 judges and they are all in different aspects of the entertainment industry, such as producers, directors, writers, actors, agents."

DOROTHY SILVER PLAYWRITING COMPETITION OF THE MANDEL

The Mandel Jewish Community Center of Cleveland, 26001 S. Woodland, Beachwood OH 44122. (216)831-0700. Fax: (216)831-7796. E-mail: dbobrow@ clevejcc.org. Website: www.clevejcc.org. **Contact:** Deborah Bobrow, competition coordinator. "All entries must be original works, not previously produced, suitable for a full-length presentation, and directly concerned with the Jewish experience." **Deadline: December 31, notification by end of March.** Prize: Cash award and a staged reading.

SOUTHEASTERN THEATRE CONFERENCE NEW PLAY PROJECT

Dept. of Theatre & Dance, Austin Peay State Univ., 681 Summer St., Clarksville TN 37044. E-mail: hardinb@apsu.edu. **Contact:** Chris Hardin, chair. "Annual award for full-length plays or related one acts. No musicals or children's plays. Submissions must be unproduced/unpublished. Readings and workshops are acceptable. Submit application, synopsis, and 1 copy of script on CD or as an e-mail attachment (preferred). Send SASE or visit website for application. Entries will be accepted between March 1st and June 1st. One submission per playwright only." Eligibility: Playwrights who reside in the SETC region (or who are enrolled in a regionally accredited educational institution in the SETC region) or who reside outside the region but are SETC members are eligible for consideration. SETC Region states include Alabama, Florida, Georgia, Kentucky, Mississippi, North Carolina, South Carolina, Tennessee, Virginia, West Virginia.

Mission: The SETC New Play Project is dedicated to the discovery, development and publicizing of worthy new plays and playwrights. **Deadline: June 1.** Prize: $1,000 and a staged reading.

Tips "Text should be in 12 pt type and in a plain font such as Times New Roman. Plays must be submitted by email attachment in Microsoft Word or PDF format with the following guidelines: Script must include page numbers at the bottom of each page. The author's name should not appear anywhere in the script. Do not include resumes, playwright biographies or a history of the play. 1 copy, Word or PDF format, attached to an email. Completed Application Form included as separate email attachment. Electronic signatures will be accepted. The decision of the panel of readers will be announced in November of each year."

SOUTHERN PLAYWRIGHTS COMPETITION

Jacksonville State University, 700 Pelham Rd. N., Jacksonville AL 36265-1602. (256)782-5469. Fax: (256)782-5441. E-mail: jmaloney@jsu.edu; swhitton@jsu.edu. Website: www.jsu.edu/depart/english/southpla.htm. **Contact:** Joy Maloney, Steven J. Whitton. Estab. 1988. "Offered annually to identify and encourage the best of Southern playwriting. Playwrights must be a native or resident of Alabama, Arkansas, District of Columbia, Florida, Georgia, Kentucky, Louisiana, Missouri, North Carolina, South Carolina, Tennessee, Texas, Virginia, or West Virginia." **Deadline: January 15.** Prize: $1,000 and production of the play.

TELEPLAY COMPETITION

Austin Film Festival, 1801 Salina St.,, Austin TX 78702. (512)478-4795. Fax: (512)478-6205. E-mail: alex@austinfilmfestival.con. Offered annually for unproduced work to discover talented television writers and introduce their work to industry professionals. Categories: drama and sitcom (must be specific scripts for currently airing cable or network shows). Contest open to writers who do not earn a living writing for television or film. **Deadline: June 1. Charges $30.** Prize: $1,000 in each category.

■ THEATRE BC'S ANNUAL CANADIAN NATIONAL PLAYWRITING COMPETITION

Theatre BC, P.O. Box 2031, Nanaimo BC V9R 6X6 Canada. (250)714-0203. Fax: (250)714-0213. E-mail: pwc@theatrebc.org. **Contact:** Robb Mowbray, executive director. Offered annually "to unpublished plays to promote the development and production of previously unproduced new plays (no musicals) at all levels of theater." Categories: Full Length (75 minutes or longer); One-Act (less than 75 minutes); and an open Special Merit (juror's discretion). Guidelines for SASE or online. Winners are also invited to New Play Festival: Up to 16 hours with a professional dramaturg, registrant actors, and a public reading in Kamloops (every Spring). Production and publishing rights remain with the playwright. Open to Canadian residents. All submissions are made under pseudonyms. E-mail inquiries welcome. **Deadline: Fourth Monday in July. Charges $40/ entry; optional $25 for written critique.** Prize: Full Length: $1,000; One-Act: $750; Special Merit: $500.

TRUSTUS PLAYWRIGHTS' FESTIVAL

Trustus Theatre, Box 11721, Columbia SC 29211-1721. (803)254-9732. Fax: (803)771-9153. E-mail: sarahkhammond@gmail.com. Website: www.trustus.org. **Contact:** Sarah Hammond, literary manager. Offered annually for professionally unproduced full-length plays; cast limit of 8. Prefers challenging, innovative dramas and comedies. No musicals, plays for young audiences, or "hillbilly" southern shows. Send SASE or consult Trustus Web site for guidelines and application. Festival for 2009 has been suspended for production of in-house play. **Deadline: for 2011 festival: December 1, 2009-February 28, 2010.** Prize: $500 and a 1-year development period with full production and travel/accommodations to attend the public opening.

UNICORN THEATRE NEW PLAY DEVELOPMENT

Unicorn Theatre, 3828 Main St., Kansas City MO 64111. (816)531-7529, ext. 22. Fax: (816)531-0421. **Contact:** Herman Wilson, literary assistant. Offered annually to encourage and assist the development of an unpublished and unproduced play. We look for nonmusical, issue-oriented, thought-provoking plays set in contemporary times (post 1950s) with a cast limit of 10. Submit cover letter, brief bio/résumé, short synopsis, complete character breakdown, complete ms, SASE. Does not return scripts. **Deadline: Ongoing.**

VAIL FILM FESTIVAL SCREENPLAY COMPETITION

Vail Film Institute, PO Box 747, Vail CO 81657. (970)476-1092. Fax: (646)349-1767. E-mail: info@vailfilmfestival.org. "The Vail Film Festival Screenplay Competition is a vehicle for aspiring screenwriters to get their script read by established film producers who are actively working at the top level of the film industry. Competition winners will have networking opportunities with some of Hollywood's top players, as well as nationwide exposure through media coverage and a Vail Film Festival press release. Screenplay submissions are judged by film industry professionals with the top three screenplays receiving prizes." Feature Scripts must be between 70-125 pages in length. Short Scripts must be between 3-45 pages in length. **October 30, 2009 (Early registration: August 31;**

Regular: Sept. 30). Charges $35-65. Prize: 2 Filmmaker Passes to the 2010 Vail Film Festival, 1 domestic air ticket to Denver, 3 night hotel accommodations in Vail, screenplay read by established film production companies. Staged reading of excerpt of winning screenplay during the Vail Film Festival April 1-4, 2010. Film industry professionals.

Tips Apply online at the website through Withoutabox link. "We have also partnered up with InkTip again. InkTip is giving our 1st place feature script winner placement of their winning script on their password-protected website for free and placement of their winning script logline in their magazine which is snail-mailed to 4500 industry professionals, and emailed to thousands more."

WICHITA STATE UNIVERSITY PLAYWRITING COMPETITION

School of Performing Arts, Wichita State University, 1845 N. Fairmount, Campus Box 153, Wichita KS 67260-0153. (316)978-3360. Fax: (316)978-3202. E-mail: brett.jones@wichita.edu. **Contact:** Bret Jones, Director of Theatre. Estab. 1974. Offered for unpublished, unproduced (a) Full-length plays in one or more acts should be a minimum of 90 minutes playing time; (b) Two or three short plays on related themes by the same author will be judged as one entry. The total playing time should be a minimum of 90 minutes; (c) Musicals should be a minimum of 90 minutes playing time and must include a CD of the accompanying music. Contestants must be graduate or undergraduate students in a US college or university. **Deadline: March 15.** Prize: Production of winning play (ACTF) Judged by a panel of faculty.

WRITERS ON THE STORM SCREENPLAY COMPETITION

Coverage, Ink., P.O. Box 899, Venice CA 90294. (310)582-5880. E-mail: writerstorm@gmail.com. Website: www.writerstorm.com. "We're all about empowering the writer, because we ARE writers. Yes, a contest that's actually by writers, for writers. Our prizes are deliberately development-heavy because we believe knowledge is power. Must be 18 years of age or older. Open to anyone who has earned less than $10,000 career earnings as a screenwriter." **Deadline: July 27, 2009. Charges $40.** Prize: $22,000 in prizes.

THE WRITERS PLACE SCREENPLAY CONTEST

525 E. 72nd St., #18A, New York NY 10021. (310)429-5181. E-mail: contact2@thewritersplace.org. **Deadline: January 1-May 15, 2009. Charges $55.**

WRITESAFE PRESENT-A-THON

3767 MC 5026, Saint Joe AR 72675. (870)449-2488. E-mail: admin@writesafe.

com. "A quarterly contest with these deadlines: The first Present-A-Thon of each year starts January 1 and ends March 31. The second Present-A-Thon of each year starts April 1 and ends June 30. The third Present-A-Thon of each year starts July 1 and ends September 30. The fourth Present-A-Thon of each year starts October 1 and ends December 31." **Deadline: March 31, June 30, September 30 and December 31.** Prize: First Prize is consideration for publication, production, or representation by a panel of experts. Second Prize is consideration for publication, production, or representation. More prizes awarded.

YEAR END SERIES (YES) FESTIVAL OF NEW PLAYS

Dept. of Theatre, Nunn Dr., Northern Kentucky University, Highland Heights KY 41099-1007. (859)572-6362. Fax: (859)572-6057. E-mail: forman@nku.edu. **Contact:** Sandra Forman, project director. "Receives submissions from May 1 until September 30 in even-numbered years for the festivals which occur in April of odd-numbered years. Open to all writers." **Deadline: October 1.** Prize: $500 and an expense-paid visit to Northern Kentucky University to see the play produced.

YOUNG PLAYWRIGHTS INC. WRITE A PLAY! NYC COMPETITION

Young Playwrights, Inc., P.O. Box 5134, New York NY 10185. (212)594-5440. Fax: (212)684-4902. E-mail: literary@youngplaywrights.org. **Contact:** Literary Department. "Offered annually for stage plays of any length (no musicals, screenplays, or adaptations) by NYC elementary, middle, and high school students only." **Deadline: April 1.** Prize: Prize varies.

ANNA ZORNIO MEMORIAL CHILDREN'S THEATRE PLAYWRITING COMPETITION

University of New Hampshire, Dept. of Theatre and Dance, PCAC, 30 Academic Way,, Durham NH 03824-3538. (603)862-3044. E-mail: mike.wood@unh.edu. **Contact:** Michael Wood. "Offered every 4 years for unpublished well-written plays or musicals appropriate for young audiences with a maximum length of 60 minutes. May submit more than 1 play, but not more than 3. All plays will be performed by adult actors and must be appropriate for a children's audience within the K-12 grades. Guidelines and entry forms available as downloads on the website. Open to all playwrights in US and Canada. All ages are invited to participate." **Deadline: March 2, 2012.** Prize: Up to $500. The play is also produced and underwritten as part of the 2013-2014 season by the UNH Department of Theatre and Dance. Winner will be notified on or after Dec. 15, 2012.

Theaters

Where TV and movies have a diminished role for writers in the collaboration that produces the final product, whether a show or a film, theater places a very high value on the playwright. This may have something to do with the role of the scripts in the different settings.

Screenplays are often in a constant state of "in progress," where directors make changes; producers make changes; and even actors and actresses make changes throughout the filming of the TV show or movie. Plays, on the other hand, must be as solid as a rock, because the script must be performed live night after night.

As a result, playwrights tend to have more involvement in the productions of their scripts, a power screenwriters can only envy. Counterbalancing the greater freedom of expression are the physical limitations inherent in live performance: a single stage, smaller cast, limited sets and lighting, and, most importantly, a strict, smaller budget. These conditions not only affect what but also how you write.

Listings

The following listings include contact information, submission details, current needs, and other helpful tips to help you find a home for your finished and polished play. As with any market, it is advised that after you pinpoint a listing that you then follow up with them to find out their most current submission policy and to ask who you should address your submission. This might seem like a lot of work, but writing plays is a competitive business. Your professionalism will go a long way in separating you from other "wannabe" playwrights.

For more information

To find out more about writing and submitting plays, contact the Dramatists

Guild (www.dramaguild.com) and the Writers Guild of America (www.wga.org). Both organizations are great for networking and for learning the basics needed to build a successful career crafting plays.

ABINGDON THEATRE CO.

312 W. 36th St., 6th Floor, New York NY 10018. (212)868-2055. Fax: (212)868-2056. E-mail: literary@abingdontheatre.org. Artistic Director: Jan Buttram. **Contact:** Literary Manager: Kim T. Sharp. Estab. 1993. Produces 2-3 Mainstage and 2-3 Studio productions/year. Professional productions for a general audience. Submit full-length script in hard copy, cast breakdown, synopsis and development history, if any. No one-act. Include SASE for return of manuscript. Responds in 4 months. Buys variable rights. Payment is negotiated.

Needs All scripts should be suitable for small stages. No musicals where the story line is not very well-developed and the driving force of the piece.

Tips "Check website for updated submission guidelines."

ACT II PLAYHOUSE

P.O. Box 555, Ambler PA 19002-0555. (215)654-0200. Fax: (215)654-9050. Frank Martin. **Contact:** Stephen Blumenthal, literary manager. Estab. 1998. Produces 5 plays/year. Submit query and synopsis. Include SASE for return of submission. Responds in 1 month. Payment negotiable.

Needs Contemporary comedy, drama, musicals. Full length. 6 character limitation; 1 set or unit set. Does not want period pieces. Limited number of scenes per act.

ACTORS THEATRE OF LOUISVILLE

316 W. Main St., Louisville KY 40202-4218. (502)584-1265. Fax: (502)561-3300. E-mail: awegener@actorstheatre.org. **Contact:** Amy Wegener, literary manager. Estab. 1964. Produces approximately 25 new plays of varying lengths/year. "Professional productions are performed for subscription audience from diverse backgrounds. Agented submissions only for full-length plays, will read 10-page samples of unagented full-length works. Open submissions to National Ten-Minute Play Contest (plays 10 pages or less) are due November 1." Responds in 9 months to submissions, mostly in the fall. Buys variable rights. Offers variable royalty.

Needs "We are interested in full-length and 10-minute plays and in plays of ideas, language, humor, experiment and passion."

Ⓐ ACT THEATRE

A Contemporary Theatre, Kreielsheimer Place, 700 Union St., Seattle WA 98101. (206)292-7660. Fax: (206)292-7670. E-mail: artistic@acttheatre.org. Kurt Beattie. Estab. 1965. Produces 5-6 mainstage plays/year. "ACT performs a subscription-based season on 3 stages: 2 main stages (a thrust and an arena) and a smaller, flexible 99-seat space. Although our focus is towards our local Seattle audience, some of our notable productions have gone on to other venues in other cities." *Agented submissions only* or through theatre professional's recommendation. No unsolicited submissions. Query and synopsis only for Northwest playwrights. Responds in 6 months. Pays 5-10% royalty.

Needs ACT produces full-length contemporary scripts ranging from solo pieces to large ensemble works, with an emphasis on plays that embrace the contradictions and mysteries of our contemporary world and that resonate with audiences of all backgrounds through strong storytelling and compelling characters.

Tips "ACT is looking for plays that offer strong narrative, exciting ideas, and well-drawn, dimensional characters that will engage an audience emotionally and intellectually. These may sound like obvious prerequisites for a play, but often it seems that playwrights are less concerned with the story they have to tell than with the way they're telling it, emphasizing flashy, self-conscious style over real substance and solid structure."

ALLEYWAY THEATRE

One Curtain Up Alley, Buffalo NY 14202. (716)852-2600. Fax: (716)852-2266. E-mail: newplays@alleyway.com. **Contact:** Literary Manager. Estab. 1980. Produces 4-5 full-length, 6-12 one-act plays/year. Submit complete script; include CD for musicals. Alleyway Theatre also sponsors the Maxim Mazumdar New Play Competition. See the Contest & Awards section for more information. Responds in 6 months. Seeks first production rights. Pays 7% royalty.

Needs "Works written uniquely for the theatre. Theatricality, breaking the fourth wall, and unusual settings are of particular interest. We are less interested in plays which are likely to become TV or film scripts."

ALLIANCE THEATRE

1280 Peachtree St. NE, Atlanta GA 30309. (404)733-4650. Fax: (404)733-4625. Website: www.alliancetheatre.org. **Contact:** Literary Intern. Estab. 1969. Produces 11 plays/year. Professional production for local audience. Only accepts agent submissions and unsolicited samples from Georgia residents only. Electronic correspondence preferred. Query with synopsis and sample or submit through agent. Enclose SASE. Responds in 9 months.

Needs Full-length scripts and scripts for young audiences no longer than 60 minutes.

Tips "As the premier theater of the southeast, the Alliance Theatre sets the highest artistic standards, creating the powerful experience of shared theater for diverse people."

⊘ AMERICAN CONSERVATORY THEATER

30 Grant Ave., 6th Floor, San Francisco CA 94108-5800. (415)834-3200. Artistic Director: Carey Perloff. **Contact:** Pink Pasdar, associate artistic director. Estab. 1965. Produces 8 plays/year. Plays are performed in Geary Theater, a 1,000-seat classic proscenium. No unsolicited scripts.

APPLE TREE THEATRE

1850 Green Bay Rd., Suite 100, Highland Park IL 60035. (847)432-8223. Fax: (847)432-5214. E-mail: info@appletreetheatre.com. **Contact:** Eileen Boevers. Estab. 1983. Produces 4 plays/year. "Professional productions intended for an adult audience mix of subscriber base and single-ticket holders. Our subscriber base is extremely theater-savvy and intellectual." Return SASE submissions only if requested. Rights obtained vary. Pays variable royalty.

Needs "We produce a mixture of musicals, dramas, classical, contemporary, and comedies." Length: 90 minutes-2 1/2 hours. Small space, unit set required. No fly space, theatre in the round. Maximum actors 5.

Tips "No farces or large-scale musicals. Theater needs small shows with 1-unit sets due to space and financial concerns. Also note the desire for nonlinear pieces that break new ground. *Please do not submit unsolicited manuscripts—send letter and description along with tapes for musicals*; if we want more, we will request it."

Ⓐ ARENA STAGE

1101 6th St. SW, Washington DC 20024. (202)554-9066. Fax: (202)488-4056. Artistic Director: Molly Smith. **Contact:** Mark Bly, senior dramaturg. Estab. 1950. Produces 8 plays/year. Only accepts scripts from writers with agent or theatrical representation.

Needs "Plays that illuminate the broad canvas of American work, with a commitment to aesthetic, cultural, and geographic diversity. Arena is committed to showcasing the past, present, and future of American theatre." Seeks only full-length plays and musicals in all genres.

ARIZONA THEATRE CO.

P.O. Box 1631, Tucson AZ 85702. (520)884-8210. Fax: (520)628-9129. **Contact:** Literary Department. Estab. 1966. Produces 6-8 plays/year. "Arizona Theatre Company is the State Theatre of Arizona and plans the season with the population of the state in mind." Only Arizona writers may submit unsolicited scripts, along with production history (if any), brief bio, and SASE. Out-of-state writers can send a synopsis, 10-page sample dialogue, production history (if any), brief bio, and SASE. Responds in 4-6 months. Payment negotiated.

Needs Full length plays of a variety of genres and topics and full length musicals. No one-acts.

Tips "Please include in the cover letter something about your current situation and goals."

ARTISTS REPERTORY THEATRE

1515 SW Morrison, Portland OR 97205. (503)241-1278. Fax: (503)241-8268. Estab. 1982. Produces Plays performed in professional theater with a subscriber-based audience. Send synopsis, résumé, and sample (maximum 10 pages). No unsolicited mss accepted. Responds in 6 months. Pays royalty.

- "We bring Portland the newest and most exhilarating plays being written today and simultaneously showcase the talents of local theater artists."

Needs Full-length, hard-hitting, emotional, intimate, actor-oriented shows with small casts (rarely exceeds 10-13, usually 2-7). Language and subject matter are not a problem. No one-acts or children's scripts.

ART STATION THEATRE

5384 Manor Dr., Stone Mountain GA 30083. (770)469-1105. E-mail: info@artstation. org. **Contact:** Jon Goldstein, program manager. Estab. 1986. Produces 3 plays/year. ART Station Theatre is a professional theater located in a contemporary arts center in Stone Mountain, GA, which is part of Metro Atlanta. Audience consists of middle-aged to senior, suburban patrons. Query with synopsis and writing samples. Responds in 1 year. Pays 5-7% royalty.

Needs Full length comedy, drama and musicals, preferably relating to the human condition in the contemporary South. Cast size no greater than 6.

ASIAN AMERICAN THEATER CO.

55 Teresita Blvd., San Francisco CA 94127. E-mail: aatcspace@gmail.com. **Contact:** Artistic Director. Estab. 1973. Produces 4 plays/year. Produces professional productions for San Francisco Bay Area audiences. Submit complete script. Payment varies.

Needs The new voice of Asian American theater. No limitations in cast, props or staging.

Tips "Looking for plays from the new Asian American theater aesthetic—bold, substantive, punchy. Scripts from Asian Pacific Islander American women and under-represented Asian Pacific Islander ethnic groups are especially welcome."

⊘ ASOLO THEATRE CO.

5555 N. Tamiami Trail, Sarasota FL 34234. (941)351-9010. Fax: (941)351-5796. **Contact:** Michael Donald Edwards, Production Artistic Dir. Estab. 1960. Produces 7-8 plays/year. A LORT theater with 2 intimate performing spaces. Negotiates rights and payment.

Needs Play must be full length. "We operate with a resident company in rotating repertory."

ATTIC THEATRE & FILM CENTRE

5429 W. Washington Blvd., Los Angeles CA 90016-1112. (323)525-0600. Website: www.attictheatre.org. Artistic Director: James Carey. **Contact:** Literary Manager. Estab. 1987. Produces 4 plays/year. "We are based in Los Angeles and play to industry and regular Joes. We use professional actors; however, our house is very small, and the salaries we pay, including the royalties are very small because of that." Send query and synopsis or check out website. Returns submissions with SASE. Responds in 4 months. Buys first producer rights. Payment is negotiated on a case by case basis.

Needs "We will consider any type of play except musicals and large cast historical pieces with multiple hard sets. One Act plays are only accepted through the Denise Ragan Wiesenmeyer One Act Marathon Competition. Please see website for contest rules and regulations. One Acts can not be any longer than 30 minutes."

Tips "Please send an SASE and read our guidelines on the website. Follow all the directions."

BAILIWICK REPERTORY

Bailiwick Arts Center, 1229 W. Belmont Ave., Chicago IL 60657-3205. (773)883-1090. Fax: (773)883-2017. E-mail: bailiwick@bailiwick.org. **Contact:** David Zak, artistic director. Estab. 1982. Produces 5 mainstage plays (classic and newly commissioned) each year; 12 one-acts in annual Directors Festival. Pride Performance Series (gay and lesbian), includes one-acts, poetry, workshops, and staged adaptations of prose. Submit year-round. One-act play fest runs July-August. Responds in 9 months for full-length only. Pays 6% royalty.

Needs "We need daring scripts that break the mold." Large casts or musicals are OK. Creative staging solutions are a must.

Tips "Know the rules, then break them creatively and boldly! Please send SASE for manuscript submission guidelines *before you submit* or get manuscript guidelines at our website."

BAKER'S PLAYS PUBLISHING CO.

45 W. 25th St., New York NY 10010. E-mail: publications@bakersplays.com. **Contact:** Managing Editor. Estab. 1845. **Publishes 20-30 straight plays and musicals. Works with 2-3 unpublished/unproduced writers annually. 80% freelance written. 75% of scripts unagented submissions.** Plays performed by amateur groups, high schools, children's theater, churches and community theater groups. Submit complete script with news clippings, resume, production history. Submit complete CD of music with musical submissions. See our website for more information about e-submissions. Responds in 3-6 months. Pay varies; negotiated royalty split of production fees; 10% book royalty.

Needs "We are finding strong support in our new division—plays from young authors featuring contemporary pieces for high school production."

Tips "We are particularly interested in adaptation of lesser-known folk tales from around the world. Also of interest are plays which feature a multicultural cast and theme. Collections of one-act plays for children and young adults tend to do very well. Also, high school students: Write for guidelines (see our website)for information about our High School Playwriting Contest."

MARY BALDWIN COLLEGE THEATRE

Mary Baldwin College, Staunton VA 24401. Fax: (540)887-7139. **Contact:** Terry K. Southerington, professor of theater. Estab. 1842. Produces 5 plays/year. 10% of scripts are unagented submissions. "An undergraduate women's college theater with an audience of students, faculty, staff and local community (adult, somewhat conservative)." Query with synopsis. Responds in 1 year. Buys performance rights only. Pays $10-50/performance.

Needs "Full-length and short comedies, tragedies, and music plays geared particularly toward young women actresses, dealing with women's issues both contemporary and historical. Experimental/studio theater not suitable for heavy sets. Cast should emphasize women. No heavy sex; minimal explicit language."

Tips "A perfect play for us has several roles for young women, few male roles, minimal production demands, a concentration on issues relevant to contemporary society, and elegant writing and structure."

BARTER THEATRE

P.O. Box 867, Abingdon VA 24212-0867. (276)628-2281. Fax: (276)619-3335. E-mail: dramaturge@bartertheatre.com. **Contact:** Catherine Bush, dramaturge. Estab. 1933. Produces 17 plays/year. "Plays performed in residency at 2 facilities, a 500-seat proscenium theater and a smaller 167-seat flexible theater. Our plays are intended for diversified audiences of all ages." Submit synopsis and dialogue sample only with SASE. Barter Theatre often premieres new works. Responds in 9 months. Pays negotiable royalty.

Needs "We are looking for good plays, comedies and dramas that entertain and are relevant; plays that examine in new and theatrical ways the human condition and contemporary issues. We prefer casts of 4-12, single or unit set. Strong language may lessen a play's appeal for Barter audiences."

Tips "We are looking for material that appeals to diverse, family audiences. We accept no one act play queries."

BLOOMSBURG THEATRE ENSEMBLE

226 Center St., Bloomsburg PA 17815. E-mail: jsatherton@bte.org. Ensemble Director:Gerard Stropnicky. **Contact:** J. Scott Atherton, manager of admin. and development. Estab. 1979. Produces 9 plays/year. Professional productions for a non-urban audience. Submit query and synopsis. Responds in 9 months. Buys negotiable rights Pays 6-9% royalty. Pays $50-70/performance.

Needs "Because of our non-urban location, we strive to expose our audience to a broad range of theatre—both classical and contemporary. We are drawn to language and ideas and to plays that resonate in our community. We are most in need of articulate comedies and cast sizes under 6."

Tips "Because of our non-urban setting we are less interested in plays that focus on dilemmas of city life in particular. Most of the comedies we read are cynical. Many plays we read would make better film scripts; static/relationship-heavy scripts that do not use the 'theatricality' of the theatre to an advantage."

BOARSHEAD THEATER

425 S. Grand Ave., Lansing MI 48933-2122. (517)484-7800, 7805. Fax: (517)484-2564. Kristine Thatcher. **Contact:** George Orban. Estab. 1966. Produces 8 plays/year (6 mainstage, 2 Young People's Theater productions inhouse), 4 or 5 staged readings. Mainstage Actors' Equity Association company; also Youth Theater—touring to schools by our intern company. Submit synopsis, character breakdown, 20 pages of sample dialogue, bio, production history (if any) via mail only. Pays royalty for mainstage productions, transport/per diem for staged readings.

Needs Thrust stage. Cast usually 8 or less; occasionally up to 20; no one-acts and no musicals considered. Prefers staging which depends on theatricality rather than multiple sets. Send materials for full-length plays (only) to Kristine Thatcher, artistic director. For Young People's Theater, send one-act plays (only); 4-5 characters.

Tips "Plays should not have multiple realistic sets—too many scripts read like film scripts. Focus on intelligence, theatricality, crisp, engaging humorous dialogue. Write a good play and prove it with 10 pages of great, precise dialogue."

BROADWAY PLAY PUBLISHING

56 E. 81st St., New York NY 10028-0202. (212)772-8334. Fax: (212)772-8358. E-mail: sara@broadwayplaypubl.com; broadwaypl@aol.com. This publisher does not read play mss. It will only publish a play if the playwright is an American-born resident; the play is not in print elsewhere; the play is full-length (at least 1 hour); the play has contemporary subject matter; the play is for at least 2 actors; the play has been professionally produced for at least 12 performances; there is acceptable color artwork for the cover; there are a few sentences from print media complimenting the play.

CELEBRATION THEATRE

7985 Santa Monica Blvd., #109-1, Los Angeles CA 90046. Fax: (323)957-1826. E-mail: celebrationthtr@earthlink.net. Artistic Director: Michael Matthews. Contact: Literary Management Team. Estab. 1983. Produces 4 plays/year. Performed in a small theatre in Los Angeles. For all audiences, but with gay and lesbian characters at the center of the plays. Submit query and synopsis. Responds in 5 months. Pays 6-7% royalty.

Needs Produce works with gay and lesbian characters at the center of the narrative. There aren't any limitations, but simple productions work best. Don't send coming-out plays/stories.

CHAMBER THEATRE

158 N. Broadway, Milwaukee WI 53202. (414)276-8842. Fax: (414)277-4477. E-mail: mail@chamber-theatre.com. **Contact:** C. Michael Wright, artistic director. Estab. 1975. Produces 5 plays/year. Plays produced for adult and student audience. Submit query and synopsis. Submissions accompanied by a SASE will be returned. Responds in 3 months. Pays royalty.

Needs Produces literary, thought-provoking, biographical plays. Plays require small-unit settings. No plays for a large cast.

CHILDSPLAY, INC.

P.O. Box 517, Tempe AZ 85280. (480)350-8101. Fax: (480)350-8584. E-mail: info@

childsplayaz.org. **Contact:** Artistic Director. Estab. 1978. Produces 5-6 plays/year. Professional touring and in-house productions for youth and family audiences. Submit synopsis, character descriptions and 7- to 10-page dialogue sample. Responds in 6 months. Pays royalty of $20-35/performance (touring) or pays $3,000-8,000 commission. Holds a small percentage of royalties on commissioned work for 3-5 years.

Needs Seeking theatrical plays on a wide range of contemporary topics. "Our biggest market is K-6. We need intelligent theatrical pieces for this age group that meet touring requirements and have the flexibility for in-house staging. The company has a reputation, built up over 30 years, of maintaining a strong aesthetic. We need scripts that respect the audience's intelligence and support their rights to dream and to have their concerns explored. Innovative, theatrical and small is a constant need." Touring shows limited to 5 actors; in-house shows limited to 6-10 actors.

Tips "No traditionally-handled fairy tales. Theater for young people is growing up and is able to speak to youth and adults. The material must respect the artistry of the theater and the intelligence of our audience. Our most important goal is to benefit children. If you wish your materials returned send SASE."

Ⓐ CLEVELAND PLAY HOUSE

8500 Euclid Ave., Cleveland OH 44106. E-mail: sgordon@clevelandplayhouse.com. Artistic Director: Michael Bloom. **Contact:** Seth Gordon, associate artistic director. Estab. 1915. Produces 10 plays/year. "We have five theatres, 100-550 seats. Submit 10-page sample with synopsis." Will return submissions if accompanied by SASE. Responds in 6 months. Payment is negotiable.

Needs All styles and topics of new plays.

COLONY THEATRE CO.

555 N. Third St., Burbank CA 91502. (818)558-7000. Fax: (818)558-7110. E-mail: colonytheatre@colonytheatre.org. **Contact:** Michael David Wadler, literary manager. Produces 6 plays/year. Professional 276-seat theater with thrust stage. Casts from resident company of professional actors. Submit query and synopsis. Negotiated rights. Pays royalty for each performance.

Needs Full length (90-120 minutes) with a cast of 4-12. Especially interested in small casts of 4 or fewer. No musicals or experimental works.

Tips "We seek works of theatrical imagination and emotional resonance on universal themes."

CREEDE REPERTORY THEATRE

P.O. Box 269, Creede CO 81130-0269. (719)658-2541. E-mail: litmgr@creederep.

com. **Contact:** Frank Kuhn, Literary Manager. Estab. 1966. Produces 6 plays/year. Plays performed for a smaller audience. Submit synopsis, 10-page dialogue sample, letter of inquiry, resume; electronic submissions only. Responds in 6 months. Royalties negotiated with each author—paid on a per performance basis.

Needs "Special consideration given to plays focusing on the cultures and history of the American West and Southwest."

Tips "We seek new adaptations of classical or older works as well as original scripts."

DALLAS CHILDREN'S THEATER

Rosewood Center for Family Arts, 5938 Skillman, Dallas TX 75231. E-mail: artie. olaisen@dct.org. **Contact:** Artie Olaisen, assoc. artistic dir. Estab. 1984. Produces 10 plays/year. "Professional theater for family and student audiences." Query with synopsis, number of actors required, any material regarding previous productions of the work, and a demo tape or lead sheets (for musicals). No materials will be returned without a SASE included. Responds in up to 8 months. Rights negotiable. Pays negotiable royalty.

Needs "Seeking substantive material appropriate for youth and family audiences. Most consideration given to full-length, non-musical works, especially classic and contemporary adaptations of literature. Also interested in social, topical, issue-oriented material. Very interested in scripts which enlighten diverse cultural experiences, particularly Hispanic and African-American experiences. Prefers scripts with no more than 15 cast members; 6-12 is ideal."

Tips "No adult experience material. We are a family theater. Not interested in material intended for performance by children or in a classroom. Productions are performed by professional adults. Children are cast in child-appropriate roles. We receive far too much light musical material that plays down to children and totally lacks any substance. Be patient. We receive an enormous amount of submissions. Most of the material we have historically produced has had previous production. We are not against perusing non-produced material, but it has rarely gone into our season unless we have been involved in its development. No phone calls."

DARLINGHURST THEATRE COMPANY

19 Greenknowe Ave., Potts Pointe NSW 2011 Australia. (61)(2)9331-3107. E-mail: theatre@darlinghursttheatre.com. Submission period ends September 15. Seeks to expose the audience to a diverse range of work, included narratives, non-narratives, Australian content, and international work. Classics are not excluded, though work new to Sydney is encouraged. Financial issues are a part of the

selection process, so discuss your proposal with Glenn Terry before submitting. If asked, send complete ms or outline. See website for more submission details.

DETROIT REPERTORY THEATRE

13103 Woodrow Wilson, Detroit MI 48238-3686. (313)868-1347. Fax: (313)868-1705. **Contact:** Barbara Busby, literary manager. Estab. 1957. Produces 4 plays/year. Professional theater, 194 seats operating on A.E.A. SPT contract Detroit metropolitan area. Submit complete ms in bound folder, cast list, and description with SASE. Responds in 6 months. Pays royalty.

Needs Wants issue-oriented works. Cast limited to no more than 7 characters. No musicals or one-act plays.

DIVERSIONARY THEATRE

4545 Park Blvd., Suite 101, San Diego CA 92116. (619)220-6830. E-mail: dkirsch@diversionary.org. **Contact:** Dan Kirsch, executive director. Estab. 1986. Produces 5-6 plays/year. "Professional non-union full-length productions of gay, lesbian, bisexual and transgender content. Ideal cast size is 2-6." Submit application and 10-15 pages of script. Responds in 6 months.

DIXON PLACE

161 Chrystie St., Ground Floor, New York NY 10002. (212)219-0736. Fax: (212)219-0761. **Contact:** Leslie Strongwater, artistic director. Estab. 1986. Produces 12 plays/year. Does not accept submissions from writers outside the NYC area. Looking for new work, not already read or workshopped in full in New York. To help us be more efficient in the reviewing of submissions, please read about our ongoing series on the website and submit proposals directly to the series you think is the "best fit". Keep in mind that you are sending an idea or proposal for a performance. Your proposal does not need to be a polished piece when you submit the work, and if selected, it should still be in a 'work-in-progress' stage when you perform it. If you would like your submission materials returned, please include a self-addressed, stamped envelope. We will not return submission materials without a SASE. Works chosen are provided an honorarium, rehearsal time, inclusion in our season brochures, website presence, and technical assistance. If you have any questions, please email us. Pays flat fee.

- "WE ARE NO LONGER ACCEPTING SUBMISSIONS FOR CONSIDERATION IN OUR FALL 09 SEASON. All incoming submissions will be directed towards early Spring 2010."

Needs Particularly interested in non-traditional, either in character, content, structure and/or themes. "We almost never produce kitchen sink, soap opera-style plays about AIDS, coming out, unhappy love affairs, getting sober or lesbian parenting. We regularly present new works, plays with innovative structure, multi-ethnic content, non-naturalistic dialogue, irreverent musicals and the elegantly bizarre. We are an established performance venue with a very diverse audience. We have a reputation for bringing our audience the unexpected. Submissions accepted year-round."

⌂ DORSET THEATRE FESTIVAL

Box 510, Dorset VT 05251-0510. (802)867-2223. Estab. 1976. Produces 5 plays/year (1 a new work). Our plays will be performed in our Equity theater and are intended for a sophisticated community. Agented submissions only. Rights and compensation negotiated.

Needs Looking for full-length contemporary American comedy or drama. Limited to a cast of 6.

Tips Language and subject matter must be appropriate to general audience.

DRAMATIC PUBLISHING

311 Washington St., Woodstock IL 60098. (800)448-7469. Fax: (800)334-5302. **Contact:** Linda Habjan, submissions editor. Publishes 40-50 titles/year. Publishes paperback acting editions of original plays, musicals, adaptations, and translations. **Receives 250-500 queries and 600 mss/year.** Catalog and script guidelines free and online. Responds in 4-6 months. Pays 10% royalty on scripts; performance royalty varies.

Needs Comedies, dramas, comedy/dramas, musicals, comedy/farce. Interested in playscripts appropriate for children, middle and high schools, colleges, community, stock and professional theaters. Send full ms.

Tips "We publish all kinds of plays for the professional, stock, amateur, high school, elementary and children's theater markets: full lengths, one acts, children's plays, musicals, adaptations."

DRAMATICS MAGAZINE

2343 Auburn Ave., Cincinnati OH 45219. (513)421-3900. Fax: (513)421-7077. E-mail: dcorathers@edta.org. **Contact:** Don Corathers, editor. Estab. 1929. For high school theater students and teachers. Submit complete script. Responds in 3 months. Buys first North American serial rights only.

- "Typically we print 10 plays, but 4 of them come from a student writing program that we do. The other 6 are by working professional playwrights. This year's crop included 3 full-lengths, 1 long one-act, and 2 ten-minute plays."

Needs "We are seeking one-acts to full-lengths that can be produced in an educational theater setting."

Tips "No melodrama, musicals, farce, children's theater, or cheap knock-offs of TV sitcoms or movies. Fewer writers are taking the time to learn the conventions of theater—what makes a piece work on stage, as opposed to film and television—and their scripts show it. We're always looking for good interviews with working theatre professionals."

EAST WEST PLAYERS

120 N. Judge John Aiso St., Los Angeles CA 90012. (213)625-7000. Fax: (213)625-7111. E-mail: jliu@eastwestplayers.org. Artistic Director: Tim Dang. **Contact:** Jeff Liu, literary manager. Estab. 1965. Produces 4 plays/year. "Professional 240-seat theater performing under LOA-BAT contract, presenting plays which explore the Asian Pacific American experience." Submit ms with title page, résumé, cover letter, and SASE. Responds in 3-9 months. Pays royalty against percentage of box office.

Needs Whether dramas, comedies, or musicals, all plays must either address the Asian American experience or have a special resonance when cast with Asian American actors.

ELDRIDGE PUBLISHING CO.

P.O. Box 14367, Tallahassee FL 32317. E-mail: editorial@histage.com. Managing Editor: Nancy Vorhis. **Contact:** Editor: Susan Shore. Estab. 1906. Publishes 65 new plays/year for junior high, senior high, church, and community audience. Query with synopsis (acceptable). Please send CD with any musicals. Responds in 1-2 months. Buys all dramatic rights. Pays 50% royalties for amateur productions, 80% for professional productions and 10% copy sales in general market. Makes outright purchase of $100-600 in religious market.

Needs "We are most interested in full-length plays and musicals for our school and community theater market. Nothing lower than junior high level, please. We always love comedies but also look for serious, high caliber plays reflective of today's sophisticated students. We also need one-acts and plays for children's theater. In addition, in our religious market we're always searching for holiday plays. No plays which belong in a classroom setting as part of a lesson plan. Unless it is for Christmas, no other religious musicals considered."

Tips "Please have your work performed, if at all possible, before submitting. The quality will improve substantially."

THE ENSEMBLE STUDIO THEATRE

549 W. 52nd St., New York NY 10019. (212)247-4982. Fax: (212)664-0041. E-mail: firman@ensemblestudiotheatre.org. Website: www.ensemblestudiotheatre.org. Artistic Director: William Carden. **Contact:** Linsay Firman, artistic director. Estab.

1972. Produces 250 projects/year for off-off Broadway developmental theater in a 100-seat house, 60-seat workshop space. Do not fax mss or resumes. Submit complete ms. Responds in 10 months.

Needs "Full-length plays with strong dramatic actions and situations and solid one-acts, humorous and dramatic, which can stand on their own. Special programs include Going to the River Series, which workshops new plays by African-American women, and the Sloan Project, which commissions new works on the topics of science and technology. Seeks original plays with strong dramatic action, believable characters and dynamic ideas. We are interested in writers who respect the power of language. No verse-dramas or elaborate costume dramas. Accepts new/unproduced work only."

ENSEMBLE THEATRE OF CINCINNATI

1127 Vine St., Cincinnati OH 45248. (513)421-3555. Fax: (513)562-4104. E-mail: lynn.meyers@cincyetc.com. **Contact:** D. Lynn Meyers, producing artistic director. Estab. 1987. Produces 12 plays/year, including a staged reading series. Professional year-round theater. Query with synopsis, submit complete ms or submit through agent. Responds in 6 months. Pays 5-10% royalty.

Needs Dedicated to good writing of any style for a small, contemporary cast. Small technical needs, big ideas.

THE ESSENTIAL THEATRE

P.O. Box 8172, Atlanta GA 30306. (404)212-0815. E-mail: pmhardy@aol.com. **Contact:** Peter Hardy, artistic director. Estab. 1987. Produces 3 plays/year. Professional theatre on a small budget, for adventurous theatre goers interested in new plays. Submit complete script by regular mail, or e-mail in Word format to: pmhardy@aol.com Include SASE for return of submission. Responds in 10 months.

Needs Accepts unproduced plays of any length by Georgia writers only, to be considered for Essential Theatre Playwriting Award.

Tips Submission deadline: April 23.

THE FOOTHILL THEATRE CO.

P.O. Box 1812, Nevada City CA 95959. (530)265-9320. Fax: (530)265-9325. E-mail: info@foothilltheatre.org. Artistic Director: Carolyn Howarth. **Contact:** Literary Manager. Estab. 1977. Produces 6-9 plays/year. We are a professional theater company operating under an Actors' Equity Association contract for part of the year, and performing in the historic 246-seat Nevada Theatre (built in 1865) and at an outdoor amphitheatre on the north shore of Lake Tahoe. We also produce a new play development program called New Voices of the Wild West that endeavors to tell the stories of the non-urban Western United States. The audience is a mix of locals and tourists. Query by e-mail. Responds in 6 months-1 year. Buys negotiable rights. Payment varies.

Needs "We are most interested in plays which speak to the region and its history, as well as to its current concerns." No melodramas. Theatrical, above all.

Tips "At present, we're especially interested in unproduced plays that speak to the rural and semi-rural American West for possible inclusion in our new play reading and development program, New Voices of the Wild West. History plays are okay, as long as they don't sound like you wrote them with an encyclopedia open in your lap. The best way to get our attention is to write something we haven't seen before, and write it well."

FOUNTAIN THEATRE

5060 Fountain Ave., Los Angeles CA 90029. (323)663-2235. Fax: (323)663-1629. E-mail: ftheatre@aol.com. Artistic Directors: Deborah Lawlor, Stephen Sachs. **Contact:** Simon Levy, dramaturg. Estab. 1990. Produces both a theater and dance season. Produced at Fountain Theatre (99-seat equity plan). *Professional recommendation only*. Query with synopsis to Simon Levy, producing director/dramaturg. Responds in 6 months. Rights acquired vary. Pays royalty.

Needs Original plays, adaptations of American literature, material that incorporates dance or language into text with unique use and vision.

THE FREELANCE PRESS

670 Centre St., Suite 8, Dover MA 02130. (617)524-7045. E-mail: info@ freelancepress.org. **Contact:** Narcissa Campion, managing director. Estab. 1979. "The musicals published by The Freelance Press are designed for music and theater educators who are seeking age-appropriate material for their students. Our plays and scores are developed by a national network of arts programs and children's theaters. Playwrights and composers, working directly with young actors and singers, have created shows to match the voices, interests and sensibilities of young people, ages 8-18." Submit complete ms with SASE. Responds in 4 months. Pays 70% of performance royalties to authors. Pays 10% script and score royalty.

Needs "We publish original musical theater to be performed by young people, dealing with issues of importance to them. Also adapt 'classics' into musicals for 8- to 16-year-old age groups to perform. Large cast, flexible."

SAMUEL FRENCH, INC.

45 W. 25th St., New York NY 10010. (212)206-8990. Fax: (212)206-1429. E-mail: publications@samuelfrench.com. **Contact:** Editorial Department. Estab. 1830.

Publishes 50-60 titles/year. Publishes paperback acting editions of plays. Receives 1,500 submissions/year, mostly from unagented playwrights. 10% of publications are from first-time authors; 20% from unagented writers. Pays 10% royalty on retail price, plus amateur and stock royalties on productions.

Needs Comedies, mysteries, children's plays, high school plays.

Tips "Broadway and Off-Broadway hit plays, light comedies and mysteries have the best chance of selling to our firm. Our market is comprised of theater producers—both professional and amateur—actors and students. Read as many plays as possible of recent vintage to keep apprised of today's market; write plays with good female roles; and be 100% professional in approaching publishers and producers. We recommend (not require) that submissions be in the format used by professional playwrights in the US, as illustrated in *Guidelines*, available for $4 (postpaid)."

WILL GEER THEATRICUM BOTANICUM

P.O. Box 1222, Topanga CA 90290. (310)455-2322. Fax: (310)455-3724. **Contact:** Ellen Geer, artistic director. Estab. 1973. Produces 4 classical and 1 new play if selected/year. Professional productions for summer theater. Botanicum Seedlings new plays selected for readings and one play each year developed. Contact: Jennie Webb. Send synopsis, sample dialogue and tape if musical. Responds in 6 months. Pays 6% royalty or $150 per show.

Needs Socially relevant plays, musicals; all full-length. Cast size of 4-10 people. "We are a large outdoor theatre—small intimate works could be difficult."

Tips "September submissions have best turn around for main season; year-round for 'Botanicum Seedlings.'"

☑ GEORGE STREET PLAYHOUSE

9 Livingston Ave., New Brunswick NJ 08901. (732)246-7717. Artistic Director: David Saint. **Contact:** Literary Associate. Produces 6 plays/year. Professional regional theater (LORT C). Proscenium/thurst stage with 367 seats. *No unsolicited scripts. Agent or professional recommendation only.*

Tips "It is our firm belief that theater reaches the mind via the heart and the funny bone. Our work tells a compelling, personal, human story that entertains, challenges and stretches the imagination."

GEVA THEATRE CENTER

75 Woodbury Blvd., Rochester NY 14607. (585)232-1366. **Contact:** Marge Betley, literary manager. Produces 7-11 plays/year. Professional and regional theater, modified thrust, 552 seats; second stage has 180 seats. Subscription and single-

ticket sales. Query with sample pages, synopsis, and resume. Responds in 3 months.

Needs Full-length plays, translations, and adaptations.

THE GOODMAN THEATRE

170 N. Dearborn St., Chicago IL 60601-3205. (312)443-3811. Fax: (312)443-3821. E-mail: artistic@goodman-theatre.org. **Contact:** Tanya Palmer, literary manager. Estab. 1925. Produces 9 plays/year. The Goodman is a professional, not-for-profit theater producing a series in both the Albert Theatre and the Owen Theatre, which includes an annual New Play Series. The Goodman does not accept unsolicited scripts, nor will it respond to synopsis of plays submitted by playwrights unless accompanied by a stamped, self-addressed postcard. The Goodman may request plays to be submitted for production consideration after receiving a letter of inquiry or telephone call from recognized literary agents or producing organizations. Responds in 6 months. Buys variable rights. Pays variable royalty.

Needs Full-length plays, translations, musicals; special interest in social or political themes.

Ⓐ GRETNA THEATRE

P.O. Box 578, Mt. Gretna PA 17064. Fax: (717)964-2189. E-mail: larryfrenock@gretnatheatre.com. **Contact:** Larry Frenock, producing director. Estab. 1927. Plays are performed at a professional equity theater during summer. Agent submissions only. Pays negotiable royalty (6-12%).

Needs "We produce full-length plays for a summer audience—subject, language and content are important. Prefer package or vehicles which have star role."

Tips No one-acts. "Given that we are a summer stock theatre, the chances of producing a new play are extremely remote, though we have produced play readings in the past."

⊕ GRIFFIN THEATRE COMPANY

13 Craigend St., Kings Cross NSW 2011 Australia. (61)(2)9332-1052. Fax: (61)(2)9331-1524. Gives consideration and feedback if the author has had a play professionally produced, has an agent, has been shortlisted for the Griffin Award, or has had a play workshopped at Griffin. "If you don't meet these requirements, you may still send a 1-page outline and a 10-page sample. If interested, we will request the full manuscript."

Ⓐ HARTFORD STAGE CO.

50 Church St., Hartford CT 06103. (860)525-5601. Fax: (860)525-4420. **Contact:** Scripts Manager. Estab. 1963. Produces 6 plays/year. Regional theater productions with a wide range in audience. Hartford Stage accepts scripts by agent submission or professional recommendation. "As a dedicated supporter of our community, we also accept scripts from Connecticut residents. Please note, we do not accept one-act plays, or unsolicited material. For questions, contact our scripts manager. If you qualify, we respond within 3-6 months."

Needs Classics, new plays, musicals.

HORIZON THEATRE CO.

P.O. Box 5376, Atlanta GA 31107. (404)523-1477. Fax: (404)584-8815. **Contact:** Literary Manager. Estab. 1983. 5+ plays/year, and workshops 6 plays as part of New South Playworks Festival Professional productions. Accepts unsolicited résumés, samples, treatments, and summaries with SASE. Responds in 1 year. Buys rights to produce in Atlanta area.

Needs "We produce contemporary plays that seek to bridge cultures and communities, utilizing a realistic base but with heightened visual or language elements. Particularly interested in comedy, satire, plays that are entertaining and topical, but thought provoking. Also particular interest in plays by women, African-Americans, or that concern the contemporary South. No more than 8 in cast."

ILLINOIS THEATRE CENTRE

371 Artists' Walk, P.O. Box 397, Park Forest IL 60466. (708)481-3510. Fax: (708)481-3693. E-mail: ilthctr@sbcglobal.net. Estab. 1976. Produces 8 plays/year. Professional Resident Theatre Company in our own space for a subscription-based audience. Query with synopsis or agented submission. Responds in 2 months. Buys casting and directing and designer selection rights. Pays 7-10% royalty.

Needs All types of 2-act plays, musicals, dramas. Prefers cast size of 6-10.

Tips "Always looking for mysteries and comedies. Make sure your play arrives between November and January when play selections are made."

INDIANA REPERTORY THEATRE

140 W. Washington St., Indianapolis IN 46204-3465. (317)635-5277. E-mail: rroberts@irtlive.com. Website: www.irtlive.com. Artistic Director: Janet Allen. Dramaturg: Richard Roberts. "Modified proscenium stage with 600 seats; thrust stage with 300 seats." Send synopsis with résumé via e-mail to the dramaturg.

No unsolicited scripts. Submit year-round (season chosen by January). Responds in 6 month.

Needs Full-length plays, translations, adaptations, solo pieces. Also interested in adaptations of classic literature and plays that explore cultural/ethnic issues with a Midwestern voice. Special program: Discovery Series (plays for family audiences with a focus on youth). Cast size should be 6-8.

Tips "The IRT employs a playwright-in-residence from whom the majority of our new work is commissioned. We occasionally place other subject-specific commissions."

INTERACT THEATRE CO.

The Adrienne, 2030 Sansom St., Philadelphia PA 19103. (215)568-8077. Fax: (215)568-8095. E-mail: pbonilla@interacttheatre.org. **Contact:** Peter Bonilla, literary associate. Estab. 1988. Produces 4 plays/year. Produces professional productions for adult audience. Query with synopsis and bio. No unsolicited scripts. Responds in 6 months. Pays 2-8% royalty or $25-100/performance.

Needs Contemporary dramas and comedies that explore issues of political, social, cultural or historical significance. "Virtually all of our productions have political content in the foreground of the drama. Prefer plays that raise interesting questions without giving easy, predictable answers. We are interested in new plays." Limit cast to 8. No romantic comedies, family dramas, agit-prop.

A INTIMAN THEATRE

201 Mercer St., Seattle WA 98109. (206)269-1901. Fax: (206)269-1928. E-mail: literary@intiman.org. Artistic Director: Bartlett Sher. **Contact:** Sheila Daniels. Estab. 1972. Produces 6 plays/year. LORT C Regional Theater in Seattle. Best submission time is October through March. *Agented submissions only* or by professional recommendation. Responds in 8 months.

Needs Well-crafted dramas and comedies by playwrights who fully utilize the power of language and character relationships to explore enduring themes. Prefers nonnaturalistic plays and plays of dynamic theatricality.

JEWEL BOX THEATRE

3700 N. Walker, Oklahoma City OK 73118-7099. (405)521-7031. Fax: (405)525-6562. **Contact:** Charles Tweed, production director. Estab. 1956. Produces 6 plays/year. Amateur productions. 3,000 season subscribers and general public. Pays $500 contest prize.

Needs Annual Playwriting Competition: Send SASE in September-October. Deadline: mid-January.

JEWISH ENSEMBLE THEATRE

6600 W. Maple Rd., West Bloomfield MI 48322. (248)788-2900. E-mail: e.orbach@
jettheatre.org. **Contact:** Evelyn Orbach, artistic director. Estab. 1989. Produces 4-6
plays/year. Professional productions at the Aaron DeRoy Theatre (season), The
Detroit Institute of Arts Theatre, and Scottish Rite Cathedral Theatre (schools),
as well as tours to schools. Submit complete script. Responds in 1 year. Obtains
rights for our season productions and staged readings for festival. Pays 6-8%
royalty for full production or honorarium for staged reading—$100/full-length
play.

Needs "We do few children's plays except original commissions; we rarely do
musicals." Cast limited to a maximum of 8 actors

Tips "We are a theater of social conscience with the following mission: to produce
work on the highest possible professional level; to deal with issues of community
& humanity from a Jewish perspective; to provide a platform for new voices and
a bridge for understanding to the larger community."

Ⓝ KITCHEN DOG THEATER

3120 McKinney Ave., Dallas TX 75204. (214)953-2258. Fax: (214)953-1873. E-mail:
admin@kitchendogtheater.org. **Contact:** Chris Carlos, co-artistic director. Estab.
1990. Produces 5 plays/year. "Kitchen Dog Theater is a place where questions
of justice, morality, and human freedom can be explored. We choose plays that
challenge our moral and social consciences, invite our audiences to be provoked,
challenged, and amazed. We have 2 performance spaces: a 100-seat black box
and a 150-seat thrust." Submit complete manuscript with SASE. Each year the
deadline for submissions is March 1 (received by). Writers are notified by May 15.
Buys rights to full production. Pays $1,000 for winner of New Works Festival.

Needs "We are interested in experimental plays, literary adaptations, historical
plays, political theater, gay and lesbian work, culturally diverse work, and small
musicals. Ideally, cast size would be 1-5, or more if doubling roles is a possibility.
No romantic/light comedies or material that is more suited for television than
the theater."

Tips "We are interested in plays that are theatrical and that challenge the
imagination—plays that are for the theater, rather than TV or film."

KUMU KAHUA

46 Merchant St., Honolulu HI 96813. (808)536-4222. Fax: (808)536-4226. E-mail:
kumukahuatheatre@hawaiiantel.net. **Contact:** Artistic Director. Estab. 1971.
Produces 5 productions, 3-4 public readings/year. Plays performed at new Kumu
Kahua Theatre, flexible 120-seat theater, for community audiences. Submit

complete script. Responds in 4 months. Pays royalty of $50/performance; usually 20 performances of each production.

Needs Plays must have some interest for local Hawai'i audiences.

LILLENAS PUBLISHING CO.

P.O. Box 419527, Kansas City MO 64141-6527. (816)931-1900. Fax: (816)412-8390. **Contact:** Kim Messer, product manager. Estab. 1926. "We publish on 2 levels: 1) Program Builders—seasonal and topical collections of recitations, sketches, dialogues, and short plays; 2) Drama Resources which assume more than 1 format: a) full-length scripts; b) one-acts, shorter plays, and sketches all by 1 author; c) collection of short plays and sketches by various authors. All program and play resources are produced with local church and Christian school in mind. Therefore there are taboos." Queries are encouraged, but synopses and complete scripts are read. This publisher is interested in collections of and individual sketches. There is also a need for short pieces that are seasonal and on current events. Responds in 3 months. First rights are purchased for Program Builders scripts. For Drama Resources, we purchase all print rights. Drama Resources are paid on a 12% royalty, whether full-length scripts, one-acts, or sketches. No advance.

Needs 98% of Program Builders materials are freelance written. Scripts selected for these publications are outright purchases; verse is minimum of 25¢/line, prose (play scripts) are minimum of $5/double-spaced page. "Lillenas Drama Resources is a line of play scripts that are, for the most part, written by professionals with experience in productions as well as writing. While we do read unsolicited scripts, more than half of what we publish is written by experienced authors whom we have already published."

Tips "All plays need to be presented in standard play script format. We welcome a summary statement of each play. Purpose statements are always desirable. Approximate playing time, cast and prop lists, etc., are important to include. Contemporary settings generally have it over Biblical settings. Christmas and Easter scripts must have a bit of a twist. Secular approaches to these seasons (Santas, Easter bunnies, and so on), are not considered. We sell our product in 10,000 Christian bookstores and by catalog. We are in the forefront as a publisher of religious drama resources. Request a copy of our newsletter and/or catalog."

A ⊘ LONG WHARF THEATRE

222 Sargent Dr., New Haven CT 06511. (203)787-4284. Fax: (203)776-2287. E-mail: gordon.edelstein@longwharf.org. **Contact:** Gordon Edelstein, artistic dir. Estab. 1965. Produces 6 plays/year on its 2 stages. "Professional regional theatre has been and continues to be an incubator of new works, including last season's

A Civil War Christmas by Paula Vogel and *Coming Home* by Athol Fugard. Long Wharf Theatre has received New York Drama Critics Awards, Obie Awards, the Margo Jefferson Award for Production of New Works and more." *Agented submissions or professional recommendations only.*

Needs Full-length plays, translations, adaptations. Special interest: Dramatic plays and comedies about human relationships, social concerns, ethical and moral dilemmas.

Tips "We no longer accept queries."

LOS ANGELES DESIGNERS' THEATRE

P.O. Box 1883, Studio City CA 91614-0883. E-mail: ladesigners@juno.com. **Contact:** Richard Niederberg, artistic dir. Estab. 1970. Produces 8-20 plays/year. "Professional shows/industry audience." Submit proposal only (i.e., 1 page in #10 SASE) We want highly commercial work without liens, 'understandings,' or promises to anyone. Does not return submissions accompanied by a SASE. Reports in 3 months (minimum) to submission. Purchases rights by negotiation, first refusal for performance/synchronization rights only. Payment varies.

Needs All types. "No limitations—We seek design challenges. No boring material. Shorter plays with musical underscores are desirable; nudity, street language, and political themes are OK."

MAGIC THEATRE

Fort Mason Center, Bldg. D, 3rd Floor, San Francisco CA 94123. (415)441-8001. Fax: (415)771-5505. E-mail: info@magictheatre.org. Artistic Director: Chris Smith. **Contact:** Mark Routhier, director of artistic development. Estab. 1967. Produces 6 mainstage plays/year, plus monthly reading series and several festivals each year which contain both staged readings and workshop productions. Regional theater. Bay area residents can send complete ms or query with cover letter, résumé, 1-page synopsis, SASE, dialogue sample (10-20 pages). Those outside the Bay area can query or submit through an agent. Responds in 6-8 months. Pays royalty or per performance fee.

Needs Plays that are innovative in theme and/or craft, cutting-edge sociopolitical concerns, intelligent comedy. Full-length only, strong commitment to multicultural work.

Tips Not interested in classics, conventional approaches and cannot produce large-cast (over 10) plays. Send query to Mark Routhier, literary manager.

⊕ MALTHOUSE THEATRE

113 Sturt St., Southbank VIC 3006 Australia. (61)(3)9685-5100. Fax: (61)(3)9685-5111. E-mail: admin@malthousetheatre.com.au. **Contact:** Michael Kantor, artistic

director. We are dedicated to contemporary Australian theatre. Writers should have had at least 1 professional production of their work. Proposals are called for on March 1, July 1, and October 1. Mail 1-page synopsis, brief author bio, and 10-page sample. Responds in 3 months if interested.

Ⓐ ⊘ MANHATTAN THEATRE CLUB

311 W. 43rd St., 8th Floor, New York NY 10036. (212)399-3000. Fax: (212)399-4329. E-mail: questions@mtc-nyc.org. Director of Artistic Development: Paige Evans. **Contact:** Raphael Martin, literary manager. Produces 7 plays/year. 1 Broadway and 2 Off-Broadway theatres, using professional actors. *Solicited and agented submissions only.* No queries. Responds within 6 months.

Needs "We present a wide range of new work, from this country and abroad, to a subscription audience. We want plays about contemporary concerns and people." All genres are welcome. MTC also maintains an extensive play development program.

Ⓐ MCCARTER THEATRE

91 University Place, Princeton NJ 08540. E-mail: literary@mccarter.org. Artistic Director: Emily Mann. **Contact:** Literary Manager. Produces 5 plays/year; 1 second stage play/year. Produces professional productions for a 1,077-seat and 360-seat theaters. Agented submissions only. Responds in 4-6 months. Pays negotiable royalty.

Needs Full length plays, musicals, translations.

⊕ MELBOURNE THEATRE COMPANY

129 Ferrars St., Southbank VIC 3006 Australia. (61)(3)9684-4500. Fax: (61)(3)9696-2627. E-mail: info@mtc.com.au. **Contact:** Aiden Fennessey, associate director. "MTC produces classic plays, modern revivals and the best new plays from Australia and overseas. Victorian work is given emphasis. MTC does not accept unsolicited manuscripts and it is our strict policy to return them unread. MTC does not produce work from previously unproduced Australian playwrights. New Australian plays generally come from three sources: by the commissioning of established writers; by the invitation to submit work to emerging writers with a track record and the potential to write for a mainstream subscription audience; and through a recommendation from an industry body, such as the Australian Script Centre or any of the major playwriting competitions." Responds in 3 months.

MERIWETHER PUBLISHING, LTD.

885 Elkton Dr., Colorado Springs CO 80907-3557. Fax: (719)594-9916. E-mail: merpcds@aol.com. President: Mark Zapel. Associate Editor: Arthur L. Zapel. **Contact:** Ted Zapel, associate editor. Estab. 1969. We publish how-to theatre materials in book and video formats. We are interested in materials for middle school, high school, and college-level students only. Query with synopsis/outline, résumé of credits, sample of style, and SASE. Catalog available for $2 postage. Responds in 1 month to queries; 2 months to full-length mss. Offers 10% royalty.

Needs Musicals for a large cast of performers, one-act or two-act comedy plays with large casts, and book mss on theatrical arts subjects. "We are now looking for scenebooks with special themes: scenes for young women, comedy scenes for 2 actors, etc. These need not be original, provided the compiler can get letters of permission from the original copyright owner. We are interested in all textbook candidates for theater arts subjects. Christian children's activity book manuscripts also accepted. We will consider elementary-level religious plays, but no elementary-level children's secular plays."

Tips "We publish a wide variety of speech contest materials for high-school students. We are publishing more full-length play scripts and musicals parodies based on classic literature or popular TV shows. Our educational books are sold to teachers and students at college and high-school levels. Our religious books are sold to youth activity directors, pastors, and choir directors. Another group of buyers is the professional theater, radio, and TV category. We will be especially interested in full-length (two- or three-act) plays with name recognition (either the playwright or the adaptation source)."

Ⓐ ⊘ METROSTAGE

1201 N. Royal St., Alexandria VA 22314. (703)548-9044. Fax: (703)548-9089. E-mail: info@metrostage.org. **Contact:** Carolyn Griffin, producing artistic director. Estab. 1984. Produces 5-6 plays/year. Professional productions for 130-seat theatre, general audience. Agented submissions only. Responds in 3 months. Pays royalty.

Needs Contemporary themes, small cast (up to 6 actors), unit set.

Tips "Plays should have *already* had readings and workshops before being sent for our review. Do not send plays that have never had a staged reading."

NEBRASKA THEATRE CARAVAN

6915 Cass St., Omaha NE 68132. Fax: (402)553-6288. E-mail: info@omahaplayhouse.com. Artistic Director: Carl Beck. **Contact:** Alena Furlong, development director. Estab. 1976. Produces 4-5 plays/year. Nebraska Theatre

Caravan is a touring company which produces professional productions in schools, arts centers, and small and large theaters for elementary, middle, high school and family audiences. Submit query and synopsis. Responds in 3 weeks. Negotiates production rights unless the work is commissioned by us. Pays $20-50/performance.

Needs All genres are acceptable bearing in mind the student audiences. "We are truly an ensemble and like to see that in our choice of shows; curriculum ties are very important for elementary and hich school shows; 75 minutes for middle/ high school shows." No sexually explicit material.

Tips "We tour eight months of the year to a variety of locations. Flexibility is important as we work in both beautiful performing arts facilities and school multipurpose rooms."

THE NEW GROUP

410 W. 42nd St., New York NY 10036. (212)244-3380. Fax: (212)244-3438. E-mail: info@thenewgroup.org. Artistic Director: Scott Elliott. **Contact:** Ian Morgan, associate artistic director. Estab. 1991. Produces 4 plays/year. Off-Broadway theater. Submit 10-page sample, cover letter, résumé, synopsis, and SASE. No submissions that have already been produced in NYC. Include SASE for return of script. Responds in 9 months to submissions. Pays royalty. Makes outright purchase.

Needs "We produce challenging, character-based scripts with a contemporary sensibility." Does not want to receive musicals, historical scripts or science fiction.

NEW JERSEY REPERTORY COMPANY.

179 Broadway, Long Branch NJ 07740. (732)229-3166. Fax: (732)229-3167. E-mail: njrep@njrep.org. Website: www.njrep.org. Artistic Director: SuzAnne Barabas. **Contact:** Literary Manager. Estab. 1997. Produces 6-7 plays/year and 20-25 script-in-hand readings. Professional productions year round. Previously unproduced plays and musicals only. Submit via e-mail with synopsis, cast breakdown, playwright bio. For musicals, e-mail mp3 of songs or send CD. Responds in 1 year if interested. Rights negotiable.

Needs Full-length plays with a cast size no more than 4. Simple set.

Tips "Annual Theatre Brut Festival of Short Plays. Previously unproduced. 1-4 actors; simple set, no more than 10 minutes in length. Theme for 2009-2010 festival: Creation."

NEW REPERTORY THEATRE

200 Dexter Ave., Waterton MA 02472. (617)923-7060. Fax: (617)923-7625. E-mail:

artistic@newrep.org. **Contact:** Rick Lombardo, producing artistic director. Estab. 1984. Produces 5 plays/year. Professional theater, general audience. Query with synopsis and dialogue sample. Buys production and subsidiary rights. Pays 5-10% royalty.

Needs Idea laden, all styles, full-length only. New musicals.

Tips No sitcom-like comedies. Incorporating and exploring styles other than naturalism.

NEW STAGE THEATRE

1100 Carlisle, Jackson MS 39202. (601)948-3533. Fax: (601)948-3538. E-mail: mail@newstagetheatre.com. **Contact:** Artistic Director. Estab. 1965. Produces 8 plays/year. Professional productions, 8 mainstage, 1 in our 'second space.' We play to an audience comprised of Jackson, the state of Mississippi and the Southeast. Submit query and synopsis. Exclusive premiere contract upon acceptance of play for mainstage production. Pays 5-8% royalty. Pays $25-60/performance.

Needs Southern themes, contemporary issues, small casts (5-8), single set plays.

NEW THEATRE

4120 Laguna St., Coral Gables FL 33146. (305)443-5373. Fax: (305)443-1642. E-mail: tvodihn@new-theatre.org. **Contact:** Tara Vodihn, literary manager. Estab. 1986. Produces 7 plays/year. Professional productions. Submit query and synopsis. Responds in 3-6 months. Rights subject to negotiation. Payment negotiable.

Needs Interested in full-length, non-realistic, moving, intelligent, language-driven plays with a healthy dose of humor. No musicals or large casts.

Tips No kitchen sink realism. Send a simple query with synopsis. Be mindful of social issues.

⊕ NEW THEATRE

542 King St., Newtown NSW 2042 Australia. (61)(2)9519-3403. Fax: (61)(2)9519-8960. E-mail: newtheatre@bigpond.com. **Contact:** Administrator. Estab. 1932. We welcome the submission of new scripts. Submissions are assessed by playreaders and the artistic director. Submit complete ms and SASE.

NEW YORK STATE THEATRE INSTITUTE

37 First St., Troy NY 12180. (518)274-3200. Fax: (518)274-3815. E-mail: nysti@ capital.net. **Contact:** Patricia DiBenedetto Snyder, producing artistic director.

Produces 6 plays/year. Professional regional productions for adult and family audiences. Submit query and synopsis. Responds in 6 weeks. Payment varies.
Needs "We are not interested in material for 'mature' audiences." Submissions must be scripts of substance and intelligence geared to family audiences.
Tips Do not submit complete script unless invited after review of synopsis.

NEW YORK THEATRE WORKSHOP

83 E. 4th St., New York NY 10003. Fax: (212)460-8996. E-mail: litern@nytw.org. Artistic Director: James C. Nicoloa. **Contact:** Literary Department. Estab. 1979. Produces 6-7 full productions and approximately 50 readings/year. "NYTW is renowned for producing intelligent and complex plays that expand the boundaries of theatrical form and in some new and compelling way address issues that are critical to our times. Plays are performed off-Broadway. Audience is New York theater-going audience and theater professionals." Prefer email submissions. Type "synopsis submission." If mailing: Query with cover letter, synopsis, 10-page dialogue sample, 2 letters of recommendation; SASE if requesting return of materials. Include tape/CD/video where appropriate. Responds in 6-10 months.
Needs Full-length plays, translations/adaptations, music theater pieces; proposals for performance projects. Socially relevant issues, innovative form, and language.
Tips No overtly commercial and conventional musicals or plays.

NORTHLIGHT THEATRE

9501 Skokie Blvd., Skokie IL 60077. (847)679-9501. Fax: (847)679-1879. E-mail: mmccarthy@northlight.org. BJ Jones. **Contact:** Meghan Beals McCarthy, dramaturg. Estab. 1975. Produces 5 plays/year. We are a professional, equity theater, LORT C. We have a subscription base of over 8,000 and have a significant number of single ticket buyers. Query with 10-page dialogue sample, synopsis, resume/bio, and SASE/SASPC for response. Responds in 3-4 months. Buys production rights, plus royalty on future mountings. Pays royalty.
Needs "Full-length plays, translations, adaptations, musicals. Interested in plays of 'ideas'; plays that are passionate and/or hilarious; accessible plays that challenge, incite, and reflect the beliefs of our society/community." Generally looking for cast size of 6 or fewer, but there are exceptions made for the right play.
Tips "As a mainstream regional theater, we are unlikely to consider anything overtly experimental or absurdist. We seek good stories, vivid language, rich characters, and strong understandings of theatricality."

⊕ ODYSSEY THEATRE ENSEMBLE

2055 S. Sepulveda Blvd., Los Angeles CA 90025-5621. (310)477-2055. Fax: (310)444-0455. Ron Sossi. **Contact:** Sally Essex-Lopresti, director of literary programs. Estab. 1969. Produces 9 plays/year. Plays performed in a 3-theater facility. All 3 theaters are Equity 99-seat theater plan. We have a subscription audience of 4,000 for a 9-play main season. No unsolicited material. Query with resume, synopsis, 10 pages of sample dialogue, and cassette if musical. Does not return scripts without SASE. Responds in 2 weeks. Buys negotiable rights. Pays 5-7% royalty.

- "Our purpose is the creation of new work, the revitalization and re-exploration of classical material, experimentation with current developments at the forefront of the "state of the art" in the international theatre world. Ultimately, the institution moves toward the creation of a larger International Experimental Theatre Center, facilitating the crosspollination of artists from different countries, cultures and disciplines, and the exposure of this collaborative work to the Southern California audience."

Needs Full-length plays only with either an innovative form and/or provocative subject matter. "We desire highly theatrical pieces that explore possibilities of the live theater experience. We are not reading one-act plays or light situation comedies."

OMAHA THEATER CO./ROSE THEATER

2001 Farnam St., Omaha NE 68102. (402)345-9718. E-mail: jlarsonotc@msn. com. **Contact:** James Larson, artistic dir. Produces 6-10 plays/year. "Our target audience is children, preschool through high school, and their parents." Submit query and synopsis. Send SASE. Responds in 9 months. Pays royalty.

Needs Plays must be geared to children and parents (PG rating). Titles recognized by the general public have a stronger chance of being produced. Cast limit: 25 (8-10 adults). No adult scripts.

Tips Unproduced plays may be accepted only after a letter of inquiry (familiar titles only!).

▓ ONE ACT PLAY DEPOT

Box 335, Spiritwood Saskatchewan S0J 2M0 Canada. E-mail: submissions@ oneactplays.net. "Accepts unsolicited submissions only in February of each year." Submit complete script by mail or via e-mail as a plain .txt file or pasted into the body of the message.

Needs Interested only in one-act plays. Does not want musicals or farces. Do not mail originals. Our main focus will be black comedy, along with well-written dramatic and comedic pieces.

O'NEILL MUSIC THEATER CONFERENCE

Eugene O'Neill Theater Center, 305 Great Neck Rd., Waterford CT 06385. (860)443-5378. Fax: (860)443-9653. E-mail: theaterlives@theoneill.org. **Contact:** Jill A. Mauritz, general manager. Estab. 1964. "At The Music Theater Conference, creative artists are in residence with artistic staff and an equity company of actors/singers. Public and private readings, script in hand, piano only." An open submission process begins in the fall of each year and concludes in May. The conference takes place in July and August at the O'Neill Theater Center. Works are accepted based on their readiness to be performed, but when there is still enough significant work to be accomplished that a fully staged production would be premature. For guidelines and application deadlines, send SASE or see guidelines online. Pays stipend, room and board.

THE O'NEILL PLAYWRIGHTS CONFERENCE

305 Great Neck Rd., Waterford CT 06385. (860)443-5378. Fax: (860)443-9653. E-mail: info@theoneill.org; playwrights@theoneill.org. **Contact:** Martin Kettling, literary manager. Estab. 1978. Produces 7-8 plays/year. The O'Neill Theater Center operates under an Equity LORT contract. Please send #10 SASE for guidelines in the fall, or check online. Decision by late April. We accept submissions September 1-October 1 of each year. Conference takes place during June/July each summer. Playwrights selected are in residence for one month and receive a four-day workshop and two script-in-hand readings with professional actors and directors. Pays stipend plus room, board and transportation.

Ⓐ ⊘ OREGON SHAKESPEARE FESTIVAL

15 S. Pioneer St., Ashland OR 97520. Fax: (541)482-0446. Artistic Director: Bill Rauch. **Contact:** Director of Literary Development and Dramaturgy. Estab. 1935. Produces 11 plays/year. OSF directly solicits playwright or agent, and does not accept unsolicited submissions.

⊕ PERTH THEATRE COMPANY

P.O. Box 3514, Adelaide Terrace, Perth WA 6832 Australia. (61)(8)9323-3433. Fax: (61)(8)9323-3455. E-mail: frontdesk@perththeatre.com.au. **Contact:** Alan Becher, artistic director. Estab. 1983. Seeks to develop new West Australian theatre and provide opportunities to talented local artists. Develops most of its scripts through the Writer's Lab program. Do not send an unsolicited ms unless it is submitted by or accompanied by a letter of recommendation from a writer's agency, script development organization, or professional theatre company. Make sure to include a SASE.

Ⓐ Ⓞ PHILADELPHIA THEATRE CO.

230 S. Broad St., Suite 1105, Philadelphia PA 19102. (215)985-1400. Fax: (215)985-5800. **Contact:** Literary Office. Estab. 1974. Produces 4 plays/year. "Under the direction of Sara Garonzik since 1982, Philadelphia Theatre Company has introduced more than 140 new plays and musicals to audiences in Philadelphia, New York and around the country, establishing the Company's national reputation for artistic quality, risk-taking and diverse programming." Agented submissions only. Responds in 6-12 months No e-mail submissions, letter of inquiry, summaries or excerpts please.

- "We have introduced countless award-winning premieres. Rather than revisit old standards, we are committed to finding the classics of the future."

Needs Philadelphia Theatre Company produces contemporary American plays and musicals.

Tips "Our work is challenging and risky—look to our history for guidance."

PIONEER DRAMA SERVICE, INC.

P.O. Box 4267, Englewood CO 80155-4267. (303)779-4035. Fax: (303)779-4315. E-mail: submissions@pioneerdrama.com. Publisher: Steven Fendrich. **Contact:** Lori Conary, submissions editor. Estab. 1963. Publishes Plays are performed by schools, colleges, community theaters, recreation programs, churches, and professional children's theaters for audiences of all ages. Query or submit complete ms All submissions automatically entered in Shubert Fendrich Memorial Playwriting Contest. Guidelines for SASE. Responds in about 2 weeks to queries; 4-6 months to submissions. Retains all rights. Pays royalty.

Needs Comedies, mysteries, dramas, melodramas, musicals and children's theater. Two-acts up to 90 minutes; children's theater (1 hour); one-acts no less than 20 minutes. Prefers large ensemble casts with many female roles, simple sets, and costumes. Plays need to be appropriate for amateur groups and family audiences. Interested in adaptations of classics of public domain works appropriate for children and teens. Also plays that deal with social issues for teens and preteens.

Tips "Check out our website to see what we carry and if your material would be appropriate for our market. Make sure to include proof of productions and a SASE if you want your material returned."

PITTSBURGH PUBLIC THEATER

621 Penn Ave., Pittsburgh PA 15222. (412)316-8200. Fax: (412)316-8216. Artistic Director: Ted Pappas. **Contact:** Dramaturg. Estab. 1975. Produces 7 plays/year. O'Reilly Theater, 650 seats, thrust seating. Submit full script through agent, or

query with synopsis, cover letter, 10-page dialogue sample, and SASE. Responds in 4 months.

- "The mission of Pittsburgh Public Theater is to provide artistically diverse theatrical experiences of the highest quality."

Needs Full-length plays, adaptations and musicals.

PLAYSCRIPTS, INC.

325 W. 38th St., Suite 305, New York NY 10018. E-mail: submissions@playscripts. com. Estab. 1998. Audience is professional, community, college, high school and children's theaters worldwide. See website for complete submission guidelines. Materials accompanied by SASE will be returned; however, e-mail submissions are preferred. Response time varies. Buys exclusive publication and performance licensing rights. Pays negotiated book and production royalties.

Needs "We are open to a wide diversity of writing styles and content." Musicals are not accepted.

Tips "Playscripts, Inc. is a play publishing company dedicated to new work by established and emerging playwrights. We provide all of the same licensing and book production services as a traditional play publisher, along with unique promotional features that maximize the exposure of each dramatic work. Be sure to view our guidelines before submitting."

THE PLAYWRIGHTS' CENTER'S PLAYLABS

2301 Franklin Ave. E., Minneapolis MN 55406. (612)332-7481. Fax: (612)332-6037. E-mail: info@pwcenter.org. Producing Artistic Director: Polly K. Carl. Estab. 1971. PlayLabs is a 2-week developmental workshop for new plays. The program is held in Minneapolis and is open by script competition. Up to 5 new plays are given reading performances and after the festival, a script sample and contact link are posted on the Center's website. Announcements of playwrights by May 1. Playwrights receive honoraria, travel expenses, room and board.

Needs "We are interested in playwrights with ambitions for a sustained career in theater, and scripts that could benefit from development involving professional dramaturgs, directors, and actors." US citizens or permanent residents only. Participants must attend entire festival. Submission deadline in October; see Web site for application and exact deadline. No previously produced materials.

PLAYWRIGHTS HORIZONS

416 W. 42nd St., New York NY 10036. (212)564-1235. Fax: (212)594-0296. Artistic Director: Tim Sanford. **Contact:** Adam Greenfield, literary manager (plays); send musicals Attn: Kent Nicholson, Director of Musical Theater. Estab. 1971. Produces 6 plays/year. Plays performed off-Broadway for a literate, urban,

it complete ms with author bio; include CD for
ₙonths. Negotiates for future rights. Pays royalty.

ₙew, full-length plays and musicals by American

acts, one-person shows, non-musical adaptations,
's, screenplays, or works by non-US writers. We
accept unsolicited manuscripts. We look for plays
age and a clear dramatic action that truly use the

FORM
oston MA 02116. **Contact:** Jerry Bisantz, producing
es approximately 50 readings/year Plays are read in
yers on Spring St. (Walthan MA). Accepts scripts on
cript and SASE (or e-mail or hand deliver). Responds

"We will not accept scripts we think are sexist or
racist. Massachusetts residents only. There are no restrictions on length or
number of characters, but it's more difficult to schedule full-length pieces.

PLAYWRIGHTS THEATRE OF NEW JERSEY

P.O. Box 1295, Madison NJ 07940-1295. (973)514-1787. Fax: (973)514-2060.
Artistic Director: John Pietrowski. **Contact:** Alysia Souder, director of program
development. Estab. 1986. Produces 3 plays/year. We operate under a Small
Professional Theatre Contract (SPT), a development theatre contract with Actors
Equity Association. Readings are held under a staged reading code. Responds in
1 year. For productions we ask the playwright to sign an agreement that gives us
exclusive rights to the play for the production period and for 30 days following.
After the 30 days we give the rights back with no strings attached, except for
commercial productions. We ask that our developmental work be acknowledged
in any other professional productions. Makes outright purchase of 750.
Needs Any style or length; full length, one acts, musicals.
Tips "We are looking for American plays in the early stages of development—plays
of substance, passion, and light (comedies and dramas) that raise challenging
questions about ourselves and our communities. We prefer plays *that can
work only on the stage* in the most theatrical way possible—plays that are not
necessarily `straight-on' realistic, but rather ones that use imagery, metaphor,
poetry and musicality in new and interesting ways. Plays can go through a 3-step

development process: A roundtable, a concert reading, and then a workshop production."

🅰 PLOWSHARES THEATRE CO.

2870 E. Grand Blvd., Suite 600, Detroit MI 48202-3146. (313)872-0279. Fax: (313)872-0067. **Contact:** Gary Anderson, producing artistic director. Estab. 1989. Produces 5 plays/year. Professional productions of plays by African-American writers for African-American audience and those who appreciate African-American culture. *Agented submissions only*. Responds in 8 months.
Tips "Submissions are more likely to be accepted if written by an African-American with the willingness to be developed. It must also be very good, and the writer should be ready to make a commitment."

PORTLAND STAGE CO.

P.O. Box 1458, Portland ME 04104. (207)774-1043. Fax: (207)774-0576. E-mail: info@portlandstage.com. Artistic Director: Anita Stewart. **Contact:** Daniel Burson, literary manager. Estab. 1974. Produces 7 plays/year. Professional productions at Portland Stage Company. Send first 10 pages with synopsis. Responds in 3 months. Buys 3- or 4-week run in Maine. Pays royalty.
Needs Developmental Staged Readings: Little Festival of the Unexpected.
Tips Work developed in Little Festival generally will be more strongly considered for future production.

🅰 PRIMARY STAGES CO., INC.

307 W. 38th St., Suite 1510, New York NY 10018. (212)840-9705. Fax: (212)840-9725. E-mail: tessa@primarystages.org. Andrew Leynse. **Contact:** Tessa LaNeve, literary manager. Estab. 1985. Produces 4 plays/year. All plays are produced professionally off-Broadway at 59E59 Theatres' 199 seat theatre. Agented submissions only Guidelines online. Pays flat fee.
• "One of the premiere theaters for the development of new work."
Needs Full-length plays, small cast (6 or fewer) musicals. New York City premieres only. Small cast (1-6), unit set or simple changes, no fly or wing space.
Tips "Best submission time: September-June. Chances: Over 1,000 scripts read, 4-5 produced. Women and minorities encouraged to submit."

PRINCE MUSIC THEATER

100 S. Broad St., Suite 650, Philadelphia PA 19110. (215)972-1000. Fax: (215)972-1020. **Contact:** Marjorie Samoff, producing artistic director. Estab. 1984. Produces 4 musicals/year. "Professional musical productions. Drawing upon operatic and

popular traditions as well as European, African, Asian and South American forms, new work and new voices take center stage." Send synopsis and sample audio tape with no more than 4 songs. Responds in 6 months. Pays royalty.

Needs Song-driven music theater, varied musical styles. Nine-member orchestra, 10-14 cast, 36x60 stage.

Tips "Innovative topics and use of media, music, technology a plus. Sees trends of arts in technology (interactive theater, virtual reality, sound design); works are shorter in length (1-1 & 1/2 hours with no intermissions or 2 hours with intermission)."

PRINCETON REP COMPANY

44 Nassau St., Suite 350, Princeton NJ 08542. E-mail: prcreprap@aol.com. **Contact:** New Play Submissions. Estab. 1984. Plays are performed in site-specific venues, outdoor amphitheatres, and indoor theatres with approximately 199 seats. Princeton Rep Company works under Actors' Equity contracts, and its directors are members of the SSDC. Query with synopsis, SASE, résumé, and 10 pages of sample dialogue. Submissions accompanied by a SASE will be returned. Responds in up to 2 years. Rights are negotiated on a play-by-play basis. Payment negotiated on a play-by-play basis.

Needs Stories that investigate the lives of middle and working class people. Love stories of the rich, famous, and fatuous. If the play demands a cast of thousands, please don't waste your time and postage. No drama or comedy set in a prep school or ivy league college.

THE PUBLIC THEATER

425 Lafayette St., New York NY 10003. (212)539-8500. Artistic Director: Oskar Eustis. **Contact:** Literary Department. Estab. 1964. Produces 6 plays/year. Professional productions. Query with synopsis,10-page sample, letter of inquiry, cassette with 3-5 songs for musicals/operas. Responds in 3 months.

Needs Full-length plays, translations, adaptations, musicals, operas, and solo pieces. All genres, no one-acts.

Ø PULSE ENSEMBLE THEATRE

248 W. 35th St., 15th Floor, New York NY 10001. (212)695-1596. Fax: (212)695-1596. E-mail: theatre@pulseensembletheatre.org. **Contact:** Brian Richardson. Estab. 1989. Produces 3 plays/year. No unsolicited submissions. Only accepts new material through the Playwright's Lab. Include SASE for return of submission. Buys variable rights. Usually pays 2% of gross.

Needs Meaningful theater. No production limitations. Does not want to see fluff or vanity theater.

THE PURPLE ROSE THEATRE CO.

137 Park St., Chelsea MI 48118. (734)433-7782. Fax: (734)475-0802. Guy Sanville. **Contact:** Guy Sanville, artistic director. Estab. 1990. Produces 4 plays/year. "PRTC is a regional theater with an S.P.T. equity contract which produces plays intended for Midwest/Middle American audience. It is dedicated to creating opportunities for Midwest theatre professionals." Query with synopsis, character breakdown, and 10-page dialogue sample. Responds in 9 months. Pays 5-10% royalty.

Needs Modern, topical full length, 75-120 minutes. Prefers scripts that use comedy to deal with serious subjects. 8 cast maximum. No fly space, unit set preferable. Intimate 168 seat 3/4 thrust house.

⊕ QUEENSLAND THEATRE COMPANY

P.O. Box 3310, South Brisbane QLD 4101 Australia. (61)(7)3010-7600. Fax: (61)(7)3010-7699. E-mail: mail@qldtheatreco.com.au. **Contact:** Michael Gow, artistic director. "Seeks timeless classics, modern classics, and new plays from Australia and overseas. Only considers unsolicited scripts if the playwright has had at least 1 play professionally produced if the script has been submitted by an agent, or recommended by a professional theatre company or script development agency." Responds in 3 months.

Needs "Works specifically aimed at child/youth audiences are less likely to be considered."

⊕ RED LADDER THEATRE CO.

3 St. Peter's Buildings, York St., Leeds LS9 1AJ United Kingdom. (44)(113)245-5311. E-mail: rod@redladder.co.uk. **Contact:** Rod Dixon, artistic director. Estab. 1969. Produces 2 plays/year. Our work tours nationally to young people, aged 13-25, in youth clubs, community venues and small scale theatres. Submit query and synopsis. Responds in 6 months. Offers ITC/Equity writers contract.

Needs One hour in length for cast size no bigger than 5. Work that connects with a youth audience that both challenges them and offers them new insights. We consider a range of styles and are seeking originality. Small scale touring. Does not want to commission single issue drama. The uses of new technologies in production (DVD, video projection). Young audiences are sophisticated.

Tips "Please do not submit full length plays. Get in touch with us first. Tell us about yourself and why you would like to write for Red Ladder. We like to hear about ideas you may have in the first instance."

RESOURCE PUBLICATIONS

160 E. Virginia St., Suite 290, San Jose CA 95112-5876. (408)286-8505. Fax:

(408)287-8748. E-mail: editor@rpinet.com. Estab. 1973. Audience includes laity and ordained seeking resources (books/periodicals/software) in Christian ministry, worship, faith formation, education, and counseling (primarily Roman Catholic, but not all). Submit query and synopsis via e-mail. Responds in 3 months.

Needs Needs materials for those in pastoral ministry, faith formation, youth ministry, and parish administration. No fiction, children's books, or music.

ROUND HOUSE THEATRE

P.O. Box 30688, Bethesda MD 20824. (240)644-1099. Fax: (240)644-1090. E-mail: roundhouse@roundhousetheatre.org. Producing Artistic Director: Blake Robison. **Contact:** Danisha Crosby, associate producer. Produces 5-7 plays/year. "Professional AEA Theatre that is recognized nationally as a center for the development of literary works for the stage. Our critically-acclaimed Literary Works Project features new adaptations of contemporary and classical novels, re-interpreted through a theatrical prism for today's audiences. We give these stories a fresh voice, a bold visual presence, and a new relevance in our ever-changing society. The project has garnered 10 Helen Hayes Award nominations and strong notices in the regional and national press." Query with synopsis; no unsolicited scripts accepted. Responds in 2-12 months. Pays negotiated percentage for productions.

SALTWORKS THEATRE CO.

569 N. Neville St., Pittsburgh PA 15213. (412)621-6150. Fax: (412)621-6010. E-mail: nalrutz@saltworks.org. **Contact:** Norma Alrutz, executive director. Estab. 1981. Produces 8-10 plays/year. Submit query and synopsis. Responds in 2 months. Obtains regional performance rights for educational grants. Pays $25/performance.

Needs Wants plays for children, youth, and families that address social issues like violence prevention, sexual responsibility, peer pressures, tobacco use, bullying, racial issues/diversity, drug and alcohol abuse (grades 1-12). Limited to 5 member cast, 2 men/2 women/1 either.

Tips Check website for current play contest rules and deadlines.

SEATTLE REPERTORY THEATRE

P.O. Box 900923, Seattle WA 98109. E-mail: bradena@seattlerep.org. Artistic Director: David Esbjornson. **Contact:** Braden Abraham, literary manager. Estab. 1963. Produces 8 plays/year. Send query, resume, synopsis and 10 sample pages. Responds in 6 months. Buys percentage of future royalties. Pays royalty.

Needs The Seattle Repertory Theatre produces eclectic programming. "We welcome a wide variety of writing."

SECOND STAGE THEATRE

307 W. 43rd St., New York NY 10036-6406. (212)787-8302. Fax: (212)397-7066. **Contact:** Sarah Bagley, literary manager. Estab. 1979. Produces 6 plays/year. "Second Stage Theatre gives new life to contemporary American plays through 'second stagings'; provides emerging authors with their Off-Broadway debuts; and produces world premieres by America's most respected playwrights. Adult and teen audiences." Query with synopsis and 10-page writing sample or agented submission. Responds in 6 months. Payment varies.

Needs "We need socio-political plays, comedies, musicals, dramas—full lengths for full production."

Tips "No biographical or historical dramas, or plays in verse. Writers are realizing that audiences can be entertained while being moved. Patience is a virtue but persistence is appreciated."

⚉ SHAW FESTIVAL THEATRE

P.O. Box 774, Niagara-on-the-Lake ON L0S 1J0 Canada. (905)468-2153. Fax: (905)468-7140. **Contact:** Jackie Maxwell, artistic director. Estab. 1962. Produces 12 plays/year. Professional theater company operating 3 theaters (Festival: 869 seats; Court House: 327 seats; Royal George: 328 seats). Shaw Festival presents the work of George Bernard Shaw and his contemporaries written during his lifetime (1856-1950) and in 2000 expanded the mandate to include contemporary works written about the period of his lifetime. Query with SASE or SAE and IRC's, depending on country of origin. "We prefer to hold rights for Canada and northeastern US, also potential to tour." Pays 5-10% royalty.

Needs "We operate an acting ensemble of up to 75 actors; and we have sophisticated production facilities. During the summer season (April-November) the Academy of the Shaw Festival organizes workshops of new plays commissioned for the company."

SOUTH COAST REPERTORY

P.O. Box 2197, Costa Mesa CA 92628-2197. (714)708-5500. Fax: (714)545-0391. Website: www.scr.org. Artistic Directors: Martin Benson and David Emmes. **Contact:** Kelly Miller, literary manager. Estab. 1964. Produces 14 plays/year. Professional nonprofit theater; a member of LORT and TCG. "We operate in our own facility which houses the 507-seat Segerstrom stage and 336-seat Julianne Argyros stage. We have a combined subscription audience of 18,000. We commit ourselves to exploring the most urgent human and social issues of our time, and to merging literature, design and performance in ways that test the bounds of theatre's artistic possibilities." Query with synopsis and 10 sample pages of dialogue, and full list of characters. Responds in 1-2 months on queries; 4-6 months on full scripts. Acquires negotiable rights. Pays royalty.

Needs "We produce full-length contemporary plays, as well as theatre for young audiences, scripts geared toward a 4th grade target audience with a running time of approximately 65 minutes. We prefer plays that address contemporary concerns and are dramaturgically innovative. A play whose cast is larger than 15-20 will need to be extremely compelling, and its cast size must be justifiable."

Tips "We don't look for a writer to write for us—he or she should write for him or herself. We look for honesty and a fresh voice. We're not likely to be interested in writers who are mindful of any trends. Originality and craftsmanship are the most important qualities we look for."

SOUTHERN APPALACHIAN REPERTORY THEATRE (SART)

Mars Hill College, P.O. Box 1720, Mars Hill NC 28754. (828)689-1384. E-mail: sart@mhc.edu. Managing Director: Rob Miller. Estab. 1975. Produces 5-6 plays/year. Since 1975 the Southern Appalachian Repertory Theatre has produced over 50 world premieres in the 166-seat Owen Theatre on the Mars Hill College campus. SART is a professional summer theater company whose audiences range from students to senior citizens. SART also conducts an annual playwrights conference in which 4-5 playwrights are invited for a weekend of public readings of their new scripts. The conference is held in March or May each year. Submissions must be postmarked by September 30. If a script read at the conference is selected for production, it will be given a fully-staged production in the following summer season. Playwrights receive honorarium and housing. Enclose SASE for return of script.

Needs Comedies, dramas and musicals. No screenplays, translations, or adaptations. Please send complete scripts of full-length plays and musicals, synopsis, and a recording of at least 4 songs (for musicals). Include name and contact information only on a cover sheet. New plays are defined as those that are unpublished and have not received a fully-staged professional production. Workshops and other readings do not constitute a fully-staged production.

STAGE LEFT THEATRE

3408 N. Sheffield, Chicago IL 60657. (773)883-8830. E-mail: scripts@stagelefttheatre.com. **Contact:** Kevin Heckman, literary manager. Estab. 1982. Produces 3-4 plays/year. "Professional productions (usually in Chicago), for all audiences (usually adult)." Submit script through an agent or query with cover letter, 10-page excerpt, 1-page synopsis, SASE, supporting material, and résumé. Responds in 3 months.

Needs Any length, any genre, any style that fits the Stage Left mission—to produce plays that raise debate on political and social issues. "We do have an emphasis on new work."

ⒶSTAMFORD THEATRE WORKS

307 Atlantic St., Stamford CT 06901. (203)359-4414. Fax: (203)356-1846. E-mail: stwct@aol.com. **Contact:** Steve Karp, producing director. Estab. 1988. Produces 4-6 plays/year. Professional productions for an adult audience. *Agented submissions* or queries with a professional recommendation. Include SASE for return of submission. Responds in 3 months. Pays 5-8% royalty.

Needs Plays of social relevance; contemporary work. Limited to unit sets; maximum cast of about 8.

ⒶSTEPPENWOLF THEATRE CO.

758 W. North Ave., 4th Floor, Chicago IL 60610. (312)335-1888. Fax: (312)335-0808. Artistic Director: Martha Lavey. **Contact:** Joy Meads, literary manager. Estab. 1976. Produces 9 plays/year. "Steppenwolf Theatre Company's mission is to advance the vitality and diversity of American theater by nurturing artists, encouraging repeatable creative relationships and contributing new works to the national canon. 500-, 250- and 100-seat performance venues. Many plays produced at Steppenwolf have gone to Broadway. We currently have 20,000 savvy subscribers." Agented submissions only with full scripts. Others please check our website for submission guidelines. Unrepresented writers may send a 10-page sample along with cover letter, bio, and synopsis. Responds in 6-8 months. Buys commercial, film, television, and production rights. Pays 5% royalty.

Needs Actor-driven works are crucial to us, plays that explore the human condition in our time. "We max at around 10 characters."

Tips No musicals, one-person shows, or romantic/light comedies. Plays get produced at STC based on ensemble member interest.

STONEHAM THEATRE

395 Main St., Stoneham MA 02180. E-mail: weylin@stonehamtheatre.org. **Contact:** Weylin Symes, artistic director. Estab. 1999. Produces 7 plays/year. Plays will be produced on-stage in our 350-seat SPT-7 theater—either as part of the Mainstage Season or our Emerging stages series of new works. Submit complete script via mail or e-mail. Submissions accompanied by a SASE will not be returned. Responds in 3 months. Rights acquired varies according to script. Pays royalty.

Needs Anything of quality will be considered. "We look for exciting new work with a fresh voice, but that can still appeal to a relatively mainstream audience." Does not want anything with a cast size over 18 for a musical or 9 for a play.

Ⓐ STUDIO ARENA THEATRE

710 Main St., Buffalo NY 14202. (716)856-8025. E-mail: jblaha@studioarena. com. **Contact:** Jana Blaha, executive assistant. Estab. 1965. Produces 6-8 plays/ year. Professional productions. Agented submissions only.

Needs Full-length plays. No fly space.

Tips "Do not fax or send submissions via the Internet. Submissions should appeal to a diverse audience. We do not generally produce musicals. Please send a character breakdown and 1-page synopsis for a faster reply."

TADA!

15 W. 28th St., 3rd Floor, New York NY 10001. (212)252-1619. Fax: (212)252-8763. E-mail: jgreer@tadatheater.com. **Contact:** Literary Manager. Estab. 1984. Produces 3 musical plays/year. TADA! produces original musicals performed by children and teens, ages 8-18. Productions are for family audiences. Submit a brief summary of the musical, 10 pages from the scripts, and a CD or cassette with songs from the score. TADA! also sponsors an annual one-act playwriting contest for their Spring Staged Reading Series. Works must be original, unproduced and unpublished one-acts. Plays must be geared toward teen audiences. Call or e-mail for guidelines. Responds in 2-3 months. Pays 5% royalty. Commission fee.

Needs Generally pieces run 1 hour long. Must be enjoyed by children and adults and performed by a cast of children ages 8-18.

Tips "No redone fairy tales or pieces where children are expected to play adults. Plays with animals and non-human characters are highly discouraged. Be careful not to condescend when writing for children's theater."

TEATRO VISIÓN

1700 Alum Rock Ave., Suite 265, San José CA 95116. (408)272-9926. Fax: (408)928-5589. E-mail: elisamarina@teatrovision.org. **Contact:** Elisa Marina Alvarado, artistic director. Estab. 1984. Produces 3 plays/year. Professional productions for a Latino population. Query with synopsis or submit complete ms. Responds in 6 months.

Needs We produce plays by Latino playwrights—plays that highlight the Chicano/ Latino experience.

◼ THE TEN-MINUTE MUSICALS PROJECT

P.O. Box 461194, West Hollywood CA 90046. E-mail: info@tenminutemusicals. org. **Contact:** Michael Koppy, producer. Estab. 1987. Produces 1-10 plays/year. "Plays performed in Equity regional theaters in the US and Canada. Deadline August 31; notification by November 30." Submit complete script, lead sheets and, cassette/CD Submission guidelines for #10 SASE. Buys first performance rights. Pays $250 royalty advance upon selection, against equal share of performance royalties when produced.

Needs Looking for complete short stage musicals lasting 7-14 minutes. Limit cast to 10 (5 women, 5 men).

THEATER AT LIME KILN

P.O. Box 1244, Lexington VA 24450. Estab. 1984. Produces 3 (1 new) plays/year. Outdoor summer theater (May through October) and indoor space (October through May, 144 seats). Submit query and synopsis. Include SASE for return of submitted materials. Responds in 3 months. Buys performance rights. Pays $25-75/performance.

Needs Plays that explore the history and heritage of the Appalachian region. Minimum set required.

Tips "Searching for plays that can be performed in outdoor space. Prefer plays that explore the cultural and/or history of the Appalachian region."

THEATER BY THE BLIND

306 W. 18th St., New York NY 10011. (212)243-4337. Fax: (212)243-4337. E-mail: gar@nyc.rr.com. **Contact:** Ike Schambelan, artistic director. Estab. 1979. Produces 2 plays/year. Off Broadway, Theater Row, general audiences, seniors, students, disabled. "If play transfers, we'd like a piece. Submit complete script." Responds in 3 months. Pays $1,000-1,500/production.

Needs Genres about blindness.

THEATRE BUILDING CHICAGO

1225 W. Belmont Ave., Chicago IL 60657. (773)929-7367 ext. 222. Fax: (773)327-1404. E-mail: jsparksco@aol.com. **Contact:** John Sparks, artistic director. "Produces readings of new musicals and Stages Festival, some works developed in our workshop. Some scripts produced are unagented submissions. Developmental readings and workshops performed in 3 small off-Loop theaters are seating 148 for a general theater audience, urban/suburban mix." Submit synopsis, sample scene, CD or cassette tape and piano/vocal score of three songs, and author bios along with Stages Festival application, available on our website. Responds in 3 months.

Needs "Musicals *only*. We're interested in all forms of musical theater including more innovative styles. Our production capabilities are limited by the lack of space, but we're very creative and authors should submit anyway. The smaller the cast, the better. We are especially interested in scripts using a younger (35 and under) ensemble of actors. We mostly look for authors who are interested in developing their scripts through workshops, readings and production. No one-man shows or 'single author' pieces."

Tips "We would like to see the musical theater articulating something about the world around us, as well as diverting an audience's attention from that world. Offers Script Consultancy—A new program designed to assist authors and composers in developing new musicals through private feedback sessions with professional dramaturgs and musical directors. For further info contact John Sparks, (773)929-7367, ext. 222."

THEATRE IV

114 W. Broad St., Richmond VA 23220. (804)783-1688. Fax: (804)775-2325. E-mail: j.serresseque@theatreivrichmond.org. **Contact:** Janine Serresseque. Estab. 1975. Produces approximately 20 plays/year. National tour of plays for young audiences—maximum cast of 5, maximum length of an hour. Mainstage plays for young audiences in 600 or 350 seat venues. Submit query and synopsis. Include SASE for return of submission. Responds in 1 month. Buys standard production rights. Payment varies.

Needs Touring and mainstage plays for young audiences. Touring—maximum cast of 5, length of 60 minutes.

THEATRE THREE

P.O. Box 512, 412 Main St., Port Jefferson NY 11777-0512. (631)928-9202. Fax: (631)928-9120. **Contact:** Jeffrey Sanzel, artistic director. Estab. 1969. We produce an Annual Festival of One-Act Plays on our Second Stage. Deadline for submission is September 30. Send SASE for festival guidelines or visit website. Include SASE. No email submissions. Guidelines online. Responds in 6 months. We ask for exclusive rights up to and through the festival. Pays $75 for the run of the festival.

Needs One-act plays. Maximum length: 40 minutes. Any style, topic, etc. "We require simple, suggested sets and a maximum cast of 6." No adaptations, musicals or children's works.

Tips "Too many plays are monologue-dominant. Please—reveal your characters through action and dialogue."

Ⓐ **THEATRE THREE**

2800 Routh St., #168, Dallas TX 75201. (214)871-3300. Fax: (214)871-3139. E-mail: admin@theatre3dallas.com. **Contact:** Jac Alder, executive producer-director. Estab. 1961. Produces 7 plays/year. Professional regional theatre, in-the-round. Audience is college age to senior citizens. Query with synopsis; agented submissions only. Responds in 6 months. Contractual agreements vary.

Needs Musicals, dramas, comedies, bills of related one-acts. Modest production requirement; prefer casts no larger than 10. Theatre Three also produces in a studio theatre (its former rehearsal hall) called Theatre Too. The space is variously configured according to demands of the show. Shows in that space include cabaret type revues, experimental work, dramas with small casts and staged readings or concert versions of musicals.

Tips "No parodies or political commentary/comedy. Most produced playwrights at Theatre Three (to show taste of producer) are Moliere, Sondheim, Ayckbourne, Miller, Stoppard, Durang (moralists and irony-masters)."

THEATRE WEST

3333 Cahuenga Blvd. W., Hollywood CA 90068-1365. (323)851-4839. Fax: (323)851-5286. E-mail: theatrewest@theatrewest.org. **Contact:** Chris DiGiovanni and Doug Haverty, moderators of the Writers Workshop. Estab. 1962. 99-seat waiver productions in our theater. Audiences are primarily young urban professionals. Residence in Southern California is vital as it's a weekly workshop. Submit script, résumé and letter requesting membership. Responds in 4 months. Contracts a percentage of writer's share to other media if produced on MainStage by Theatre West. Pays royalty based on gross box office.

Needs Full-length plays only, no one-acts. Uses minimalistic scenery, no fly space.

Tips "Theatre West is a dues-paying membership company. Only members can submit plays for production. So you must first seek membership to the Writers Workshop. We accept all styles of theater writing, but theater only—no screenplays, novels, short stories or poetry will be considered for membership."

THEATREWORKS

P.O. Box 50458, Palo Alto CA 94303. (650)463-1950. Fax: (650)463-1963. E-mail: kent@theatreworks.org. **Contact:** Kent Nicholson, new works director. Estab. 1970. Produces 8 plays/year. Specializes in development of new musicals. Plays are professional productions intended for an adult audience. Submit synopsis, 10 pages of sample dialogue, and SASE. Include SASE for return of submission. Responds in 6-8 months. Buys performance rights. Payment varies per contract.

Needs TheatreWorks has a high standard for excellence. "We prefer well-written, well-constructed plays that celebrate the human spirit through innovative productions and programs inspired by our exceptionally diverse community. There is no limit on the number of characters, and we favor plays with multi-ethnic casting possibilities. We are a LORT C company. Plays are negotiated per playwright. Does not want one-acts, plays with togas. We are particularly interested in plays with musical elements."

Tips Guidelines are online—check out our website for Submission Checklist Request and the New Works Program under New Works.

☑ THEATREWORKS/USA

151 W. 26th St., 7th Floor, New York NY 10001. (212)647-1100. Fax: (212)924-5377. Estab. 1961. Produces 3-4 plays/year. "The theatre is an arena for previously unproduced plays, and works towards their future development. Professional equity productions for young audiences. Weekend series at Equitable Towers, NYC. Also, national and regional tours of each show." Submit query and synopsis only. *No unsolicited submissions.* Responds in 1 month. Obtains performing rights. Pays 6% royalty.

UNICORN THEATRE

3828 Main St., Kansas City MO 64111. (816)531-7529 ext. 23. Fax: (816)531-0421. Producing Artistic Director: Cynthia Levin. **Contact:** Herman Wilson, literary assistant. Produces 6-8 plays/year. "We are a professional Equity Theatre. Typically, we produce plays dealing with contemporary issues." Send complete script (to Herman Wilson) with brief synopsis, cover letter, bio, character breakdown. Send #10 SASE for results. Does not return scripts. Responds in 4-8 months.

Needs Prefers contemporary (post-1950) scripts. Does not accept musicals, one-acts, or historical plays.

URBAN STAGES

555 8th Avenue #1800, New York NY 10018. (212)421-1380. Fax: (212)421-1387. E-mail: urbanstage@aol.com. **Contact:** Frances Hill. Estab. 1986. Produces 2-4 plays/year. Professional productions off Broadway—throughout the year. General audience. Submit complete script. Enter Emerging Playwright Award competition. There is a reading fee of $10 per script. Prize is $1,000, plus NYC production. Responds in 4 months. If produced, option for 1 year. Pays royalty.

Needs Full-length; generally 1 set or styled playing dual. Good imaginative, creative writing. Cast limited to 3-6.

Tips "We tend to reject `living-room' plays. We look for imaginative settings.

Be creative and interesting. No one acts. No e-mail submissions, scripts are not returned."

UTAH SHAKESPEAREAN FESTIVAL

New American Playwright's Project, 351 W. Center St., Cedar City UT 84720-2498. (435)586-7884. Fax: (435)865-8003. Founder/Executive Producer Emeritus: Fred C. Adams. **Contact:** Charles Metten, director. Estab. 1993. Produces 9 plays/year. Travelling audiences ranging in ages from 6-80. Programming includes classic plays, musicals, new works. Submit complete script; no synopsis. No musicals. Returns submissions accompanied by a SASE. Responds in 3-4 months. Pays travel, housing, and tickets for USF productions only.

Needs "The USF is only interested in material that explores characters and ideas that focus on the West and our western experience, spirit, and heritage. Preference is given to writers whose primary residence is in the western United States. New plays are for staged readings only. These are not fully mountable productions. Cast size is a consideration due to the limited time of rehearsal and the actors available during the USF production period. Does not want plays that do not match criteria or plays longer than 90 pages."

Tips "We want previously unproduced plays with western themes by western playwrights."

WALNUT STREET THEATRE

Ninth and Walnut Streets, Philadelphia PA 19107. (215)574-3550. Fax: (215)574-3598. Producing Artistic Director: Bernard Havard. **Contact:** Literary Office. Estab. 1809. Produces 10 plays/year. Our plays are performed in our own space. WST has 3 theaters—a proscenium (mainstage), 1,052 seats; and 2 studios, 79-99 seats. We have a subscription audience—the largest in the nation. If you have written a play or musical that you feel is appropriate for the Walnut Street Theatre's Mainstage or Independence Studio on 3, please send the following: 1-2 page synopsis, 5-10 page excerpt from the scrip, a character breakdown, bios for the playwright, composer, lyricist, and any other artistic collaborators, Demo CD with tracks clearly labeled (musicals only). Include SASE for return of materials. Responds in 5 months. Rights negotiated per project. Pays negotiable royalty or makes outright purchase.

Needs Full-length dramas and comedies, musicals, translations, adaptations, and revues. The studio plays must have a cast of no more than 4 and use simple sets.

Tips "Bear in mind that on the mainstage we look for plays with mass appeal, Broadway-style. The studio spaces are our off-Broadway. No children's plays.

Our mainstage audience goes for work that is entertaining and light. Our studio season is where we look for plays that have bite and are more provocative."

WILLOWS THEATRE CO.

636 Ward St., Martinez CA 94553-1651. Artistic Director: Richard Elliott. Produces 6 plays/year. Professional productions for a suburban audience. Accepting only commercially viable, small-medium size comedies right now. Guidelines are online at website. Send synopsis, character breakdown, resume, SASE. Do not send full script unless invited to do so. Do not email submission or email the office for information on your submission. Responds in 6 months to scripts. Pays standard royalty.

Needs Commercially viable, small-medium size musicals or comedies that are popular, rarely produced, or new. Certain stylized plays or musicals with a contemporary edge to them (e.g., *Les Liasons Dangereuses, La Bete, Candide*). No more than 15 actors. Unit or simple sets with no fly space, no more than 7 pieces. We are not interested in 1-character pieces.

Tips "Our audiences want light entertainment, comedies, and musicals. Also, have an interest in plays and musicals with a historical angle."

Ⓐ THE WILMA THEATER

265 S. Broad St., Philadelphia PA 19107. (215)893-9456. Fax: (215)893-0895. E-mail: wcb@wilmatheater.org. **Contact:** Walter Bilderback, dramaturg and literary manager. Estab. 1980. Produces 4 plays/year. LORT-C 300-seat theater, 7,500 subscribers. *Agented submissions only* for full mss. Accepts queries with cover letter, résumé, synopsis, and sample if recommended by a literary manager, dramaturg, or other theater professional. Responds in 6 months.

Needs Full-length plays, translations, adaptations, and musicals from an international repertoire with emphasis on innovative, bold staging; world premieres; ensemble works; works with poetic dimension; plays with music; multimedia works; social issues, particularly the role of science in our lives. Prefers maximum cast size of 12. Stage 44' × 46'.

Tips "Before submitting any material to The Wilma Theater, please research our production history. Considering the types of plays we have produced in the past, honestly assess whether or not your play would suit us. In general, I believe researching the various theaters to which you send your play is important in the long and short run. Different theaters have different missions and therefore seek out material corresponding with those goals. In other words, think through what is the true potential of your play and this theater, and if it is a compatible relationship."

WOMEN'S PROJECT AND PRODUCTIONS

55 West End Ave., New York NY 10023. (212)765-1706. Fax: (212)765-2024. **Contact:** Megan E. Carter, Associate Artistic Director. Estab. 1978. Produces 3 plays/year. Professional Off-Broadway productions. Agented submissions only. Please see website for submission guidelines and details.

Needs "We are looking for full-length plays written by women."

Ⓐ WOOLLY MAMMOTH THEATRE CO.

641 D St. NW, Washington DC 20004. (202)289-2443. E-mail: elissa@ woollymammoth.net. Artistic Director: Howard Shalwitz. **Contact:** Elissa Goetschius, literary manager. Estab. 1980. Produces 5 plays/year. Produces professional productions for the general public. Solicited submissions only. Responds in 6 months to scripts; very interesting scripts often take much longer. Buys first- and second-class production rights. Pays variable royalty.

Needs "We look for plays with a distinctive authorial voice. Our work is word and actor driven." One-acts and issue-driven plays are not used. Cast limit of 5.

Conferences

Writing is a solitary task. It means a lot of time sitting at the computer, researching facts online, checking your e-mail, and staring at a chapter you've rewritten 18 times that still doesn't seem to work. If you want to be a writer, you're going to spend plenty of time alone, but at the same time, you need to understand the importance of networking and making friends who are fellow scribes. That's where writers' conferences come in.

Conferences are rare and invaluable opportunities to simply get out there—to mingle, network, have fun, and meet new contacts that can help further your career. They are events where writers gather to meet one another and celebrate the craft and business of writing. Attendees listen to authors and professionals who present sessions on various topics of interest. Each day is filled with presentations regarding all aspects of writing, and attendees will likely have a choice of which sessions to attend.

Perhaps the most valuable aspect of a conference for writers is the opportunity to meet power players and decision makers in both the entertainment and publishing worlds. In addition, writers can make contacts and form partnerships with fellow scribes. Agents, managers and production executives attend conferences for a specific reason: to find good writers. They are bombarded with pitches and request writing samples from those attendees who dazzle them with a good idea or pitch. Short of an excellent referral, conferences are the best way to snag a rep, so take advantage of meeting one.

Usually it works like this: You schedule a short amount of time to pitch your idea to a rep or executive. Your "elevator pitch" should be relatively short and then there's some time for the professional to ask you questions about the script. If they're interested in seeing some of your work, they will pass you a business card and request part or all of your script. If the agent is not interested, she will say so. When an agent requests pages, you can send it in and put "Requested Material" on the envelope (or in the e-mail) so it gets past the slush pile.

Conferences usually have either a general focus on all subjects of writing, or a more narrow purpose. With some looking, you can find conferences devoted to screenwriting, playwriting, romance, mysteries, fantasy, science fiction, medical thrillers, and more.

SUBHEADS

Each listing is divided into subheads to make locating specific information easier. In the first section, you'll find contact information for conference contacts. You'll also learn conference dates, specific focus, and the average number of attendees. Finally, names of agents who will be speaking or have spoken in the past are listed along with details about their availability during the conference. Calling or e-mailing a conference director to verify the names of speakers and agents in attendance is always a good idea.

Costs: Looking at the price of events, plus room and board, may help writers on a tight budget narrow their choices.

Accommodations: Here conferences list overnight accommodations and travel information. Often conferences held in hotels will reserve rooms at a discount rate and may provide a shuttle bus to and from the local airport.

Additional Information: This section includes information on conference-sponsored contests, individual meetings, the availability of brochures, and more.

AGENTS AND EDITORS CONFERENCE

Writers' League of Texas, 1501 W. Fifth St., Suite E-2, Austin TX 78703. (512)499-8914. Fax: (512)499-0441. E-mail: wlt@writersleague.org. Website: www.writersleague.org. Estab. 1982. Annual conference held in the summer. Conference duration: 3 days. Average attendance: 300. Provides writers with the opportunity to meet top literary agents and editors from New York and the West Coast. Topics include: finding and working with agents and publishers, writing and marketing fiction and nonfiction, dialogue, characterization, voice, research, basic and advanced fiction writing, the business of writing, and workshops for genres. Speakers have included Malaika Adero, Stacey Barney, Sha-Shana Crichton, Jessica Faust, Dena Fischer, Mickey Freiberg, Jill Grosjean, Anne Hawkins, Jim Hornfischer, Jennifer Joel, David Hale Smith and Elisabeth Weed.
Costs $309 member/$439 nonmember.
Accommodations 2009 event is at the Austin Sheraton Hotel, 701 East 11th St., Austin. Check back often for new information.
Additional Information June 26-28, 2009. Contests and awards programs are offered separately. Brochures are available upon request.

ALGONKIAN WRITER WORKSHOPS

2020 Pennsylvania Ave. NW, Suite 43, Washington DC 20006. (800)250-8290. E-mail: algonkian@webdelsol.com. Website: http://www.algonkianconferences.com/. Estab. 2001. "Conference duration: 5 days. Average attendance: 15/craft workshops; 60/pitch sessions. Workshops on fiction, short fiction, and poetry are held 12 times/year in various locations. Speakers have included Paige Wheeler, Elise Capron, Deborah Grosvenor and Kathleen Anderson. Agents will be speaking and available for meetings with attendees."
Costs Housing costs vary depending on the workshop's location.
Additional Information "These workshops are challenging and are not for those looking for praise. Guidelines and dates are available online or via e-mail."

AMERICAN CHRISTIAN WRITERS CONFERENCES

P.O. Box 110390, Nashville TN 37222-0390. (800)219-7483. Fax: (615)834-7736. E-mail: acwriters@aol.com. Website: www.acwriters.com. Estab. 1981. Conference duration: 2 days. Average attendance: 60. Annual conferences promoting all forms of Christian writing (fiction, nonfiction, scriptwriting). Conferences are held throughout the year in 36 US cities.
Costs Approximately $209, plus meals and accommodations.
Accommodations Special rates are available at the host hotel (usually a major chain like Holiday Inn).
Additional Information Send a SASE for conference brochures/guidelines.

AMERICAN INDEPENDENT WRITERS (AIW) SPRING WRITERS CONFERENCE

1001 Connecticut Ave. NW, Suite 701, Washington DC 20036. (202)775-5150. Fax: (202)775-5810. E-mail: info@aiwriters.org. Website: www.aiwriters.org. **Contact:** Taryn Carrino. Estab. 1975. Annual conference held in June. Average attendance: 350. Focuses on fiction, nonfiction, screenwriting, poetry, children's writing, and technical writing. Gives participants the chance to hear from and talk with dozens of experts on book and magazine publishing, as well as on the craft, tools, and business of writing. Speakers have included Erica Jong, John Barth, Kitty Kelley, Vanessa Leggett, Diana McLellan, Brian Lamb, and Stephen Hunter. New York and local agents attend the conference.

Additional Information See the Web site or send a SASE in mid-February for brochures/guidelines and fees information.

Anhinga Writers' Studio Workshops

Gainesville Association for the Creative Arts, P.O. Box 357154, Gainesville FL 32635. (352) 379-8782. Fax: (352) 380-0018. E-mail: info@anhingawriters.org. Website: www.anhingawriters.org. Estab. 1997. Formerly Writing the Region. Annual conference held in July. 2009 dates: July 29-August 1. Conference duration: 4 days. Average attendance: 100. Conference concentrates on fiction, writing for children, poetry, nonfiction, drama, screenwriting, writing with humor, setting, character, and more. Held at the Hilton Hotel and Conference Center across from the University of Florida in Gainesville. Speakers have included Anne Hawking, Doris Booth, Sarah Bewley, Bill Maxwell, and Robert Fulton. Agent/editor appointments are available.

Costs Costs available online. Lower costs for half-day and one-day registration.

Accommodations Special rates are available at the Holiday Inn, University Center and the Residence Inn, Marriott.

ANTIOCH WRITERS' WORKSHOP

P.O. Box 494, Yellow Springs OH 45387. (937)475-7357. E-mail: info@ antiochwritersworkshop.com. Website: www.antiochwritersworkshop.com. **Contact:** Sharon Short. Estab. 1986. Annual one-week conference held in July. Average attendance: 80. Workshop focuses on poetry, scholarly nonfiction, literary fiction, mystery, memoir, and screenwriting. Workshop is located in the charming village of Yellow Springs, Ohio, on the edge of the Glen Helen Nature Preserve. Speakers have included Sue Grafton, Natalie Goldberg, Sena Jeter Naslund, Sigrid Nunez, Mary Kay Andrews and William Least Heat Moon. Agents will be speaking and available for meetings with attendees.

Costs $735, regular tuition; $675, alumni/locals.

Accommodations Accommodations are available at local hotels and in local homes.

Additional Information Optional ms critique is $75.

ASJA WRITERS CONFERENCE

American Society of Journalists and Authors, 1501 Broadway, Suite 302, New York NY 10036. (212)997-0947. Fax: (212)768-7414. E-mail: staff@asja.org; director@asja.org. Website: www.asja.org/wc. **Contact:** Alexandra Owens, exec. dir.. Estab. 1971. Annual conference held in April. Conference duration: 2 days. Average attendance: 600. Covers nonfiction and screenwriting. Held at the Grand Hyatt in New York. Speakers have included Dominick Dunne, James Brady, and Dana Sobel. Agents will be speaking at the event. Largest gathering of nonfiction freelance authors in the country.

Costs $200 +, depending on when you sign up (includes lunch). Check website for updates.

Accommodations The hotel holding our conference always blocks out discounted rooms for attendees.

Additional Information Brochures available in February. Registration form is on the Web site. Inquire by e-mail or fax. Sign up for conference updates on website.

ASPEN SUMMER WORDS LITERARY FESTIVAL & WRITING RETREAT

Aspen Writers' Foundation, 110 E. Hallam St., #116, Aspen CO 81611. (970)925-3122. Fax: (970)925-5700. E-mail: info@aspenwriters.org. Website: www.aspenwriters.org. Estab. 1976. Annual conference held the fourth week of June. Conference duration: 5 days. Average attendance: 150 at writing retreat; 300 + at literary festival. Retreat for fiction, creative nonfiction, poetry, magazine writing, food writing, and literature. Festival includes author readings, craft talks, panel discussions with publishing industry insiders, professional consultations with editors and agents, and social gatherings. Retreat faculty members in 2007: Andrea Barzi, Katherine Fausset, Anjali Singh, Lisa Grubka, Amber Qureshi, Joshua Kendall, Keith Flynn, Robert Bausch, Amy Bloom, Percival Everett, Danzy Senna, Bharti Kirchner, Gary Ferguson, Dorianne Laux. Festival presenters include (in 2007): Ngugi Wa Thiong'o, Wole Soyinka, Chimamanda Ngozi Adichie, Alaa Al Aswany, Henry Louis Gates, Jr., Leila Aboulela, and many more!

Costs Check website each year for updates.

Accommodations Discount lodging at the conference site will be available. See updates each year.

Additional Information Workshops admission deadline is April 20 for the

2009 conference, or until all workshops are filled. Juried admissions for some workshops; writing sample required with application to juried workshops. Mss will be discussed during workshop. Literary festival and some retreat programs are open to the public on first-come, first-served basis; no mss required. Brochure, application and complete admissions information available on Web site, or request by phone, fax or e-mail. Include mailing address with all e-mail requests.

ASSOCIATED WRITING PROGRAMS ANNUAL CONFERENCE

Mail Stop 1E3, George Mason University, Fairfax VA 22030-4444. (703)993-4301. Fax: (703)993-4302. E-mail: conference@awpwriter.org. Website: www.awpwriter. org. Estab. 1992. Annual conference held between February and April. Average attendance: 5,000. The conference focuses on fiction, poetry, and creative writing and features 400 presentations—including readings, lectures, panel discussions and forums—plus hundreds of book signings, receptions, dances, and informal gatherings. In 2010, AWP will bring its annual conference and bookfair back to Denver, Colorado at the Hyatt Regency Denver & the Colorado Convention Center. Speakers have included Walter Mosley, Tim O'Brien, Denis Johnson, Tony Hoagland, Jane Hirshfield, Donald Hall, Naomi Shihab Nye, Chitra Divakaruni, B.H. Fairchild, and Marie Howe.

Costs See website.

Accommodations Offers overnight accommodations at a discounted rate. For 2010: $189 a night for a single/double occupancy room. Telephone for reservations: 1-800-233-1234. Website reservations: Hyatt's AWP webpage. To receive the special conference rate, contact the Hyatt Regency Denver directly and identify yourself as an AWP Conference attendee. You must make your reservations no later than Monday, March 15, 2010.

AUSTIN FILM FESTIVAL & CONFERENCE

1145 W 5th St., Suite 210, Austin TX 78703. (512)478-4795. Fax: (512)478-6205. Website: www.austinfilmfestival.com. **Contact:** Maya Perezz, conference director. Estab. 1994. Annual conference held in October. Conference duration: 4 days. Average attendance: 2,200. This festival is the first organization of its kind to focus on writers' unique creative contribution to the film and television industries. The conference takes place during the first four days of the festival. The event presents more than 75 panels, round tables and workshops that address various aspects of screenwriting and filmmaking. The Austin Film Festival is held in downtown Austin at the Driskill and Stephen F. Austin hotels. The AFF boasts a number of events and services for emerging and professional writers and filmmakers. Past participants include Robert Altman, Wes Anderson, James L. Brooks, Joel & Ethan Coen, Russell Crowe, Barry Levinson, Darren Star, Robert Duvall, Buck Henry,

Dennis Hopper, Lawrence Kasdan, John Landis, Garry Shandling, Bryan Singer, Oliver Stone, Sandra Bullock, Harold Ramis, Danny Boyle, Judd Apatow, Horton Foote, and Owen Wilson.

Costs Approximately $300 for early bird entries(includes entrance to all panels, workshops, and roundtables during the 4-day conference, as well as all films during the 8-night film exhibitions and the opening and closing night parties). Go online for other offers.

Accommodations Discounted rates on hotel accommodations are available to attendees if the reservations are made through the Austin Film Festival office.

Additional Information The Austin Film Festival is considered one of the most accessible festivals, and Austin is the premier town for networking because when industry people are here, they are relaxed and friendly. The Austin Film Festival holds annual screenplay/teleplay and film competitions, as well as a Young Filmmakers Program. Check online for competition details and festival information. Inquire via e-mail or fax.

N ⊕ AUSTRALIAN POETRY FESTIVAL

2/370 Darling St., P.O. Box 91, Balmain NSW 2041 Australia. (61)(2)9818-5366. Fax: (61)(2)9818-5377. E-mail: info@poetsunion.com; martinlangford@bigpond. com. Website: www.poetsunion.com. Estab. 1998. Biennial conference held in September. The festival includes workshops, readings, and panel sessions.

N BACKSPACE AGENT-AUTHOR SEMINAR

P.O. Box 454, Washington MI 48094-0454. (732)267-6449. Fax: (586)532-9652. E-mail: karendionne@bksp.org. Website: www.bksp.org. Estab. 2006. 2009 conference is over and was a success. Main conference duration: 1 day. Average attendance: 100. Annual seminar held in November. Panels and workshops designed to educate and assist authors in search of a literary agent to represent their work. Only agents will be in program. Past speakers have included Scott Hoffman, Dan Lazar, Scott Miller, Michael Bourret, Katherine Fausset, Jennifer DeChiara, Sharlene Martin and Paul Cirone.

Costs $165.

Additional Information The Backspace Agent-Author Seminar offers plenty of face time with attending agents. This casual, no-pressure seminar is a terrific opportunity to network, ask questions, talk about your work informally and listen from the people who make their lives selling books.

BACKSPACE WRITERS CONFERENCE

P.O. Box 454, Washington MI 48094-0454. (732)267-6449. Fax: (586)532-9652. E-mail: chrisg@bksp.org. Website: www.backspacewritersconference.

com. Estab. 2005. The 2010 conference will be held in New York City in May. Conference duration: 2 days. Average attendance: 150. Conference focuses on all genres of fiction and nonfiction. Offers query letter workshop, writing workshop, and panels with agents, editors, marketing experts, and authors. Speakers have included Pulitzer-Prize-winning playwright Douglas Wright, Michael Cader, David Morrell, Lee Child, Gayle Lynds, Ron McLarty, C. Michael Curtis, Jeff Kleinman, Richard Curtis, Noah Lukeman, Jenny Bent, Dan Lazar and Kristin Nelson.

Costs $355 for Backspace members, $395 for non-members (includes 2-day, 2-track program and refreshments on both days, as well as a cocktail reception).

Additional Information This is a high-quality conference, with much of the program geared toward agented and published authors. Afternoon mixers each day afford plenty of networking opportunities. Go online for brochure, or request information via fax or e-mail.

BALTIMORE WRITERS' CONFERENCE

PRWR Program, LInthicum Hall 218K, Towson University, 8000 York Rd., Towson MD 21252. (410)704-5196. E-mail: prwr@towson.edu. Website: www.towson. edu/writersconference. Estab. 1994. "Annual conference held in November. Nov. 14 for 2009 at Townson University's University Union. Conference duration: 1 day. Average attendance: 150-200. Covers all areas of writing and getting published. Held at Towson University. Session topics include fiction, non-fiction, poetry, magazine and journals, agents and publishers. Sign up the day of the conference for quick critiques to improve your stories, essays, and poems." KEYNOTE SPEAKER for 2009 is Mark Bowden. Mark Bowden is the author of the books *Black Hawk Down* and *The Best Game Ever: Giants vs. Colts, 1958*.

Costs $75-95 (includes all-day conference, lunch and reception). Student special rate of $35 before Oct. 17, $50 thereafter.

Accommodations Hotels are close by, if required.

Additional Information Writers may register through the BWA Web site. Send inquiries via e-mail.

☒ BAY AREA WRITER'S LEAGUE ANNUAL CONFERENCE

P.O. Box 580007, Houston TX 77058. E-mail: info@bawl.org. Website: www. bawl.org. The Bay Area Writer's League, known locally as BAWL, has returned to its two-day format with this past year's Writers Conference, which was called "Texas Writers Rock." The Conference was held at the Univ. of Houston Clear Lake, in the Bayou Building. Writers, Dayna Steele and Tammy Kling were Keynote speakers. Workshops were held during the conference on such topics as Author Organization, Memoir Journaling, Scriptwriting Techniques, What's New in the

Publishing World, Websites for Authors, Keeping a Writers Notebook, Poetry, and many others. The Conference fee was $125, all inclusive. Past speakers have included Robin T. Popp (author), Leslie Kriewaldt (Barnes & Noble), Brian Klems (*Writer's Digest*), and Margie Lawson (author).

Costs $50/members; $65/nonmembers.

BIG SUR WRITING WORKSHOPS

Henry Miller Library, Highway One, Big Sur CA 93920. Phone/Fax: (831)667-2574. E-mail: magnus@henrymiller.org. Website: www.henrymiller.org/CWW. Annual workshops held in December (Dec. 4-6, 2009) for children's/young adult writing and in March for adult fiction and nonfiction.

Accommodations See location online at website. It has changed.

BLACK WRITERS REUNION & CONFERENCE

BWRC/Pentouch, P.O. Box 542711, Grand Prairie TX 75054-2711. E-mail: bwrc@blackwriters.org. Website: www.blackwriters.org. Estab. 2000. Annual conference held in August. Conference focuses on the craft of writing, publishing, fiction, poetry, romance, Christian fiction, playwriting, and screenwriting. Agent/editor critiques and pitch sessions are also offered. Speakers have included Vincent Alexandria, Venise Berry, Mondella Jones, Shana Murph, and Kat Smith.

Costs $225/full conference (includes workshops, breakfast buffet, luncheon); $100/day for workshops only.

Accommodations Offers $75/night rate at the Raddison Hotel & Suites in Dallas.

Additional Information The next Black Writers Reunion & Conference is scheduled to be held in Las Vegas, Nevada, June 18-19, 2009. Advance registration is now closed. Walk-up registration will open at the hotel on Thursday, June 18, at 10:30 a.m. at walk-up registration rates.

◪ BLOODY WORDS

64 Shaver Ave., Toronto ON M9B 3T5 Canada. E-mail: carosoles@rogers.com; cheryl@freedmanandsister.com; amummenhoff@rogers.com; info@bloodywords.com. Website: www.bloodywords.com. **Contact:** Caro Soles. Estab. 1999. Annual conference held in June. 2009 dates: June 6-8. Conference duration: 3 days. Average attendance: 250. Focuses on mystery fiction and aims to provide a showcase for Canadian mystery writers and readers, as well as provide writing information to aspiring writers. We will present 3 tracks of programming: Just the Facts, where everyone from coroners to toxicologists to tactical police units present how things are done in the real works; and What's the Story - where panelists discuss subjects of interest to readers; and the Mystery Cafe, where 12

authors read and discuss their work. Bloody Words is Canada's oldest and largest gathering of mystery readers and authors. The conference has become *the* June event to look forward to for people who enjoy genre conventions.

Costs $125+ (Canadian). $115 (US). Includes banquet. If paying by mail, send to Caro Soles, 12 Roundwood Ct., Toronto, ON, M1W 1Z2, Canada.

Accommodations A special rate will be available at The Downtown Hilton Hotel in Toronto, Ontario.

Additional Information Registration is available online. Send inquiries via e-mail.

BLUE RIDGE MOUNTAIN CHRISTIAN WRITERS CONFERENCE

No public address available, E-mail: ylchman@bellsouth.net. Website: www. lifeway.com/christianwriters. Annual conference held in May. Conference duration: Sunday through lunch on Thursday. Average attendance: 400. A training and networking event for both seasoned and aspiring writers that allows attendees to interact with editors, agents, professional writers, and readers. Workshops and continuing classes in a variety of creative categories are also offered.

Costs 2009: $375 (includes sessions and a banquet). See website for next year's costs.

Accommodations $54-84, depending on room size, at the LifeWay Ridgecrest Conference Center near Asheville, North Carolina.

Additional Information The event also features a contest for unpublished writers and ms critiques prior to the conference.

BOOKEXPO AMERICA/WRITER'S DIGEST BOOKS WRITERS CONFERENCE

4700 E. Galbraith Rd., Cincinnati OH 45236. (513)531-2690. Fax: (513)891-7185. E-mail: publicity@fwmedia.com. Website: www.writersdigest.com/bea. Estab. 2003. Annual conference held in May the day before BookExpo America starts. The conference is at the same location as BEA. Average attendance: 500+. The conference offers instruction on the craft of writing, as well as advice for submitting work to publications, publishing houses, and agents. We provide breakout sessions on these topics, including expert advice from industry professionals, and offer workshops on fiction and nonfiction. We also provide agents to whom attendees can pitch their work. The conference is part of the BookExpo America trade show. Registration for the conference does not allow you access to the trade show. Speakers have included Jodi Picoult, Jerry Jenkins, Steve Almond, John Warner, Donald Maass, Noah Lukeman and Jennifer Gilmore. The conference finishes with a large Agent Pitch Slam, with up to 60 agents and editors taking pitches from writers. The slam is the largest of its kind. The conference portion of the week is sponsored by F+W Media. Annual

BOUCHERCON

World Mystery Convention, Bouchercon 2009 c/o The Mystery Company, 233 Second Ave. SW, Carmel IN 46032. E-mail: registration@bouchercon2009.com. Website: www.bouchercon.com. Estab. 1970. Annual convention held in late September/early October. The 40th Bouchercon World Mystery Convention will be held in Indianapolis, Indiana, October 15 - 18, 2009. Expecting 2,000. Co-chairs: Jim Huang, Mike Bursaw. Average attendance: 1,500. Focus is on mystery, suspense, thriller, and true crime novels. Speakers have included Lawrence Block, Jeremiah Healy, James Lee Burke, Ruth Rendell, Ian Rankin, Michael Connelly, Eileen Dreyer, and Earl Emerson. Agents will be speaking and available for informal meetings with attendees.

Costs $150 registration fee. Visit registration page.

Accommodations See online for hotel info. Attendees must make their own transportation arrangements.

Additional Information "This will be the first time that a Bouchercon will include sessions specifically for younger readers and their families. Read more on Children's Program page. During each session, attendees normally have 3-5 choices of programs to choose from. Types of programs include panel discussions on specific aspects of the genre, lectures, classes, demonstrations, book discussion groups, interviews, and more."

BREAD LOAF WRITERS' CONFERENCE

Middlebury College, Middlebury VT 05753. (802)443-5286. Fax: (802)443-2087. E-mail: ncargill@middlebury.edu. Website: www.middlebury.edu/blwc. Estab. 1926. Annual conference held in late August. Conference duration: 11 days. Average attendance: 230. Offers workshops for fiction, nonfiction, and poetry. Agents, editors, publicists, and grant specialists will be in attendance.

Costs $2,345 (includes tuition, housing).

Accommodations Bread Loaf Campus in Ripton, Vermont.

Additional Information 2009 Conference Dates: Wednesday, August 12 - Sunday, August 23. "Please note that all application deadlines for the 2009 session have now passed."

⊕ BRISBANE WRITERS FESTIVAL

P.O. Box 3453, 12 Merivale St., South Brisbane QLD 4101 Australia. (61)(7)3255-0254. Fax: (61)(7)3255-0362. E-mail: info@brisbanewritersfestival.com.au. Website: www.brisbanewritersfestival.com.au. **Contact:** Jane O'Hara, Artistic Director. Annual festival held in September. This event draws on local, national, and international guests for an eclectic mix of panels, discussions, debates, launches and interviews.

⊕ BYRON BAY WRITERS FESTIVAL

Northern Rivers Writers' Centre, P.O. Box 1846, 69 Johnson St., Byron Bay NSW 2481 Australia. 040755-2441. E-mail: jeni@nrwc.org.au. Website: www. byronbaywritersfestival.com. **Contact:** Jeni Caffin, dir.. Estab. 1997. Annual festival held the first weekend in August at Becton's Byron Bay Beach Resort. Conference duration: 3 days. Celebrate and reflect with over 100 of the finest writers from Australia and overseas. Workshops, panel discussions, and poetry readings will also be offered. The Byron Bay Writers Festival is organised by the staff and Committee of the Northern Rivers Writers' Centre, a member based organisation receiving core funding from Arts NSW.

Costs See costs online under Tickets. Early bird, NRWC members and students, kids.

Additional Information "2009 Festival dates are 7-9 August and discounted Early Bird 3 day passes are now on sale at our website or through Jetset Byron Bay on 02 6685 6262."

BYU WRITING AND ILLUSTRATING FOR YOUNG READERS WORKSHOP

348 HCEB, Brigham Young University, Provo UT 84602. (801)422-2568. E-mail: cw348@byu.edu. Website: wfyr.byu.edu. Estab. 2000. Annual workshop held in June 2010. Conference duration: 5 days. Average attendance: 100. "Learn how to write/illustrate and publish in the children's and young adult fiction and nonfiction markets. Beginning and advanced writers/illustrators are tutored in a small-group setting by published authors/artists and receive instruction from editors, a major publishing house representative and a literary agent." Held at Brigham Young University's Harmon Conference Center. Speakers have included Edward Necarsulmer, Stephen Fraiser, Krista Marino, and Margaret Miller.

Costs Costs available online.

Accommodations A block of rooms is reserved at the Super 8 Motel and Marriott Courtyard at BYU conference discounted price.

Additional Information Guidelines and registration are on the Web site.

CALIFORNIA CRIME WRITERS CONFERENCE

cosponsored by Sisters in Crime/Los Angeles and the Southern California Chapter of Mystery Writers of America, No public address available, E-mail: sistersincrimela@yahoo.com. Website: www.sistersincrimela.com. Estab. 1995. Annual conference held in June. (2009 conference will be at the Hilton Pasadena, 168 S. Los Robles Ave., Pasadena, on the weekend of June 13 and 14, 2009.

The keynote speakers will be Robert Crais, author of *The Watchman* and *L.A. Requiem*, and Laurie R. King, who brings us *A Grave Talent* and *Folly* as well as the Mary Russell series.) Average attendance: 150. Conference on mystery and crime writing. Offers craft and forensic sessions, a keynote speaker, a luncheon speaker, author and agent panels, and book signings.

Additional Information Conference information is available on the Web site.

🌐 CANBERRA READERS & WRITERS FESTIVAL

ACT Writers Centre, Gorman House, Ainslie Avenue, Braddon ACT 2612 Australia. (61)(2)6262-9191. E-mail: admin@actwriters.org.au. Website: www.actwriters. org.au. Annual conference held in late August. Local, national, and international writers will give readings, participate in workshops, and sign books.

Costs Most events are free and open to the public.

Additional Information This year's festival is July 10-12, 2009. Seminars: *Working with your publisher*; *Words Change Worlds*; *Readers, Critics, Writers*. See programs online.

CHATTANOOGA FESTIVAL OF WRITERS

Arts & Education Council, 3069 S. Broad St., Suite 2, Chattanooga TN 37408. (423)267-1218. Fax: (423)267-1018. E-mail: info@artsedcouncil.org. Website: www.artsedcouncil.org/page/chattanooga-festival-of-writers. Estab. 2006. Biennial conference held in late March. Conference duration: 2 days. Average attendance: 250. This conference covers fiction, nonfiction, drama and poetry through workshops and keynote. Held in downtown Chattanooga. Speakers have included Suzette Francis, Richard Bausch, David Magee, Philip Gerard, Elizabeth Kostova and Robert Morgan.

Costs $65-175 (depending on attendees participation in workshops, luncheon and dinner).

Additional Information Held during the off years of the AEC Conference on Southern Literature, the 2nd biennial Chattanooga Festival of Writers was March 28 and 29, 2008.

CHRISTOPHER NEWPORT UNIVERSITY WRITERS' CONFERENCE & WRITING CONTEST

1 University Place, Center for Community Learning, Newport News VA 23606-2988. (757)594-7938. Fax: (757)594-8736. E-mail: challiday@cnu.edu. Website: writers.cnu.edu/. Estab. 1981. Conference held in March. This is a working conference. Presentations made by editors, agents, fiction writers, poets and more. Breakout sessions in fiction, nonfiction, poetry, juvenile fiction and publishing.

Previous panels included Publishing, Proposal Writing, Internet Research. Brings together published and aspiring authors.

Accommodations Provides list of area hotels.

Additional Information Save the date: 29th Annual Writers' Conference & Writing Contest, March 12-13, 2010. Explore your love of writing by joining us for this annual event that brings together published and aspiring authors. Full contest info will be available online.

⊕ CLARION SOUTH WRITERS WORKSHOPS

Fantastic Queensland, Inc., P.O. Box 1394, Toowong QLD 4101 Australia. E-mail: info@clarionsouth.org. Website: www.clarionsouth.org. Six-week workshop held in January for writers preparing for a professional career in speculative fiction, science fiction, fantasy, or horror. Each week, a different professional writer/editor conducts the workshop; mornings are devoted to critiquing stories and afternoons/evening/weekends are for individual writing, private conferences, and social activities. Participants produce new work and receive feedback on structure, style, and substance. Writers must apply to the workshop by submitting up to 6,000 words of their fiction.

Costs Check online (includes tuition and accommodations). Scholarships, bursaries, and other forms of financial aid are available.

Accommodations Griffith University, Nathan Campus dorms.

Additional Information "Clarion South runs every 2 years in Brisbane, Australia and is the most intensive professional development program for speculative fiction writers in the southern hemisphere. The next workshop will run January-February 2011."

CLARION WEST WRITERS' WORKSHOP

340 15th Ave. E, Suite 350, Seattle WA 98112-5156. (206)322-9083. E-mail: info@clarionwest.org. Website: www.clarionwest.org. Clarion West is an intensive 6-week workshop for writers preparing for professional careers in science fiction and fantasy, held annually in Seattle, Washington, USA. Usually goes from late June through early July. Conference duration: 6 weeks. Average attendance: 18. Held near the University of Washington. Deadline for applications is March 1. Agents are invited to speak to attendees. This year's workshop will be held from June 21 - July 31, 2009.

Costs $3200 (for tuition, housing, most meals). $100 discount if application received prior to March 1. Limited scholarships are available based on financial need.

Additional Information This is a critique-based workshop. Students are encouraged to write a story every week; the critique of student material produced at the workshop forms the principal activity of the workshop. Students and instructors critique mss as a group. Students must submit 20-30 pages of ms to qualify for admission. Conference guidelines are available for a SASE. Visit the Web site for updates and complete details.

CLARKSVILLE WRITERS CONFERENCE

1123 Madison St., Clarksville TN 37040. (931)645-2317. E-mail: corneliuswinn@bellsouth.net. Website: www.artsandheritage.us/writers/. Annual conference held in the summer. The conference features a variety of presentations on fiction, nonfiction and more. Our keynote speaker for 2009 will be John Egerton. Others attending: Darnell Arnoult, Earl S. Braggs, Christopher Burawa, Susan Gregg Gilmore, James & Lynda O'Connor, Katharine Sands, George Singleton, Bernis Terhune, p.m. terrell. Our presentations and workshops are valuable to writers and interesting to readers. This fun, affordable, and talent-laden conference is presented at Austin Peay State University and the Clarksville Country Club. Annual

Costs Costs available online; prices vary depending on how long attendees stay and if they attend the banquet dinner.

Accommodations Hotel specials provided every year. For 2009, discounted lodging package at Riverview Inn, a luxury hotel located in historic downtown Clarksville, is available for Clarksville Writers' Conference participants only. Call toll-free at 1-877-487-4857 to make reservations. Pay $74.00 per night plus tax, running July 10-12, 2008 (breakfast included). www.theriverviewinn.com

Additional Information Clarksville Writers Conference 2009 information is being updated as it becomes available. Please check back frequently for updates. The Fifth Annual Clarksville Writers' Conference is July 22 - 25, 2009.

DESERT DREAMS

Phoenix Desert Rose Chapter No. 60, PO Box 27407, Tempe AZ 85285. (866)267-2249. E-mail: info@desertroserwa.org; desertdreams@desertroserwa.org. Website: www.desertroserwa.org. Estab. 1986. Conference held every other April. Conference duration: 3 days. Average attendance: 250. Covers marketing, fiction, screenwriting, and research. Keynote speakers: New York Times Bestselling Author Linda Lael Miller and Brad Schreiber VP of Storytech (The Writer's Journey with Chris Vogler).

Costs $218 + (includes meals, seminars, appointments with agents/editors).

Accommodations Discounted rates for attendees is negotiated at the Crowne Plaza San Marcos Resort in Chandler, Ariz.

Additional Information Send inquiries via e-mail. Visit Web site for updates and complete details.

Conferences

DINGLE WRITING COURSES

Ballintlea, Ventry Co Kerry Ireland. Phone/Fax: (353)(66)915-9815. E-mail: info@dinglewritingcourses.ie. Website: http://www.dinglewritingcourses.ie. Estab. 1996. Workshops held in September and October. Average attendance: 14. Creative writing weekends for fiction, poetry, memoir, novel, starting to write, etc. Our courses take place over a weekend in a purpose-built residential centre at Inch on the Dingle peninsula. They are designed to meet the needs of everyone with an interest in writing. All our tutors are well-known writers, with experience tutoring at all levels. See courses and tutors online at website.

Costs 420-445 euros. Some bursaries are available from county arts officers.

Accommodations Provides overnight accommodations.

Additional Information Some workshops require material to be submitted in advance. Accepts inquiries by e-mail, phone, and fax.

EAST OF EDEN WRITERS CONFERENCE

P.O. Box 3254, Santa Clara CA 95055. E-mail: vp@southbaywriters.com; pres@southbaywriters.com. Website: www.southbaywriters.com. Estab. 2000. Biannual conference held in September. Average attendance: 300. Writers of all levels are welcome. Pitch-sessions to agents and publishers are available, as are meetings with authors and editors. Workshops address the craft and the business of writing. Location: Salinas, Calif. - Steinbeck Country.

Costs Costs vary. The full conference (Friday and Saturday) is approximately $250; Saturday only is approximately $175. The fee includes meals, workshops and pitch/meeting sessions. Optional events extra.

Accommodations Negotiated rates at local hotels - $85 per night, give or take.

Additional Information The East of Eden conference is run by writers/volunteers from the California Writers Club, South Bay Branch. The Salinas Community Center's Sherwood Hall has been reserved for September 24-26, 2010 for the next conference. For details, please visit our Web site or send an SASE.

EAST TEXAS CHRISTIAN WRITERS CONFERENCE

The School of Humanities, Dr. Jerry L. Summers, Dean, Scarborough Hall, East Texas Baptist Univ., 1209 N. Grove, Marshall TX 75670. (903)923-2269. E-mail: jhopkins@etbu.edu. Website: www.etbu.edu/News/CWC. Estab. 2002. Average attendance: 60. Conference offers: contact, conversation, and exchange of ideas with other aspiring writers; outstanding presentations and workshop experiences with established authors; potential publishing and writing opportunities; networking with other writers with related interests; promotion of both craft and faith; and consultations with agents, editors, and publishers. Speakers have included Mike and Susan Farris, Denny Boultinghouse, Pamela Dowd, and Mary Lou Redding.

Costs Visit Web site.

Accommodations Visit Web site for a list of local hotels offering a discounted rate.

Additional Information Next one will be held April 9-10, 2010.

FALL WRITERS' SEMINAR

Council for the Written Word, P.O. Box 298, Franklin TN 37065. (615)591-2947. E-mail: info-fallseminar@cww-writers.org. Website: www.asouthernjournal. com/cww. Annual conference held in September. The Sept. 12, 2009 session is named *The Unbridled Pen*. "Michael Martone will slice & dice your work in his interactive 'Cross-Sectional Workshop' revealing what comprises the best of titles, first lines, closing paragraphs, as well as narrative, plot, structure, and other elements of strong writing. Peggy Godfrey will discuss breathing 'geothermal' life into your prose & poetry in her workshop, 'Turning Experience Into Descriptive Prose & Poetry/the Author's Voice.' She will also discuss translating the passion & meaning of your work when reading to an audience."

Costs Fee is $73 ($65 is postmarked by June 30, 2009). Covers pre-event reception, workshop, continental breakfast & lunch during workshop.

Additional Information Pre-event Reception held at Landmark Bookshop; workshop held at Christ UMC, 508 Franklin Rd., Franklin, TN.

FESTIVAL OF FAITH AND WRITING

Department of English, Fine Arts Center, Calvin College, 1795 Knollcrest Circle SE, Grand Rapids MI 49546. (616)526-6770. E-mail: ffw@calvin.edu. Website: www.calvin.edu/academic/engl/festival.htm. Estab. 1990. Biennial festival held in April. Conference duration: 3 days. The festival brings together writers, editors, publishers, musicians, artists, and readers to discuss and celebrate insightful writing that explores issues of faith. Focuses on fiction, nonfiction, memoir, poetry, drama, children's, young adult, academic, film, and songwriting. Past speakers have included Joyce Carol Oates, Salman Rushdie, Patricia Hampl, Thomas Lynch, Leif Enger, Marilynne Robinson and Jacqueline Woodson. Agents and editors attend the festival.

Costs Estimated at $170; $85/students (includes all sessions, but does not include meals, lodging, or evening concerts).

Accommodations Shuttles are available to and from local hotels. Shuttles are also available for overflow parking lots. A list of hotels with special rates for conference attendees is available on the festival Web site. High school and college students can arrange on-campus lodging by e-mail.

Additional Information Online registration opens in October. Accepts inquiries by e-mail, phone, and fax.

Conferences

⚡ FESTIVAL OF WORDS

217 Main St. N., Moose Jaw SK S6J 0W1 Canada. (306)691-0557. Fax: (306)693-2994. E-mail: word.festival@sasktel.net. Website: www.festivalofwords.com. Estab. 1997. Annual festival held in July. 2009 dates: July 16-19. Conference duration: 4 days. Average attendance: 1,500.

Accommodations A list of motels, hotels, campgrounds, and bed and breakfasts is provided upon request.

Additional Information "Our festival is an ideal place for people who love words to mingle, promote their books, and meet their fans. Brochures are available; send inquiries via e-mail or fax."

FLATHEAD RIVER WRITERS CONFERENCE

P.O. Box 7711, Kalispeil MT 59904-7711. E-mail: answers@authorsoftheflathead.org. Website: www.authorsoftheflathead.org. Estab. 1990. Annual conference held in early mid-October. Average attendance: 100. We provide several small, intense 3-day workshops before the general weekend conference. Workshops, panel discussions, and speakers focus on novels, nonfiction, screenwriting, short stories, magazine articles, and the writing industry. Formerly held at the Grouse Mountain Lodge in Whitefish, Montana. Past speakers have included Sam Pinkus, Randy Wayne White, Donald Maass, Ann Rule, Cricket Pechstein, Marcela Landres, Amy Rennert, Ben Mikaelsen, Esmond Harmsworth, Linda McFall, and Ron Carlson. Agents will be speaking and available for meetings with attendees.

Accommodations Rooms are available at a discounted rate. Whitefish is a resort town, so less expensive lodging can be arranged.

Additional Information Our 19th Annual Flathead River Writers' Conference will be reduced in scope and duration. It will be a one-day conference on October 3, 2009 at Flathead Valley Community College and will be **free for paid-up members** of Authors of the Flathead. It is our hope that by doing this we can relieve some of the pressures on your pocketbooks and still make it possible for us to get together this year—affordably. We will soon announcing the agenda for our conference and the particulars. Watch our website for details. Here are some added decisions/details: The conference will be by reservation only. Go online to sign up. Send inquiries via e-mail.

FLORIDA CHRISTIAN WRITERS CONFERENCE

2344 Armour Ct., Titusville FL 32780. (321)269-5831. Fax: (321)264-0037. E-mail: billiewilson@cfl.rr.com. Website: www.flwriters.org. Estab. 1988. Annual conference held in March. Conference duration: 4 days. Average attendance:

275. Covers fiction, nonfiction, magazine writing, marketing, Internet writing, greeting cards, and more. Conference is held at the Christian Retreat Center in Brandenton, Florida.

Costs $575 (includes tuition, meals).

Accommodations We provide a shuttle from the Orlando airport. $725/double occupancy; $950/single occupancy.

Additional Information "Each writer may submit 2 works for critique. We have specialists in every area of writing. Brochures/guidelines are available online or for a SASE."

FLORIDA SUNCOAST WRITERS' CONFERENCE

University of South Florida, Continuing Education, 4202 E. Fowler Ave., NEC16, Tampa FL 33620-6758. (813)974-2403. Fax: (813)974-5421. E-mail: dcistaff@admin.usf.edu. Website: english.cas.usf.edu/fswc. Estab. 1970. Annual conference held in February. Conference duration: 3 days. Average attendance: 400. Conference covers poetry, short stories, fiction, nonfiction, science fiction, detective, travel writing, drama, TV scripts, photojournalism, and juvenile. Also features panels with agents and editors. We do not focus on any one particular aspect of the writing profession, but instead offer a variety of writing-related topics. The conference is held on the picturesque university campus fronting the bay in St. Petersburg, Floriday. Speakers have included Lad P.D. James, William Styron, John Updike, Joyce Carol Oates, Francine Prose, Frank McCourt, David Guterson, Jane Smiley, Augusten Burroughs, Billy Collins, and Heather Sellers.

Costs See updates.

Accommodations Special rates are available at area motels. All information is contained in our brochure.

Additional Information Participants may submit work for critiquing (costs $50). Inquire via e-mail or fax.

FRONTIERS IN WRITING

7221 Stagecoach Trail, Amarillo TX 79124. (806)383-4351. E-mail: fiw2006@hotmail.com; panhandleprowriters@yahoo.com. Website: www.panhandleprowriters.org. Estab. 1920. Annual conference held in June. Conference duration: 2 days. Average attendance: 125. Covers screenwriting, children's writing, nonfiction, poetry, and fiction (mystery, romance, mainstream, science fiction, fantasy). Speakers have included Devorah Cutler Rubenstein and Scott Rubenstein (editor/broker for screenplays), Andrew Brown (children's literary agent), Elsa Hurley (literary agent), and Hillary Sears (Kensington Books).

Costs Constantly updating website.

Conferences

Accommodations Special room rates are available.

Additional Information Sponsors a contest. Guidelines available online or for a SASE.

FUN IN THE SUN

P.O. Box 550562, Fort Lauderdale FL 33355. E-mail: frw_registration@yahoo. com. Website: www.frwriters.org. Estab. 1986. Biannual conference held in February. Features intensive workshops on the craft of writing taught by an array of published authors; a marketing and publicity boot camp; an open-to-the-public book signing for all attending published authors; one-on-one editor/agent pitch sessions; and special events.

Costs See website for updates, depending on membership status and registration date.

Additional Information Ours is the longest-running conference of any RWA chapter. Brochures/registration are available online, by e-mail, or for a SASE.

⊕ GENEVA WRITERS CONFERENCE

Geneva Writers Group, Switzerland. E-mail: info@GenevaWritersGroup.org. Website: www.genevawritersgroup.org/conference.html. Estab. 2002. Conference held in Geneva, Switzerland. Conference duration: 2 days. Past speakers and presenters have included Thomas E. Kennedy, Nahid Rachlin, Jeremy Sheldon, Kwame Kwei Armah, Philip Graham, Mimi Schwartz, Susan Tiberghien, Jo Shapcott, Wallis Wilde Menozzi, David Applefield, Laura Longrigg, Bill Newlin, Zeki Ergas, D-L Nelson, Sylvia Petter, Alistair Scott Annual

THE GLEN WORKSHOP

Image, 3307 Third Avenue W., Seattle WA 98119. (206)281-2988. Fax: (206)281-2335. E-mail: glenworkshop@imagejournal.org; jmullins@imagejournal.org. Website: www.imagejournal.org/glen. Estab. 1991. Annual workshop held in August. Conference duration: 1 week. Workshop focuses on fiction, poetry, spiritual writing, playwriting, screenwriting, songwriting, and mixed media. Writing classes combine general instruction and discussion with the workshop experience, in which each individual's works are read and discussed critically. Held at St. John's College in Santa Fe, New Mexico. Faculty has included Scott Cairns, Jeanine Hathaway, Bret Lott, Paula Huston, Arlene Hutton, David Denny, Barry Moser, Barry Krammes, Ginger Geyer, and Pierce Pettis. The Glen Workshop combines an intensive learning experience with a lively festival of the arts. It takes place in the stark, dramatic beauty of the Sangre de Cristo mountains and within easy reach of the rich cultural, artistic, and spiritual traditions of northern New Mexico. Lodging and meals are included with registration at affordable rates. A low-cost "commuter" rate is also available for those who wish to camp, stay with friends, or otherwise find their own food and lodging. The next Glen Workshop will take place July 26 through August 2, 2009. The theme for the week will be "Fully Human." Faculty, speakers, and more here.

Costs See costs online. A limited number of partial scholarships are available.

Accommodations Offers dorm rooms, dorm suites, and apartments.

Additional Information Like *Image*, the Glen is grounded in a Christian perspective, but its tone is informal and hospitable to all spiritual wayfarers. Depending on the teacher, participants may need to submit workshop material prior to arrival (usually 10-25 pages).

GLORIETA CHRISTIAN WRITERS CONFERENCE

CLASServices, Inc., 3311 Candelaria NE, Suite 1, Albuquerque NM 87107-1952. (800)433-6633. Fax: (505)899-9282. E-mail: info@classervices.com. Website: www.glorietacwc.com. Estab. 1997. Annual conference held in October. Conference duration: Wednesday afternoon through Sunday lunch. Average attendance: 350. Includes programs for all types of writing. Agents, editors, and professional writers will be speaking and available for meetings with attendees. Annual

Costs For costs, see Web site. Critiques are available for an additional charge.

Accommodations Hotel rooms are available at the LifeWay Glorieta Conference Center. Santa Fe Shuttle offers service from the Albuquerque or Santa Fe airports to the conference center. Hotel rates vary. We suggest you make airline and rental car reservations early due to other events in the area.

Additional Information Brochures are available April 1. Inquire via e-mail, phone, or fax, or visit the Web site.

GOTHAM WRITERS' WORKSHOP

WritingClasses.com, 555 Eighth Ave., Suite 1402, New York NY 10018. (212)974-8377. Fax: (212)307-6325. E-mail: dana@write.org. Website: www.writingclasses.com. Estab. 1993. Online classes are held throughout the year. There are four terms of NYC classes, beginning in January, April, June/July, and September/October. Offers craft-oriented creative writing courses in general creative writing, fiction writing, screenwriting, nonfiction writing, article writing, stand-up comedy writing, humor writing, memoir writing, novel writing, children's book writing, playwriting, poetry, songwriting, mystery writing, science fiction writing, romance writing, television writing, article writing, travel writing, business writing and classes on freelancing, selling your screenplay, hot to blog, nonfiction book proposal, and getting published. Also, Gotham Writers' Workshop offers a teen program, private instruction, mentoring program, and classes on selling your work. Classes are held at various schools in New York City as well as online at www.writingclasses.com. Agents and editors participate in some workshops.

Costs $395/10-week workshops; $125 for the four-week online selling seminars and 1-day intensive courses; $295 for 6-week creative writing and business writing classes.

THE GREAT AMERICAN PITCHFEST & SCREENWRITING CONFERENCE

Twilight Pictures, 12400 Ventura Blvd. #735, Studio City CA 91604. (877)255-2528. E-mail: info@pitchfest.com. Website: pitchfest.com/index.shtml. Conference duration: 3 days. Our companies are all carefully screened, and only the most credible companies in the industry are invited to hear pitches. They may include: agents, managers, distributors and sales agents, Hollywood production companies, Canadian production companies, international production companies, advertisers and agencies, funding organizations, broadcasters and networks, studio representatives.

Costs Prices varies, depending on everything that an attendee wants to take part in. See online.

Accommodations All activities will be held at the Burbank Marriott Hotel & Convention Center, 2500 N. Hollywood Way, Burbank, CA 91505.

Additional Information June 12-14, 2009.

GREAT LAKES WRITER'S WORKSHOP

Alverno College, 3400 S. 43rd St., P.O. Box 343922, Milwaukee WI 53234-3922. (414)382-6176. Fax: (414)382-6088. Website: www.alverno.edu. Estab. 1985. Annual workshop held in June. Average attendance: 100. Workshop focuses on a variety of subjects, including fiction, writing for magazines, freelance writing, writing for children, poetry, marketing, etc. Participants may select individual workshops or opt to attend the entire weekend session. The workshop is held at Alverno College in Milwaukee, Wisconsin.

Costs In the past, the entire program cost $115 (early bird) (includes breakfast and lunch with the keynote author). June 27, 2009 workshop now $129. Deadline to register is June 23, 2009.

Accommodations Attendees must make their own travel arrangements. Accommodations are available on campus; rooms are in residence halls. There are also hotels in the surrounding area.

Additional Information View brochure online or send SASE after March. Send inquiries via fax.

GREEN LAKE CHRISTIAN WRITERS CONFERENCE

W2511 State Road 23, Green Lake Conference Center, Green Lake WI 54941-9599. (920)294-3323. E-mail: janwhite@glcc.org. Website: www.glcc.org. Estab. 1948. August 23-28, 2009. Conference duration: 1 week. Attendees may be well-published or beginners, may write for secular and/or Christian markets. Leaders are experienced writing teachers. Attendees can spend 11.5 contact hours in the workshop of their choice: fiction, nonfiction, poetry, inspirational/devotional. Seminars include specific skills: marketing, humor, songwriting, writing for children, self-publishing, writing for churches, interviewing, memoir writing, the magazine market. Evening: panels of experts will answer questions. Social and leisure activities included. GLCC is in south central WI, has 1,000 acres, 2.5 miles of shoreline on Wisconsin's deepest lake, and offers a resort setting.

Additional Information Brochure and scholarship info from website or contact Jan White (920-294-7327). To register, call 920-294-3323.

GREEN MOUNTAIN WRITERS CONFERENCE

47 Hazel St., Rutland VT 05701. (802)236-6133. E-mail: ydaley@sbcglobal.net. Website: www.vermontwriters.com. Estab. 1999. Annual conference held in the summer; 2009 dates are July 27-31. Covers fiction, creative nonfiction, poetry, journalism, nature writing, essay, memoir, personal narrative, and biography. Held at an old dance pavillion on on a remote pond in Tinmouth, Vermont. Speakers have included Joan Connor, Yvonne Daley, David Huddle, David Budbill, Jeffrey Lent, Verandah Porche, Tom Smith, and Chuck Clarino.

Costs $500 before July 1; $525 after July 1. Partial scholarships are available.

Accommodations We have made arrangements with a major hotel in nearby Rutland and 2 area bed and breakfast inns for special accommodations and rates for conference participants. You must make your own reservations.

Ⓝ GULF COAST WRITERS CONFERENCE

P.O. Box 35038, Panama City FL 32412. (850)639-4848. E-mail: MichaelLister@mchsi.com. Website: www.gulfcoastwritersconference.com/. Estab. 1999. Annual conference held in September in Panama City, Fla. Conference duration: 2 days. Average attendance: 100+. This conference is deliberately small and writer-centric with an affordable attendance price. Speakers include writers, editors and agents. Cricket Pechstein Freeman of the August Agency is often in attendance. The 2009 keynote speaker is mystery writer Michael Connelly.

HARRIETTE AUSTIN WRITERS CONFERENCE

Georgia Center for Continuing Education, The University of Georgia, Athens GA

30602-3603. Website: harrietteaustin.org/default.aspx. Annual conference held in July. Sessions cover fiction, poetry, freelance writing, computers, how to get an agent, working with editors, and more. Editors and agents will be speaking. Ms critiques and one-on-one meetings with an evaluator are available for $50.
Costs Cost information available online.
Accommodations Accommodations at the Georgia Center Hotel (georgiacenter. uga.edu).

HAWAII WRITERS CONFERENCE

P.O. Box 1118, Kihei HI 96753. (808)879-0061. Fax: (808)879-6233. E-mail: writers@hawaiiwriters.org. Website: https://www.hawaiiwriters.org/conference. php. Estab. 1993. Formerly the Maui Writers Conference. Annual conference held at the end of August or beginning of September (Labor Day weekend). Conference duration: 4 days. Average attendance: 600. Covers fiction, nonfiction, poetry, screenwriting, children's/young adult writing, horror, mystery, romance, science fiction, and journalism. Though previously held in Maui, the conference moved to Honolulu in 2008. Speakers have included Kimberley Cameron (Reece Halsey North), Susan Crawford (Crawford Literary Agency), Jillian Manus (Manus & Associates), Jenny Bent (Trident Media Group), Catherine Fowler (Redwood Agency), James D. Hornfischer (Hornfischer Literary Management), and Debra Goldstein (The Creative Culture). Annual
Costs $600-1,000. See the Web site for full information.
Additional Information "We offer a comprehensive view of the business of publishing, with more than 1,500 consultation slots with industry agents, editors, and screenwriting professionals, as well as workshops and sessions covering writing instruction. Consider attending the MWC Writers Retreat immediately preceding the conference. Write, call, or visit our Web site for current updates and full details on all of our upcoming programs."

HEART TALK

Women's Center for Ministry, Western Seminary, 5511 SE Hawthorne Blvd., Portland OR 97215-3367. (503)517-1931 or (800)517-1800, ext. 1931. Fax: (503)517-1889. E-mail: western@westernseminary.edu; kstein@westernseminary.edu. Website: www.westernseminary.edu/women. Estab. 1998. Biannual conference held in March. Conference alternates between writing one year and speaking the next. Provides inspiration and techniques for writing fiction, nonfiction, children's books, websites, blogs, etc. Editors/publicists available for one-on-one consultations. Past speakers have included Robin Jones Gunn, Deborah Hestrom-Page, Patricia Rushford, Sally Stuart, and many more. 2010 speaker's conference with Carol Kent and SpeakUp with Confidence team; 2011 next writer's conference.

Additional Information 2011 next writer's conference. Conference information is available by e-mail, phone, fax, or online.

HEDGEBROOK

2197 Millman Road, Langley WA 98260. (360)321-4786. Fax: (360)321-2171. E-mail: info@hedgebrook.org; kimberto@hedgebrook.org. Website: www.hedgebrook. org. **Contact:** Vito Zingarelli, residency director. Estab. 1988. "Hedgebrook is a retreat for women writers on Whidbey Island on 48 beautiful acres, near Seattle, where writers of diverse cultural backgrounds working in all genres, published or not, come from around the globe to write, rejuvenate, and be in community with each other. Writers stay in one of 6 handcrafted cottages for two to six weeks at no cost to the writer." Guidelines: women writers, ages 18 and up, unpublished; women of color encouraged to apply. Application procedure: application, project description, work sample and 425 fee; download appication from website beginning June 2009. Submission deadline: September 25, 2009.

Additional Information Go online for more information.

HIGHLAND SUMMER CONFERENCE

Box 7014, Radford University, Radford VA 24142-7014. (540)831-5366. Fax: (540)831-5951. E-mail: dcochran7@radford.edu; jasbury@radford.edu. Website: www.radford.edu/~arsc. Estab. 1978. Annual conference held in June. 2009 date: June 8-19. Conference duration: 2 weeks. Average attendance: 25. Covers fiction, nonfiction, poetry, and screenwriting. This year's Highland Summer Conference will be conducted the first week by Crystal Wilkinson, who is the author of *Water Street* and *Blackberries, Blackberries*. The second week of the Conference will be conducted by author Cathy Smith Bowers, whose works include *The Love that Ended Yesterday in Texas, A Book of Minutes, and Traveling in Time of Danger*. Special evening readings by Sharyn McCrumb and Jim Minick. Go to website for more information.

Costs The cost is based on current Radford tuition for 3 credit hours, plus an additional conference fee. On-campus meals and housing are available at additional cost. In 2007, conference tuition was $717/in-state undergraduates, $1,686/for out-of-state undergraduates, $780/in-state graduates, and $1,434/out-of-state graduates.

Accommodations We do not have special rate arrangements with local hotels. We do offer accommodations on the Radford University campus in a recently refurbished residence hall. The 2005 cost was $26-36/night.

Additional Information Conference leaders typically critique work done during the 2-week conference, but do not ask to have any writing submitted prior to the conference. Conference brochures/guidelines are available in March for a SASE. Inquire via e-mail or fax.

HIGHLIGHTS FOUNDATION FOUNDERS WORKSHOPS

814 Court St., Honesdale PA 18437. (570)253-1172. Fax: (570)253-0179. E-mail: contact@highlightsfoundation.org. Website: www.highlightsfoundation.org. Estab. 2000. Conference duration: 3-7 days. Average attendance: limited to 10-14. Genre specific workshops and retreats on children's writing: fiction, nonfiction, poetry, promotions. "Our goal is to improve, over time, the quality of literature for children by educating future generations of children's authors." Highlights Founders' home in Boyds Mills, PA. Faculty/speakers in 2003 included Joy Cowley, Patricia Lee Gauch, Carolyn Yoder, Andrea Early, Stephen Swinburne, Juanita Havill, Sandy Asher, Eileen Spinelli, Rich Wallace, Neil Waldman, Kent L. Brown, Jr. and Peter Jacobi. Workshops held seasonally in March, April, May, June, September, October, November.

Costs 2009 costs ranged from $795-1195, including meals, lodging, materials, and much more.

Accommodations Coordinates pickup at local airport. Offers overnight accommodations. Participants stay in guest cabins on the wooded grounds surrounding Highlights Founders' home adjacent to the house/conference center.

Additional Information Some workshops require pre-workshop assignment. Brochure available for SASE, by e-mail, on website, by phone, by fax. Accepts inquiries by phone, fax, e-mail, SASE. Editors attend conference. "Applications will be reviewed and accepted on a first-come, first-served basis, applicants must demonstrate specific experience in writing area of workshop they are applying for - writing samples are required for many of the workshops."

HIGHLIGHTS FOUNDATION WRITERS WORKSHOP AT CHAUTAUQUA

814 Court St., Honesdale PA 18431. (570)253-1192. Fax: (570)253-0179. E-mail: contact@highlightsfoundation.org. Website: www.highlightsfoundation.org. Estab. 1985. Annual conference held July 17-24, 2010. Average attendance: 100. Workshops are geared toward those who write for children at the beginner, intermediate, and advanced levels. Offers seminars, small group workshops, and one-on-one sessions with authors, editors, illustrators, critics, and publishers. Workshop site is the picturesque community of Chautauqua, New York. Speakers have included Bruce Coville, Candace Fleming, Linda Sue Park, Jane Yolen, Patricia Gauch, Jerry Spinelli, Eileen Spinelli, Joy Cowley and Pam Munoz Ryan.

Costs $2,400 (includes all meals, conference supplies, gate pass to Chautauqua Institution).

Accommodations We coordinate ground transportation to and from airports, trains, and bus stations in the Erie, Pennsylvania and Jamestown/Buffalo, New York area. We also coordinate accommodations for conference attendees.

Additional Information "We offer the opportunity for attendees to submit a manuscript for review at the conference. Workshop brochures/guidelines are available upon request."

HOFSTRA UNIVERSITY SUMMER WRITING WORKSHOPS

University College for Continuing Education, 250 Hofstra University, Hempstead NY 11549-2500. (516)463-5993. Fax: (516)463-4833. E-mail: uccelibarts@hofstra. edu. Website: www.hofstra.edu/ucce/summerwriting. Estab. 1972. Annual conference held in mid-July. 2009: July 6-17 ($550). Conference duration: 2 weeks. Average attendance: 65. Conference offers workshops in short fiction, nonfiction, poetry, and occasionally other genres such as screenplay writing or writing for children. Site is the university campus on Long Island, 25 miles from New York City. Speakers have inluded Oscar Hijuelos, Robert Olen Butler, Hilma and Meg Wolitzer, Budd Schulberg, Cynthia Ozick, and Rebecca Wolff.

Costs Check Web site for current fees. Credit is available for undergraduate and graduate students. Continental breakfast daily; tuition also includes the cost of the banquet. All workshops include critiquing. Each participant is given one-on-one time for a half hour with a workshop leader. More details will be available in March. Accepts inquiries via fax and e-mail.

Accommodations Free bus operates between Hempstead Train Station and campus for those commuting from New York City on the Long Island Rail Road. Dormitory rooms are available.

Additional Information Students entering grades 9-12 can now be part of the Summer Writers Program with a special section for high school students. Through exercises and readings, students will learn how to use their creative impulses to improve their fiction, poetry and plays and learn how to create cleaner and clearer essays. During this intensive 2-week course, students will experiment with memoir, poetry, oral history, dramatic form and the short story, and study how to use character, plot, point of view and language.

HOLLYWOOD PITCH FESTIVAL

Fade In Magazine, 287 S. Robertson Blvd., #467, Beverly Hills CA 90211. (800)646-3896. E-mail: inquiries@fadeinonline.com. Website: hollywoodpitchfestival. com/. Estab. 1996. 2009: August 1 & 2, at Bergamot Station, Santa Monica, CA. Register online or Call To Register (800) 646-3896. Conference duration: Two days. This is a pitch event that provides non-stop pitch meetings over a two-day period - with 200 of Hollywood's top buyers/representatives under one roof.

HPF only has one class - a pitch class taught by a professional A-list filmmaker on Saturday morning, and it is optional. Each attendee will received by e-mail a list of the companies/industry representatives attending, what each company is currently looking to produce (i.e., genre, budget), along with each company's credits. We also post a genre list at each event for cross-reference. Annual **Costs** Our ticket prices are flat fees that cover each attendee's entire weekend (including food and drink). There are no other extra, added costs (i.e., no per pitch meeting fees) involved (unless you're adding hotel rooms).

IDAHO WRITERS LEAGUE WRITERS' CONFERENCE
P.O. Box 492, Kootenai, ID 83840. (208)290-8749. E-mail: president@ idahowritersleague.com. Website: www.idahowritersleague.com/Conference. html. Estab. 1940. Annual floating conference. Next conference: The Twin Falls Chapter will host the 2009 League Conference. Dates are beginning Thursday, September 24, 2009 for registration. The workshops will run Friday, September 25 and Saturday, September 26, 2009. The conference will be at the Red Lion Canyon Springs Hotel and Convention Center in Twin Falls. As we receive information on the conference schedule, presenters, and other related information, we will add them to our Web page. Average attendance: 80+. We have such writers as magazine freelance and children's book author, Kelly Milner Halls; and author of the 2006 Christian Women's Fiction Book of the Year, Nikki Arana.
Costs Cost: $125. Check for updates on cost.
Additional Information Check out our website at www.idahowritersleague.com.

IMAGINATION WRITERS WORKSHOP AND CONFERENCE
Cleveland State University, English Department, 2121 Euclid Ave., Cleveland OH 44115. (216)687-4522. Fax: (216)687-6943. E-mail: imagination@csuohio.edu. Website: www.csuohio.edu/imagination/. Estab. 1990. Annual conference is held in late June/early July. Conference duration: 6 days. Average attendance: 60. Program includes intensive workshops, panels, lectures on poetry, fiction, creative nonfiction, playwriting, and the business of writing by noted authors, editors and agents. Held at Trinity Commons, an award-winning urban renovation and ideal conference center adjacent to the CSU campus. Available both not-for-credit and for university credit.
Additional Information This year the conference will be held Tuesday Evening, July 7, through Sunday Afternoon, July 12, 2009. Application deadline: May 20.

INDIANA UNIVERSITY WRITERS' CONFERENCE
464 Ballantine Hall, Bloomington IN 47405. (812)855-1877. E-mail: writecon@ indiana.edu. Website: www.indiana.edu/~writecon. Estab. 1940. Annual

conference held in June. 2009: June 14-19. The Indiana University Writers' Conference, now in its 69th year, invites prominent writers who are equally skilled and involved teachers. Participants in the week-long conference join faculty-led workshops (fiction, poetry, and creative nonfiction), take classes, engage in one-on-one consultation with authors, and attend a variety of readings and social events. Previous speakers have included Raymond Carver, Mark Doty, Robert Olen Butler, Aimee Bender, Li-Young Lee, and Brenda Hillman.
Costs Costs available online.
Additional Information In order to be accepted in a workshop, the writer must submit the work they would like critiqued. Work is evaluated before the applicant is accepted. Go online or send a SASE for guidelines.

INTERNATIONAL MUSEUM PUBLISHING SEMINAR

University of Chicago, Graham School of General Studies, 1427 E. 60th St., Chicago IL 60637. (773)702-1682. Fax: (773)702-6814. E-mail: s-medlock@ uchicago.edu. Website: grahamschool.uchicago.edu. Estab. 1988. Biennial conference. Conference duration: 2 1/2 days. Average attendance: 250. Primarily covers nonfiction, writing, and editing in museums. Recent themes have included selecting an attractive books cover, artful strategies for cutting costs, digital imaging, a survival guide, and more. The conference moves to a new city each year and is co-sponsored by the university with different museums.
Costs $600-650
Accommodations See Web site for hotel options.
Additional Information Send a SASE in January for brochure/guidelines. Inquire via e-mail or fax.

IN THE COMPANY OF WRITERS, WEBINARS AND TELESEMINARS

1071 Steeple Run, Lawrenceville GA 30043. (678)407-0703. Fax: (678)407-9917. E-mail:info@inthecompanyofwriters.com. Website:www.inthecompanyofwriters. com. Estab. 2006. Weekly and monthly classes via teleseminars and webinars starting in February (six-week, 12-hour class). Sessions range from two hours to six weeks. Learn from the nation's top experts, covering all genres and aspects of the writing life for inspiration, information, publication, marketing and more. Presented via telephone, online media and e-books. There's no traveling, no hotels and no expensive meals out. Presenters include Dr. Brian J. Corrigan, Bobbie Christmas, mystery writer Fran Stewart, memoirist Sara Harrell Banks, poet Collin Kelley.
Costs Varies; the cost is free to some and can be up to $247 for others depending on subject and duration.

Additional Information "Join online in order to receive our FREE E-Lert Newsletter bringing you updates on courses, writing tips, and information, including markets, contests."

IOWA SUMMER WRITING FESTIVAL

C215 Seashore Hall, University of Iowa, Iowa City IA 52242. (319)335-4160. Fax: (319)335-4743. E-mail: iswfestival@uiowa.edu. Website: www.uiowa. edu/~iswfest. Estab. 1987. "Annual festival held in June and July. Conference duration: Workshops are 1 week or a weekend. Average attendance: Limited to 12 people/class, with over 1,500 participants throughout the summer. We offer courses across the genres: novel, short story, poetry, essay, memoir, humor, travel, playwriting, screenwriting, writing for children, and women's writing. Held at the University of Iowa campus. Speakers have included Marvin Bell, Lan Samantha Chang, John Dalton, Hope Edelman, Katie Ford, Patricia Foster, Bret Anthony Johnston, Barbara Robinette Moss, among others."

Costs $500-525/week; $250/weekend workshop. Housing and meals are separate. See registration info online.

Accommodations Iowa House: $75/night; Sheraton: $88/night (rates subject to change).

Additional Information Brochures are available in February. Inquire via e-mail or fax.

IWWG EARLY SPRING IN CALIFORNIA CONFERENCE

International Women's Writing Guild, P.O. Box 810, Gracie Station, New York NY 10028-0082. (212)737-7536. Fax: (212)737-9469. E-mail: iwwg@iwwg.org. Website: www.iwwg.org. Estab. 1982. Annual conference held the second week in March. Average attendance: 50. Conference promotes creative writing, personal growth, and voice. Site is a redwood forest mountain retreat in Santa Cruz, California.

Costs $350/members; $380/nonmembers for weekend program with room and board; $125 for weekend program without room and board.

Accommodations All participants stay at the conference site or may commute.

Additional Information Brochures/guidelines are available online or for a SASE. Inquire via e-mail or fax.

IWWG Meet the Agents/Meet the Authors plus One Day Writing Workshop

c/o International Women's Writing Guild, P.O. Box 810, Gracie Station, New York NY 10028-0082. (212)737-7536. Fax: (212)737-9469. E-mail: iwwg@iwwg. org. Website: www.iwwg.org. Estab. 1980. Workshops are held the second weekend in April and October. Average attendance: 200. Workshops promote creative writing and professional success. A 1-day writing workshop is offered on Saturday. Sunday morning includes a discussion with up to 10 recently published IWWG authors and a book fair during lunch. On Sunday afternoon, up to 10 literary agents introduce themselves, and then members of the audience speak to the agents they wish to meet. Many as-yet-unpublished works have found publication in this manner. Speakers have included Meredith Bernstein, Rita Rosenkranz, and Jeff Herman.

Costs $130/members for the weekend; $160/nonmembers for the weekend; $90/100 for Saturday; $80/105 for Sunday.

Additional Information Information (including accommodations) is provided in a brochure. Inquire via fax or e-mail.

JACKSON HOLE WRITERS CONFERENCE

PO Box 1974, Jackson WY 83001. (307)413-3332. E-mail: tim@ jacksonholewritersconference.com. Website: jacksonholewritersconference. com/. Estab. 1991. Annual conference held in June. For 2009: June 25-28. Conference duration: 4 days. Average attendance: 70. Covers fiction and creative nonfiction and offers ms critiques from authors, agents, and editors. Agents in attendance will take pitches from writers. Paid manuscript critique programs are available.

Costs $360-390

Additional Information Held at the Center for the Arts in Jackson, Wyoming.

JAMES RIVER WRITERS CONFERENCE

P.O. Box 25067, Richmond VA 23260. (804)474-3575. E-mail: fallconference@ jamesriverwriters.com. Website: www.jamesriverwriters.com. Estab. 2003. Annual conference held in October. For 2009: Oct. 9-10. Average attendance: 250. The conference is held at the Library of Virginia, located in downtown Richmond. Some events planned include panel discussions on freelancing, historical fiction, how to create dialogue, and nonfiction. Speakers discuss the craft and profession of writing and publishing and present many genres—from fiction, nonfiction, and screenwriting, to poetry, children's literature, and science fiction. New York agents, bestselling authors, and major publishers usually attend.

Costs $150 (early bird) for 2 days of speakers, panels/discussions, an agent meeting (if available), and a continental breakfast and box lunch on both days. Parking is not included.

Accommodations Overnight accommodation information is available on the Web site. A block of hotel rooms is also reserved at the Holiday Inn Central, located near downtown.

Additional Information Brochures/guidelines are available online or for a SASE. Send inquiries via e-mail.

KARITOS CHRISTIAN ARTS CONFERENCE

1122 Brentwood Ln., Wheaton IL 60189. (847)925-8018. E-mail: bob@karitos. com. Website: www.karitos.com. Estab. 1996. Annual conference held each summer. 2009: July 16-18. Average attendance: 300-400. Karitos is a celebration and teaching weekend for Christian artists and writers. Writing Division will focus on teaching the craft of writing, beginning and advanced, fiction and nonfiction. Site for this year's conference is Living Waters Community Church in the Chicago suburb of Bolingbrook, Faculty has included Lori Davis, John DeJarlais, Eva Marie Everson, Lin Johnson, Patricia Hickman, Elma Photikarm, Rajendra Pillai, Jane Rubietta, Travis Thrasher and Chris Wave.
Costs See website for costs.

KEENE STATE COLLEGE WRITERS CONFERENCE

Continuing Education and Extended Studies, 229 Main St., Keene, NH 03435-2605, (603)358-2290. Fax: (603)358-2569. Website: www.keene.edu/conted/writerconf/. 2009 dates: July 26-August 1. Conference duration: one week. Whether your interest lies in fiction, nonfiction, poetry or all three, this summer conference will help writers with their work. There are daily workshops, writings sessions, individual meetings, craft talks, readings, informal after-hours gatherings, and, above all, time to write. Annual
Costs Approximately $990. Additional costs for college credit, room, meals.
Additional Information Please register early. Space is limited.

KENYON REVIEW WRITERS WORKSHOP

The Kenyon Review, Kenyon College, Gambier OH 43022. (740)427-5207. Fax: (740)427-5417. E-mail: reacha@kenyon.edu. Website: www.kenyonreview.org. Estab. 1990. Annual 8-day workshop held in June. Participants apply in poetry, fiction, or creative nonfiction, and then participate in intensive daily workshops which focus on the generation and revision of significant new work. Held on the campus of Kenyon College in the rural village of Gambier, Ohio. Workshop leaders have included David Baker, Ron Carlson, Rebecca McClanahan, Rosanna Warren and Nancy Zafris.
Costs $1,995 (includes tuition, housing, meals).
Accommodations Participants stay in Kenyon College student housing.

KEY WEST LITERARY SEMINAR

718 Love Ln., Key West FL 33040 (December-April). (888)293-9291. E-mail: mail@kwls.org. Website: www.keywestliteraryseminar.org. 16 Prayer Ridge Rd., Fairview NC 28730 (May-November). Annual conference held in January. 2010: Jan. 7-10 at San Carlos Institute. See website for topics. 2010 conference is a celebration of 60 years of American poetry.

Costs $495/seminar; $450/writers workshop (Jan. 10-14, 2010).

Accommodations A list of nearby lodging establishments is made available.

ℕ KILLALOE HEDGE-SCHOOL OF WRITING

4 Riverview, Ballina, Killaloe Co. Clare Ireland. (353)(61)375-217. Fax: (353)(61)375-487. Website: www.killaloe.ie/khs. Estab. 1999. Conference duration: 2 days. Holds workshops on 6 different topics.

Costs €235/course.

Accommodations There is a list of hotels and bed and breakfasts on the Web site.

KILLER NASHVILLE

P.O. Box 680686, Franklin TN 37068-0686. (615)599-4032. E-mail: contact@killernashville.com. Website: www.killernashville.com. Estab. 2006. Annual conference held in August. Next conference: Aug. 14-16, 2009. Conference duration: 3 days. Average attendance: 180+. Conference designed for writers and fans of mysteries and thrillers, including fiction and nonfiction authors, playwrights, and screenwriters. There are many opportunities for authors to sign books. Authors/panelists have included Michael Connelly, Bill Bass, J.A. Jance, Carol Higgins Clark, Hallie Ephron, Chris Grabenstein, Rhonda Pollero, P.J. Parrish, Reed Farrel Coleman, Kathryn Wall, Mary Saums, Don Bruns, Bill Moody, Richard Helms, Brad Strickland and Steven Womack. Literary agents and acquisitions editors attend and take pitches from writers. The conference is sponsored by American Blackguard, Barnes and Noble, Mystery Writers of America, Sisters in Crime and the Nashville Scene, among others. Representatives from the FBI, TBI, ATF, police department and sheriff's department present on law enforcement procedures to the general public.

LA JOLLA WRITERS CONFERENCE

P.O. Box 178122, San Diego CA 92177. (858)467-1978. Fax: (858)467-1971. E-mail: jkuritz@san.rr.com. Website: www.lajollawritersconference.com. Estab. 2001. Annual conference held in October/November. Conference duration: 3 days. Average attendance: 200. In addition to covering nearly every genre, we also take particular pride in educating our attendees on the business aspect of the book industry by having agents, editors, publishers, publicists, and distributors teach classes. Our conference offers 2 types of classes: lecture sessions that run for 50 minutes, and workshops that run for 110 minutes. Each block period is dedicated to either workshop or lecture-style classes. During each block period, there will be 6-8 classes on various topics from which you can choose to attend. For most workshop classes, you are encouraged to bring written work for review. Literary agents from The Andrea Brown Literary Agency, The Dijkstra Agency, The McBride Agency and Full Circle Literary Group have participated in the past.

Costs Costs are available online.

Accommodations We arrange a discounted rate with the hotel that hosts the conference. Please refer to the Web site.

Additional Information "Our conference is completely non-commercial. Our goal is to foster a true learning environment. As such, our faculty is chosen based on their expertise and willingness to make themselves completely available to the attendees. Brochures are online; send inquiries via e-mail or fax."

LAS VEGAS WRITERS CONFERENCE

Henderson Writers Group, 614 Mosswood Drive, Henderson NV 89015. (702)564-2488. E-mail: info@lasvegaswritersconference.com. Website: www. lasvegaswritersconference.com/. Annual conference just outside of Las Vegas. Conference duration: 3 days. Average attendance: 140. Join writing professionals, agents, industry experts and your colleagues for four days in Las Vegas, NV, as they share their knowledge on all aspects of the writer's craft. One of the great charms of the Las Vegas Writer's Conference is its intimacy. Registration is limited to 140 attendees so there's always plenty of one-on-one time with the faculty. While there are formal pitch sessions, panels, workshops, and seminars, the faculty is also available throughout the conference for informal discussions and advice. Plus, you're bound to meet a few new friends, too. Workshops, seminars and expert panels will take you through writing in many genres including fiction, creative nonfiction, screenwriting, poetry, journalism and business and technical writing. There will be many Q&A panels for you to ask the experts all your questions. Annual

Accommodations Sam's Town Hotel and Gambling Hall.

LEAGUE OF UTAH WRITERS ANNUAL CONFERENCE AND ROUNDUP

P.O. Box 18430, Kearns UT 84118. Website: www.luwrite.com. Estab. 1935. Annual conference held in September. (2009: Sept. 18-19, Heber Valley, UT)

Conference duration: 2 days. Offers up to 16 workshops, a keynote speaker, and an awards banquet. Speakers cover subjects from generating ideas, to writing a novel, to working with a publisher.

Additional Information This conference is held in a different site in Utah each year. See the Web site for updated information.

▥ LIGONIER VALLEY WRITERS CONFERENCE

P.O. Box B, Ligonier PA 15658. (724)593-7294. E-mail: jgallagher@LHTC.net. Website: www.lvwonline. Annual conference held last weekend in July. 2009: July 18, 2009. Details will be posted on their site: lvwonline. Readings, seminars, and workshops cover nonfiction, fiction, children's, poetry, creative nonfiction, playwriting, screenwriting, memoir, travel, historical, fantasy, science fiction, romance, journaling, nature, horror, plot development, and editing. Speakers have included Julia Kasdorf, Paola Corso, Randall Silvis, David Walton, Hilary Masters, Amanda Lynch, and Kathleen George.

Costs See costs for members/nonmembers at lvwonline.

Accommodations A special rate is available at the Ramada Inn of Ligonier.

Additional Information Attendees can submit up to 20 pages for a critique.

LOVE IS MURDER

E-mail: hanleyliz@wideopenwest.com. Website: www.loveismurder.net. Annual conference held in February for readers, writers, and fans of mystery, suspense, thriller, romantic suspense, dark fiction, and true crime. Published authors provide ms critiques; editors/agents participate in pitch sessions. Attorneys, criminal justice experts, forensic scientists, and physicians also attend.

Additional Information Sponsors Reader's Choice Awards for best first novel, historical novel, series, crime-related nonfiction, private investigator/police procedural, paranormal/science fiction/horror, traditional/amateur sleuth, suspense thriller, romance/fantasy, and short story.

THE MACDOWELL COLONY

100 High St., Peterborough NH 03458. (603)924-3886. Fax: (603)924-9142. E-mail: admissions@macdowellcolony.org. Website: www.macdowellcolony.org. Estab. 1907. Open to writers, playwrights, composers, visual artists, film/video artists, interdisciplinary artists and architects. Applicants send information and work samples for review by a panel of experts in each discipline. See application guidelines for details.

Costs Financial assistance is available for participants of the residency, based on need. There are no residency fees.

MAGNA CUM MURDER

The Mid America Crime Writing Festival, The E.B. and Bertha C. Ball Center, Ball State University, Muncie IN 47306. (765)285-8975. Fax: (765)747-9566. E-mail: magnacummurder@yahoo.com; kennisonk@aol.com. Website: www. magnacummurder.com. Estab. 1994. Annual conference held in October. Average attendance: 350. Festival for readers and writers of crime writing. Held in the Horizon Convention Center and Historic Hotel Roberts. Dozens of mystery writers are in attendance and there are presentations from agents, editors and professional writers. The Web site has the full list of attending speakers.
Costs Check website for updates.

MALICE DOMESTIC

PO Box 8007, Gaithersburg MD 20898-8007. Fax: (301)432-7391. E-mail: malicechair@malicedomestic.org. Website: www.malicedomestic.org/. Estab. 1989. 2010 dates: April 30 - May 2, 2010. The conference is for mystery writers of all kinds and always held in the Washington, DC regional area. The conference includes authors and literary agents.
Costs See website for additional information.

MANHATTANVILLE SUMMER WRITERS' WEEK

2900 Purchase St., Purchase NY 10577-0940. (914)323-5239. Fax: (914)694-0348. E-mail: gps@mville.edu; dowdr@mville.edu. Website: www.mville.edu. Estab. 1983. Annual conference held in late June. 2009: June 22-26. Conference duration: 5 days. Average attendance: 100. Workshops are offered in fiction, nonfiction, personal narrative, poetry, children's/young adult, and literature/playwriting. Held at a suburban college campus 30 miles from New York City. Workshop sessions are held in a 19th century Norman castle, which serves as the college's administration building. Speakers have included Brian Morton, Valerie Martin, Ann Jones, Mark Matousek, Major Jackson, Linda Oatman High, Jeffrey Sweet, Alice Quinn (*The New Yorker*), Georgia Jelatis Hoke (MacIntosh & Otis), Paul Cirone (Aaron Priest Literary Agency), and Emily Saladino (Writer's House). Agents will be speaking and available for meetings with attendees.
Costs $650/noncredit (includes all workshops, craft seminars, readings, keynote lecture); $1,040/2 graduate credits. Participants may purchase meals in the college cafeteria or cafe.
Accommodations A list of hotels in the area is available upon request. Overnight accommodations are also available in the college residence halls.
Additional Information Brochures are available online or for a SASE at the end of February. Inquire via e-mail or fax.

⧉ ⧉ MARITIME WRITERS' WORKSHOP

UNB Art Centre, Box 4400, Fredericton NB E3B 5A3 Canada. (506)452-6360. E-mail: rhona.sawlor@unb.ca. Website: www.unb.ca/extend/writers. **Contact:** Allison Howells. Estab. 1976. Annual workshop held in July. Average attendance: 50. Offers workshops in 4 areas: fiction, poetry, nonfiction, and writing for children. Site is the University of New Brunswick, Fredericton campus.

Costs $115 per workshop, or $460 for the week.

Accommodations $725/single occupancy; $705/double occupancy. Meals are included.

Additional Information Participants must submit 10-20 manuscript pages for workshop discussions. Brochures are available after March (no SASE necessary). Accepts inquiries via e-mail.

MARYMOUNT MANHATTAN COLLEGE WRITERS' CONFERENCE

Marymount Manhattan College, 221 E. 71st St., New York NY 10021. (212)774-4810. E-mail: lfrumkes@mmm.edu. Estab. 1993. Annual conference held in June. 2009 keynote speakers: Joseph O'Neill (Netherland), Christopher Reich (Rules of Deception), Peter Scoblic (Managing Editor, *The New Republic*). Conference duration: 1 day. Average attendance: 200. We present workshops on several different writing genres and panels on fiction and nonfiction, literary agents, memoir and more. Over 60 distinguished authors, agents, and publicists attend. Keynote speakers have included Lewis Lapham and Joyce Carol Oates.

Costs $165 before June 1; $185 after June 1 (includes lunch, reception).

MAUMEE VALLEY FREELANCE WRITERS' CONFERENCE

Lourdes College, Franciscan Center, 6832 Convent Blvd., Sylvania OH 43560. (800)878-3210, ext. 3707. E-mail: gburke@lourdes.edu. Website: www.maumeevalleywritersconference.com/. Estab. 1997. Annual conference held in May. Sessions include: Freelance Writing for Magazines, Jumpstart your Stalled Novel, Personal Essays, and Asking the Right Questions: the Art of the Interview. Speakers have included Craig Holden, Matt Betts, Russ Franzen, Benjamin Gleisser, Nicole Hunter, and Jack Lessenberry. Agents and editors participate in the conference.

Costs $99 (includes lunch); $49/students; $30/ms critique.

MENDOCINO COAST WRITERS CONFERENCE

1211 Del Mar Dr., Fort Bragg CA 95437. (707)962-2600, ext. 2167. E-mail: info@mcwc.org. Website: www.mcwc.org. Estab. 1988. Annual conference held in August.

Conferences

Average attendance: 90. Provides workshops for fiction, nonfiction, scriptwriting, children's, mystery, and writing for social change. Held at a small community college campus on the northern Pacific Coast. Speakers have included Jandy Nelson, Paul Levine, Sally Werner, John Lescroart, and Maxine Schur. Agents will be speaking and available for meetings with attendees.

Costs $450+ (includes panels, meals, 2 socials with guest readers, 1 public event, 1 day intensive in 1 subject and 2 days of several short sessions).

Accommodations Information on overnight accommodations and shared rides from the San Francisco Airport is made available.

Additional Information Emphasis is on writers who are also good teachers. Brochures are online or available with a SASE after January. Send inquiries via e-mail.

MIDWEST WRITERS WORKSHOP

Department of Journalism, Ball State University, 2800 Bethel Ave., Muncie IN 47306. (765)282-1055. Fax: (765)285-5997. E-mail: info@midwestwriters.org. Website: www.midwestwriters.org. **Contact:** Jama Bigger, registrar. Estab. 1974. Annual workshop held last weekend in July. Conference duration: 3 days. Covers fiction, nonfiction, poetry, writing for children, how to find an agent, memoirs, Internet marketing and more. Speakers have included best selling authors, literary agents, and editors.

Costs $100-295; $25/ms evaluation

MONTROSE CHRISTIAN WRITERS' CONFERENCE

5 Locust St., Montrose PA 18801. (570)278-1001 or (800)598-5030. Fax: (570)278-3061. E-mail: mbc@montrosebible.org. Website: www.montrosebible.org. Estab. 1990. Annual conference held in July. Offers workshops, editorial appointments, and professional critiques. We try to meet a cross-section of writing needs, for beginners and advanced, covering fiction, poetry, and writing for children. It is small enough to allow personal interaction between attendees and faculty. Speakers have included William Petersen, Mona Hodgson, Jim Fletcher, and Terri Gibbs.

Costs $150/tuition; $35/critique for 2008.

Accommodations Housing and meals are available on site.

MOUNT HERMON CHRISTIAN WRITERS CONFERENCE

37 Conference Drive, Mount Hermon CA 95041. E-mail: info@mounthermon.org. Website: www.mounthermon.org/writers. Estab. 1970. Annual conference held in the spring. 2008 dates were March 14-16. Average attendance: 450. We are a broad-ranging conference for all areas of Christian writing, including fiction,

children's, poetry, nonfiction, magazines, books, inspirational and devotional writing, educational curriculum and radio and TV scriptwriting. This is a working, how-to conference, with many workshops within the conference involving on-site writing assignments. The conference is sponsored by and held at the 440-acre Mount Hermon Christian Conference Center near San Jose, California, in the heart of the coastal redwoods. The faculty-to-student ratio is about 1 to 6. The bulk of our more than 60 faculty members are editors and publisher representatives from major Christian publishing houses nationwide. Speakers have included T. Davis Bunn, Debbie Macomber, Jerry Jenkins, Bill Butterworth, Dick Foth and others.

Accommodations Registrants stay in hotel-style accommodations. Meals are buffet style, with faculty joining registrants.

Additional Information "The residential nature of our conference makes this a unique setting for one-on-one interaction with faculty/staff. There is also a decided inspirational flavor to the conference, and general sessions with well-known speakers are a highlight. Registrants may submit 2 works for critique in advance of the conference, then have personal interviews with critiquers during the conference. Brochures/guidelines are available December 1. All conference information is now online only. Send inquiries via e-mail or fax. Tapes of past conferences are also available."

MUSE AND THE MARKETPLACE

160 Boylston St., 4th Floor, Boston MA 02116. (617)695.0075. E-mail: info@grubstreet.org. Website: www.grubstreet.org. The conferences are held in the late spring, such as early May. Conference duration: 2 days. Average attendance: 400. Dozens of agents are in attendance to meet writers and take pitches. Previous keynote speakers include Jonathan Franzen. The conferences has workshops on all aspects of writing. Annual

Costs Approx. $250-400 depending on if you're a Member or Non-Members (includes 6 workshop sessions and 2 Hour of Power sessions with options for the Manuscript Mart and a Five-Star lunch with authors, editors and agents). Other passes are available for Saturday only and Sunday only guests.

NASHVILLE SCREENWRITERS CONFERENCE

(615)254-2049. Website: nashscreen.com/nsc/. This is a three-day conference dedicated to those who write for the screen. Nashville is a city that celebrates its writers and its creative community, and every writer wants to have a choice of avenues to increase their potential for success. In this memorable weekend, conference participants will have the opportunity to attend various writing panels led by working professionals and participate in several special events. Annual

NATCHEZ LITERARY AND CINEMA CELEBRATION

P.O. Box 1307, Natchez MS 39121-1307. (601)446-1208. Fax: (601)446-1214. E-mail: carolyn.smith@colin.edu. Website: www.colin.edu/NLCC. Estab. 1990. Annual conference held in February. Conference duration: 5 days. Conference focuses on all literature, including film scripts. Each year's conference deals with some general aspect of Southern history. Speakers have included Eudora Welty, Margaret Walker Alexander, William Styron, Willie Morris, Ellen Douglas, Ernest Gaines, Elizabeth Spencer, Nikki Giovanni, Myrlie Evers-Williams, and Maya Angelou.

NATIONAL WRITERS ASSOCIATION FOUNDATION CONFERENCE

P.O. Box 4187, Parker CO 80134. (303)841-0246. Fax: (303)841-2607. E-mail: natlwritersassn@hotmail.com. Website: www.nationalwriters.com. Estab. 1926. Annual conference held the second week of June in Denver. Conference duration: 1 day. Average attendance: 100. Focuses on general writing and marketing.
Costs Approximately $100
Additional Information Awards for previous contests will be presented at the conference. Brochures/guidelines are online, or send a SASE.

🌐 NATIONAL YOUNG WRITERS FESTIVAL

3/231 King St., Newcastle NSW 2300 Australia. (61)(2)4927-1475. Fax: (61)(2)4927-0470. E-mail: submissions.nywf@gmail.com. Website: www. youngwritersfestival.org. Estab. 1998. Annual festival held in September/October. Conference duration: 5 days. "Poets, editors, comic creators, spoken word artists, script writers, journalists, and all-and-sundry 'friends of the word' gather for workshops, discussions, performances, and collaborations. The National Young Writers' Festival is part of a coalition of festivals called This Is Not Art that occurs over the same 5 days in Newcastle and offers a vibrant and unique mix of experimental and independent arts and media events. All sessions are free of charge.
Costs All sessions are free of charge.

NATJA ANNUAL CONFERENCE & MARKETPLACE

North American Travel Journalists Association, 531 Main St., #902, El Segundo CA 90245. (310)836-8712. Fax: (310)836-8769. E-mail: chelsea@natja.org; elizabeth@natja.org. Website: www.natja.org/conference. Estab. 2003. Annual conference held in May or June. Conference duration: 3 days. Average attendance: 250. Provides professional development for travel journalists and gives them the chance to market themselves to destinations and cultivate relationships to further their careers. Previous speakers have included Lisa Lenoir (*Chicago Sun-Times*), Steve Millburg (*Coastal Living*) and Peter Yesawich. The dates and location of this event change each year, so checking the Web site is the best way to go. Annual

Accommodations Different destinations host the conference each year, all at hotels with conference centers.

Additional Information E-mail, call, or go online for more information.

NEBRASKA SUMMER WRITERS' CONFERENCE

Department of English, University of Nebraska, Lincoln NE 68588-0333. (402)472-1834. E-mail: nswc@unl.edu. Website: www.nswc.org. Annual conference held in June. Conference duration: 1 week. Faculty include Sara Gruen, Ron Hansen, Li-Young Lee, Sean Doolittle, Lee Martin, Dorianne Laux, Jim Shepard, Judith Kitchen, Joe Mackall, Hilda Raz, William Kloefkorn, agent Sonia Pabley, Timothy Schaffert, Brent Spencer, Stan Sanvel Rubin, agent Emma Sweeney, Jane Von Mehren (vice president, Random House). An agent is usually in attendance to take pitches.

Costs Costs available online.

NECON

Northeastern Writers Conference, 330 Olney St., Seekonk MA 02771. (508)557-1218. E-mail: daniel.booth77@gmail.com. Website: www.campnecon.com. Estab. 1980. Annual conference typically held in July. Conference duration: Four days. Average attendance: 200. The conference is dedicated to those who write fiction. Held at Roger Williams University in Bristol, RI. Themes vary from year to year. Agents attend the workshop each year. Annual

Costs $350-450. This includes meals and lodging.

Accommodations Attendees stay on campus in the dorm rooms. This housing cost is in the registration fee.

Additional Information Shuttle service provided to the convention site as well as the airport and train station. We are a very laid back, relaxed convention. However, work is accomplished each year and it's a good opportunity to network.

NETWO WRITERS ROUNDUP

Northeast Texas Writers Organization, P.O. Box 411, Winfield TX 75493. (903)856-6724. E-mail: netwomail@netwo.org. Website: www.netwo.org. Estab. 1987. Annual conference held in April. Conference duration: 2 days. Presenters include agents, writers, editors, and publishers. Agents in attendance will take pitches from writers. The conference features a writing contest, pitch sessions, critiques from professionals, as well as dozens of workshops and presentations.

Costs $60+ (discount offered for early registration).

Additional Information Conference is co-sponsored by the Texas Commission on the Arts. See Web site for current updates.

NEW-CUE WRITERS' CONFERENCE & WORKSHOP IN HONOR OF RACHEL CARSON

New-Cue, Inc., Methodist College, Clark Hall, 5300 Ramsey St., Fayetteville NC 28311. (845)630-7047 or (910)630-7046. Fax: (910)630-7221. E-mail: info@new-cue.org. Website: www.new-cue.org. Estab. 1999. Biannual conference held in June. Next one will be in 2010. Conference duration: 4 days. Average attendance: 100. This interdisciplinary event will be a blend of scholarly presentations, readings, informal discussions, and writing workshops. Held at The Spruce Point Inn in Boothbay Harbor, Maine. Speakers have included Lawrence Buell, Bill McKibben, Carl Safina and Linda Lear.

Costs Registration costs include sessions, meals and keynote reception.

Accommodations Special rates are available for participants at the Spruce Point Inn. Transportation and area information is available through the Boothbay Harbor Chamber of Commerce.

NEW JERSEY ROMANCE WRITERS PUT YOUR HEART IN A BOOK CONFERENCE

P.O. Box 513, Plainsboro NJ 08536. E-mail: njrwconfchair@yahoo.com; njrw@njromance writers.org. Website: www.njromancewriters.org. Estab. 1984. Annual conference held in October. Average attendance: 500. Workshops are offered on various topics for all writers of romance, from beginner to multi-published. Speakers have included Nora Roberts, Kathleen Woodiwiss, Patricia Gaffney, Jill Barnett and Kay Hooper. Appointments are offered with editors/agents. Annual

Accommodations Special rate available for conference attendees at the Sheraton at Woodbridge Place Hotel in Iselin, New Jersey.

Additional Information Conference brochures, guidelines, and membership information are available for SASE. Massive bookfair is open to the public with authors signing copies of their books.

THE NEW LETTERS WEEKEND WRITERS CONFERENCE

University of Missouri-Kansas City, 5101 Rockhill Rd., Kansas City MO 64110-2499. (816)235-1168. Fax: (816)235-2611. E-mail: newletters@umkc.edu. Website: www.newletters.org. **Contact:** Betsey Beasley. Estab. 1970s (as The Longboat Key Writers Conference). Annual conference held in late June. Conference duration: 3 days. Average attendance: 60. The conference brings together talented writers in many genres for seminars, readings, workshops, and individual conferences. The emphasis is on craft and the creative process in poetry, fiction, screenwriting, playwriting, and journalism, but the program also deals with matters of psychology, publications, and marketing. The conference is appropriate for both advanced and beginning writers. The conference meets at the university's beautiful Diastole Conference Center. Two- and 3-credit hour options are available by special permission from the Director Robert Stewart.

Costs Participants may choose to attend as a noncredit student or they may attend for 1 hour of college credit from the University of Missouri-Kansas City. Conference registration includes Friday evening reception and keynote speaker, Saturday and Sunday continental breakfast and lunch.

Accommodations Registrants are responsible for their own transportation, but information on area accommodations is available.

Additional Information Those registering for college credit are required to submit a ms in advance. Ms reading and critique are included in the credit fee. Those attending the conference for noncredit also have the option of having their ms critiqued for an additional fee. Brochures are available for a SASE after March. Accepts inquiries by e-mail and fax.

◉ NEW ZEALAND POST WRITERS AND READERS WEEK

New Zealand International Arts Festival, P.O. Box 10-113, Level 2, Anvil House, 138-140 Wakefield St., Wellington New Zealand. (04)(4)473-0149. Fax: (04)(4)471-1164. E-mail: nzfestival@festival.co.nz. Website: www.nzfestival.telecom.co.nz. **Contact:** Sue Paterson. Biennial festival held in March. 2010: Feb. 26-Mar. 21. Conference duration: 5 days. Focuses on fiction, poetry, and serious nonfiction. Participants are selected by a committee of writers and other book professionals. Held at the Embassy Theatre and other venues.

Costs Tickets range from $13-50.

Additional Information Sign up for newsletter online.

NIMROD AWARDS CELEBRATION & WRITING WORKSHOP

University of Tulsa, 800 S. Tucker Drive., Tulsa OK 74104-3189. (918)631-3080. Fax: (918)631-3033. E-mail: nimrod@utulsa.edu. Website: www.utulsa.edu/nimrod. Estab. 1978. Annual conference held in October. Conference duration: 1 day. Offers one-on-one editing sessions, readings, panel discussions, and master classes in fiction, poetry, nonfiction, memoir, and fantasy writing. Speakers have included Myla Goldberg, B.H. Fairchild, Colleen McElroy, Gina Ochsner, Kelly Link, Rilla Askew, Matthew Galkin, and A.D. Coleman.

Additional Information Full conference details are online in August.

NORTH CAROLINA WRITERS' NETWORK FALL CONFERENCE

P.O. Box 954, Carrboro NC 27510-0954. (919)967-9540. Fax: (919)929-0535. E-mail: mail@ncwriters.org. Website: www.ncwriters.org. Estab. 1985. "Annual conference held in November in Research Traingle Park (Durham, North Carolina). Average attendance: 450. This organization hosts two conferences: one in the spring and one in the fall. Each conference is a weekend full of workshops, panels, book signings, and readings (including open mic). There will be a keynote speaker, along with sessions on a variety of genres, including fiction, poetry, creative nonfiction, journalism, children's book writing, screenwriting, and playwriting. We also offer craft, editing, and marketing classes. We hold the event at a conference center with hotel rooms available. Speakers have included Donald Maass, Noah Lukeman, Joe Regal, Jeff Kleinman, and Evan Marshall. Some agents will teach classes and some are available for meetings with attendees."

Costs Approximately $250 (includes 2 meals).

Accommodations Special rates are available at the Sheraton Hotel, but conferees must make their own reservations.

Additional Information Brochures/guidelines are available online or by sending your street address to mail@ncwriters.org. You can also register online.

ⓃNORTHERN COLORADO WRITERS CONFERENCE

108 East Monroe Dr., Fort Collins CO 80525. (970)556-0908. E-mail: kerrie@ncwc.biz. Website: www.ncwc.biz/. Estab. 2006. Annual conference held in the spring in Colorado. Conference duration: 2 days. The conference features a variety of speakers, agents and editors. There are workshops and presentations on fiction, nonfiction, screenwriting, staying inspired, and more. Previous agents who have attended and taken pitches from writers include Jessica Regel, Kristen Nelson, Rachelle Gardner, Andrea Brown, Jessica Faust, Jon Sternfeld, and Jeffrey McGraw. Each conference features more than 30 workshops from which to choose from. Annual

Costs $200-300, depending on what package the attendee selects.

Accommodations The conference is hosted at the Fort Collins Hilton, where rooms are available at a special rate.

NORWESCON

P.O. Box 68547, Seattle WA 98168-9986. (206)270-7850. Fax: (520)244-0142. E-mail: info@norwescon.org. Website: www.norwescon.org. Estab. 1978. Annual conference held in April. (Norwescon 33 will be held April 1-4, 2010.) Average attendance: 2,800. General multitrack convention focusing on science fiction and fantasy literature with wide coverage of other media. Tracks cover science, sociocultural, literary, publishing, editing, writing, art, and other media of a science fiction/fantasy orientation. Agents will be speaking and available for meetings with attendees.

Accommodations Conference is held at the Seatec Doubletree Hotel.

Additional Information Brochures are available online or for a SASE. Send inquiries via e-mail.

ODYSSEY FANTASY WRITING WORKSHOP

P.O. Box 75, Mont Vernon NH 03057. E-mail: jcavelos@sff.net. Website: www. odysseyworkshop.org. Estab. 1996. Annual workshop held in June (through July). Conference duration: 6 weeks. Average attendance: 16. A workshop for fantasy, science fiction, and horror writers that combines an intensive learning and writing experience with in-depth feedback on students' mss. Held on the campus of Saint Anselm College in Manchester, New Hampshire. Speakers have included George R.R. Martin, Elizabeth Hand, Jane Yolen, Harlan Ellison, Melissa Scott and Dan Simmons.

Costs $1,900/tuition; $700-1,400/on-campus apartment; approximately $550/on-campus meals. Scholarships are available.

Additional Information Prospective students must include a 15-page writing sample with their application. Accepts inquiries by SASE, e-mail, fax and phone. Application deadline April 8.

OKLAHOMA WRITERS' FEDERATION CONFERENCE

1213 E. 9th, Sand Springs OK 74063. (918)519-6707. Fax: (918)519-6707. E-mail: conferenceinfo@owfi.org; rangerjudy@cox.net. Website: www.owfi.org. Estab. 1968. Annual conference held in May. Average attendance: 500. Features writers, editors, agents, and informative programs to help authors write well and get published. Editor/agent appointments are available. Speaker have included Daniel Lazar (Writer's House), Robyn Russell (Amy Rennert Agency), Bryan Painter (*The Oklahoman*), and Mike Sanders (Alpha Books).

Costs $60-200 depending on if attendee partakes in dinners and sessions, as well as the attendee's registration date.

Accommodations Embassy Suites Hotel in Oklahoma City (within walking distance of the airport).

Additional Information We have a writing contest with 27 categories that pay cash prizes.

OPEN WRITING WORKSHOPS

Creative Writing Program, Department of English, Bowling Green State University, Bowling Green OH 43403. (419)372-6864. Fax: (419)372-6805. E-mail: masween@

bgnet.bgsu.edu. Website: www.bgsu.edu/departments/creative-writing/wshop.html. **Contact:** Mary Ann Sweeney. Estab. 1999. Annual workshops held in the Spring and Fall. Conference duration: 1 day. Average attendance: 10-20/workshop. Intensive manuscript-based workshops designed for fiction writers and poets of all levels of experience who are working in a variety of genres. Writers in the workshops share their work in a professional studio setting and receive commentary on works in progress from published writers and editors.

Additional Information Participants need to submit workshop material prior to conference.

OUTDOOR WRITERS ASSOCIATION OF AMERICA ANNUAL CONFERENCE

158 Lower Georges Valley Rd., Spring Mills PA 16875. (814)364-9557. Fax: (814)364-9558. E-mail: eking@owaa.org. Website: www.owaa.org. Estab. 1927. Annual conference held in June. (Held June 13-16, 2009 in Grand Rapids.) Conference duration: 4 days. Sessions concentrate on outdoor topics for all forms of media. Held in Lake Charles, Louisiana. Speakers have included Jill Adler, Eric Chaney, Todd Smith, Risa Weinreb-Wyatt, Bob Marshall, and Kathleen Kudlinski.

Costs See website.

Accommodations A block of rooms is held at a special rate.

OZARK CREATIVE WRITERS CONFERENCE

ETSU-Box 23115, Johnson City TN 37614. (423)439-6024. E-mail: ozarkcreativewriters@earthlink.net. Website: www.ozarkcreativewriters.org. Estab. 1975. Annual conference held the second weekend in October, in Eureka Springs, AR. Includes programs for all types of writing. Speakers have included Dan Slater (Penguin Putnam), Stephan Harrigan (novelist/screenwriter), and Christopher Vogler. At least one literary agent is in attendance each year to take pitches.

Costs Approximately $150.

Accommodations Special rates are available at the Inn of the Ozarks in Eureka Springs, Arkansas.

Additional Information The conference has a friendly atmosphere and conference speakers are available. Many speakers return to the conference for the companionship of writers and speakers. Brochures are available for a SASE.

⊕ PARIS WRITERS WORKSHOP

WICE, 7, Cité Falguiére, Paris 75015 France. (33)(14)566-7550. Fax: (33)(14)065-9653. E-mail: pww@wice-paris.org. Website: www.wice-paris.org. Estab. 1987. Annual conference held in July. Conference duration: 1 week. Average attendance:

12/section. Each participant chooses one workshop section - creative nonfiction, novel, poetry, or short story—which meets for a total of 15 classroom hours. Writers in residence have included Vivian Gornick, Lynne Sharon Schwartz, Liam Rector, Ellen Sussman, and Katharine Weber. Located in the heart of Paris, the site consists of 4 classrooms, a resource center/library, and a private terrace.
Costs See website for more information.
Accommodations Hotel information is on the Web site.

WILLIAM PATERSON UNIVERSITY SPRING WRITER'S CONFERENCE

English Department, Atrium 232, 300 Pompton Rd., Wayne NJ 07470. (973)720-3067. Fax: (973)720-2189. E-mail: parrasj@wpunj.edu. Website: http://euphrates. wpunj.edu/writersconference. Annual conference held in April. Conference duration: 1 day. Average attendance: 100-125. Panels address topics such as writing from life, getting your work in print, poetry, playwriting, fiction, and creative nonfiction. Sessions are led by William Paterson faculty members and distinguished writers and editors of verse and prose. Speakers have included Alison Lurie and Edward Hower.
Costs $50 (includes lunch).

PENNWRITERS ANNUAL CONFERENCE

E mail: conferenceco@pennwriters.org. Website. www.pennwriters.org. Estab. 1987. Annual conference held the third weekend of May. Conference duration: 3 days. Average attendance: 120. Offers agent and editor panel and workshops on marketing, fiction, romance, networking, and more. Speakers have included Evan Marshall, Nancy Martin, Evan Fogelman, Cherry Weiner, and Karen Solen. Agents will be speaking and available for meetings with attendees.
Costs $150+ (includes all workshops and panels, as well as any editor or agent appointments). There is an additional charge for Friday's keynote dinner and Saturday night's dinner activity.
Accommodations We arrange a special rate with the hotel; details will be in our brochure.
Additional Information We are a multi-genre group encompassing the state of Pennsylvania and beyond. Brochures available in February for SASE. Send inquiries via e-mail or visit the Web site for current updates and details.

PHILADELPHIA WRITERS' CONFERENCE

121 Almatt Terrace, Philadelphia PA 19115-2745. E-mail: info@pwcwriters.org. Website: www.pwcwriters.org. Estab. 1949. Annual conference held in June. Conference duration: 3 days. Average attendance: 150+. Workshops cover short

stories, poetry, travel, humor, magazine writing, science fiction, playwriting, memoir, juvenile, nonfiction, and fiction. Speakers have included Ginger Clark (Curtis Brown), Sara Crowe (Harvey Klinger), Samantha Mandor (Berkley), Nancy Springer, Susan Guill, Karen Rile, Gregory Frost, and John Volkmer. Editor/agent critiques are available.
Costs Costs available online.

PIKES PEAK WRITERS CONFERENCE

4164 Austin Bluffs Pkwy., #246, Colorado Springs CO 80918. (719)531-5723. E-mail: info@pikespeakwriters.com. Website: www.pikespeakwriters.com. Estab. 1993. Annual conference held in April. Conference duration: 3 days. Average attendance: 400. Workshops, presentations, and panels focus on writing and publishing mainstream and genre fiction (romance, science fiction/fantasy, suspense/thrillers, action/adventure, mysteries, children's, young adult). Agents and editors are available for meetings with attendees on Saturday.
Costs $300-500 (includes all meals).
Accommodations Marriott Colorado Springs holds a block of rooms at a special rate for attendees until late March.
Additional Information Readings with critiques are available on Friday afternoon. Also offers a contest for unpublished writers; entrants need not attend the conference. Deadline: November 1. Registration and contest entry forms are online; brochures are available in January. Send inquiries via e-mail.

PIMA WRITERS' WORKSHOP

Pima College, 2202 W. Anklam Road, Tucson AZ 85709-0170. (520)206-6084. Fax: (520)206-6020. E-mail: mfiles@pima.edu. Website: www.pima.edu. **Contact:** Meg Files, director. Estab. 1988. Annual conference held in May. Conference duration: 3 days. Average attendance: 300. Covers fiction, nonfiction, poetry, and scriptwriting for beginner or experienced writers. The workshop offers sessions on writing short stories, novels, nonfiction articles and books, children's and juvenile stories, poetry, and screenplays. Sessions are held in the Center for the Arts on Pima Community College's West campus. Speakers have included Larry McMurtry, Barbara Kingsolver, Jerome Stern, Connie Willis, Jack Heffron, Jeff Herman, and Robert Morgan. Agents will be speaking and available for meetings with attendees.
Costs $80 (can include ms critique). Participants may attend for college credit, in which case fees are $117 for Arizona residents and $340 for out-of-state residents. Meals and accommodations are not included.
Accommodations Information on local accommodations is made available. Special workshop rates are available at a specified motel close to the workshop

site (about $70/night).

Additional Information The workshop atmosphere is casual, friendly, and supportive, and guest authors are very accessible. Readings and panel discussions are offered, as well as talks and manuscript sessions. Participants may have up to 20 pages critiqued by the author of their choice. Mss must be submitted 3 weeks before the workshop. Conference brochure/guidelines available for SASE. Accepts inquiries by e-mail.

PNWA SUMMER WRITERS CONFERENCE
PMB 2717, 1420 NW Gilman Blvd., Issaquah WA 98027. (425)673-2665. E-mail: pnwa@pnwa.org. Website: www.pnwa.org. Estab. 1955. All conferences are held in July. Conference duration: 4 days. Average attendance: 400. Attendees have the chance to meet agents and editors, learn craft from authors and uncover marketing secrets. Speakers have included J.A. Jance, Sheree Bykofsky, Kimberley Cameron, Jennie Dunham, Donald Maass, Jandy Nelson, Robert Dugoni and Terry Brooks. Annual

Costs For cost and additional information, please see the Web site.

Accommodations The conference is held at the Hilton Seattle Airport & Conference Center.

Additional Information "PNWA also holds an annual literary contest every February with more than $12,000 in prize money. Finalists' manuscripts are then available to agents and editors at our summer conference. Visit the Web site for further details."

PORT TOWNSEND WRITERS' CONFERENCE
Box 1158, Port Townsend WA 98368. (360)385-3102. Fax: (360)385-2470. E-mail: info@centrum.org. Website: www.centrum.org/writing. Estab. 1974. Annual conference held in mid-July. Average attendance: 180. Conference promotes poetry, fiction, and creative nonfiction and features many of the nation's leading writers. All conference housing and activities are located at beautiful Fort Worden State Park, a historic fort overlooking the Strait of Juan de Fuca, with expansive views of the Olympic and Cascade mountain ranges.

Costs See website for cost and accommodation information.

Additional Information The conference focus is on the craft of writing and the writing life, not on marketing. Guidelines/registration are available online or for SASE.

ROBERT QUACKENBUSH'S CHILDREN'S BOOK WRITING & ILLUSTRATING WORKSHOP
460 E. 79th St., New York NY 10075-1443. (212)744-3822. Fax: (212)861-2761.

E-mail: rqstudios@aol.com. Website: www.rquackenbush.com. Estab. 1982. Annual workshop held during the second week in July. Conference duration: 4 days. Average attendance: Enrollment limited to 10. Workshops promote writing and illustrating books for children and are geared toward beginners and professionals. Generally focuses on picture books, easy-to-read books, and early chapter books. Held at the Manhattan studio of Robert Quackenbush, author and illustrator of more than 200 books for children. All classes led by Robert Quackenbush.

Costs $750 tuition covers all the costs of the workshop, but does not include housing and meals. A $100 nonrefundable deposit is required with the $650 balance due two weeks prior to attendance.

Accommodations A list of recommended hotels and restaurants is sent upon receipt of deposit.

READERS & WRITERS HOLIDAY CONFERENCE

Central Ohio Fiction Writers, P.O. Box 1981, Westerville OH 43086-1981. E-mail: mollygbg@columbus.rr.com. Website: www.cofw.org. Estab. 1991. Annual conference held in October. The conference is designed to address the needs of writers in all genres of fiction. It explores fiction-writing trends and discusses the business and craft of writing.

Accommodations Attendees are given discounted hotel accommodations.

Additional Information See website for location, costs, and other information.

REMEMBER THE MAGIC

International Women's Writing Guild, P.O. Box 810, Gracie Station, New York NY 10028-0082. (212)737-7536. Fax: (212)737-9469. E-mail: iwwg@iwwg.org. Website: www.iwwg.org. Estab. 1978. Annual conference held in June. Average attendance: 400. Conference to promote creative writing and personal growth, professional know-how and contacts, and networking. Site is the campus of Skidmore College in Saratoga Springs, New York (near Albany). Approximately 65 workshops are offered each day. Conferees have the freedom to make their own schedule.

Costs $1,085 single/$945 double for members; $1,130 single/$990 double for nonmembers. These fees include the 7-day program and room and board for the week. Rates for a 5-day stay and a weekend stay, as well as commuter rates, are also available.

Additional Information Conference brochures/guidelines are available online or for a SASE. Inquire via e-mail or fax.

RETREAT FROM HARSH REALITY

Mid-Michigan RWA Chapter, 6845 Forest Way, Harbor Springs MI 49740. E-mail: retreat@midmichiganrwa.org. Website: www.midmichiganrwa.org/retreat.html. Estab. 1985. Annual conference held in April. Average attendance: 50. Conference focusing on romance and fiction writing. Speakers have included Rosanne Bittner, Debra Dixon, Bettina Krahn, Ruth Ryan Langan, Elizabeth Bevarly, Julie Kistler, Merline Lovelace, and Elizabeth Grayson.

ROCKY MOUNTAIN FICTION WRITERS COLORADO GOLD

Rocky Mountain Fiction Writers, P.O. Box 545, Englewood CO 80151. E-mail: conference@rmfw.org. Website: www.rmfw.org/default.aspx. Estab. 1983. Annual conference held in September/October. Conference duration: 3 days. Average attendance: 250. Themes include general novel-length fiction, genre fiction, contemporary romance, mystery, science fiction/fantasy, mainstream, and history. Speakers have included Terry Brooks, Dorothy Cannell, Patricia Gardner Evans, Diane Mott Davidson, Constance O'Day, Connie Willis, Clarissa Pinkola Estes, Michael Palmer, Jennifer Unter, Margaret Marr, Ashley Krass, and Andren Barzvi. Approximately 4 editors and 5 agents attend annually.
Costs Costs available online.
Accommodations Special rates will be available at a nearby hotel.
Additional Information Editor-conducted workshops are limited to 10 participants for critique, with auditing available.

ROMANCE WRITERS OF AMERICA NATIONAL CONFERENCE

16000 Stuebner Airline Rd., Suite 140, Spring TX 77379. (832)717-5200. Fax: (832)717-5201. Website: www.rwanational.com. Estab. 1981. Annual conference held in July. Average attendance: 2,000. More than 100 workshops on writing, researching, and the business side of being a working writer. Publishing professionals attend and accept appointments. The keynote speaker is a renowned romance writer. Held at the Hyatt Regency in Dallas.
Costs $340-550 depending on your membership status as well as when you register.
Additional Information Annual RTA awards are presented for romance authors. Annual Golden Heart awards are presented for unpublished writers.

ROMANTIC TIMES CONVENTION

55 Bergen St., Brooklyn NY 11201. (718)237-1097 or (800)989-8816, ext. 12. Fax: (718)624-2526. E-mail: jocarol@rtconvention.com. Website: www.rtconvention. com. Annual conference held in April. Features 125 workshops, agent and editor

appointments, a book fair, and more.

Costs See website for pricing and other information.

ROPEWALK WRITERS' RETREAT

University of Southern Indiana, 8600 University Blvd., Evansville IN 47712. (812)464-1863. E-mail: ropewalk@usi.edu; lcleek@usi.edu. Website: www. ropewalk.org. Estab. 1989. Annual conference held in June. Conference duration: 1 week. The retreat gives participants an opportunity to attend workshops and to confer privately with one of 4 or 5 prominent writers. Held at the historic New Harmony Inn and Conference Center in Indiana. Faculty members have included Stephen Dobyns, Heather McHugh, Ellen Bryant Voigt, Susan Neville, and Bob Shacochis.

Costs $645 (includes workshops, individual conference, readings, receptions, meals); 10% discount for Indiana residents. Scholarships are available.

Accommodations A block of rooms is reserved at the New Harmony Inn ($96-606) and at The Barn Abbey ($25/night).

⊠ SAGE HILL WRITING EXPERIENCE

Box 1731, Saskatoon SK S7K 2Z4 Canada. Phone/Fax: (306)652-7395. E-mail: sage.hill@sasktel.net. Website: www.sagehillwriting.ca. Annual workshops held in late July/August and May. Conference duration: 10-14 days. Average attendance: 40/summer program; 8/spring program. Sage Hill Writing Experience offers a special working and learning opportunity to writers at different stages of development. Top-quality instruction, low instructor-student ratio, and the beautiful Sage Hill setting offer conditions ideal for the pursuit of excellence in the arts of fiction, poetry and playwriting. The Sage Hill location features individual accommodations, in-room writing areas, lounges, meeting rooms, healthy meals, walking woods, and vistas in several directions. Classes being held (may vary from year to year) include: Introduction to Writing Fiction & Poetry, Fiction Workshop,; Writing Young Adult Fiction Workshop, Poetry Workshop, Poetry Colloquium, Fiction Colloquium, Novel Colloquium, Playwriting Lab, Fall Poetry Colloquium, and Spring Poetry Colloquium. Speakers have included Nicole Brossard, Steven Galloway, Robert Currie, Jeanette Lynes, Karen Solie and Colleen Murphy.

Costs Summer program: $1,095 (includes instruction, accommodation, meals). Fall Poetry Colloquium: $1,375. Scholarships and bursaries are available.

Accommodations Located at Lumsden, 45 kilometers outside Regina.

Additional Information For Introduction to Creative Writing, send a 5-page sample of your writing or a statement of your interest in creative writing and a list of courses taken. For workshop and colloquium programs, send a résumé of your writing career and a 12-page sample of your work, plus 5 pages of published work. Guidelines are available for SASE. Inquire via e-mail or fax.

SANDHILLS WRITERS CONFERENCE

Augusta State University, Department of Communications and Professional Writing, 2500 Walton Way, Augusta GA 30904-2200. E-mail: akellman@aug.edu. Website: www.sandhills.aug.edu. Annual conference held the fourth weekend in March. Covers fiction, poetry, children's literature, nonfiction, plays, and songwriting. Located on the campus of Augusta State University in Georgia. Agents and editors will be speaking at the event.

Accommodations Several hotels are located near the university.

SAN DIEGO STATE UNIVERSITY WRITERS' CONFERENCE

SDSU College of Extended Studies, 5250 Campanile Dr., San Diego State University, San Diego CA 92182-1920. (619)594-2517. Fax: (619)594-8566. E-mail: jgreene@mail.sdsu.edu; rbrown2@mail.sdsu.edu. Website: www.ces.sdsu.edu/writers. Estab. 1984. Annual conference held in January/February. 2010 dates: Jan. 29-31. Conference duration: 2 days. Average attendance: 375. Covers fiction, nonfiction, scriptwriting and e-books. Held at the Doubletree Hotel in Mission Valley. Each year the conference offers a variety of workshops for the beginner and advanced writers. This conference allows the individual writer to choose which workshop best suits his/her needs. In addition to the workshops, editor reading appointments and agent/editor consultation appointments are provided so attendees may meet with editors and agents one-on-one to discuss specific questions. A reception is offered Saturday immediately following the workshops, offering attendees the opportunity to socialize with the faculty in a relaxed atmosphere. Last year, approximately 60 faculty members attended.

Costs Approximately $365-485 (2010 costs will be published with a fall update of the Web site).

Accommodations Doubletree Hotel (800)222-TREE. Attendees must make their own travel arrangements.

SANDY COVE CHRISTIAN WRITERS CONFERENCE

Sandy Cove Ministries, 60 Sandy Cove Rd., North East MD 21901. (410)287-5433. Fax: (410)287-3196. E-mail: info@sandycove.org. Website: www.sandycove.org. Estab. 1991. Annual conference held the first week in October. Conference duration: 4 days. Average attendance: 200. There are major workshops in fiction, article writing, and nonfiction books for beginner and advanced writers. The conference has plans to add tracks in screenwriting and musical lyrics. Workshops offer a wide variety of hands-on writing instruction in many genres. While Sandy

Cove has a strong emphasis on available markets in Christian publishing, all writers are more than welcome. Speakers have included Francine Rivers, Lisa Bergen, Ken Petersen (Tyndale House), Linda Tomblin (*Guideposts*), and Karen Ball (Zondervan).

Costs Call for rates.

Accommodations Sandy Cove is a full-service conference center located on the Chesepeake Bay. All the facilities are first class, with suites, single rooms, and double rooms available.

Additional Information "Conference brochures/guidelines are available. Visit the Web site for exact conference dates."

SAN FRANCISCO WRITERS CONFERENCE

1029 Jones St., San Francisco CA 94109. (415)673-0939. Fax: (415)673-0367. E-mail: sfwriterscon@aol.com. Website: www.sfwriters.org. **Contact:** Michael Larsen, director. Estab. 2003. Annual conference held President's Day weekend in February. Average attendance: 400 + . Top authors, respected literary agents, and major publishing houses are at the event so attendees can make face-to-face contact with all the right people. Writers of nonfiction, fiction, poetry, and specialty writing (children's books, cookbooks, travel, etc.) will all benefit from the event. There are important sessions on marketing, self-publishing, technology, and trends in the publishing industry. Plus, there's an optional 3-hour session called Speed Dating for Agents where attendees can meet with 20 + agents. Speakers have included Jennifer Crusie, Richard Paul Evans, Lalita Tademy, Jamie Raab, Mary Roach, Jane Smiley, Debbie Macomber, Firoozeh Dumas, Zilpha Keatley Snyder. More than 20 agents and editors participate each year, many of whom will be available for meetings with attendees.

Costs $600 + with price breaks for early registration (includes all sessions/ workshops/keynotes, Speed Dating with Editors, opening gala at the Top of the Mark, 2 continental breakfasts, 2 lunches). Optional Speed Dating for Agents is $50.

Accommodations The Intercontinental Mark Hopkins Hotel is a historic landmark at the top of Nob Hill in San Francisco. Elegant rooms and first-class service are offered to attendees at the rate of $139/night. The hotel is located so that everyone arriving at the Oakland or San Francisco airport can take BART to either the Embarcadero or Powell Street exits, then walk or take a cable car or taxi directly to the hotel.

Additional Information "Present yourself in a professional manner and the contact you will make will be invaluable to your writing career. Brochures and registration are online."

SANTA BARBARA WRITERS CONFERENCE

P.O. Box 6627, Santa Barbara CA 93160. (805)964-0367. E-mail: info@sbwriters. com. Website: www.sbwriters.com. Estab. 1973. Annual conference held in June. Average attendance: 450. Covers poetry, fiction, nonfiction, journalism, playwriting, screenwriting, travel writing, young adult, children's literature, chick lit, humor, and marketing. Speakers have included Kenneth Atchity, Michael Larsen, Elizabeth Pomada, Bonnie Nadell, Stuart Miller, Angela Rinaldi, Katherine Sands, Don Congdon, Mike Hamilburg, Sandra Dijkstra, Paul Fedorko, Andrea Brown and Deborah Grosvenor. Agents appear on a panel, plus there will be an agents and editors day when writers can pitch their projects in one-on-one meetings.

Accommodations Fess Parker's Doubletree Resort.

Additional Information Individual critiques are also available. Submit 1 ms of no more than 3,000 words in advance (include SASE). Competitions with awards are sponsored as part of the conference. E-mail or call for brochure and registration forms.

SANTA FE WRITERS CONFERENCE

Southwest Literary Center, 826 Camino de Monte Rey, A3, Santa Fe NM 87505. (505)577-1125. Fax: (505)982-7125. E-mail: litcenter@recursos.org. Website: www.santafewritersconference.com. **Contact:** Ellen Bradbury, director. Estab. 1985. Annual conference held in June. Conference duration: 5 days. Average attendance: 50. Conference offering intimate workshops in fiction, poetry, and creative nonfiction. Speakers have included Lee K. Abbott, Alice Adams, Lucille Adler, Francisco Alarcon, Agha Shahid Ali, Rudolfo Anaya, Max Apple, Jimmy Santiago Baca, Madison Smartt Bell, Marvin Bell, Molly Bendall, Elizabeth Benedict, Roo Borson, Robert Boswell, Kate Braverman, Mei-Mei Berssenbrugge, Ron Carlson, Denise Chavez, Lisa D. Chavez, Alan Cheuse, Ted Conover, Robert Creeley, C. Michael Curtis, Jon Davis, Percival Everett, Jennifer Foerster, Richard Ford, Judith Freeman, Samantha Gillison, Natalie Goldberg, Jorie Graham, Lee Gutkind, Elizabeth Hardwick, Robert Hass, Ehud Havazelet, Elizabeth Hightower, Tony Hillerman, Brenda Hillman, Tony Hoagland, Garrett Hongo, Lewis Hyde, Mark Irwin, Charles Johnson, Diane Johnson, Teresa Jordan, Donald Justice, Laura Kasischke, Pagan Kennedy, Brian Kiteley, William Kittredge, Carolyn Kizer, Verlyn Klinkenborg, Karla Kuban, Mark Levine, Alison Lurie, Tony Mares, Kevin McIlvoy, Christopher Merrill, Jane Miller, Mary Jane Moffat, Carol Moldow, N. Scott Momaday, David Morrell, Antonya Nelson, Susan Neville, John Nichols, Sharon Niederman, Naomi Shahib Nye, Grace Paley, Ann Patchett, Margaret Sayers Peden, Michael Pettit, Robert Pinsky, Melissa Pritchard, Annie Proulx, Ron Querry, Judy Reeves, Katrina Roberts, Janet Rodney, Pattiann Rogers, Suzanna Ruta, David St. John, Scott Sanders, Bob Shacochis, Julie Shigekuni,

John Skoyles, Carol Houck Smith, Gibbs M. Smith, Roberta Smoodin, Marcia Southwick, Kathleen Spivack, Gerald Stern, Robert Stone, Arthur Sze, Elizabeth Tallent, Nathaniel Tarn, James Thomas, Frederick Turner, Leslie Ullman, David Wagoner, Larry Watson, Rob Wilder, Eleanor Wilner, Diane Williams, Kimberly Witherspoon, Charles Wright, Dean Young, Norman Zollinger.
Costs $575 + .
Accommodations A special rate is offered at a nearby hotel.
Additional Information Brochure are available online or by e-mail, fax, or phone.

SCBWI SOUTHERN BREEZE FALL CONFERENCE

P.O. Box 26282, Birmingham AL 35260. E-mail: jskittinger@bellsouth.net. Website: www.southern-breeze.org. Estab. 1992. Annual conference held on the third Saturday in October (2009: Oct. 17). Conference duration: 1 day. Geared toward the production and support of quality children's literature. Offers approximately 28 workshops on craft and the business of writing, including a basic workshop for those new to the children's field. Manuscript and portfolio critiques are offered. Agents and editors participate in the conference. Speakers include editors, agents, art directors, authors and illustrators.
Accommodations We have a room block with a conference rate. The conference is held at a nearby school.

SCENE OF THE CRIME CONFERENCE

Kansas Writers Association, P.O. Box 2236, Wichita KS 67201. (316) 618-0449; (316)208-6961. E-mail: info@kwawriters.org. Website: www.kwawriters.org/sceneofthecrime.htm. Biennial conference held in April. Features agent/editor consultations, mixer, banquet and two days of speaker sessions with detectives, government agents, CSI professionals, editors, agents and authors. A full list of each year's speakers is available to see in full on the Web site. Annual
Accommodations Wichita Airport Hilton.

❖ THE SCHOOL FOR WRITERS SUMMER WORKSHOP

The Humber School for Writers, Humber Institute of Technology & Advanced Learning, 3199 Lake Shore Blvd. W., Toronto ON M8V 1K8 Canada. (416)675-6622. E-mail: antanas.sileika@humber.ca; hilary.higgins@humber.ca. Website: www. creativeandperformingarts.humber.ca/content/writers.html. Annual workshop held second week in July. Conference duration: 1 week. Average attendance: 100. New writers from around the world gather to study with faculty members to work on their novel, short stories, poetry, or creative nonfiction. Agents and editors participate in conference. Include a work-in-progress with your registration.

Faculty has included Martin Amis, David Mitchell, Rachel Kuschner, Peter Carey, Roddy Doyle, Tim O'Brien, Andrea Levy, Barry Unsworth, Edward Albee, Ha Jin, Mavis Gallant, Bruce Jay Friedman, Isabel Huggan, Alistair MacLeod, Lisa Moore, Kim Moritsugu, Francine Prose, Paul Quarrington, Olive Senior, and D.M. Thomas.

Costs $949/Canadian residents before June 12; $1,469/non-Canadian residents before June 12; $999/Canadian residents after June 12; $1,519/non-Canadian residents after June 12 (includes panels, classes, lunch). Scholarships are available.

Accommodations $480/week for a modest college dorm room. Nearby hotels are also available.

Additional Information Accepts inquiries by e-mail, phone, and fax.

THE SCREENWRITING CONFERENCE IN SANTA FE, LLC

P.O. Box 29762, Santa Fe NM 87592. (866)424-1501. Fax: (505)424-8207. E-mail: writeon@scsfe.com. Website: www.scsfe.com. Estab. 1999. "SCSFe was the first screenwriting conference in the world." Annual conference held the week following Memorial Day. Average attendance: 175. The conference is divided into 2 components: The Screenwriting Symposium, designed to teach the art and craft of screenwriting, and The Hollywood Connection, which speaks to the business aspects of screenwriting. Held at The Lodge in Santa Fe.

Costs $695 for The Screenwriting Symposium; $245 for The Hollywood Connection. Early discounts are available. Includes 9 hours of in-depth classroom instruction, over 2 dozen seminars, panel discussions, a screenplay competition, academy labs for advanced screenwriters, live scene readings, and social events.

SCREENWRITING EXPO

6404 Hollywood Blvd., Suite 415, Los Angeles CA 90028. E-mail: info@creativescreenwriting.com. Website: www.screenwritingexpo.com/. Conference duration: 3-4 days. The Screenwriting Expo is produced by Creative Screenwriting Magazine. The expo is a large conference and trade show for writers. Speaker lists frequently include A-list screenwriters and academy award winners. Recent special guests include William Goldman (*All the President's Men*), David Koepp (*Spider-Man*) and Paul Haggis (*Crash*).

SEAK FICTION WRITING FOR PHYSICIANS CONFERENCE

P.O. Box 729, Falmouth MA 02541. (508)548-7023. Fax: (508)540-8304. E-mail: mail@seak.com. Website: www.seak.com. Annual conferences held on Cape Cod. The medical seminar is taught by *New York Times* bestselling authors Michael Palmer, MD and Tess Gerritsen, MD. Session topics include writing fiction that sells, screenwriting, writing riveting dialogue, creating memorable characters, getting your first novel published, and more. Agents will be speaking and available for one-on-one meetings.

SEWANEE WRITERS' CONFERENCE

735 University Ave., 123 Gailor Hall, Stamlor Center, Sewanee TN 37383-1000. (931)598-1141. E-mail: cpeters@sewanee.edu. Website: www.sewaneewriters. org. **Contact:** Cheri B. Peters, Creative Writing Programs Manager. Estab. 1990. Annual conference held in the second half of July. Conference duration: 12 days. Average attendance: 144. "We offer genre-based workshops in fiction, poetry, and playwriting. The conference uses the facilities of Sewanee: The University of the South. The university is a collection of ivy-covered Gothic-style buildings located on the Cumberland Plateau in mid-Tennessee. Editors, publishers, and agents structure their own presentations, but there is always opportunity for questions from the audience." 2009 faculty included fiction writers Richard Bausch, Tony Earley, Diane Johnson, Randall Kenan, Jill McCorkle, Alice McDermott, Erin McGraw, and Steve Yarbrough; poets Daniel Anderson, Claudia Emerson, Debora Greger, Andrew Hudgins, William Logan, Alan Shapiro, Dave Smith, and Greg Willimson; and playwrights Lee Blessing and Dan O'Brien. Visiting agents include Gail Hochman and Georges Borchardt. A score of writing professionals will visit.

Costs $1,700 (includes tuition, board, single room, sports and fitness center access).

Accommodations Participants are housed in single rooms in university dormitories. Bathrooms are shared by small groups. Motel or B&B housing is available, but not abundantly so.

Additional Information "Complimentary chartered bus service is available from the Nashville Airport to Sewanee and back on the first and last days of the conference. We offer each participant (excepting auditors) the opportunity for a private manuscript conference with a member of the faculty. These manuscripts are due 1 month before the conference begins. Brochures/guidelines are free. The conference provides a limited number of fellowships and scholarships; these are awarded on a competitive basis."

SOCIETY OF CHILDREN'S BOOK WRITERS & ILLUSTRATORS ANNUAL SUMMER CONFERENCE ON WRITING AND ILLUSTRATING FOR CHILDREN

8271 Beverly Blvd., Los Angeles CA 90048-4515. (323)782-1010. Fax: (323)782-1892. E-mail: scbwi@scbwi.org. Website: www.scbwi.org. Estab. 1972. Annual conference held in early August. Conference duration: 4 days. Average attendance:

1,000. Held at the Century Plaza Hotel in Los Angeles. Speakers have included Andrea Brown, Steven Malk , Scott Treimel, Ashley Bryan, Bruce Coville, Karen Hesse, Harry Mazer, Lucia Monfried, and Russell Freedman. Agents will be speaking and sometimes participate in ms critiques.

Costs Approximately $400 (does not include hotel room).

Accommodations Information on overnight accommodations is made available.

Additional Information Ms and illustration critiques are available. Brochure/guidelines are available in June online or for SASE.

SOUTH CAROLINA WRITERS WORKSHOP

P.O. Box 7104, Columbia SC 29202. (803)413-5810. E-mail: conference@myscww.org. Website: www.myscww.org/. Estab. 1991. Annual conference in October held at the Hilton Myrtle Beach Resort in Myrtle Beach, SC. Conference duration: 3 days. The conference features critique sessions, open mic readings, presentations from agents and editors and more. The conference features more than 50 different workshops for writers to choose from, dealing with all subjects of writing craft, writing business, getting an agent and more. Agents will be in attendance.

SOUTH COAST WRITERS CONFERENCE

Southwestern Oregon Community College, P.O. Box 590, 29392 Ellensburg Avenue, Gold Beach OR 97444. (541)247-2741. Fax: (541)247 6247. E mail: ocwc@socc. edu. Website: www.socc.edu/scwriters. Estab. 1996. Annual conference held President's Day weekend in February. Conference duration: 2 days. Covers fiction, historical, poetry, children's, nature, and marketing. Larry Brooks is the next scheduled keynote speaker and presenters include Shinan Barclay, Jim Coffee, Linda Crew, Roger Dorband, Jayel Gibson, Phil Hann, Rachel Ellen Koski, Bonnie Leon, John Noland, Joanna Rose and J.D. Tynan.

Additional Information See website for cost and additional details.

SOUTHEASTERN WRITERS WORKSHOP

P.O. Box 82115, Athens GA 30608. E-mail: info@southeasternwriters.com. Website: www.southeasternwriters.com. Estab. 1975. Held annually the third week in June at Epworth-by-the-Sea, St. Simons Island, Georgia. Conference duration: 4 days. Average attendance: Limited to 100 students. Classes are offered in all areas of writing, including fiction, poetry, nonfiction, inspirational, juvenile, specialty writing, and others. The faculty is comprised of some of the most successful authors from throughout the southeast and the country. Agent-in-Residence is available to meet with participants. Up to 3 free ms evaluations and critique sessions are also available to participants if mss are submitted by the deadline.

Costs Costs change each year. See the Web site.

Additional Information Multiple contests with cash prizes are open to participants. Registration brochure is available in March—e-mail or send a SASE. Full information, including registration material, is on the Web site.

SOUTHERN CALIFORNIA WRITERS' CONFERENCE

1010 University Ave., #54, San Diego CA 92103. (619)303-8185. Fax: (619)303-7428. E-mail: wewrite@writersconference.com. Website: www.writersconference.com. Estab. 1986. Annual conference held in February in San Diego and in September in Los Angeles. The conference is also held periodically in Palm Springs (dates to be announced). Conference duration: 3 days. Average attendance: 250. Covers fiction and nonfiction, with a particular emphasis on reading and critiquing conferees' manuscripts. Offers extensive reading and critiquing workshops by working writers, plus over 3 dozen daytime workshops and late-night sessions that run until 3-4 a.m. Agents will be speaking and available for meetings with attendees.

Additional Information Brochures are available online or for SAE. Inquire via e-mail or fax.

SOUTHERN LIGHTS CONFERENCE

First Coast Roance Writers, P.O. Box 32456, Jacksonville FL 32237. (352)687-3902. E-mail: conference@firstcoastromancewriters.com. Website: www.firstcoastromancewriters.com. Estab. 1995. Annual conference held in late March/early April. Conference duration: 2 days. Offers workshops, author panels, industry expert sessions, editor/agent appointments, and a keynote address. Speakers have included Joan Johston, Steven K. Brown, Tracy Montoya, Kristy Dykes, and Caren Johnson (Firebrand Literary).

SOUTHWEST WRITERS CONFERENCE MINI-CONFERENCE SERIES

3721 Morris St. NE, Suite A, Albuquerque NM 87111. (505)265-9485. E-mail: swwriters@juno.com. Website: www.southwestwriters.org. Estab. 1983. Annual mini-conferences held throughout the year. Average attendance: 50. Speakers include writers, editors, agents, publicists, and producers. All areas of writing, including screenwriting and poetry, are represented.

Costs Fee includes conference sessions and lunch.

Accommodations Usually have official airline and hotel discount rates.

Additional Information Sponsors a contest judged by authors, editors from major publishers, and agents from New York, Los Angeles, etc. There are 16 categories. Deadline: May 1; late deadline May 15. Entry fee ranges from $20-60. There are quarterly contests with various themes - $10entry fee. See Web site for details.

Brochures/guidelines are available online or for a SASE. Inquire via e-mail or phone. A one-on-one appointment may be set up at the conference with the editor or agent of your choice on a first-registered, first-served basis.

SPACE COAST WRITERS GUILD ANNUAL CONFERENCE
No public address available, (321)956-7193. E-mail: scwg-jm@cfl.rr.com. Website: www.scwg.org/conference.asp. Annual conference held in January along the east coast of central Florida. Conference duration: 2 days. Average attendance: 150 +. This conference is hosted each winter in Florida and features a variety of presenters on all topics writing. Critiques are available for a price, and agents in attendance will take pitches from writers. Previous presenters have included Davis Bunn (writer), Ellen Pepus (agent), Miriam Hees (editor), Lauren Mosko (editor), Lucienne Diver (agent) and many many more. Annual
Accommodations The conference is hosted on a beachside hotel, where rooms are available.

SPRINGFED WRITING RETREAT
P.O. Box 304, Royal Oak MI 48068-0304. (248)589-3913. Fax: (248)589-9981. E-mail: johndlamb@ameritech.net. Website: www.springfed.org. Estab. 1999. Annual conference held in October. Average attendance: 75. "Focus includes fiction, poetry, screenwriting and nonfiction." Past faculty included Billy Collins, Michael Moore, Jonathan Rand, Jacquelyn Mitchard, Jane Hamilton, Thomas Lux, Joyce Maynard, Jack Driscoll, Dorianne Laux, and Cornelius Eady.
Costs $625, $560 (3 days, 2 nights, all meals included). $360 non-lodging.
Accommodations The Birchwood Inn, Harbor Spring, MI. "Attendees stay in comfortable rooms, and seminars are held in conference rooms with fieldstone fireplaces and dining area." Shuttle rides from Traverse City Airport or Pellston Airport. Offers overnight accommodations. Provides list of area lodging options.
Additional Information "Optional: Attendees may submit 3 poems or 5 pages of prose for conference with a staff member. Brochures available mid-June by e-mail, on Web site, or by phone. Accepts inquiries by SASE, e-mail, phone. "

SPRING WRITER'S FESTIVAL
University of Wisconsin-Milwaukee, School of Continuing Education, 161 W. Wisconsin Ave., Suite 6000, Milwaukee WI 53203. (414)227-3311. Fax: (414)227-3146. E-mail: sce@uwm.edu. Website: www3.uwm.edu/sce. Annual conference held in April. Features readings, craft workshops, panels, ms reviews, preconference intensive workshops, and pitch sessions with literary agents. Speakers have included Joanna MacKenzie, Alec Yoshio MacDonald, A. Manette Ansay, Liam Callanan, C.J. Hribal, and Kelly James-Enger.

Conferences

Costs See website for more information on cost and accommodations.

SPRING WRITERS' WORKSHOP
Council for the Written Word, P.O. Box 298, Franklin TN 37065. (615)591-7516. E-mail: publicity@cww-writers.org. Website: www.cww-writers.org. Annual workshop held in March. An intensive, half-day event with instruction and hands-on experience in a specific genre.

SQUAW VALLEY COMMUNITY OF WRITERS WORKSHOP
P.O. Box 1416, Nevada City CA 95959-1416. (530)470-8440. E-mail: info@ squawvalleywriters.org. Website: www.squawvalleywriters.org/writers_ws.htm. Estab. 1969. Annual conference held the first full week in August. Conference duration: 1 week. Average attendance: 124. Covers fiction, nonfiction, and memoir. Held in Squaw Valley, California—the site of the 1960 Winter Olympics. The workshops are held in a ski lodge at the foot of this spectacular ski area. Literary agent speakers have recently included Betsy Amster, Julie Barer, Michael Carlisle, Elyse Cheney, Mary Evans, Christy Fletcher, Theresa Park, B.J. Robbins and Peter Steinberg. Agents will be speaking and available for meetings with attendees.
Costs $750 (includes tuition, dinners). Housing is extra.
Accommodations Single room: $550/week; double room: $350/week per person; multiple room: $210/week per person. The airport shuttle is available for an additional cost.
Additional Information Brochures are available online or for a SASE in March. Send inquiries via e-mail.

STEAMBOAT SPRINGS WRITERS CONFERENCE
Steamboat Springs Arts Council, P.O. Box 774284, Steamboat Springs CO 80477. (970)879-8079. E-mail: info@steamboatwriters.com. Website: www. steamboatwriters.com. **Contact:** Susan de Wardt. Estab. 1982. Annual conference held in mid-July. Conference duration: 1 day. Average attendance: approximately 35. Attendance is limited. Featured areas of instruction change each year. Held at the restored train depot. Speakers have included Carl Brandt, Jim Fergus, Avi, Robert Greer, Renate Wood, Connie Willis, Margaret Coel and Kent Nelson.
Costs $50 prior to May 21; $60 after May 21 (includes seminars, catered lunch). A pre-conference dinner is also available.
Additional Information Brochures are available in April for a SASE. Send inquiries via e-mail.

STELLARCON

Box 4, Brown Annex, Elliott University Center, UNCG, Greensboro NC 27412. (336)294-8041. E-mail: info@stellarcon.org. Website: www.stellarcon.org. Estab. 1976. Annual conference held in March. Average attendance: 500. Conference focuses on general science fiction, fantasy, horror with an emphasis on literature, and comics. Held at the Radisson Hotel in High Point, North Carolina.

STONECOAST WRITERS' CONFERENCE

University of Southern Maine, P.O. Box 9300, Portland ME 04104. (207)228.8393. Website: www.usm.maine.edu/summer/stonecoastwc/. **Contact:** Justin Tussing. Estab. 1979. Annual conference held in mid-July. Conference duration: 10 days. Average attendance: 90-100. Concentrates on fiction, poetry, popular fiction, and creative nonfiction. Held at Wolfe's Neck on Casco Bay in Freeport, Maine. Speakers have included Christian Barter, Brian Turner, Chun Yu, Margo Jefferson, Mike Kimball, and Jack Neary.

Costs See website for tuition and cost of accommodations.

STONY BROOK SOUTHAMPTON SCREENWRITING CONFERENCE

Stony Brook Southampton, 239 Montauk Highway, Southampton NY 11968. (631)632 5030. E mail: southamptonwriters@notes.cc.sunysb.edu. Website: www. sunysb.edu/writers/screenwriting/. The Southampton Screenwriting Conference welcomes new and advanced screenwriters, as well as all writers interested in using the language of film to tell a story. The five-day residential Conference will inform, inspire, challenge, and further participants' understanding of the art of the screenplay and the individual writing process. Our unique program of workshops, seminars, panel presentations, and screenings will encourage and motivate attendees under the professional guidance of accomplished screenwriters, educators, and script analysts. Annual

Costs $1,000 + .

Additional Information Space is limited.

SUNSHINE COAST FESTIVAL OF THE WRITTEN ARTS

Box 2299, Sechelt BC V0N 3A0 Canada. (604)885-9631 or (800)565-9631. Fax: (604)885-3967. E-mail: info@writersfestival.ca. Website: www.writersfestival. ca. Estab. 1983. Annual festival held in August. Conference duration: 3½ days. Average attendance: 3,500. The festival does not have a theme. Instead, it showcases 25 or more Canadian writers in a variety of genres each year. Held at the Rockwood Centre. Speakers have included Jane Urquhart, Sholagh Rogers,

David Watmough, Zsuzsi Gartner, Gail Bowen, Charlotte Gray, Bill Richardson, P.K. Page, Richard B. Wright, Madeleine Thien, Ronald Wright, Michael Kusugak, and Bob McDonald.

Accommodations A list of hotels is available.

Additional Information The festival runs contests during the event. Prizes are books donated by publishers. Brochures/guidelines are available. Visit the Web site for current updates and details.

◪ SURREY INERNATIONAL WRITERS' CONFERENCE

10707 146th St., Surrey BC V3R 1T5 Canada. (640)589-2221. Fax: (604)589-9286. Website: www.siwc.ca. Estab. 1992. Annual conference held in October. Conference duration: 3 days. Average attendance: 600. Conference for fiction, nonfiction, scriptwriting, and poetry. Held at the Sheraton Guildford Hotel. Speakers have included Donald Maass, Meredith Bernstein, Charlotte Gusay, Denise Marcil, Anne Sheldon, Diana Gabaldon, and Michael Vidor. Agents will be speaking and available for one-on-one meetings with attendees.

Costs See Web site for full cost information and list of upcoming speakers for the next year.

Accommodations Attendees must make their own hotel and transportation arrangements.

⊕ SYDNEY WRITERS' FESTIVAL

10 Hickson Rd., The Rocks NSW 2000 Australia. (61)(2)9252-7729. Fax: (61)(2)9252-7735. E-mail: info@swf.org.au. Website: www.swf.org.au. Estab. 1997. Annual festival held in May. The event celebrates books, reading, ideas, writers, and writing.

Costs Over 70% of events are free.

TAOS SUMMER WRITERS' CONFERENCE

Department of English Language and Literature, MSC 03 2170, University of New Mexico, Albuquerque NM 87131-0001. (505)277-5572. Fax: (505)277-2950. E-mail: taosconf@unm.edu. Website: www.unm.edu/~taosconf. Estab. 1999. Annual conference held in July. Conference duration: 7 days. Offers workshops in novel writing, short story writing, screenwriting, poetry, creative nonfiction, travel writing, historical fiction, memoir, and revision. Participants may also schedule a consultation with a visiting agent/editor.

Costs $325/weekend; $625/week; discounted tuition rate of $275/weekend workshop with weeklong workshop or master class registration.

Accommodations $69-109/night at the Sagebrush Inn; $89/night at Comfort Suites.

THRILLERFEST

PO Box 311, Eureka CA 95502. E-mail: infocentral@thrillerwriters.org. Website: www.thrillerwriters.org/thrillerfest/. **Contact:** Shirley Kennett. Estab. 2006. 2010 conference: July 7-10 in Manhattan. Conference duration: 4. Average attendance: 700. Conference "dedicated to writing the thriller and promoting the enjoyment of reading thrillers." Speakers have included David Morrell, Sandra Brown, Eric Van Lustbader, David Baldacci, Brad Meltzer, Steve Martini, R.L. Stine, Katherine Neville, Robin Cook, Andrew Gross, Kathy Reichs, Brad Thor, Clive Cussler, James Patterson, Donald Maass, and Al Zuckerman. Two days of the conference is CraftFest, where the focus is on writing craft, and two days is ThrillerFest, which showcases the author-fan relationship. Also featured are an Awards Banquet, and AgentFest, a unique event where authors can pitch their work face-to-face to forty top agents in one afternoon. There is also AgentFest, where authors can pitch their work to agents in attendance. Annual
Costs Price will vary from $200 to $1,000 dollars depending on which events are selected. Various package deals are available, and Early Bird pricing is offered beginning August 2009.
Accommodations Grand Hyatt in New York City.

TMCC WRITERS' CONFERENCE

5270 Neil Road, #216, Reno NV 89502. (775)829-9010. Fax: (775)829-9032. E-mail: wdce@tmcc.edu. Website: wdce.tmcc.edu. Estab. 1991. Annual conference held in April. Average attendance: 125. Focuses on fiction, poetry, and memoir, plus an assortment of other forms of writing, such as screenwriting, thrillers, mysteries, and nonfiction. There is always an array of speakers and presenters with impressive literary credentials, including agents and editors. Speakers have included Dorothy Allison, Karen Joy Fowler, James D. Houston, James N. Frey, Gary Short, Jane Hirschfield, Dorrianne Laux, Kim Addonizio, Amy Rennert, and Laurie Fox.
Costs $99 for a full-day seminar; $15 for 15 minute one-on-one appointment with an agent or editor.
Accommodations The Nugget offers a special rate and shuttle service to the Reno/Tahoe International Airport, which is less than 20 minutes away.
Additional Information "The conference is open to all writers, regardless of their level of experience. Brochures are available online and mailed in the fall. Send inquiries via e-mail."

UCLA EXTENSION WRITERS' PROGRAM

10995 Le Conte Ave., #440, Los Angeles CA 90024. (310)825-9415 or (800)388-UCLA. Fax: (310)206-7382. E-mail: writers@uclaextension.edu. Website:

www.uclaextension.org/writers. Estab. 1891. "As America's largest and most comprehensive continuing education creative writing and screenwriting program, the UCLA Extension Writers' Program welcomes and trains writers at all levels of development whose aspirations range from personal enrichment to professional publication and production. Taught by an instructor corps of 250 professional writers, the Writers' Program curriculum features 530 annual open-enrollment courses onsite and online in novel writing, short fiction, personal essay, memoir, poetry, playwriting, writing for the youth market, publishing, feature film writing, and television writing, and is designed to accommodate your individual writing needs, ambitions, and lifestyle. Special programs and services include certificate programs in creative writing, feature film writing, and television writing; a four-day Writers Studio which attracts a national and international audience; nine-month master classes in novel writing and feature film writing; an online screenwriting mentorship program; one-on-one script and manuscript consultation services; literary and screenplay competitions; advisors who help you determine how best to achieve your personal writing goals; and free annual public events such as Writers Faire and Publication Party which allow you to extend your writing education and network with the literary and entertainment communities."

Costs Depends on length of the course.

Accommodations Students make their own arrangements. Out-of-town students are encouraged to take online courses.

Additional Information Some advanced-level classes have ms submittal requirements; see the UCLA Extension catalog or see website.

UNIVERSITY OF NORTH DAKOTA WRITERS CONFERENCE

Department of English, 110 Merrifield Hall, 276 Centennial Drive, Stop 7209, Grand Forks ND 58202. (701)777-3321. E-mail: english@und.edu. Website: www.undwritersconference.org. Estab. 1970. Annual conference held in March. Offers panels, readings, and films focused around a specific theme. Almost all events take place in the UND Memorial Union, which has a variety of small rooms and a 1,000-seat main hall. Future speakers include Stuart Dybek, Mary Gaitskill, Li-Young Lee, Timothy Liu, Leslie Adrienne Miller, Michelle Richmond, Miller Williams and Anne Harris.

Costs All events are free and open to the public. Donations accepted.

UNIVERSITY OF WISCONSIN AT MADISON WRITERS INSTITUTE

21 N. Park St., Madison WI 53715-1218. (608)262-3447. Website: www.dcs.wisc.edu/lsa. Estab. 1990. Annual conference held in April. (The 2010 conference is

set for April 23-25, 2010.) Average attendance: 200. Conference on fiction and nonfiction held at the University of Wisconsin at Madison. Guest speakers are published authors, editors, and agents.

Costs Approximately $245 for the weekend; $145 per day; critiques and pitch meetings extra.

Accommodations Information on accommodations is sent with registration confirmation.

Additional Information Critiques are available. Go online for conference brochure.

VIRGINIA FESTIVAL OF THE BOOK

Virginia Foundation for the Humanities, 145 Ednam Dr., Charlottesville VA 22903. (434)924-6890. Fax: (434)296-4714. E-mail: vabook@virginia.edu. Website: www.vabook.org. Estab. 1995. Annual festival held in March. 2010 dates: March 17-21. Average attendance: 26,000. Festival held to celebrate books and promote reading and literacy.

WESLEYAN WRITERS CONFERENCE

Wesleyan University, 294 High St., Room 207, Middletown CT 06459. (860)685-3604. Fax: (860)685-2441. E-mail: agreene@wesleyan.edu. Website: www.wesleyan.edu/writers. Estab. 1956. Annual conference held the third week of June. Average attendance: 100. Focuses on the novel, fiction techniques, short stories, poetry, screenwriting, nonfiction, literary journalism, memoir, mixed media work and publishing. The conference is held on the campus of Wesleyan University, in the hills overlooking the Connecticut River. Features a faculty of award-winning writers, seminars and readings of new fiction, poetry, nonfiction and mixed media forms - as well as guest lectures on a range of topics including publishing. Both new and experienced writers are welcome. Participants may attend seminars in all genres. Speakers have included Esmond Harmsworth (Zachary Schuster Agency), Daniel Mandel (Sanford J. Greenburger Associates), Dorian Karchmar, Amy Williams (ICM and Collins McCormick), Mary Sue Rucci (Simon & Schuster), Denise Roy (Simon & Schuster), John Kulka (Harvard University Press), Julie Barer (Barer Literary) and many others. Agents will be speaking and available for meetings with attendees. Participants are often successful in finding agents and publishers for their mss. Wesleyan participants are also frequently featured in the anthology *Best New American Voices*.

Accommodations Meals are provided on campus. Lodging is available on campus or in town.

Additional Information Ms critiques are available, but not required. Scholarships and teaching fellowships are available, including the Joan Jakobson Awards for fiction writers and poets; and the Jon Davidoff Scholarships for nonfiction writers and journalists. Inquire via e-mail, fax, or phone.

WESTERN RESERVE WRITERS' CONFERENCE

Lakeland Community College, 7700 Clocktower Dr., Kirtland OH 44060-5198. (440)525-7116 or (800)589-8520. E-mail: deencr@aol.com. Website: www. deannaadams.com. Estab. 1983. Biannual conference held in March and September. Average attendance: 120. Conference covers fiction, nonfiction, business of writing, children's writing, science fiction/fantasy, women's fiction, mysteries, poetry, short stories, etc. Classes take place on a community college campus. Editors and agents will be available for meetings with attendees. Biannual

Costs $69 for March mini-conference (half day); $95 for September all-day conference, including lunch. There is an additional fee for agent consultations.

Additional Information Presenters are veterans in their particular genres. There will be a prestigious keynote speaker at the September conference. Check Web site 6 weeks prior to the event for guidelines and updates. Send inquiries via e-mail.

WHIDBEY ISLAND WRITERS' CONFERENCE

Whidbey Island Writers' Association, P.O. Box 1289, Langley WA 98260. (360)331-6714. E-mail: wiwa@whidbey.com. Website: http://writeonwhidbey. org. Annual conference held in February/March. Conference duration: 2 days. Average attendance: 250. Annual conference, located near Seattle, combines pre-conference workshops, signature fireside chats, professional instruction and island hospitality to encourage and inspire writers. Check out this year's upcoming talent on our Web site. Covers fiction, nonfiction, screenwriting, writing for children, poetry, travel, and nature writing. Class sessions include Dialogue That Delivers and Putting the Character Back in Character. Held at a conference hall, with break-out fireside chats held in local homes near the sea. Past speakers included Elizabeth George, Maureen Murdock, Steve Berry, M.J. Rose, Katharine Sands, Doris Booth, Eva Shaw, Stephanie Elizondo Griest.

Costs See website for costs and early registration deadlines.

Additional Information Brochures are available online or for a SASE. Send inquiries via e-mail.

WILDACRES WRITERS WORKSHOP

233 S. Elm St., Greensboro NC 27401. (336)370-9188. E-mail: judihill@aol. com. Website: www.wildacres.com. Estab. 1985. Annual workshop held in July. Conference duration: 1 week. Average attendance: 90. Workshop focuses on

novel, short story, flash fiction, poetry, and creative nonfiction. Held at a retreat center in the Blue Ridge Mountains of North Carolina. Speakers have included Gail Adams, Rand Cooper, Philip Gerard, Luke Whisnant, and Janice Fuller.
Costs See website for pricing.
Additional Information Include a 1-page writing sample with your registration. See the Web site for information.

WILLAMETTE WRITERS CONFERENCE

9045 SW Barbur, Suite 5-A, Portland OR 97219. (503)452-1592. Fax: (503)452-0372. E-mail: wilwrite@willamettewriters.com. Website: www.willamettewriters.com. Estab. 1968. Annual conference held in August. Average attendance: 600. "Williamette Writers is open to all writers, and we plan our conference accordingly. We offer workshops on all aspects of fiction, nonfiction, marketing, the creative process, etc. Also, we invite top-notch inspirational speakers for keynote addresses. We always include at least 1 agent or editor panel and offer a variety of topics of interest to screenwriters and fiction and nonfiction writers." Speakers have included Laura Rennert, Kim Cameron, Paul Levine, Angela Rinaldi, Robert Tabian, Joshua Bilmes and Elise Capron. Agents will be speaking and available for meetings with attendees.
Costs Pricing schedule available online.
Accommodations If necessary, arrangements can be made on an individual basis. Special rates may be available.
Additional Information Brochure/guidelines are available for a catalog-sized SASE.

WINTER & SUMMER FISHTRAP

Fishtrap, Inc., P.O. Box 38, 400 Grant St., Enterprise OR 97828. (503)426-3623. Fax: (503)426-9075. E-mail: rich@fishtrap.org. Website: www.fishtrap.org. Estab. 1988. Annual gatherings held in February and July. Fishtrap gatherings are about writing and the West (there is a theme for each conference). They are about ideas more than the mechanics and logistics of writing/publishing. Workshops are not ms reviews, but rather writing sessions. Fishtrap events meet at Wallowa Lake Lodge in Joseph, Oregon. Previous faculty has included Donald Snow, Suan Power, Aimee Pham, Judith Barrington, Laurie Lewis (songwriter), and Michael Wiegers (Copper Canyon). Agents and editors occasionally participate in conference.
Costs See website for pricing and details on accommodations.
Additional Information Five fellowships are given annually for Summer Fishtrap. Submit 8 pages of poetry or 2,500 words of prose (no name on ms) by February 6. Entries are judged by a workshop instructor. Inquire via e-mail or phone.

WINTER POETRY & PROSE GETAWAY IN CAPE MAY

No public address available, (609)823-5076. E-mail: info@wintergetaway.com. Website: www.wintergetaway.com. Estab. 1994. Annual workshop held in January. Conference duration: 4 days. Offers workshops on short stories, memoirs, creative nonfiction, children's writing, novel, drama, poetry and photography. Classes are small, so each person receives individual attention for the new writing or work-in-progress that they are focusing on. Held at the Grand Hotel on the oceanfront in historic Cape May, New Jersey. Speakers have included Stephen Dunn (recipient of the 2001 Pulitzer Prize for poetry), Christian Bauman, Kurt Brown, Catherine Doty, Douglas Goetsch, James Richardson, Robbie Clipper Sethi and many more.

WISCONSIN BOOK FESTIVAL

222 S. Bedford St., Suite F, Madison WI 53703. (608)262-0706. Fax: (608)263-7970. E-mail: alison@wisconsinbookfestival.org. Website: www.wisconsinbookfestival. org. Estab. 2002. Annual festival held in October. Conference duration: 5 days. The festival features readings, lectures, book discussions, writing workshops, live interviews, children's events, and more. Speakers have included Michael Cunningham, Grace Paley, TC Boyle, Marjane Satrapi, Phillip Gourevitch, Myla Goldberg, Audrey Niffenegger, Harvey Pekar, Billy Collins, Tim O'Brien and Isabel Allende.

Costs All festival events are free.

WISCONSIN REGIONAL WRITERS' ASSOCIATION CONFERENCES

No public address available, E-mail: vpresident@wrwa.net. Website: www. wrwa.net. Estab. 1948. Annual conferences are held in May and September. Conference duration: 1-2 days. Provides presentations for all genres, including fiction, nonfiction, scriptwriting, and poetry. Presenters include authors, agents, editors, and publishers. Speakers have included Jack Byrne, Michelle Grajkowski, Benjamin Leroy, Richard Lederer, and Philip Martin.

Additional Information Go online for brochure or make inquiries via e-mail or with SASE.

THE WOMEN WRITERS CONFERENCE

232 E. Maxwell St., Lexington KY 40506. (859)257-2874. E-mail: wwk.info@gmail.com. Website: www.thewomenwritersconference.org. Estab. 1979. The conference switches months and dates each year. Programming is presented in a festival atmosphere and includes small-group workshops, panel discussions,

master classes, readings, film screenings, and performances. Presenters include Sara Vowell, Patricia Smith, Hayden Herrera, Diane Gilliam Fisher, Jawole Willa Jo Zollar and the Urban Bush Woman, Sonia Sanchez, Heather Raffo, Mabel Maney, Phoebe Gloeckner, Lauren Weinstein, Kim Ganter, Jane Vandenburgh, and Alex Beauchamp. Annual

Additional Information Visit the Web site to register and get more information.

WOMEN WRITING THE WEST

8547 Araphoe Rd., Box J-541, Greenwodd Village CO 80112-1436. E-mail: wwwadmin@lohseworks.com. Website: www.womenwritingthewest.org. Annual conference held in September. Covers research, writing techniques, multiple genres, marketing/promotion, and more. Agents and editors will be speaking and available for one-on-one meetings with attendees. Conference location changes each year.

Accommodations See website for location and accommodation details.

WORDS & MUSIC

624 Pirates Alley, New Orleans LA 70116. (504)586-1609. Fax: (504)522-9725. E-mail: info@wordsandmusic.org. Website: www.wordsandmusic.org. Estab. 1997. Annual conference held the first week in November. Conference duration: 5 days. Average attendance: 300. Presenters include authors, agents, editors and publishers. Past speakers included agents Deborah Grosvenor, Judith Weber, Stuart Bernstein, Nat Sobel, Jeff Kleinman, Emma Sweeney, Liza Dawson and Michael Murphy; editors Lauren Marino, Webster Younce, Ann Patty, Will Murphy, Jofie Ferrari-Adler, Elizabeth Stein; critics Marie Arana, Jonathan Yardley, and Michael Dirda; fiction writers Oscar Hijuelos, Robert Olen Butler, Shirley Ann Grau, Mayra Montero, Ana Castillo, H.G. Carrillo. Agents and editors critique manuscripts in advance; meet with them one-on-one during the conference.

Costs See website for a costs and additional information on accommodations.
Accommodations Hotel Monteleone in New Orleans.

WRANGLING WITH WRITING

Society of Southwestern Authors, P.O. Box 30355, Tucson AZ 85751-0355. (520)546-9382. Fax: (520)751-7877. E-mail: Carol Costa (Ccstarlit@aol.com). Website: www.ssa-az.org/conference.htm. **Contact:** Carol Costa. Estab. 1972. Sept. 26-27, 2009. Conference duration: 2 days. Average attendance: 300. Conference offers 36 workshops covering all genres of writing, plus pre-scheduled one-on-one interviews with 30 agents, editors, and publishers representing major book houses and magazines. Speakers have included Ray Bradbury, Clive Cussler, Elmore Leonard, Ben Bova, Sam Swope, Richard Paul Evans, Bruce Holland

Rogers and Billy Collins. Annual

Costs 2007 costs were $275/members; $350/nonmembers. Five meals included.

Additional Information Brochures/guidelines are available as of July 15 by e-mail address above. Two banquets will include editor and agent panels for all attendees, and Saturday evening winning plays from contestants will be presented.

⚑ WRITE! CANADA

The Word Guild, P.O. Box 487, Markham ON L3P 3R1 Canada. (905)294-6482. E-mail: events@thewordguild.com. Website: www.writecanada.org. Conference duration: 3 days. Annual conference for writers of all types and at all stages. Offers solid instruction, stimulating interaction, exciting challenges, and worshipful community.

WRITE ON THE SOUND WRITERS' CONFERENCE

Edmonds Arts Commission, 700 Main St., Edmonds WA 98020. (425)771-0228. Fax: (425)771-0253. E-mail: wots@ci.edmonds.wa.us. Website: www. ci.edmonds.wa.us/ArtsCommission/wots.stm. Estab. 1985. Annual conference held in October. Conference duration: 2.5 days. Average attendance: 200. Features over 30 presenters, a literary contest, ms critiques, a reception and book signing, onsite bookstore, and a variety of evening activities. Held at the Frances Anderson Center in Edmonds, just north of Seattle on the Puget Sound. Speakers have included Elizabeth George, Dan Hurley, Marcia Woodard, Holly Hughes, Greg Bear, Timothy Egan, Joe McHugh, Frances Wood, Garth Stein and Max Grover.

Costs See website for more information.

Additional Information Brochures are available Aug. 1. Accepts inquiries via phone, e-mail and fax.

WRITERS@WORK CONFERENCE

P.O. Box 540370, North Salt Lake UT 84054-0370. (801)292-9285. E-mail: lisa@ writersatwork.org. Website: www.writersatwork.org. Estab. 1985. Annual conference held in June. Conference duration: 5 days. Average attendance: 250. Morning workshops (3-hours/day) focus on novel, advanced fiction, generative fiction, nonfiction, poetry, and young adult fiction. Afternoon sessions will include craft lectures, discussions, and directed interviews with authors, agents, and editors. In addition to the traditional, one-on-one manuscript consultations, there will be many opportunities to mingle informally with agents/editors. Held at Spiro Arts Community at Silver Star, Park City, Utah. Speakers have included Steve Almond, Bret Lott, Shannon Hale, Emily Forland (Wendy Weil Agency), Julie Culver (Folio Literary Management, Chuck Adams (Algonquin Press), and Mark A. Taylor (Juniper Press).

Costs See website for pricing information.

Accommodations Onsite housing in luxury condos available. Can choose between 2, 3, or 4 bedroom suites. Secondary offer includes lower-priced condos a short walk away. Additional lodging and meal information is on the Web site.

WRITERS AT THE BEACH: SEAGLASS WRITERS CONFERENCE

Writers at the Beach, PO Box 1326, Rehoboth Beach DE 19971. (302)226-8210. E-mail: contactus@rehobothbeachwritersguild.com. Website: www.writersatthebeach.com/. Annual conference held in the spring. 2010 dates: March 26-28. Conference duration: 3 days. Annual conference on the Delaware coast featuring a variety of editors, agents and writers who present workshops on fiction writing, nonfiction writing and more. Manuscript readings are available, and a 'Meet the Authors' sessions takes place. The beachcoast conference is a great opportunity to learn and charge your batteries. Some proceeds from the conference go to charity.

Accommodations Held at the Atlantic Sands Hotel. See website for pricing, details, and to join mailing list.

WRITERS RETREAT WORKSHOP

E-mail: wrw04@netscape.net. Website: www.writersretreatworkshop.com. Estab. 1987. Annual workshop held in August. Conference duration: 10 days. Focuses on fiction and narrative nonfiction books in progress (all genres). This is an intensive learning experience for small groups of serious-minded writers. Founded by the late Gary Provost (one of the country's leading writing instructors) and his wife Gail (an award-winning author). The goal is for students to leave with a solid understanding of the marketplace, as well as the craft of writing a novel. Held at the Marydale Retreat Center in Erlanger, Kentucky (just south of Cincinnati, Ohio). Speakers have included Becky Motew, Donald Maass, Jennifer Crusie, Michael Palmer, Nancy Pickard, Elizabeth Lyon, Lauren Mosko (Writer's Digest Books), Adam Marsh (Reece Halsey North), and Peter H. McGuigan (Sanford J. Greenburger Literary Agency).

Costs $1,725 (includes meals, housing, consultations, materials). Scholarships are available.

WRITERS WORKSHOP IN SCIENCE FICTION

English Department/University of Kansas, Lawrence KS 66045-2115. (785)864-3380. Fax: (785)864-1159. E-mail: jgunn@ku.edu. Website: www.ku.edu/~sfcenter. Estab. 1985. Annual workshop held in late June/early July. Average attendance: 15. Conference for writing and marketing science fiction.

Classes meet in university housing on the University of Kansas campus. Workshop sessions operate informally in a lounge. Speakers have included Frederik Pohl, Kij Johnson, James Gunn, and Chris McKitterick.

Costs See website for tuition rates, dormitory housing costs, and deadlines.

Accommodations Housing information is available. Several airport shuttle services offer reasonable transportation from the Kansas City International Airport to Lawrence.

Additional Information Admission to the workshop is by submission of an acceptable story. Two additional stories should be submitted by the middle of June. These 3 stories are distributed to other participants for critiquing and are the basis for the first week of the workshop. One story is rewritten for the second week. Send SASE for brochure/guidelines. This workshop is intended for writers who have just started to sell their work or need that extra bit of understanding or skill to become a published writer.

WRITE-TO-PUBLISH CONFERENCE

WordPro Communication Services, 9118 W Elmwood Dr., #1G, Niles IL 60714-5820. (847)296-3964. Fax: (847)296-0754. E-mail: lin@writetopublish.com. Website: www.writetopublish.com. Estab. 1971. Annual conference held June 2-5, 2010. Conference duration: 4 days. Average attendance: 250. Conference on writing fiction, nonfiction, devotions, and magazine articles for the Christian market. Held at Wheaton College in Wheaton, Illinois. Speakers have included Dr. Dennis E. Hensley, agent Chip MacGregor, David Long (Bethany House), Carol Traver (Tyndale House), Dave Zimmerman (InterVarsity Press), Ed Gilbreath (Urban Ministries), Ken Peterson (WaterBrook Multnomah).

Costs $470 (includes all sessions, Saturday night banquet, 1 ms evaluation); $105/meals.

Accommodations Campus residence halls: $260/double; $340/single. A list of area hotels is also on the Web site.

WRITING FOR THE SOUL

Jerry B. Jenkins Christian Writers Guild, 5525 N. Union Blvd., Suite 200, Colorado Springs CO 80918. (866)495-5177. Fax: (719)495-5181. E-mail: paul@ christianwritersguild.com. Website: www.christianwritersguild.com/conferences. **Contact:** Paul Finch, admissions manager. Annual conference held in February. Workshops and continuing classes cover fiction, nonfiction, magazine writing, children's books, and teen writing. Appointments with more than 30 agents, publishers, and editors are also available. The keynote speakers are nationally known, leading authors. The conference is hosted by Jerry B. Jenkins.

Costs $649/guild members; $799/nonmembers.

Accommodations $159/night at the Grand Hyatt in Denver.

WRITING TODAY

Birmingham-Southern College, Box 549066, Birmingham AL 35254. (205)226-4922. Fax: (205)226-4931. E-mail: agreen@bsc.edu. Website: www.writingtoday.org. Estab. 1978. Annual conference held during the second weekend in March. The 2010 dates and location have yet to be determined. Conference duration: 2 days. Average attendance: 300-350. Conference hosts approximately 18 workshops, lectures, and readings. We try to offer sessions in short fiction, novels, poetry, children's literature, magazine writing, songwriting, and general information of concern to aspiring writers, such as publishing, agents, markets, and research. The event is held on the Birmingham-Southern College campus in classrooms and lecture halls. Speakers have included Eudora Welty, Pat Conroy, Ernest Gaines, Ray Bradbury, Erskine Caldwell, John Barth, Galway Kinnell, Edward Albee, Horton Foote, and William Styron and other renowned writers.

Costs To be determined. Please check website or join mailing list for upcoming information.

Accommodations Attendees must arrange own transportation and accommodations.

Additional Information For an additional charge, poetry and short story critiques are offered for interested writers who request and send mss by the deadline. The conference also sponsors the Hackney Literary Competition Awards for poetry, short stories, and novels.

Glossary

#10 Envelope. Standard business-size envelope used for 8.5 x 11 sheets of paper.

A-List. The most famous and bankable talent of the current times—usually in reference to actors.

Above the Line. Costs of a film prior to the actual shoot.

Acting Credits. An actor's previous professional work.

Adaptation. The process of rewriting a composition (e.g., novel, article) into a form suitable for some other medium, such as TV or the stage.

Advance. A sum of money paid to a writer prior to publication or production. An advance is made based on anticipated profits not yet realized.

Adventure. A genre of fiction in which action and location are the key elements.

ADR (Automatic Dialogue Replacement). Dialogue that is added or rerecorded in post-production.

AFI. The American Film Institute.

Agent. A writer's business representative who secures work and negotiates contracts in exchange for a portion of the money the writer makes.

All Rights. Complete rights to a work, meaning that the writer now owns nothing—including the characters, concept and dialogue.

Angel. A wealthy individual or private investor who can bankroll a project and provide production capital.

Antagonist. The primary character (or force) in a story with whom the protagonist is in conflict.

Arbitration. A form of legal dispute resolution which forgoes court judgment to determine an award or disputed screenplay credit.

At Rise. The description of setting at the beginning of a stage play.

Auction. A bidding war for the acquisition, purchase or option of a script.

Beat. (1)A one-count pause in the action or in a character's speech. (2) The smallest unit of a story; a moment in which something dramatic occurs.

Beat Sheet. The breakdown of key scenes contained in a screenplay.

Before Rise. What's happening onstage before the curtain opens and a play begins.

Below the Line. Actual production costs of a film.

Bible. A master reference for a television series containing character information and projected storylines.

Bidding War. An instance where two or more studios are trying to outbid one another in terms of money to secure a certain property.

Bio. Short for biography. This term usually identifies a relatively concise paragraph detailing who the writer/producer is.

Blurb. A brief statement, such as one from a reviewer, which accompanies a movie for market and advertising appeal.

Boffo. A box office success.

Boilerplate. A standardized contract in which there is no variance from general terms and conditions offered between one project and another.

Bomb. A box office failure.

Budget. A detailed listing of expenses, potential and actual, for the making of a movie. The budget is used to determine the estimated total cost of the project from screenplay to post-production and distribution.

Character Arc. The emotional journey of a character that details how they change from a story's beginning to end.

Climax. The pinnacle of action and conflict in a story, usually just before the end.

Concept. The general idea regarding a story—i.e., what the story is about on a basic level.

Copyediting. The process of fixing faulty grammar, formatting, spelling and punctuation.

Copyright. A means to protect an author's work.

Cover Page. A one-page sheet before the first page of your script. The cover page lists the title of the work, the author's name, and all pertinent contact information—whether that's for the writer or a representative.

Coverage. A reader's written thoughts and critique of a script created so producers can digest the material quickly. Coverage includes a logline, a synopsis, and the reader's compliments/criticism of the work.

Critiquing Service. Serving the same purpose as a script doctor, this is a service where a professional will help edit a writer's manuscript for a fee.

Curtain. (1) A fabric or screen separating the audience from the setting. (2) A term used to indicate the opening or closing of a scene.

Deal Memo. A rough draft of a contract that comes before the real contract.

Deus ex Machina. Latin for "God from the machine." This term is used to describe a story ending where an impossible scenario is miraculously fixed thanks to a illogical happening or intervention.

Development. The process of bringing a story to the screen. If a script has been commissioned, or is in rewrites, that project is in development.

Development Hell. When the development phase of creating a movie is delayed by endless script changes, delays, and other problems.

Developmental Workshop. When a play is given several rehearsals and performed by actors.

Direct to Video. A movie released to the public for home viewing, bypassing theaters.

Docudrama. A combination of the genres of documentary and drama. The docudrama uses a script, actors, and a set in order to portray real events, either current or historical.

Electronic Rights. Rights pertaining to the Internet and other electronic media.

Elements. (1) The format of a movie script such as headers, character names, dialogue, and narrative. (2) The talent involved in creating a movie or play, such as screenwriters, director, actors, and props.

El-Hi (Elementary-High School). A term used to refer to the publications of books and plays as school texts for adolescents from kindergarten through 12th grade.

Episodic Television. Series television.

Ethnic. A story in which the central characters are typically caught between two conflicting ways of life: mainstream American culture and his or her own ethnic heritage.

Evaluation Fees. Fees charged by agents and companies to consider a manuscript. No WGA-endorsed reps will ask for them.

Exclusive. Rights or privileges granted to one body that are not awarded to others, usually lasting a specified period of time.

Executive Producer. Someone who provides financing or represents the financial backing for a film. The executive producer is charged with keeping production within the targeted budget.

Experimental. A method of presenting a story in a new way, such as through style or exploring new themes and concepts.

Exposition. Communicating information by explaining something to the audience. In movies and plays, exposition is usually explained through dialogue, and kept to a minimum to keep the story moving.

Family Saga. A story that unfolds over generations through interwoven tales of several members of a genealogical line.

Fantasy. A genre containing magical and supernatural elements such as mythical creatures and legendary characters.

Feature. A full-length film, usually running 90-150 minutes.

Film Noir. A genre of film featuring gritty, dark stories set in urban areas. Other aspects include police detectives, corruption, plot twists and turns, and a femme fatale.

Film Rights. For a book, film rights concern the right to turn the story into a screenplay and produce it.

First Look Deal. Also known as "first right of refusal" in which a deal is struck providing one person or entity the first chance to develop a screenplay or film. If that entity chooses to pass on the opportunity, the offer can then be opened to others.

Foreign Rights. Rights of selling a writer's work in other countries.

Free Option. When a studio options a script from a writer at no cost.

Genre. A method of categorization based on elements contained within the story, its subject, or the style that is used. Traditional genres in playwriting are tragedy, comedy, romance, and irony; modern genres continue to expand those, including historical, adventure, science fiction, fantasy, western, family, musical, horror, mystery, and so forth. Sub-genres often combine elements of two or more of the genres, such as romantic comedy (rom-com), or action-adventure.

Ghostwriting. The process of writing/rewriting a story for a set fee but receiving little to no credit. Books by celebrities and politicians are usually ghostwritten.

Gofer/Gopher. An employee who handles menial and typically inglorious tasks, such as delivering scripts and fetching coffee.

Graphic Novel. A publication similar in format to comic books, but usually containing a longer, more complex storyline or series of stories. Usually sold in bookstores and bound using the same methods as traditional books.

Green Light. The phrase used to approve a project and let pre-production commence.

Handshake Deal. A deal with no contracts—relying on the "older" practice of two parties and their word.

Hard Sell. A movie without an easy explanation or high concept that will be more difficult to sell.

High Concept. Used to describe a movie with a remarkable idea that is easily summarized.

Hi-Lo. High concept, low budget films.

Historical. A film or story in which the setting and events occur sometime in the past. Historical films are often referred to as "period films" when the events occur during a time frame with specific, recognizable cultural traits.

Hook. Element of the story that grabs attention and compels the viewer's interest in following the story to its resolution.

Horror. Genre of story containing dark themes and in which the intention is to inspire fear or dread.

Hot. Anything that's getting attention or buzz at the moment, such as a script that's deemed a "hot read."

Inciting Incident. An incident or event or happening (usually early in the script) that sets the story in motion.

Independent Producers. A person involved with the production of film or television but is not affiliated with a major company or studio.

Indie. Short for independent. A film created by an individual or smaller company; commonly refers to films that are more experimental or targeted to a specific audience.

Ink Session. A meeting where contracts are signed.

Intermission. A distinct break during a play—usually at the half-way point, lasting approximately 15 minutes.

IRC. International reply coupon, which is used instead of stamps when a writer needs materials sent back from a foreign country.

Joint Contract. A legal agreement in which two or more parties agree to complete a project or perform a service, or may benefit from the completion of a project or performance of service.

Libel. Written words that defame or cause damage through misrepresentation to someone living.

Logline. A concise, one-sentence description of a story that is used to pique interest.

Manager. In screenwriting terms, a representative who will not only rep your work, but also help edit and guide writers on a career path. A manager lacks the legal license to sell a work, and collects a small percentage of any money the writer makes.

Memoir. A story about a person's life written by that person.

Miniseries. A story that borrows the sequential nature of television shows but retains the pacing, resolution, and ending of a movie, usually unfolding in two to four parts.

Montage. A series of shots or short vignettes spliced together in rapid succession to convey the passage of time or to encompass a theme too unwieldy to film in completion.

MOW. Movie of the week.

Multiple Contract. A contract by which the theater/studio agrees to publish, and the author agrees to have produced, two or more consecutive works by the writer.

Musical. A stage production in which songs are used to reinforce the major points of the story being acted out.

Mystery. A story in which one or more elements remain unknown or unexplained until the end of the story.

Narration. The method used to tell a story. In screenplays, this is usually through first-person ("I") or voice-over.

Net Receipts. The amount of money received on the sale of a project after discounts, special sales, etc.

Novelization. The act of creating a novel from a popular movie.

Offscreen. A term used to indicate a sound or voice heard, but not seen, by the audience. It is represented in a script by the letters "O.S."

On Book. A phrase used to describe a play performance where actors still have scripts in hand.

One-Act Play. A form of stage play with a length between 20 and 60 minutes.

Option. A fee paid to a writer for exclusive rights to a script for a certain period of time.

Option Clause. Also called "the right of first refusal," this clause in a contract allows the purchaser to have the first opportunity to review the writer's next similar work.

Orphaned. Used to describe a script/project that was under consideration but is now of little interest to a studio.

Package. A deal that brings together various elements in order to sell a script or product. An agency specializing in package deals will usually attempt to utilize as much of their talent roster as possible.

Pass. The act of officially saying no to a project.

Pitch. Concisely explaining what the story is about in the hopes to pique interest and have the full manuscript requested/read.

Platform. A writer's visibility, and the avenues he or she has to sell their work to the audience(s) who will buy it.

Play. (1) A live performance of a script using actors and setting. (2) A script or book formatted to be performed live containing characters, setting, and dialogue, divided up into acts and scenes.

Plot. The sequence in which an author arranges a series of carefully devised and interrelated incidents so as to form a logical pattern and achieve an intended effect. A plot can also be called the structure, backbone or framework of fiction.

Producer. Person responsible for bringing together all the elements of a film from inception to completion. The producer is responsible for the entire movie, from hiring scriptwriters, directors, and actors to the completion of the project.

Proofreading. The process of reading a work and identifying errors in copy.

Property. Term used to describe a script or other written material.

Proscenium. The walls and arch found in some theaters that contains the curtain and divides the stage area from the audience.

Protagonist. The central character of a story.

Public Domain. Material not protected by copyright, patent or trademark, and therefore available to the general public for use without fee.

Query. A one-page letter designed to interest the reader (agent, editor, etc.) in a story idea.

Reader. (1) The consumer of a written work at whom the story is aimed. (2) The person whose job is to read and evaluate scripts.

Regional Premiere. (1) A formal viewing of a movie in a specific locale, often with a significance to the movie-making process, such as setting or film location. (2) A play or musical's first full production in an area of the country.

Release. (1) To distribute a television show or movie into public either for a limited or general viewing, such as "release date." (2) To give written permission to use a likeness, either pictorial or descriptive, to a script or film without incurring liability.

Residuals. Payments awarded by a union to creative talent in addition to that covered by their contracts.

Resolution. The point at which a solution to the central conflict or driving plot is applied and the story reaches a conclusion.

Romance. A genre in which the plot is centered around two persons having to overcome some obstacle(s) to fall in love.

Royalties. Money received from the individual performance, sale, or use of a published work; for example, the sale of movies for home viewing. Royalties are a percentage of the actualized profits.

SASE. Self-addressed stamped envelope. This is an envelope addressed to oneself and stamped for the return of materials sent with a submission.

Science Fiction. A genre containing impossible or supernatural elements, often set in futuristic or off-world settings. This genre is distinguished from fantasy in that it is technology that makes events occur.

Script. The written version of a film, TV episode or stage play.

Script Doctor. A freelance editor paid to consult on a script.

Script Polish. A final edit or rewrite of a script, usually by a professional who is not the original writer.

Shooting Script. The final version of a script used on set by actors and crew.

Showrunner. The individual(s) responsible for overseeing day-to-day operations on a show—in other words, he or she who "runs the show." The term is sometimes interchanged with "executive producer."

Simultaneous Submission. The act of submitting a query or work to more than one market/agent at the same time.

Sitcom. Short for situation comedy.

Slasher Film. A horror flick with lots of deaths, blood and gore.

Slice of Life. A type of story designed to show a particular way of life in a certain area or time period.

Slug Line. A line in a script designed to show where a scene is taking place. The slug line always begins with EXT. or INT., immediately telling readers whether the scene is set outside or inside.

Slush Pile. A term used to refer to the pile of unsolicited manuscripts received by publishers and/or producers that have not been read or rejected.

Spec Script. A script written "on speculation," meaning that it has not been contracted or commissioned, and no money is assured when writing it.

Staged Reading. A gathering of actors to read a script, so that the writer can hear the dialogue spoken aloud by professionals.

Subplot. A plot line that runs along a story but is smaller in scope and importance than the true plot.

Subsidiary Rights. Also called subrights, these rights refer to a variety of things, such as merchandising, film rights, foreign rights and more.

Subtext. In dialogue, what is meant but never explicitly said aloud.

Synopsis. A summary of a script's plot. It can be as brief as a few lines or several paragraphs long and include explanations of characters, subplots, conflict and resolution.

Tagline. A clever line on a movie poster designed to pique interest.

Theme. The implicit meaning, message, concept, or idea contained within the story; often contains some universal lesson about life, death, love, or human nature.

Thriller. A genre of story dealing with suspense, cat-and-mouse chases, killers, close calls and high-adrenaline storytelling.

Treatment. A loose and somewhat incomplete version of a script that is completed from beginning to end, but lacks details and dialogue in scenes.

Unsolicited Manuscript. A completed work that has not been requested by a studio, person or theater.

Vehicle. A project developed for a specific movie star.

Voice-over. Vocal narration that is spoken by an offscreen character.

Westerns/Frontier. A genre set in western or frontier regions, usually set in the past and dealing with things such as cowboys, train robberies, Native Americans and the natural beauty of open spaces.

White Space. Plenty of empty space on a script page. Preferable to "too much black."

Work-for-Hire. When a writer is contracted and paid to do a specific work or rewrite. This is in contrast to writing a work on speculation.

World Premiere. A play term referring to the first full production of a work.

Agents & Managers Specialties Index

The subject index is divided into script subject categories and formats. To find an agent interested in the type of scripts you've written, see the appropriate sections under the subject headings that best describe your work.

FICTION

Adventure

Comic

Confession

Detective

Specialties Index

Plays

Kubler Auckland Management 223

Sherman & Associates, Ken 236

Poetry

Sherman & Associates, Ken 236

Poetry Trans

Sherman & Associates, Ken 236

Psychic

Niad Management 229

Sherman & Associates, Ken 236

Regional

Anderson Literary, TV & Film
  Agency, Darley 203

Sherman & Associates, Ken 236

Religious

AEI 201

Anderson Literary, TV & Film
  Agency, Darley 203

Author Literary Agents 204

Sherman & Associates, Ken 236

Romance

Anderson Literary, TV & Film
  Agency, Darley 203

Author Literary Agents 204

Niad Management 229

Sheil Land Associates, Ltd 235

Sherman & Associates, Ken 236

Science

AEI 201

Anderson Literary, TV & Film
  Agency, Darley 203

Author Literary Agents 204

Communications and Entertainment,
  Inc. 210

MBA Literary Agents, Ltd 226

Miller Co., The Stuart M. 227

Sherman & Associates, Ken 236

Short

Sherman & Associates, Ken 236

Spiritual

Sherman & Associates, Ken 236

Sports

Anderson Literary, TV & Film
  Agency, Darley 203

Miller Co., The Stuart M. 227

Sherman & Associates, Ken 236

Thriller

AEI 201

Anderson Literary, TV & Film
  Agency, Darley 203

Author Literary Agents 204

Communications and Entertainment,
  Inc. 210

E S Agency, The 214

Miller Co., The Stuart M. 227

Niad Management 229

Sheil Land Associates, Ltd 235

Sherman & Associates, Ken 236

Specialties Index

Computers

AEI 201

Author Literary Agents 204

Miller Co., The Stuart M. 227

Sherman & Associates, Ken 236

Cooking

Anderson Literary, TV & Film
   Agency, Darley 203

Author Literary Agents 204

Sheil Land Associates, Ltd 235

Sherman & Associates, Ken 236

Crafts

Sherman & Associates, Ken 236

Current affairs

AEI 201

Miller Co., The Stuart M. 227

Richards Agency, The Lisa 233

Sherman & Associates, Ken 236

Education

Author Literary Agents 204

Sherman & Associates, Ken 236

Ethnic

AEI 201

Sherman & Associates, Ken 236

Film

Communications and Entertainment,
   Inc. 210

Sherman & Associates, Ken 236

Gardening

Sheil Land Associates, Ltd 235

Sherman & Associates, Ken 236

Gay

Sherman & Associates, Ken 236

Government

AEI 201

Miller Co., The Stuart M. 227

Sherman & Associates, Ken 236

Health

AEI 201

Creswell, Cameron 212

Miller Co., The Stuart M. 227

Sherman & Associates, Ken 236

History

AEI 201

Author Literary Agents 204

Capel & Land Ltd 207

Communications and Entertainment,
   Inc. 210

Creswell, Cameron 212

MBA Literary Agents, Ltd 226

Miller Co., The Stuart M. 227

Richards Agency, The Lisa 233

Sheil Land Associates, Ltd 235

Sherman & Associates, Ken 236

How to

AEI 201

Miller Co., The Stuart M. 227

Sherman & Associates, Ken 236

Humor

AEI 201

Author Literary Agents 204

Sheil Land Associates, Ltd 235

Sherman & Associates, Ken 236

Interior

Sherman & Associates, Ken 236

Language

Author Literary Agents 204

Sherman & Associates, Ken 236

Medicine

RCW 231

Memoirs

AEI 201

Anderson Literary, TV & Film
   Agency, Darley 203

Creswell, Cameron 212

MBA Literary Agents, Ltd 226

Miller Co., The Stuart M. 227

Richards Agency, The Lisa 233

Sherman & Associates, Ken 236

Military

AEI 201

Miller Co., The Stuart M. 227

Sheil Land Associates, Ltd 235

Sherman & Associates, Ken 236

Money

AEI 201

Sherman & Associates, Ken 236

Multicultural

Sherman & Associates, Ken 236

Music

Author Literary Agents 204

Communications and Entertainment,
   Inc. 210

Sherman & Associates, Ken 236

Nature

AEI 201

Author Literary Agents 204

Sherman & Associates, Ken 236

Newage

Sherman & Associates, Ken 236

Philosophy

Sherman & Associates, Ken 236

Photography

Sherman & Associates, Ken 236

Popular Culture

AEI 201

Anderson Literary, TV & Film
   Agency, Darley 203

MBA Literary Agents, Ltd 226

Richards Agency, The Lisa 233

Specialties Index

Agents Index

To find the individual pages of these agents and agencies, you can cross-reference the agency names in the General Index (page 416) or you can find the agencies in alphabetical order in the Agents & Managers market section of this book (page 197).

Agents Index

M

N

General Index

General Index